THE CAPITALIST UNCONSCIOUS

THE CAPITALIST UNCONSCIOUS

FROM KOREAN UNIFICATION TO TRANSNATIONAL KOREA

HYUN OK PARK

COLUMBIA UNIVERSITY PRESS   New York

COLUMBIA UNIVERSITY PRESS

PUBLISHERS SINCE 1893

NEW YORK   CHICHESTER, WEST SUSSEX

cup.columbia.edu

Copyright © 2015 Columbia University Press
Paperback edition, 2018

This publication project was supported by the Korea Foundation.

Library of Congress Cataloging-in-Publication Data
Park, Hyun Ok.
The capitalist unconscious : from Korean unification to transnational Korea /
Hyun Ok Park.
pages cm
Includes bibliographical references and index.
ISBN 978-0-231-17192-2 (cloth : alk. paper) | ISBN 978-0-231-17193-9 (pbk. : alk. paper) |
ISBN 978-0-231-54051-3 (ebook)
1. Korea (South)—Social conditions. 2. Capitalism—Social aspects—Korea
(South) 3. Korea (North)—Social conditions. 4. Socialism—Korea (North)
5. Korean reunification question (1945-) I. Title.
HN730.5.A8P39 2015
306.3′4209519—dc23
2015010090

COVER IMAGE: Cho Chonhyun, Footsteps on the Border
COVER DESIGN: Chang Jae Lee

For Michael Burawoy and Harry Harootunian

CONTENTS

PREFACE

Korea is already unified in a transnational form by capital. The prevailing ability to overlook flows of people, goods, and ideas crossing the borders of South Korea, China, and North Korea—beyond economic aid and the widely publicized trail of North Korean refugees—attests to the continued reign of the Cold War's legacy and a seemingly undeniable sense of capitalism's victory over socialism. Recognition of transnational Korea requires a historical approach that consigns the current Korean nation formation to the history of Korea and the Korean diaspora in the twentieth century. The ongoing transnational interaction of Koreans is constituted by asynchronous adoption of neoliberal reforms in Korean communities, each of which imagines them as a new democratic order. *The Capitalist Unconscious* presents the postcolonial and Cold War history of socialism and capitalism as the history of the neoliberal present. During the Cold War, rivalry between the two Koreas contrived their territorial integration as the normative vision of Korean ethnic and national sovereignty. Despite the tenacity of this Cold War formula, the current capitalist and democratic integration of Koreans across borders has once again destabilized ethnic and national relations of Koreans, which have been a vortex of the Asian order ever since the large-scale migration of Koreans to Manchuria (northeast China) and neighboring countries from Japanese rule. In turn, the unfolding disagreements over the identity and rights of border-crossing Koreans within each community and across them expose the unevenness and disjuncture of the current capitalist expansion on a global scale, which each Korean community construes as a transition from socialism to capitalism or from military dictatorship to democracy.

The purportedly hegemonic spread of neoliberal capitalism is in fact the latest response of each Korean community to its singular crisis during the Cold War era that shaped nation formation, whether socialist or capitalist.

The border between North Korea and the world is not another Berlin Wall. The German model of national unification is not suitable for Korea. Unlike East Germany during the Cold War, two key forces have integrated North Korea into the global capitalist system in the post–Cold War era: Its new economic relationship with China and South Korea and the border-crossing migratory labor of North Koreans, both of which are inextricable from socioeconomic changes within North Korea. The German experience pertains to the Cold War context. Adopting it for Korea would mean disregarding the massive political, socioeconomic, and cultural changes in North Korea since the 1990s. North Korea and the United States and its allies may well agree on the importance of capital investment in North Korea. One might ask what is preventing us not only from recognizing that North Korea has already combined socialist ideology and capitalist economic development, as China has done, but also from accepting their consequent synergy that is to be determined by the society and the state. North Korea, in fact, has been on that thorny road for decades. Even if the North Korean regime falls in the near future, the politics and history of the neoliberal capitalist and democratic present discussed in this book will continue to inform an important strand of unfolding change in its society.

The booming field of North Korean studies regards the state's capricious marketization and its clash with the people's desire for privatization and democracy as the defining reality of North Korea in the current moment. However, this book interprets the latest conflict of the state and society as the newest instance of their repeated struggle to reconcile the continued contradiction between socialist construction and pursuit of rapid industrialization under postcolonial condition and national division. Given that this contradiction was integral to socialist experiences during the twentieth century, *The Capitalist Unconscious* provides a comparative account of North Korean socialism in light of the history of permanent and continued revolution in the Soviet Union and China. Today's politics concerning North Korea pits economic engagement with North Korea against protecting the human rights of North Koreans. Called the Sunshine Policy, trade and other forms of economic cooperation between the two Koreas are adopted as the means for peaceful reconciliation and gradual political change by progressive leftist South Korean governments. The protection of the human rights of North Koreans through the means of regime change is advocated by forces as various as South Korean and global NGOs, converted former pro–North Korean radicals, Christian evangelists, and the United States–led war on terrorism. This political antinomy in the approach to North Korea obscures their consensus on the capitalist market system and the rule of law as cornerstones of democratization. The vehemently opposed proposals for North Korea are spectacles of neoliberal capitalism, in which Korean and global communities displace their own contradictions arising from capitalist consensus and deepened socioeconomic inequality at home onto the task of democratizing North Korea.

The neoliberal capitalist and democratic present in the Korean peninsula is entwined with the Korean Chinese community in northeast China through the cascading labor migration of Koreans from China to South Korea and from North Korea to China. In South Korea, Korean Chinese migrant workers provide cheap labor in caring of children, the elderly, and the sick, as well as in restaurants and karaoke places. Apart from working in coastal regions of China in factories owned by South Koreans, North Korean migrant workers not only farm land of Korean Chinese farmers who left for South Korea but also work in the thriving service sectors opened up by Korean Chinese with their remittances from South Korea. Neoliberal capitalist reforms ruptured the promise of a welfare society in South Korea; low-paid Korean Chinese labor contributes to maintaining its facade. Some Korean Chinese make sense of their experience of migratory work in South Korea by remembering the Chinese Cultural Revolution as intra-ethnocide. Remembrance in South Korea of this deeply repressed history authorizes an investigation into the Chinese revolution as the history of their present-day relationship with South Koreans. The double inversion of Koreans from anticolonial revolutionaries to counterrevolutionaries, and from partners of socialist internationalism to national enemies characterizes the tumultuous process of Koreans becoming a national minority in the People's Republic of China. The repeated construction of Koreans as others has coexisted with the history of Korean leadership during the anticolonial revolutionary struggle in Manchuria and Koreans' extensive participation in the socialist construction. This paradox has unsettled their national identities and rights, although it is often shrouded by the ready-made narrative of the model minority. Constructed primordial attributes of Korean ethnicity supplied the *content* for exclusion of, and violence against, Korean Chinese. Yet the repeated "otherization" of Koreans was the *form* through which they became a national minority: Korean and Chinese revolutionaries in China vainly continued to resolve the contradiction between the socialist dictum and the intensified drive for industrialization;

and this impossibility was inverted into the construction of Koreans as others. When the state calls privatization the reparation of socialist wrongs, the current diasporic migratory work of Korean Chinese in South Korea becomes the mechanism of reparation in unexpected ways. Savings and remittances from their work in South Korea reverse the construction of their status as others and victims. Their migratory work actualizes socialist promises for housing, healthcare, and education as commodities.

The history of Korean migration to Manchuria under Japanese colonialism becomes an ur-history of transnational Korea. Narrative and affective memories of colonial migration are exchanged among Koreans across borders, as they negotiate with each other the terms of migration, work, and rights. As North Korean migrants and Korean Chinese become undocumented labor respectively in China and South Korea, their evoked memories of colonial migration tame their struggles with exploitation and uncertainty and keep the capitalist dream alive. Both the ethnic compassion and perversion that migrant Koreans express toward their Korean employers and middlemen need to be understood in the context of their transnational capitalist present. Moreover, the language of reparation of colonial wrongs enabled South Korean activists to identity Korean Chinese migrants as colonial returnees, contesting the terms of their return and "recovery" of (South) Korean citizenship. This advocacy of Korean Chinese as ethnic nationals clashed with advocacy of non-Korean migrant workers that was framed in cosmopolitanism. Reparation for Korean Chinese was criticized for discriminating against non-Korean migrant workers.

The politics of reparation, the promotion of peace and reconciliation, and the advocacy of human rights constitute three repertoires of neoliberal democracy. I conceptualize them as market utopia and delineate utopian impulses behind the historical shift toward neoliberal democracy. Neoliberal democratic politics postulates diverse groups of migrant workers as anyone other than laborers: non-Koreans as cosmopolitan beings, Korean Chinese as colonial returnees, and North Koreans as refugees. This fragmented representation of migrant workers masks their shared ties with one another and with South Korean workers under conditions of neoliberal capitalist production. It also helps NGOs and the South Korean state to manage them as productive laborers by legalizing their work and yet denying their right to change workplace. The analysis of the democratic politics of migrant workers makes this book a study of labor in the putative postlabor era. I discern the capitalist consensus, discursive or unconscious, which resides in ethnic, national, and democratic politics of border-crossing Koreans.

Focused on Korea and Asia, this book concerns the issues of ethnicity and nationalism in the current era of global capitalism and political sovereignty. This book was completed at another moment of sweeping ethnic and national violence in world politics and widespread expropriation of people from their communities. Diagnoses of current events are often made in reference to earlier occurrences of civil war, apartheid, ethic separatism, and the Cold War. Prescriptions to resolve the violence are envisaged using modalities from historical examples. This mode of historical repetition in popular discourses and political consciousness is a primary concern of this book. *The Capitalist Unconscious* demonstrates that the historical content of each instance of ethnic and national politics is revealed when the concept of repetition is interrogated as a form whose mundane and haunting recurrence needs to be deciphered in conjunction with ongoing changes in global capitalism and global democratic politics.

NOTES ON ROMANIZATION AND TRANSLATION

I follow the McCune-Reischauer system and Pinyin system for the romanization of Korean and Chinese respectively, except for works and names that have their own specific conventions, for example, Kim Dae Jung. All translations from Korean and Chinese materials and interviews are my own unless otherwise noted.

ACKNOWLEDGMENTS

This book draws on years of ethnographic and archival research in South Korea and northeast China. It would have been simply impossible without all of the migrants in South Korea and China who gave their time and shared their experiences with me, even as they faced daily challenges and uncertainties. Community organizers, policy makers, and scholars in Seoul and Yŏn'gil also set aside their immediate tasks to explain their work and introduce me to their community. I am especially grateful to Lim Kwangbin, Chon Sinja, and Son Ch'unil. Going beyond acts of friendship and collegiality, they helped me at many stages of my research in finding important resources and contacts. I appreciate the generosity of Cho Ch'ŏnhyŏn, who showed me his video stills and photographs and made them available for this book.

The research and writing of this book is imprinted with decades of learning and inspiration from Michael Burawoy and Harry Harootunian. Their different intellectual thoughts and modes of interpretation have provided the enriching foundation from where I ventured into diverse theoretical and philosophical traditions and developed the sociopolitical and historical problematics explored in this work. Since my embarking on the research for this book in Ann Arbor, many friends and colleagues listened to my thoughts and offered me invaluable feedback and encouragement. I am especially grateful to Gay Seidman, George Steinmetz, Julia Adams, Rebecca Karl, Yukiko Hanawa, Ken Kawashima, Janet Poole, Hong Kal, Jesook Song, Janice Kim, Pak Kyongtae, Lee Yonghee, Chang Yongsok, Yi Jin-kyung, Goh Byeonggwon, and Ko misuk. My special gratitude goes to Andre Schmid who made Korean studies in Toronto an open intellectual space. I thank Lee Chunja and

Lee Hyunju for delicious meals and support in Seoul and Toronto. I am also grateful for institutional and intellectual support from York University and its sociology department, especially Peter Vandergeest, Radhika Mongia, Peter Landstreet, Himani Bannerji, Hira Singh, Philip Walsh, Fuyuki Kurasawa, Luin Goldring, Lesley Wood, Larry Lam, Nancy Mandell, Margaret Beare, Jackie Siebert, Rita Kanarek, Tom Cohen, David McNally, and the former dean, Robert Drummond.

The momentum for this book project was sustained over the years by presentations in lectures and workshops, where I tried out my emerging ideas and received critique and support, at the University of California in Berkeley, Stanford University, University of Iowa, Cornell University, University of Illinois in Urbana and Champaign, University of Toronto, McGill University, University of British Columbia, University of Manitoba, Columbia University, National Chiao Tung University, Hanyang University, Duke University, and the Institute for Advanced Study in Princeton. I am particularly grateful to their organizers, including Jennifer Chun, Judy Han, Elaine Kim, Gi-Wook Shin, Sonia Ryang, Michael Shin, Nancy Abelmann, Andre Schmid, Janet Poole, Adrienne Hurley, Tina Chen, Tani Barlow, Rosalind Morris, Joyce Liu, Cheehyung Kim, Nicola Di Cosmo, and Michael van Walt van Praag. This book also grew alongside teaching seminars on capitalism, global modernity, memory, and the philosophy of history. I appreciate very much the insights of all my students, especially Jonathan Adjemian and Alex Wolfson at York with whom I mulled over difficult texts. I extend my wholehearted gratitude to Lise McKean for her support and editing of this book manuscript draft after draft in its variant incarnations.

The research for this book was supported by the MacArthur Foundation's Program on Global Security and Sustainability, the American Council of Learned Societies, and later the Academy of Korean Studies. The writing of the book began at the Institute for Advanced Study in Princeton, and years later I returned there to complete it. At the Institute I found my deepest thoughts, and my scholarship matured into an otherwise unimaginable form. I attribute them to the intellectual engagement beyond immediate utilities and received rules of scholarship, for which I am grateful to the faculty of the School of Historical Studies. Nicola Di Cosmo's pastoral support for fellows created an environment where writing became as ordinary as sharing meals and laughter. I appreciate Nicola's suggestion for a new title of the book, leading to the present one. Together with my thanks to Caroline Bynum's support, I express my sincere gratitude to Piet Hut in the Program in Interdisciplinary Studies for extending my stay and allowing me to complete the book in such a reflective environment. The many hours spent each day in the Institute's library acquired a collective flair in the company of Heinrich von Staden, Christopher Jones, and Sabine Schmidtke. I also would like to thank the Institute's library staff, especially Kirstie Venanzi, for all the books that arrived at my desk, as well as other staff members for many nourishing treats and pleasant rides to downtown. I enjoyed conversation with a diverse group of scholars, including Carol Gluck, David Lurie, Ching Kwan Lee, Jos de Mul, Mark Driscoll, Diane Nelson, Weirong Shen, Moon-Kie Jung, David Eng, Yannis Hamilakis, Chen-Pang Yeang, Aihe Wang, Anna Krylova, Nikolay Tsyrempilove, Yucel Yanikdag, Barbara Walker, and Judi Byfield. The incredible summer writing camp with Jungwon Kim, also at the Institute, enabled me to muster loose and overflowing ideas and complete the revision in time; words are inadequate for conveying my gratitude for her earnest faith in the book and beyond.

I extend my deep gratitude to Jennifer Crewe at Columbia University Press for her enthusiasm and commanding support for the book. Jonathan Fiedler has taken care of details in the production process with a great ease. I am grateful to the two exceptional reviewers selected by the Press for their generous intellectual engagement with different scholarly orientations and for their incisive reading on both historical and theoretical fronts.

My siblings and my extended family in South Korea and the United States fill my life with love and perspective, and the period of researching and writing this book project is no exception. Through well-orchestrated webs of daily talks, Mija, Yoon Duckkeun, Sookja, Scott Saki, Namkyu, Kim Miheh, Hyun-Sook, Stan Young, Hyun Joo, Moon Seongho, Jiyon, Hyewon, Yonghoon, Justin, Minjae, Minkyong, Amanda, Caroline, Seonghyun, Jooyoung, and Terry have showered me with blissful surprises and given me strength. I also thank my uncle Kim Hyongju for his embrace of my study. Living in our midst and in my heart are my parents, Park Ro Tack and Kim Yang Rye. The detailed notes on everyday wisdom and knowledge they left behind bear their extraordinary times with the twentieth-century Korea. This history and its inflection with the current condition are the subject of this book.

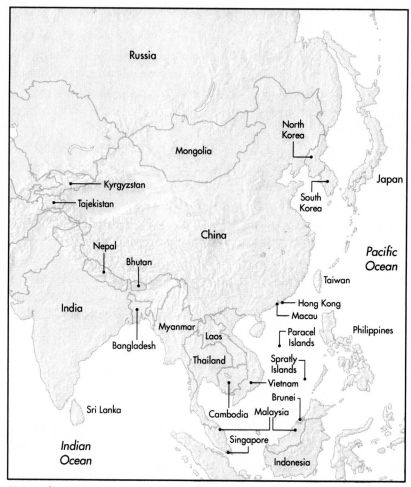

Map 1: Asia

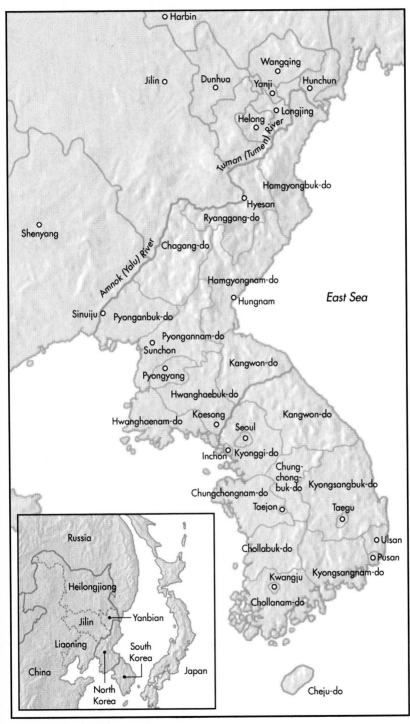

Map 2: Korea and Yanbian

PART I
CRISIS

1

THE CAPITALIST UNCONSCIOUS: THE KOREA QUESTION

Korean unification is the quintessential problematic of the Cold War order in East Asia and concerns the national quest for decolonization. This book presents a new conceptual approach to Korean unification that observes a metamorphosis from a rapprochement between the two Koreas to the formation of a transnational community that includes Korean diasporic communities as major participants. Routine questions on Korean unification ask whether and when the two Koreas will be unified. The book's thesis is that capital has already unified Korea in a transnational form. This form of unification is not shaped by the long-awaited form of territorial integration and family union but rather is driven by the exchange of capital, labor, and ideas across the borders of Korean communities, including the Korean diaspora. The national division of Korea and the superpowers' rivalry over it was the bedrock of the Cold War. Since the 1990s, the transnational Korean migration across the two Koreas and China constitutes a privileged venue of Korean unification, a new capitalist democratic order in East Asia, and an immanent link between them. The colonial migration from Korea to northeast China (Manchuria) in the first half of the twentieth century becomes an ur-history that Koreans in North Korea, South Korea, and China draw on to reinforce and challenge the terms of their capitalist integration.

Transnational Korea does not involve a convergence of Korean communities on the modular form of neoliberal capitalism despite the hegemonic role of capital. Instead, local meanings for transnational Korea are constituted by asynchronous constellations of old and new socioeconomic and emancipatory projects within each community. The rise of transnational Korea does not result from South Korea's victory in its rivalry with North Korea.

It ensues from each involved Korean community's simultaneous experiences of socioeconomic crisis and crisis resolution by means of privatization, deregulation, and border-crossing labor migration. Transnational Korea is formed under the specific historical conditions of crisis in industrial development in Korean communities. A new capitalist network among Korean communities is transforming their inimical relations of the Cold War era into socioeconomic exchanges aimed at resolving the crisis. This book focuses particular attention on the cascading labor migration of Korean Chinese and North Koreans that integrates radically different economies: Korean Chinese migrate to South Korean cities to work in the expanding service economy, and North Koreans migrate to China for agricultural work formerly performed by Korean Chinese and for work in cities in burgeoning small businesses made possible by their remittances from South Korea.

I theorize capitalist experience as an unconscious that consists of the sociopolitical and historical unconscious. Market utopia is the sociopolitical unconscious that represents the capitalist experience in narrative, corporeal, and sensorial practices in quotidian life. The experience of expropriation, exploitation, inequality, and border crossing becomes the basis for a social construction of democracy that I conceptualize as market utopia. Whether in socialism or welfare capitalism, the vision of democracy during the industrial era concerned the power of the masses attesting to their critical role in consolidating mass production, mass consumption, and the dream of collective sovereignty. Market utopia is an alternative democratic practice that corresponds to the hegemonic domination of neoliberal and financial capitalism. Notwithstanding their importance, narrative constructions neither exhaust their experience nor entirely integrate with other experiences of socioeconomics, such as everyday routines, predicaments, and contradictions that Korean migrants register through bodily expression involving work, protest, emotion, and illness. Market utopia entails three repertoires of democratic politics—reparation, peace and reconciliation, and human rights—whose shared capitalist logic is explicated in this book.

The historical unconscious concerns the memory form of history and the temporal structure of subjectivity. When one is preoccupied with discerning new capitalist and democratic logics, such attention to the new may inadvertently foster a historicism that projects a rupture or a transition as if the old disappears. I examine how this historicism is authorized by the problematic concept of epochal transition and bring history to the forefront of the inquiry. Different economic sectors have undergone disparate changes in the putative era of financial capital. For example, the industrial sector shrank, but not all factories moved overseas or closed down. Instead of proclaiming the demise of the industrial sector, we need to delve into the new nexus between industrial capital and financial capital that is forged with the changed vision about the state. Furthermore, earlier utopian ideals have not vanished but returned as unscheduled revenants, haunting the hegemonic neoliberal democracy. Thus, the issue is about not only how to create a new politics but also how to recognize it when it emerges. History takes up philosophical status, since history is a matter not of aggregating events but of understanding and experiencing time through narrative, corporeality, and memory. I place the capitalist unconscious within the framework of historical repetition to examine the form and content in which the capitalist unconscious appeared at different historical moments.

FROM KOREAN UNIFICATION TO TRANSNATIONAL KOREA

Since the 1990s, capital has spearheaded the transnational form of Korean unification. This new form eludes even watchful eyes because of the fixation on the unification of territorial nation-states as envisaged during the Cold War. Unification discourses and practices offer few clues for recognizing the new transnational form of Korean unity. Old and new tropes of Korean unification transpose the trauma of national division into a substance for reestablishing an organic national whole. The Cold War notion of returning to an undivided past through territorial union continues to inform unification politics in the aftermath of the Cold War. The imposition of national division by foreign superpowers against Koreans' will was a powerful Cold War narrative. Accordingly, the dissolution of the global Cold War is commonly understood as removing foreign opposition to Korean reunification. Thus the collapse of North Korea is considered imminent, with Korean unification only a matter of time. The German experience is held up as the model for assessing the economic capacity needed by South Korea for the peaceful integration of North Korea. Brief and tearful reunions of families separated since the Korean War have galvanized moral calls for reunification and fortified their normative imperative. Given the post–Cold War allure of the imminent realization of national union, cultural differences between the two Koreas resulting from decades-long separation rather than military enmity are perceived as creating barriers to genuine reunion and threatening reunification—even if territorial integration is achieved. These forays into the return to an undivided whole obfuscate the fact that Korean ethnic sovereignty assumes a new form of transnational community that eschews belabored forms of family reunion and the singular nation-state.

In my approach, the current form of Korean unification is not merely a matter of national and familial reconciliation. Rather, it is constitutive of a new capitalist and democratic order in post–Cold War Asia. During the Cold War, the Korean national division was paradoxically consolidated by diametrically opposed states that elevated unification to the sublime objective of national independence and used it to consolidate military dictatorship (Cumings 1981; Koo 1994; Bleiker 2005). Each state participated in an intensified race for military armament and state-led industrialization. If the Cold War is to be understood not just as a military rivalry between superpowers but also as an American project of establishing capitalist hegemony, then the post–Cold War does not negate the Cold War order but reconfigures a global capitalist order marked by porous borders and neoliberal democracy. Paik Nak-chung (1998), a renowned literary critic in South Korea, has offered a rare account of the role of capital in transforming the Korean division in the post–Cold War era. Writing soon after the 1997 financial crisis, Paik observed that investment and trade with North Korea by South Korean conglomerates riled but fell short of annihilating the national division. This resilience of the Korean division, he argued, underscores that the national division has become "the system" (ch'eje) with its own mechanisms of reproduction, which in this case are military and political forces within and beyond the Korean peninsula that sustain the Korean division. In my view, Paik has underestimated the unruly changes in the post–Cold War capitalist system that are accompanied by changes in national and global politics of sovereignty.

Capital-driven transnational Korea offers a missing link between the normalized task of Korean unification and the prevalent disenchantment with unification in South Korea. Democratized public space in South Korea is marked by indifference and skepticism over the viability of Korean unification, as well as by defeatism among activists whose roles in unification efforts no longer gave them prominence. Scientific surveys and opinion polls on unification conducted by the government and research institutes affirm the demise of the wish for unification, which seems to be interrupted only by intermittent family unions hosted by the two states. Without a prospect of meeting again, family unions turn the decades-long awaited moment into a spectacle of human tragedy. The public's disaffection with unification in South Korea is often attributed to concern over its economic cost. Accordingly, the economics of unification needs to be seriously interrogated. I consider this economic disenchantment with unification to be a phenomenological index of the global capitalist integration of the two Koreas and the Korean diaspora. Even then, global capitalist integration repeats sentiments of a necessary yet impossible union in the future. The exchange of capital and labor satisfies long-standing aspirations for reconciliation among Koreans while taming the urgency of Korean unification into regularized enactments of market exchange. The missing link is that Korea is already unified in a transnational form by capital. Transnational Korea coheres under the act of commodity exchange across Korean communities. This material substance is conceived, enacted, and reproduced as the new everyday reality of the post–Cold War era. The border crossings of people, goods, and money bear with them fantastic desires for wealth, security, and the primordial belonging. Capital occupies the transnational space of Korean interactions through the affective politics of the ethnic nation.

Transnational Korea locates a new form of Korean ethnic sovereignty within capitalist crisis and its historically specific response to the crisis and discerns within it a new cultural-political register of democracy. Buck-Morss (2002:39) argues that "if the era of the Cold War is over, it is perhaps less because one side has won than because the legitimation of each political discourse found itself fundamentally challenged by material developments themselves." Similarly, the Korean Cold War has subsided since the 1990s despite perennial military tension between the two Koreas. This is less because South Korea won the Cold War than because the two Koreas simultaneously faced crises that were bound up with a global capitalist crisis. An analysis of the capitalist crisis and its attempted resolution in each place is necessary to make legible the emergent transnational Korea. As much as the global capitalist crisis at the end of World War II laid the political economic foundation of the Cold War and the Korean division, a new global crisis of industrial accumulation provided the momentum for the waning of the Cold War. This means that Korean unification is a problematic of global capitalism and its corollary regime of democracy rather than an a priori question of ethnic sovereignty.

Led by South Korean capital, transnational Korea signifies a distinctively uneven integration of East Asia in the post–Cold War era, which belies both the prevalent imaginaries of regional unity and the persistent strength of nation-states. South Korea grants Korean Americans de facto dual citizenship while constraining the rights of Korean Chinese to visit and work in South Korea. Inequality between the two Korean diasporic communities has become the most contentious issue together with the status of North Korea in the formation of the deterritorialized Korea. Devoid of capitalist exchanges with South Korea, Koreans in Japan and Russia remain invisible in transnational Korea. A hierarchical transnational community is anomalous with the ethnic principle of citizenship and the dichotomy of home and diaspora.

Postcoloniality

Conceptualizing the national question as a postcolonial question is key to understanding the shift in the imagined Korean community from Korean unification to transnational Korea. The two Koreas' Cold War rivalry for territorial integration of the nation has a postcolonial character. The division of Korea after liberation from Japanese rule was not simply the result of intervention by the superpowers. It was also the result of the domestic struggle over social reforms to address the inequalities exacerbated by colonization. The Cold War fixed the decolonization struggle as a competition between state socialism and military capitalism. Under the banner of permanent revolution, the North proceeded with a socialist form of decolonization, conducting land reform, purging colonial collaborators, and consecrating the memory of anticolonial struggle as the basis of its *Juche* (self-reliance) ideology. The South developed a military state that delayed land reform and reinstated collaborators with Japanese power in key administrative and military positions. The interlocking relationship in South Korea of military dictatorship, American influence, and capitalist development formed the central question in the social formation debate of the 1980s. Postcolonial politics in the Korean peninsula, with its fixation on the Cold War division of the nation, is similar to the politics in postwar Japan, where defeat and US occupation led to Japan's becoming engrossed with its relationship with the United States. In Young's (2012) observation, the postimperialist history of Japan was reduced to postwar history, mainly determining responsibility for the war. In building a Cold War bloc in Asia, the United States in the early 1960s led the South Korean state to agree to Japan's offer of a one-time monetary settlement in order to bury the issue of colonization and compensation.

The post–Cold War era has reconfigured postcolonial desire, constructing the Korean nation in transnational form. The issue of reparation of colonial wrongs has been reopened in South Korea in the post–Cold War context, most notably in conjunction with reparation for women who were mobilized by the Japanese state as sex-workers for its military during the colonial era. Marx's observation that history repeats itself the first time as tragedy and the next time as farce is apropos of the Korean context. If Koreans in China and North Korea enjoyed amicable relations as communist brothers in the past, their uneven capitalist integration since the 1990s has produced hierarchical relations defined by the market exchange of money and labor. Their hierarchical relations with South Koreans are mapped onto new repertoires of democratic politics in hegemonic South Korea, namely, reparation, peacemaking, and humanitarianism. In this conjuncture, the colonial history of migration to Manchuria becomes the ur-history of transnational Korea. Memories of Japanese colonization provide Korean Chinese and North Koreans with a discourse for articulating quotidian experiences and actions (see Park 2005). The repeated migration of Koreans in these two historical moments does not mean that the pattern of Korean migration then and now is similar. Instead, it discloses the repeated paradoxical tension of territorializing and deterritorializing forces that arises from the interplay between global capitalist expansion and the state's role in it.

Historical repetition is more than resemblance and memory. Recognition of repetition interrupts the linear historical temporality that frames neoliberal democracy, at the same time pointing to the very logic of capitalist expansion that triggers repetition. Buck-Morss (2002:31) notes that "unlike Hegelian or Marxist philosophies of history, the conception of the ur-form presumes no continuum of historical development and no deterministic necessity as to the outcome." Similarly, the colonial history of migration as the ur-form of transnational Korea requires an approach beyond the thesis of colonial modernity. The latter locates the origin of capitalist development in the colonial era, implicating the origin of Korean modernity in what was called Western modernity, which Japan simultaneously sought to imitate and overcome in its metropole and colonies (e.g., Shin and Robinson 2001). My analysis reveals instead that the colonial history of migration to Manchuria provides a basis for identification and disidentification with the neoliberal democratic order. The book examines the present, in which emerging global capitalist and democratic regimes rupture the lives of border-crossing Koreans. Memories of colonial migration configure experiences of capitalist and democratic changes. Koreans across borders comprehend and contest the hierarchy among their communities through their articulations of new memories.

Transnationalism

Transnational Korea reveals its instability as soon as it is explored substantively. Conflicts and contradictions arise from practices and narratives over Koreans' border-crossing interactions. Ethnicity, nation, cosmopolitanism, peace, and human rights are key spatial sites of political economic and cultural exchanges of Koreans across borders. Neither here nor there, these spatial sites are liminal zones whose principal function is to offer the time and place for capitalist transactions. With its inherent contradictions, transnational Korea rests on cosmopolitanism and nationalism, both of which provide crucial, though not always functional, services for capitalist expansion. Nongovernmental organizations in South Korea, for instance, espouse cosmopolitanism in defining migrants' rights as human rights while bringing nationalism in through the back door. Nation-states and migrants also appeal to transnational as well as national ties.

Transnational Korea exceeds the framework of diaspora studies and transnational migration studies, which take the nation-state as the unit of analysis by regarding diaspora as the extension or transcendence of the nation-state. Theories of transnationalism revolve around ethnic and global homogeneity, such as Appadurai's (1996) "ethnoscape" and the global human rights regime, and local differentiation such as diasporic culture (Clifford 1992; Gupta and Ferguson 1997; Braziel 2003). However, neither pole of this theoretical polemic explains the hierarchical structure of the Korean transnational community. This hierarchy also challenges the principle of ethnic citizenship, which postulates symmetrical inclusion of all members of the same putative ethnic group regardless of differences in social status, residence, or citizenship (Brubaker 1998). The notion of long-distance nationalism conceptualizes overseas members as an extension of the home nation-state (Anderson 1992). However, studies of diaspora and transnational migrants present them as others of nation-states, who disperse across borders, live in interstitial spaces of states, and make no fixed commitment to either home or host states, but instead develop multiple, hybrid identities (Schiller, Basch, and Blanc 1995; Soysal 1995). Thus, an important concern in these studies of diasporic and transnational migration is the status of the nation-state and its membership system within contemporary globalization. As a result, the studies present a dyadic analysis of home/host nation-state and diasporic migrants, which regards the latter as a whole and the others of the nation-state. This dyadic framework is adopted in the proliferating studies of foreign migrant workers in South Korea, the Korean Chinese diaspora, and North Korean migrants for investigating discrimination in South Korea, diasporic networks, ethnic and national membership, and multiple belongingness (Sŏl 1999; Cho 2008; Pak Kyŏngt'ae 2008; Ryang 2008; Jaeeun Kim 2011).

Current studies of citizenship and transnational migration do not adequately address the complexity associated with these hierarchical relationships across transnational Korea. Different positions, rights, and bargaining powers of Korean diasporic communities as compared with South Korea, as well as in relation to one another, demand an analytic framework that goes beyond the conventional dyadic analysis of the home state and diaspora and instead takes the home/host nation-states, non-Korean migrants, and different diasporic Korean communities together. When one observes diasporic communities *one by one*, the position of Korean Americans in transnational Korea resembles that of Hong Kong Chinese investors in China, where the Beijing government welcomes their investment but treats them like married daughters whose loyalty no longer belongs to their natal family (Ong 1999). The status of Korean Chinese working in South Korea is similar to that of Japanese descendants who returned to Japan from Brazil in the 1970s (Linger 2001; Lesser 2003). I argue that it is possible to observe a hierarchy among them only when we examine Korean diasporic communities all together. This book demonstrates that transnational Korea is inextricable from the capitalist imperatives that shape the hierarchical relations among involved Korean communities.

My analysis of the global scale of Korean capitalism and its hierarchical structure also considers the problem of the instrumental logic of capital. I probe South Koreans' portrayal of North Koreans and Korean Chinese as cheap laborers and consumers of surplus commodities. My analysis links global Korean capitalism and its form to the *simultaneous* crisis of industrial accumulation in the two Koreas and China and their conjoined struggles to resolve the crisis through the exchange of capital and labor among them and imagine such exchange as a process of democratization. The problem of capitalist crisis must be investigated thoroughly in order to recognize the new form of Korean unification. In the Hegelian formula, the crisis of global capitalism is found in the transnational form of Korean sovereignty that emerged out of the effort to overcome the crisis. Or conversely, the analysis of the Korean transnational community demonstrates global capitalism's universal logic and intrinsic crisis. This suggests that the index of Korean ethnic sovereignty is not ethnic and national content nor ideological motifs (cultural differences, ethnic purity, or level of economic development). Rather, it is articulated first and foremost in its commodity form.

CRISIS, SOCIALISM, AND SOVEREIGNTY

To explain the capitalist logic of transnational Korea, I offer an analysis of capitalism, particularly its valorization and the historical expressions of its immanent crisis. Transnational Korea involves a simultaneous crisis in South Korea,

North Korea, and China, and their interlocking process of crisis resolution. A thorough analysis of crisis in capitalism and socialism is therefore warranted. My discussion focuses on the shifting characterization of socialism, especially on the gap between its utopian vision and actuality, as its relationship with capitalism has been theoretical and political terrain for envisioning emancipatory politics. The law of value and the state-capital nexus are two axes of the debate on the crisis of capitalism and the construction of socialism as an alternative. I integrate analyses of global capitalism and biopolitics as a framework for the study of living and dead labor in this book.

Capitalist Crisis and Socialism

Theoretical and historical assessments of capitalist crisis concern the issues of how crisis originates in the very processes of large-scale industrial capitalism and whether the resolution of the crisis requires revolution or reform (Lenin 1917; Marx 1976; Steger 1997). Rejecting market equilibrium as a solution to crisis, Keynes (1936) regarded creating a demand for consumption as a means to forestall declines in the sale of goods. In leftist circles the crisis of capitalism has three structural sources. One is underconsumption, since the masses' consumption power decreases in proportion to capital accumulation that depends on reducing wages (Luxemburg 1913). Another is overproduction, as the monopolistic capitalists are driven to invest in technology and machinery, expand capacity for production, and enhance labor productivity (Lenin 1917). A third source of crisis is a tendency of falling rate of profit: the constant capital spent on buildings, technology, and other costs of production increases disproportionately over variable capital spent on labor costs; and reductions in the workforce cause the rate of profit to fall, since profit requires surplus value, that is, unpaid labor, even when capitalists increase the mass quantity of profit through this process (Marx 1992).

Socialist reformers Bernstein and Kausky argued that the crisis of overproduction could be averted by the state's fiscal and monetary policies and by imperialist means, respectively (Salvadori 1990; Steger 1997). In contrast, Luxemburg (1900) argued that the credit system could exacerbate the crisis by encouraging capitalists to expand without regard to limits of consumption and that imperialism's creation of world-scale markets as the solution to underconsumption would globalize the crisis rather than solve it. The increasing coalescence between banks and industrial capital and the consequent tendency to create monopolies through cartels and trusts produced the well-known synergy and disagreement between Hilferding (1910) and Lenin (1917) on finance capital as the new or highest stage of imperialism. Hilferding located crisis in the dominance of finance capital that engenders disequilibrium between supply and demand, and figures imperialism as necessary to alleviate the crisis. In contrast, Lenin saw finance capitalists as parasites or rentiers whose speculative activities would arrest economic development, at the same time arguing that export of finance capital would lead to wars among imperialistic nation-states and thus intensify political and economic crisis and revolutionary struggle in advanced countries.

The history of socialist economies reveals the complexity of the idea of socialism and its realization. The idea that socialism is a permanent solution to capitalist crisis is rooted in the belief that replacing private property rights with public ownership would bring equality and freedom and that state planning would rationalize production according to the society's needs. Yet assessment of the actual socialist economy depended on the vertiginous implications of the bureaucratization of the state and the continued commodity production and regulation of labor in the process of realizing a socialist economy. A key concern in debates is whether the law of value operates in a socialist economy and if so, how it coexists with state economic planning. The law of value establishes commodified labor power as the means of creating value, and unpaid labor as surplus value that equates to profits. This thesis is at the crux of Marx's (1976) critique of political economists, that is, of his contemporaries who postulated investment in production as the source of profit in capitalism. According to the law of value, application of labor power to other means of production valorizes money into capital. This valorization process is undergirded by private property ownership that commodifies labor. Because propertyless workers own nothing but their labor, they must sell it to survive and must work under regulations designed to maximize the use of their labor power. Through legal contracts employers appropriate the value of work performed by a worker beyond the worth of the worker's wage.

Specific concerns about the law of value in socialist countries address the triad of property ownership, commodity production, and economic distribution. Debates center on whether a change in property ownership is necessary but insufficient for establishing new social relations. Commodity production is seen as vital during the period of transition to socialism. Economic distribution is to be based on the amount and quality of labor needed to enhance productivity. These debates reflect a historical context in which socialist revolution under conditions of underdevelopment caused the development of productive forces to become an imperative of state planning. Called "a strategic retreat," Lenin's New Economic Policy in 1921 permitted peasants free trade, private property ownership of land, and in-kind taxation in order for dispersed peasants to recover from a series of wars. Stalin replaced the New Economic Policy with sweeping collectivization of agriculture and heavy industrialization while insisting that commodity production existed only in the countryside where peasants were allowed to own seed and sell their products. Critics questioned this duality in the Soviet economy and observed that for decades commodity production operated in all facets of the socialist economy (Ali 1984).[1] Stalin justified the state's power as the means to break out of underdevelopment, pursue heavy industrialization, and thereby secure the conditions for socialism in the USSR. Despite his condemnation of bureaucracy, Trotsky conceded that to overcome underdevelopment, the state needed to create the conditions for capitalist expansion in society and ultimately realize socialism by abolishing the subsistence-oriented peasant economy and increasing technological development and the productivity of industrial labor. According to Žižek (Trotsky 2007:viii–ix), this emphasis on the role of the state makes Trotsky a precursor to Stalin despite their fundamental disagreements. Using the metaphor of the cocoon becoming a butterfly, Trotsky (1984:35) reasoned that "in order to become social, private property must inevitably pass through the pupal stage . . . [and yet] myriads of pupae perish without ever becoming butterflies." The transformation of the socialist economy into its butterfly stage depends on the ability of workers to establish their power in the party. This conviction allowed him to state that the October revolution was betrayed but not yet overthrown.

When workers experienced intensified regulation of their labor under the piecework system, shock brigades, and the Stakhanov movement, Stalin (1951) declared that the law of value operated in the USSR without any regulating function except influencing production; he even argued that it could teach business executives and planners to calculate production and its magnitude. Characterizing the Soviet economy as a transitional phase and "the lower stage of communism," Trotsky (1984:37) noted that Soviet workers were still paid according to "bourgeois norms—that is, in dependent upon skill, intensity, and so on"—and that wage differences in the Soviet Union were thus greater and even more barbarous than in capitalist countries. When, however, other critics saw the exploitation of labor as a sign that the Soviet economy had become state capitalism, Trotsky parted with them because of his conviction about permanent revolution against the bureaucratic Thermidorian turn. On a different note, Dunayevskaya (1944), Trotsky's associate and a leader of the Fourth International exiled in the United States, argued that workers in the Soviet Union were subject to the socially necessary labor time set to extract surplus value. For her, the state's paying of wages according to labor, rather than according to need, signified the continued operation of the capitalist law of value in the USSR.

In China, Mao Tse-tung asserted the key role of the political struggle against the bureaucratization of the state and the party in China. Critiquing Stalin for reducing the people to "things" or tools for developing productive forces, Mao emphasized the role of the people in transforming the superstructure of politics. Yet this vision of permanent revolution was also caught in the drive to develop productive forces, as he created a motto about catching up with English industrialization even during the Cultural Revolution. Variant reformers since the 1970s sought to reconcile distribution according to labor and commodity production as necessary for boosting individual incentives within the system of state ownership and planning. In the end, Chinese reforms since the 1990s theoretically separated state ownership from socialism, legitimating the introduction of diverse property ownership systems and thus authorizing private property ownership while keeping the name of socialism (Rozman 1987; Sun 1995:89–107). This book rethinks this Chinese history from the experience of Korean minority. It also demonstrates that North Korea is not an exception to the contradiction arising from the utopian socialist ideal and the pursuit of developing productive forces. I interpret Juche ideology as part and parcel of North Korea's distinctive formula of permanent revolution.

Politics of History: Transition and Unevenness

Deindustrialization and financialization of global capitalism since the late twentieth century further blur the distinction of socialism and capitalism and continue to characterize them as twins—but this time as twins of industrial capitalism. Succeeding the leftist standpoint of the 1970s (Cliff 1974; Binns, Cliff, and Harman 1987), Harman (2010) has argued that capitalist and socialist societies of the twentieth century, despite their respective differences as market and state monopolies, share the same monopolistic tendency of capital, with the crisis of overproduction dictating industrial production. Burawoy (1985) offered a comparative study of the Fordist industrial regime across socialist and capitalist divides. Buck-Morss (2002) has delineated the common construction of state sovereignty in the United States and the USSR, namely, their political imaginaries of the collective figure of the people and its human omnipotence. She has embedded their similar imaginaries in the material conditions of twentieth-century industrial production such as technological development, an unprecedented scale of mass production, and mass labor power.

While these recent and earlier analyses of socialist societies have sought to historicize them, another more recent verdict declares socialist societies to be failures, as if socialism is a thing of the past with no place in the present (Badiou 2005; Russo 2005; Douzinas 2010). Scholars variously characterize this new present as the era of financial capitalism, whose logic of capital accumulation differs from that of the industrial era. This premise of a historical rupture between the industrial and financial stages of capitalism is the assumption underlying the idea of salvaging communism from failed socialism as the renewed form of utopian ideal. Specifically, Hardt and Negri (2011) have called the latest capitalism the biopolitical metropolis, which commodifies sociocultural practices such as language, information, and communication, as well as affects, passions, and other modes of sociality. The central figures in this new capitalist regime are immaterial and intellectual labor and the precarious workforce, especially women and migrant laborers, clashing with moral, nationalist, and racist ideologies. Harvey (2011) has called the state-finance nexus the "central nerve system" of capital accumulation under neoliberalism. Both Harvey and McNally (2010) have documented that manufacturing corporations now derive a large proportion of their profits from financial activities. For example, the profits of the consumer finance divisions of General Motors equal if not surpass profits from the production and sales of vehicles and place the corporation among the largest private holders of property mortgages.

Moreover, the law of competition in financial deregulation motivates financiers to invent new financial products such as credit default swaps, currency derivatives, and interest rate swaps and to engage in short-term, highly speculative, and at times deceptive investment. According to Harvey (2011), the expropriation of the people from the commons, which Marx calls the process of primitive accumulation, is reinvented in the era of neoliberal and financial capitalism as accumulation by dispossession of the commons by privatization, deregulation, and attack on labor power. This latest expropriation involves two broad groups, namely, workers with precarious jobs and dependency on credit, and the group of peasants and indigenous people who become migratory workers in order to survive. For Sassen (2014), current financial capitalism is driven by the logic of expulsion in both the global south and north: Refugee camps in sub-Saharan Africa are flooded with people displaced by global financial capitalists' investment in extracting natural resources for vast short-term profit; in the capitalist north, subprime and other mortgage schemes exploit middle-class and minority homeowners and cause financial destitution. In other words, whereas industrial capitalism creates jobs, economic growth, and socioeconomic mobility within a country, capitalism in its current form for Sassen renders it more predatory on workers and resources.

Recent philosophical discussions return to communism through the endeavor to discern the logic of financial capitalism. For Harvey (2011), communism is an alternative to capitalism, while socialism is a particular democratic form of industrial capitalism. Hardt and Negri (2011; see also Hardt 2010) have found a new basis for communism in the material conditions of the global financial capitalism, given that easily shared and reproducible ownership of commodities, knowledge, and information can make it difficult to police ownership and enforce property rights. Badiou (2010) has approached communism as truth, that is, the utopian idea that is to be repeatedly put into practice despite its historical failures. For Badiou and his interlocutors repeated practice is a central concept for opening the dialectics of politics to indeterminacy beyond the earlier historical materialism.

The notion of historical rupture that is intrinsic to the various postulations about the earlier socialism and the current neoliberal and financial capitalism is problematic. It is one thing to discern the new logic of capital accumulation. It is quite another to explain the institutionalization and experience of the new, given that social relations consist of the new intertwined with the old and that experience is subject to representation and interpretation. Therefore, I shift analytic focus in the study of global financial capitalism from political economic transition to history and politics. Declarations that historic forms of socialism have failed run the risk of leaving out history in a move toward pure politics. They assume that the arrival of the new banishes earlier structures and experiences. This historical consciousness resembles the enduring ideology of capitalism, which represents itself as a revolutionizing force and inaugurates the old as the new through repeated production and circulation. Corollaries of the invoked transition to capitalism since the 1980s are the shift in politics from class struggle to identity and biopolitics and the shift in the idea of democracy from collective emancipation to the rule of law and self-empowerment. These shifts in accounts of socioeconomics, politics, and culture seemingly free history from economic determinism and move it toward fluidity, indeterminacy, and contingency. At the same time, they address knowledge production and cross-class identity formation in the construction of power. These shifts conjure the present historical conjuncture as an era of "transition" that posits a break between the past and the present. I inquire into this prevailing notion of historical transition. Asymmetrical change across economic sectors contradicts the posited sweeping transition to a new form of capitalism. Moreover, historical imagination about an alternative future remains bound to the past whether through negation, nostalgia, or other modes of memory.

What characterizes the present is the uneven relationship between industrial and financial capital, and not a linear transition from the former to the latter. This uneven relationship departs from the modern problematic of the uneven relationship of countryside and city that has defined history and politics since the emergence of industrial capitalism. In the conventional formulation, industrial capitalism began with the expropriation of peasants and herders from the land, which brought an end to their subsistence livelihood. The state and investors legitimated this expropriation on the ground of private property ownership. When the development of urban factories did not keep pace with the need to employ peasants displaced from the countryside, the state feared unrest and imposed laws that banned vagabondage and transformed displaced former peasants into refugees and slaves. For this reason Marx (1976:875) called this process of primitive accumulation a history written in "letters of blood and fire." The violence underpinning capital accumulation is overshadowed by a view of historical progress that imagines technology, market exchange, consumption, and sheer concentration of the people as the grounds for freedom and equality. Benjamin (1969, 2002) discerned ruin and cataclysm in industrial capitalism's ceaseless expansion and optimism about human history. Socialism in the twentieth century was an idea borne of industrial capitalism, whose crisis led pundits to postulate the necessity and inevitability of socialist revolution and the subsequent transition from socialism to communism. However, analyses of historically existent socialism reveal that the imperative of heavy industrialization was not an exception in the making of socialism. Industrialization and labor disciplines also became a mantra in the twentieth-century Third World that perpetuated the dream of socialism. Politics during the industrial era was defined by the hegemonic relationship of workers and intellectuals over peasants and other sectors of the population. The ideology of industrialism legitimates the displacement of peasants from their means of living. Current postulation of a shift from industrial capitalism to financial capitalism functions similarly as an ideology that legitimates dispossessing workers of what they have struggled for with some success under twentieth-century Fordism, namely, secure jobs, higher wages, and rights to collective action.

The hegemonic dominance of finance capital ushers in the uneven changes not only because of the gap between economic sectors but also because of the entwined relationship between economics and politics. On the economics side is the new nexus between industrial capital and finance capital. During the industrial era, finance capital was valorized in relation to the turnover time of industrial capital, for the return on profits in the form of interest on loans is dependent on the process of extracting surplus value from commodified labor production. Instead of positing a transition from industrial to financial capitalism, I follow the ways that manufacturing firms use financial institutions to devise strategies for maximizing profit, even contriving a new crisis as a rationale for laying off workers. As chapter 2 shows, accounting firms help companies to devise ways to devalue constant capital, at least on the books, so as to restructure the production process to benefit capital at the expense of labor. I pay particular attention to the rise of private property rights as a key feature of neoliberal financialization, as well as to its constitutive effects on workers and their desires and struggles, which I analyze within the parameters of the history of the industrial capitalist system and its aftermath.

On the cultural and ideological side is the politics of crisis that constructs capitalism as the imperative force in the making of democracy. This book investigates how the sense of crisis comes to permeate facets of social life under neoliberalization, what new utopian ideals of democracy are, and how earlier utopian dreams play havoc on the present. Whereas sources and logics of capitalist crisis are primary concerns in the literature, I also follow the experience of crisis that is mediated by politics and culture. When observers of today's capitalist system regard migrant workers as paradigmatic subjects displaced by the neoliberal and financial capitalist system, Koreans from China and North Korea working in South Korea and China are emblematic of such displacement. They are subject to the notion that factory work is a thing of the past, while their experiences are also shaped by their own desires for private property rights, wealth, and freedom, all of whose meanings are contingent on their memories of earlier socialist experiences. Given that South Korean workers are also subject to the ideology of postindustrialism, their struggle involves both the negation of earlier mass politics and flashbacks to it. Putatively outdated ideals such as pride in hard work, emancipatory politics, and ethnicity summon a return of the past to the present.

Biopolitics and Global Capitalism

Relating utopian democratic visions to capitalist crisis, I integrate the two canonical paradigms of modern sovereignty: a framework of biopolitics that accounts for the state's exceptional sovereignty within and beyond the law and considers refugees as both others and mirrors of citizens; and a materialist framework of living and dead labor that locates the inalienable sovereignty of the people in their labor power, a source of wealth in the modern history called capitalism. Schmitt (1985) located the sovereignty of the liberal democratic state in its ability to declare a state of exception and sanctify it by law. Arendt (1951) was concerned about refugees who are expelled by the state's violence and dispossessed of the right to have rights. The figure of the refugee reveals a paradox inherent in the modern nation-state system, which inscribes human rights to citizenship and simultaneously endows the nation-state with the power to withhold the rights of citizens. This distinction of refugee and citizen dissolves in Agamben's elaboration of Schmitt's theory of sovereignty. According to Agamben (1998), modern sovereignty renders refugees not just as others of citizens for residing outside of the nation-state and lacking the right to have rights but also as mirrors of citizens whose rights can be suspended by the state's sovereignty. Foucault's (1978) accounts of the modern state and its production and management of life have allowed the discussion of exceptional sovereignty to become a central concern in the study of biopolitics in recent years. For Foucault, the production of knowledge and norms about birth, health, sexuality, and other fundamental aspects of life enables the state's power to pervade the everyday life of individuals. Studies of governmentality under the most recent form of neoliberal democracy concentrate on discourses of power that constitute individuals' worldviews, subjectivities, and desires (see Campbell and Sitze 2013).

I extend the inquiry of biopolitics into the realm of socioeconomics, arguing that the bearers of rights called sovereign subjects are the owners of private property. In the current neoliberal era, the right to private property is more sanctified than ever before by the rule of law, which itself has become equated with democracy. The state's defense of private property rights holds a key to understanding the state's power and its putative withdrawal from socioeconomic affairs. The historically specific feature of the state's sovereignty over the social life of the people is to be analyzed through its relationship with the system of rights to private property. Ideas about the rights of man need to be discussed in relation to the rise and transformation of man as the owner of private property in modern capitalist society. In other words, seeing biopolitics through the prism of history authorizes to connect modern sovereignty with the historical development of capitalism and its institutions.

In turn, the meaning of *living labor* needs further consideration, given the extensive theorization of the politics of life and death as the grounds of modern sovereignty. In Marx's (1976) accounts of capitalism, capitalists buy labor, not labor power, so they impose various social regulations on labor processes in an effort to maximize productivity. This production of socially necessary labor defines the politics of living labor, in which the loss of workers' sovereignty or their death is to be overcome by eliminating the private property system and establishing socialism. Marx's dichotomy between living and dead labor offers original grounds for considering the sovereign subject in capitalism. Marx's characterization of constant capital as dead labor underscores his theorization of surplus labor as a source of profit. I expand the analytic terrain of living or socially necessary labor into the realm of biopolitics. The framework of biopolitics allows us to go beyond the dichotomization of life and death to see them as different sides of the sociopolitical production of labor. The life and death of labor constitute the metamorphosis of socially necessary labor whose contradiction unfolds in the struggle for sovereignty between capital and labor. Discourses about rights, the desire for freedom, and the pursuit of equality are intertwined with the life and death of workers under capitalist conditions.

My analysis of the biopolitics of labor goes beyond a sociological analysis of the political economy of labor. Sociological studies of labor regimes explore regulated, socially necessary labor time in terms of the organization of labor processes, the state, and ideology (e.g., Burawoy 1985; Seidman 1994; Lee 2007; Chun 2009). I establish the sovereignty of labor as an area for historical and philosophical inquiry into capitalism and its crisis. Accounts of neoliberal and financial capitalism postulate capital as the subject of capitalism by attending to capital's strategies to resolve the crisis through privatization, deregulation, and attacks on the collective power of labor (e.g., Aglietta 2001; Sassen 2014). Observers of capitalist crisis see it as a necessity: the inevitable expression of contradictions within the process of accumulation (Clarke 1988, 1993; Marx 1992), and the need for capitalism to resolve overproduction by dumping excess capital through devaluation such as bankruptcy (Harman 2010). This necessity does not mean that crisis necessarily will lead to the breakdown of capitalism and subsequently to revolution. Its manifestation is observed as an occasion for capital and the state to devise new strategies for capital accumulation. Interrupting this framework of capital as the subject of capital accumulation and crisis resolution, Harvey (2011) takes the matter back to a different Marxist ground, namely, labor as the sovereign subject and labor power as the source of its inalienable right. Harvey argues that focus on capital's strategies for crisis resolution obscures the fact that the neoliberal turn since the late 1970s in the West is capital's class struggle to restore and consolidate its class power and that capital transmits its own crisis in profit making into the struggle of workers to maintain employment and economic security. The class nature of neoliberalism is masked by the rhetorics of individual freedom, liberty, and personal responsibility and the virtues of privatization, the free market, and free trade. For Harvey, an unforeseen and ironic effect of this class struggle is that the process of accumulation by dispossession spearheaded by neoliberalization produces numerous interests other than labor that oppose the power of finance capital.

I approach workers' sovereignty by making three entwined modifications in the materialist inquiry: I move from the realm of class struggle, as in Harvey's (2011) approach, to the terrain of the production of surplus value; I extend accounts of the production of surplus value from the law of value and its political economy to delve into biopolitics and its production of life and death; and I expand the terrain of biopolitics from its discursive domain of the production of knowledge and power to include corporeal experiences and historical memories and attend to the historicity of power in the latest turn in capitalism. At the center of the law of value in Marx's accounts of capitalism is the private property system that commodifies labor power and legalizes capitalists' social regulation of labor and their appropriation of unpaid labor. His concept of commodity fetishism underlines the abstraction of social relations into things in that individuals are reduced to values exchanged in the market. Biopolitics expands the space of the social relations of things, given its illumination of lived experience and subjectivities inscribed on the body.

Virno (2004) has offered a rare integration of biopolitics with an analysis of the commodification of labor power. He rethinks Marx's concept of intellectual labor in his investigation of labor in the culture industry under the post-Fordist regime that commodifies intellect, skill, and aptitude. Virno reflects on the concept of social cooperation in these historical conditions and the political meaning of this latest bind of intellectual and manual labor whose hitherto separation has defined the commodification of labor during the industrial era. He unveils the limits of the state's production of life by mapping biopolitics on the problematic that a worker's labor power is sold only as potential. Like Virno, I embed the biopolitics of state sovereignty in the realm of labor power and its incomplete commodification. However, when Virno explicates a new logic of postindustrial capitalism, I explicate the next nexus between industrial and finance capital. Whereas Virno reflects philosophically on the meaning of the ontological sovereignty of labor, I analyze specific cases of Korean migrant laborers, follow their bodily experience of life and death, and conceptualize the cotemporality of different political regimes.

In a conversation with Butler on neoliberalism and economic crisis in and beyond Greece, Athanasiou (Butler and Athanasiou 2013) has approached private property rights as a form of biopolitics, drawing on Fanon's work on the double consciousness of the colonized. Fanon (1967) has probed the constitutive effect of the skin and bodily senses on the lived experience and subjectivities of the colonized, who see their existence through the racialized gaze of the colonizer. According to Athanasiou, when colonial conditions made whiteness and maleness the requirement for property ownership, the body became the terrain of a struggle for recognition, which attests to the struggle's instability and its inevitable determination by material conditions of dispossession. Athanasiou (2013:13) has explored the constitutive effect of private property rights on personhood, belongingness, and identity arising from the ontological linkage of being and having: "Being is defined as having; having is constructed as an essential prerequisite for proper human being." In a similar move, while attending to the constitutive effects of private property rights on the subjectivities of labor, I relate the changing politics of private property ownership to the historical nexus of state, industrial capital and finance capital. These series of steps in integrating the frameworks of biopolitics and living labor guide my analysis of the capitalist unconscious.

THE CAPITALIST UNCONSCIOUS

The Capitalist Unconscious provides a conceptual framework for the study of the sociocultural symbolization of the capitalist system and the ideological and historical character of such representation. For Jameson (1981), the concept of political unconscious allows recognition of symbolic representations of economics and historicizes culture and politics by detecting the repressed and buried reality of history in the present. Similarly, the concept of capitalist unconscious as developed in this book recognizes the economic sources of crisis and its representation in socialist and capitalist economies. Jameson's focus on narratives of ideology and culture reflects his seminal thesis of modernity as a narrative category. My accounts of capitalist utopian ideas expand the unconscious beyond narrative analysis into other corporeal, sensorial, and temporal symbolizations.

Sociopolitical Unconscious: Market Utopia

Market utopia is the sociopolitical symbolization of the latest form of capitalism. The conjectured metamorphosis of the global capitalist system from the industrial age to financial domination corresponds to that of the envisaged democracy from mass utopia to market utopia. Mass production and consumption in the industrial age constituted political subjects as the masses. Imagined possibilities of technology, machinery, and other means for developing the forces of production primed workers to zealously pursue their potential and unleash their imaginations about the future. Linking Benjamin's critique of industrial capitalism and Schmitt's theory of political sovereignty, Buck-Morss (2002:xiii) has asked whether democracy can ever be compatible with a notion of state sovereignty based on violence; she defines the political imaginary of mass power as the visual field of state sovereignty during the industrial era. Both the United States and the USSR embedded the power of the state in the construction of mass power by formulating a common enemy and waging war on behalf of the people's sovereign agency. The notion of mass power is, according to Buck-Morss, a cultural and political construction of the people drawn from utopian imaginaries of industrialization, e.g., new politics and cultures associated with the gigantic scale of production, new organization of labor process, mass consumption, everyday leisure, architecture, and art. Buck-Morss argues that through this process, industrial modernity begets twin worlds: capitalist and socialist. The capitalist world dreamed that the people's democratic sovereignty would manifest itself through material abundance and consumer choice, whereas the socialist world dreamed that the state would provide total security. Under the capitalist system in the twentieth century, the system of private property and the law of competition failed to fulfill social needs and created the illusion that consumption would provide instant gratification. Under the socialist system during the twentieth century, the people also remained imaginary masses, since the state never handed over control of the means of production. She attributes the failure of realizing utopian visions to an inherent contradiction between the political imagery and its socioeconomic conditions, and between global capitalism and the nation-state system. In other words, the Cold War ended with the breakdown of political legitimacy in capitalist and socialist systems alike.

Market utopia has emerged to repair breakdowns in industrial capitalism and mass utopia. Observers note that the mantra of mass power and collective struggle has been replaced by new ideals of personal responsibility, individual freedom, and liberty. According to Ranciere (1999, 2009), democracy has descended into consensus and differential inclusion of people without disruption to the social order, at the same time devolving from the people to the few, namely, the state, technocrats, and experts. Harvey (2011) has seen interests other than labor emerging to fight against the power of financial capital. Abensour (2011) has issued a call to reclaim the act of critiquing and challenging social order in order to separate democracy from procedural democracy and state dictatorship. I conceptualize the notion of market utopia in order to comprehend the construction of capitalism as the market system and rule of law that sanctifies private property rights of individuals. Modern mass utopia derived from the dreamed image associated with the scale of industrial production and consumption and was concerned with the issue of collective human liberation with the state as an instrument. The most recent incarnation of free market capitalism revives the eighteenth-century notion of the market as the basis of the social contract and peace. The return of this belief is at best ironic, because it is remote from the reality of the market's operations under financial capital's predatory strategy of maximizing profits. Market utopia imagines an all-encompassing power of the market and is concerned with the individual's freedom, legal rights, and protections from state violence. Market utopia rests on the market's logic of homogenization rather than technology and mass power, as well as on the idea of the market as a self-regulating institution. Speaking of the earlier liberal capitalist system, Polanyi (1944) noted that the market is seen to regulate itself and freely permeate any barrier, making the previously imagined omnipotence of the collective into passive accessories. Similarly, market utopia in the present envisions the transgression of established political, cultural, and economic borders. It refers to a place without territoriality, that is, to a legal and moral zone of extraterritoriality.

Market utopia entails three repertoires of democratic politics that emerged in the post–Cold War era: reparation, peace, and human rights. I trace their shared capitalist logic of democratic sovereignty. As the most celebrated form of post–Cold War democratic politics, reparation politics aims at correcting wrongs committed by the state in the name of modernization, economic development, and national unity. In places across the continents from South Africa, Congo, Eastern Europe, and North America to South Korea, special laws and truth commissions were set up to document violence and identify victims; reconciliation is enacted through official apologies, monetary and symbolic compensation, and amendments to official history (e.g., Klug 2000; Torpey 2006). This momentous project of correcting history is, however, a form of forgetting or redressing that is a technique of state governance. According to Brown (1995), in reparation politics the liberal opposition between the state and its victims, the people, lumps together all forms of violence and imputes them to the previous state without distinguishing types and sources of violence. Reparation bestows moral legitimacy on the current state by attributing violence to the previous state. Brown's critique uncovers the continuity of power disguised as a historical break. My analysis of reparation as a market utopia brings her critique of the political to its socioeconomic underpinnings and historical representation.

As a metonym of capitalism, the market is envisaged as a mechanism of peace and reconciliation in the neoliberal era. Neoliberal capitalism restores an earlier notion of the market as a mechanism of peace. Intercapitalist competition and state protectionism fueled rivalry and war during the nineteenth century and the first half of the twentieth century. While imperial power was changing hands and decolonization gave rise to new nation-states, the creation of the United Nations and other institutional arrangements such as the Bretton Woods Agreement of 1944 brought about new rules for international trade and set the terms for peace. During the Cold War, the United States and the USSR offered military support and the status of privileged trading partner to those who aligned with them ideologically. The post–Cold War era has reinforced trade as the mechanism of peace, obscuring domination and exploitation across former Cold War fault lines. According to Dean (2009:55), the fantasy of free trade as a form of exchange promises to serve everyone and obscures persistent market failure, intensified inequalities, and increasing monopolies in the market. Conceptualizing this fantasy of free trade as market utopia locates its capitalist logic in the commodification of people. Social relations become commodited when the notion of free trade disaggregates the sovereignty of the people into free individuals who engage in market exchange. The market's logic of homogenization transforms the sovereignty of the people into the freedom of individuals whose histories and differences have been erased. Polanyi (1944) explained the peace of the nineteenth century in terms of the dual movement of commodification and society's utopian responses. My analysis shows that such social responses to crises are not autonomous, as Polanyi assumed, but are implicated in capitalist logic.

Humanism in the age of neoliberal capitalism hinges on the legal protection of the individual's right to the freedom of expression and association. The notion of community here refers to the liberal tenet that the public constitutes a communicative dialogue of disaggregated individuals and their negotiating power with the state (Habermas 1991).[2] In the last century mass utopia drew on the political mobilization of the masses for street protest and collective action as a routine repertoire of politics, whether mobilizing for the right to unionize or for freedom of association. In contrast, market utopia in the current era constitutes politics as a legal process that defines litigation at various levels of courts, including the Constitutional Court, as a new repertoire of politics and thus threatens to remove the political process from everyday life. In the neoliberal era, protection of human rights is exalted as the most sublime value; it transcends the jurisdiction of the nation-state and warrants putative supranational power. I transform the inquiry of human rights advocacy into its relationship with the global capitalist system and its legal foundation such as private property rights.

Market utopia is a new aesthetics of politics, pledging to reclaim politics from the earlier mass politics. Having momentarily overcome enemies—until the rise of antiterrorism in the mid-2000s—the modern state's violence during the post–Cold War era has emerged as a new enemy. Market utopia negates the very act of grounding sovereignty in the state's production of the collective that Schmitt (1976) theorized as the political par excellence. It instead defines two new enemies, namely, the modern state's violence involved in making of the collective, and individuals' complicity with the state. I discern the renunciation of the state's violence as a shared property of reparation politics, peace and reconciliation, and human rights advocacy. The new politics in the post–Cold War era appeals to fight against "the enemies within us" and blurs the boundary of us and them. Market utopia is an instance of this new politics that redefines the distinction between Left and Right.

Everydayness, spontaneous politics, and ethics constitute market utopian politics. Market utopian politics pillories metanarratives of social change led by the state, the party, and social movement organizations on the grounds that such politics suffocate individuality and standardize the process of politics. Market utopia rejects the political and moral leadership of organized political groups in defense of the individual's spontaneity and open-ended action. Instead, abstract moral or ethical concerns become the harbinger of reconciliation, peace, and human rights. Everyday life becomes the zone of pure politics, which harbors unmediated, immediate, and even pristine experience. Rejecting the politics as a unitary whole, the politics against violence by the state, wars, and human rights abuses develops a synergy with identity politics and neoliberal politics of self-improvement. I analyze the ways that the politics of quotidian life and morality enters into a consensus with capitalism.

Law is the technique of sovereignty in market utopia. Victims and refugees become a sublime and simulated corporeality as they become themselves a sign of the intrinsic limit to citizenship rights. Democracy comes to mean legal rights of individuals in relation to the state, while erasing the meaning of collective sovereignty. It is instructive to compare law with cinema that is a technique of sovereignty in mass utopia. For Buck-Morss (2002:149), cinema is "the means of social control [that is] not organizational but mimetic," as phenomena exist as images on the cinema screen, as well as in advertisements and propaganda posters; this technique of doubling turns the anxiety of alienation or meaninglessness of individuals into illusory fulfillment. Law confers a similar dreamlike character on market utopia, albeit in the realm of expertise and lobbying rather than that of collective politics. The cinematic screen provides a prosthetic experience of mass power; the advocacy for the constitutional rights of victims moves politics from the streets to the courts.

When the law is equated with truth and justice, it is instrumental in privatizing common goods and public assets. This capitalist aspect of the law underpins primitive accumulation and accumulation by dispossession. Thus, an account of the cotemporality of legalism and the neoliberal capitalist system is in order. In fact, the victimization of individuals is at best a phenomenal representation of violence that entails a complex constellation of modernity—capitalism, imperialism, a vision of historical progress, and emancipatory politics. Conceptualizing "legal fetishism," Pashukanis (1924), a Soviet scholar of law and Marxism, approached law not only as a matter of the political interests of class actors or a state institution but also as an institution intrinsic to capitalism. Legal fetishism concerns homogenization of the people into aggregates of individuals whose rights vis-à-vis one another are equal under the law. According to Pashukanis, this legal basis is intrinsic to commodity fetishism, for it authorizes the transaction of labor power as equal exchange and thus permits appropriation of surplus value. Whereas legal fetishism risks economic reductionism, Comaroff and Comaroff (2009) have grasped the indeterminate interaction of legalism and capitalist domination. In their observation, native populations in the United States and South Africa in the neoliberal capitalist turn commodified their culture and ethnic identity in the operation of casinos and the creation of their practice as intellectual property. According to the Comaroffs, this "Ethnicity, Inc." does not entirely reify their culture and identity, but offers an unexpected moment for native Indians to develop their sovereign power against the state through the economic and legal means afforded by profits from their ethnic enterprises.

Expanding the inquiry of sovereignty into the inquiry of law and capitalism, I analyze the ways current democratic politics abstracts the capitalist character of the law and follow the narrative construction of law and constitutionalism and their limits.

Historical Unconscious: History as Repetition

Market utopia signifies a transition in democratic politics. Market utopia evokes not so much historical progress as the move toward a new universal history in the form of ethics. I critique the transition thesis about global capitalism as well as the thesis about market utopia on the grounds that they ignore history and politics. I demonstrate that earlier democratic ideals unleash their spell over the politics of market utopia. For instance, nationalism and collectivism refuse to disappear but return through the back door to coexist with the new ethics of individual responsibility, cosmopolitanism, and plural belongingness. Although socialist and revolutionary politics are renounced in the age of identity politics and contingent politics, their unrealized ideals add bewilderment to the presumed historical transition. The history of mass sovereignty is deposited in one's memory and bodily sensory system. It is released, à la Benjamin (1969, 2002), without consciousness or intention as the political potential capable of disrupting the status quo.

The transition paradigm involves not just the changes in capitalism and democratic politics but also the changes in the state. It has become conventional in the West and beyond to observe a shift from the Keynesian welfare state to the neoliberal state. The welfare state frames social security measures as common goods necessary for generating economic growth and expanding democracy. In contrast, the neoliberal state enforces privatization, deregulation, and other neoliberal economic measures through laws and legal proceedings that sanctify private property rights and individual freedom over the common good and social justice. The neoliberal state prioritizes cutting public spending, particularly on social welfare, while advocating a smaller government bureaucracy in the name of increasing efficiency and reducing public expenditure. In that conjuncture, scholars seek to transform the paradigm of the developmental state from an earlier model of facilitating capital accumulation as an engine for job creation and economic growth to a new model of a state that strengthens human capabilities (Sen 1999; Evans 2014). With deindustrialization, theorists seek to find institutions that are conducive to generating growth and improving workers' prospects (e.g., Rodrik, Subramanian, and Trebbi 2004).

Despite the importance of transforming the paradigm of the modern state, I conceptualize the changing visions of the modern state as "repetition" by relating them to capitalist crisis. The concept of history as repetition authorizes comprehension of the temporality of historical change beyond the transition paradigm. In Schmitt's footsteps, Löwith recognized the contiguity of democracy and totalitarianism. He attributed the transformation of bourgeois democracy into regimes of totalitarian rule, including socialist Russia, fascist Italy, and National Socialist Germany, to the development of mass industrial democracy that politicizes all domains of life from work to spirituality (cited from Agamben 1998:120–21). For Agamben (1998:121–23), this contiguity of democracy and fascism also develops in a reverse order from fascist regimes back into parliamentary democratic systems in twentieth-century Europe.[3] This contiguity of different political regimes arises, argues Agamben, from the shared belief in the modern state's production and management of life despite the state's different contents. Instead, I approach the comparability of various states not in terms of contiguity but in terms of historical repetition. When the philosophical discussions about the contiguity of various states are based on the biopolitics of modern state sovereignty, I consider this inquiry a problematic of the capitalist crisis. Namely, crisis repeatedly generates the impossibility of overcoming itself, and this impossibility fuels repeated attempts to find adequate political forms to contain its effects. Historical repetition in this book does not refer to the business cycle of prosperity, crisis, recession, and recovery, but instead to the manifestation of the crisis immanent in capitalism in political form, thus making repetition symptomatic of crisis. The impossibility of completely containing crises immanent to capitalism triggers repeated attempts to invent political forms. While socialist dictatorship emerged as a political force that aimed to replace capitalism with a new utopian system, neoliberal representative democracy is the latest attempt in repeated efforts to overcome global capitalist crises.

Karatani (2012) has conceptualized the historical repetition arising from the simultaneous necessity and impossibility of political resolutions as "repetition compulsion." In his reading of Marx's *The Eighteenth Brumaire of Louis Bonaparte* (1968), Karatani has argued that the appearance of revolution in the form of the emperor in the book attests not merely to a return of the old in the present, as in conventional readings of *The Eighteenth Brumaire*, but rather to the very crisis of capitalism represented in an old political form. With a focus on the market circulation of goods, Karatani bases his understanding of crisis on the business cycle of boom and bust in the history of the West and Japan. This cyclical nature of business cannot, however, adequately explain repetition of political forms, that is, the inability of political regimes to permanently stabilize capitalism. In my view, the immanence of crisis in production, not the business cycle of boom and bust, is key to understanding the repetition of political forms that Karatani set out to explain. The seemingly stable period of capital accumulation in the United States during the 1950s and 1960s relied on the state's role in securing class compromises and social security necessary to stabilize production and consumption by workers. This stabilizing arrangement, called Fordism, was short lived, and its alternatives such as post-Fordism and just-in-time production remain largely unsuccessful (Harvey 1991; Aglietta 2001). The limit of the state's role results from the contradictory dynamics inherent in capitalist expansion: capital not only benefits from the state's enforcement of private property rights and regulation of labor but also deterritorializes its production and circulation.

Political regimes are fetishized, which, according to Žižek (2002), exposes the relationship between actual social relations and their idealized expression and authorizes a separation of form and content. Despite the seemingly contrasting and incompatible contents of each state, they share the same form because they share important yet futile roles in resolving capitalist crises. If the socialism of the twentieth century became a spectacle for the violent nature of the socialist state that nullified the utopian revolutionary zeal of the masses, gulags were its evident contents. Socialism is, I argue, a political form that was envisaged to remedy the ills and crises of industrial capitalism. That is, the dictatorship of the socialist state was grounded in the social process of pursuing industrial accumulation. The socialist state created institutions to close the gap between actual social conditions and its utopian social vision by imposing homogeneous reforms of the state-planned economy and collectivization. It also attempted to close the gap between a utopian vision of production and distribution and the actual requirement of surplus appropriation that was deemed necessary for facilitating productive forces and economic development—the race to catch up with English industrialization, according to Mao Tse-tung (Schram 1971). Military dictatorship, the welfare state, and neoliberal democracy are other political forms that had similar political functions of representing and resolving capitalist crisis.

My analysis of political form does not reduce politics to economics but rather exposes the shared logic of different political regimes. This means that capitalist crises contribute to the establishment of political forms and that socialism, communism, or democracy is more than a political ontology or theorem. Political form paradoxically attests to the irreducibility of the economic to the political: While capital accumulation depends on the liberal state and other political forms for institutionalizing social conditions that valorize capital, such as law and policies on property and labor rights, its immanent crises can only temporally be contained. According to Žižek (2002), French post-Marxism insists on the irreducibility of politics to economics in fear of losing the openness and contingency constitutive of the political field. The cultural turn and identity studies also launched a similar political critique of Marxism over recent decades. In this book, I attend to the fidelity of logic and history, which, helps us to recognize the important mediation of the socio-economics of capitalism and the limits of such mediation (see Harootunian 2012). Derrida (1994) observes this fidelity in terms of the spectral manifestation of the real. In *The Capitalist Unconscious*, the real is the socioeconomic logic of the valorization of capital that manifests only through mediation, and such mediation is always partial and repeated through spectrality.

Chapter Outlines

This book is intended to be read as a whole. Throughout the text, local and national histories in the three places—South Korea, North Korea, and China—are woven together in order to discern the dynamics of transnational Korea despite the important complexity of each history. As a multi-site analysis of border-crossing labor migration, this book is based on my archival and ethnographic research begun in 1996, with the concentration on the period from 2001 to 2007, which is the volatile formative period of transnational Korea. Ethnographic materials from this period come from my participation in meetings and forums organized by legislators and activists as well as from in-depth interviews with more than 120 people, including migrant workers, policy makers, legislators, and activists in South Korea and China. Activists and local residents introduced me to undocumented Korean Chinese and North Koreans. Archival sources comprise official, unpublished, and censored documents issued by governments, political parties, and social organizations. They include socialist documents, including North Korean archival materials and highly censored Chinese records on the Korean Chinese minority and its participation in the Chinese revolution. The research process offered an occasion to rethink the meaning of democratization in doing historical research: Consensus as a mode of democratic politics circumscribes the diversity of perspectives despite freer access.

I analyze institutional, legal, and political processes in South Korea, in which policy makers, NGOs, leftists, and evangelists in partnership with the United States and global NGOs construct identities and rights of Korean migrants from North Korea and China in relation to those of non-Korean migrant laborers from other parts of Asia. These analyses of South Korean politics are paired with the politics and history of the socialist revolution and privatization in China and North Korea, as well as with migrants' own politics. South Korean politics does not completely determine this capitalist integration of the two Koreas and the Korean diaspora. The multisite analysis demonstrates the extent to which neoliberal capitalist measures were adopted simultaneously in these different places yet generated meanings specific to each site's different local history. This analysis in turn provides the basis for understanding the state's language and everyday politics of privatization and deregulation in each Korean community.

The outlines of chapters in this book are as follows. Part I presents a historical and theoretical framework for the book. Chapter 1 formulates a transnational approach to the Korea question and embeds it in the larger historical and theoretical inquiry into modern sovereignty, the crisis of capitalism, and the temporality of historical change. Chapter 2 examines the cotemporality of political regimes, recognition of which leads to formulating the cotemporality of hitherto fragmented groups of labor, including unionized domestic workers, nonunionized irregular workers, foreign migrant workers, and ethnic returnees. In the putatively democratic and neoliberal era, flashbacks to occasions of violence perpetrated by the military state create new political moments that break down the prevailing periodization of pre- and post-democratization in democratic politics.

Part II focuses on reparation as a mode of market utopia by expounding the formation of transnational Korea under the crises of South Korea and Korean Chinese community. Chapter 3 examines the ways that debates on hierarchical transnational Korea entail reparation politics for Korean Chinese. Their unexpected return to South Korea as migrant workers is constructed as a moment of decolonization for South Korea. I discern liberal and capitalist logics in this inverted decolonization that jettisons the rights of Korean Chinese as migrant workers. Chapter 4 approaches Korean Chinese migratory work as a form of socialist reparation that transmutes unfulfilled socialist promises into commodities. The Chinese state characterizes economic privatization as reparation for the violence of socialist revolution. I investigate the new forms of violence involved in the capitalist integration of Korean Chinese, with a focus on their corporeal experience of migratory work and their narratives of dual nationality. Chapter 5 interprets the involuntary recollections of the Chinese Cultural Revolution that arose among Korean Chinese while working in South Korea as a sign of the historical repetition of violence. The trope of intraethnocide in their memory is explored as inverting the violence that was integral to the Chinese socialist revolution into ethnic trauma. Repeated articulation of dual nationality during the socialist revolution and the current privatization is a metanarrative of Korean Chinese experiences of migration.

Part III presents advocacy of peace and human rights as other modes of market utopia, taking account of the formation of transnational Korea in the tripartite relationship of the two Koreas and Korean Chinese. Chapter 6 approaches Korean unification as the question of democratic politics in South Korea, which changes from national utopia to market utopia during the post–Cold War era. I uncover the consensus underlying heated opposition within unification politics between advocacy of peace and reconciliation and advocacy of human rights and regime change in North Korea. I disclose the shared capitalist logic of the two polemical visions of Korean unification that are mapped on the disparate new imaginaries of the Asian community. In chapter 7 the construction of North Korea in these new unification politics is juxtaposed with the North Korean state's own crisis-ridden construction of socialism from the 1950s to the present. As in the Soviet Union and China, socialist construction in North Korea developed the contradiction between rapid heavy industrialization and the socialist ideals of sovereignty and equality, which I locate in its socioeconomic institutions and the processes of socialist transition. This historical approach to the current crisis in North Korea embeds its putative transition to capitalism in the crisis-ridden history of its socialist transition. Addressing the capitalist and democratic integration of North Koreans with South Korea and Korean Chinese community, chapter 8 elucidates the everyday experience and subjectivity of North Koreans in their migration to China and South Korea. The narrative of their migration, "I didn't have to come [to China and South Korea] but still [I did] . . ." authorizes a shift in analytic focus from their refugee status, as in unification politics, to their commodification. I conceptualize their cascading migration to China and on to South Korea as a Hegelian negation of the negation of commodification, attending to its mediation by ethnic and religious relations with Korean Chinese. Finally, I identify aleatory subjects whose vagabondage, manual labor, and desire for a stateless nation harbor subversive critiques of socialism and capitalism.

2

THE AESTHETICS OF DEMOCRATIC POLITICS: LABOR, VIOLENCE, AND REPETITION

This chapter investigates the inversion of democracy into the rule of law in South Korea since the 1990s, which sanctifies the private property system. Whereas South Korea's military state (1961–1988) assumed supreme power over the law and legal proceedings, the representative democratic state (1988–present) espouses the rule of law as the source of its power. The democracy movement against the military dictatorship formulated nationalist and socialist visions of a future to counter the partnership of the state, monopoly capital, and American imperialism. On July 29, 1987, popular protests forced the military power to accede to the demand for a direct election, making this event a turning point for democratization. The democracy movement since then moved toward an expansion of the rights of citizens and the autonomy of civil society. In this chapter I analyze the paradox in this momentous political transition in terms of the continuous dominance of capital and its mechanisms.

I conceptualize this new mode of democracy as the capitalist unconscious. A tragedy of the military dictatorship was its appropriation of nationalism, which legitimated its discipline of capitalists and workers as national assets. A farce in democratization since 1987 is the sublimation of private property ownership in the name of the rule of law. My inquiry focuses on the representation of private property rights in discourses and politics of capitalist crises, democracy, and historical progress. In order to elucidate the ideological character of the latest democracy movement, it is crucial to identify, notwithstanding their striking differences, the *cotemporality* of the military dictatorship and the representative democratic state as two political forms of capital accumulation. Proof of this cotemporality lies in the limit of democracy under each government. The rule of law not only legitimates the suspension of individual rights by invoking the supremacy of universal will but also guarantees private property ownership to validate the violence of capital. Recognition of this limit of representative democracy dissolves an enduring schema of the political that provides the basis for the distinction between the two political forms. This limit to democracy under the representative regime is structural precisely because of the privatization and deregulation of capital: capital is released from nationalism and other collective appearances, becomes freer and more ruthless, and spirals into its innate crises of competition and monopoly. I analyze the new regime of capital and its everyday transformation by examining their mediation by the politics of historical transition.

The latest politics of democracy since 1987 distinguishes among three figures of workers: Chŏn T'aeil, a martyr of the labor struggle, who represented workers under the despotic labor regime during the military dictatorship and whose suicide galvanized the popular minjung (people's) democracy struggle of the 1980s; foreign migrant workers (hereafter migrant workers) whose undocumented status and inhumane working and living conditions spurred the civil society movement, especially during putatively progressive governments (1998–2008); and Korean workers (hereafter domestic workers), whose rights to unionization and to political empowerment since 1987 symbolize democratization, and yet who are subjected to layoffs as part of neoliberal restructuring and the brutal suppression of their strikes once again. The latest politics of democracy maps three labor figures on the order of disparate spatiotemporalities that separate them from one another in terms of political regime, labor regime, citizenship, race, and unionization. I explicate narratives and practices of the fragmented democratic politics in terms of political subjects, vision of their emancipation, and repertoires of struggle. I approach the fragmented democratic politics as a sociopolitical symbolization of neoliberal capitalist rule. The cotemporality of the three labor figures is an excess that is repressed by the fragmented democratic politics. The cotemporality denotes that capital and disparate political regimes continue capital accumulation by deploying broad-ranging techniques of labor discipline. Two instances of cotemporality are important for my analysis, which simultaneously underscores their shared experience of commodification and highlights historically specific modes of discipline and labor regulation. One instance concerns military and democratic (progressive and conservative) governments, both of which enforce the valorization of capital and the commodification of labor. The other instance of cotemporality involves illegal migrant workers and unionized workers of the democratic era, who are both oppressed under the rule of law. The spatiotemporality of these laborers concerns the cultural and ideological representation of capitalist accumulation in democratic politics. It is situated within concrete material conditions, namely, the bifurcated structure of capital that shaped the uneven crisis and crisis-resolution strategies of conglomerates and small- and medium-sized firms during the military era and that continues to shape them.

I begin this chapter by raising the question of the temporality of three labor figures, which illustrates the importance of linking capitalist crisis, democratic representation, and commodification. Next I explore the politics of migrant workers employed in small- and medium-sized factories, which demonstrates the shift of democratic politics from a popular mass movement to an identitarian civil society movement. This analysis of migrant workers is followed by accounts of unionized workers' struggles over their discharge under neoliberal restructuring. The politics of these two groups of labor embody aesthetics of the new democratic politics and its excesses. Then, I examine two modes of contemporary historicism in South Korea, the 1987 thesis and the 1997 thesis, as narratives of the crisis that seek to reconcile neoliberal capitalism with democracy by envisaging historical progress in terms of transition. I theorize an alternative notion of history, that is, historical repetition, in order to probe capital's historically changing modes of violence and explain the cotemporality of the three labor figures.

SPATIOTEMPORALITY OF THREE FIGURES OF LABOR

"How long have I waivered and agonized over this decision? Now at this moment I made a near absolute decision. I must return. I definitely must return. To my wretched brothers and sisters. To my heart's home. To the young children's mind in the P'yŏnghwa Market that is my whole ideal. . . . I return to them, forsaking myself and killing myself. I entirely dedicate my weak being in order not to leave all of you" (Chŏn T'aeil kinyŏm'gwan kŏllip wiwŏnhoe 1983). On November 13, 1970, about three months after writing this resolution in his diary, Chŏn T'aeil set himself on fire on the streets of the market. Soon to become a martyr of the labor struggle under the military dictatorship, this twenty-two-year-old tailor in the P'yŏnghwa (Peace) Market shouted the slogans until he lost consciousness: "Observe the Labor Standards Act! Workers Are Not Machines! Let Us Rest On Sundays!" Twenty-five years later on January 9, 1995, thirteen Nepali migrant workers began their nine-day sit-in-protest at the

Myŏngdong Cathedral, a long-standing cradle of the democracy movement, which marked the beginning of the upcoming sporadic struggle of migrant workers. They shackled their necks with iron chains to depict their slavelike working conditions. They appealed:

> Since we didn't have jobs in our own countries, we came to South Korea as industrial trainees to escape poverty. . . . While we came with a hopeful dream in our heart, we now suffer indescribably. . . . Our families back home haven't received any money, while employment agencies have already seized our wages for six months with the promise of sending them to our families on our behalf. On a daily basis we are abused verbally and beaten up, and never receive wages directly. . . . We are treated as less valuable than machines. We learned that the South Korean government systematically facilitates such a situation. . . . Although we suffer like slaves in South Korea, our existence itself as humans is not indigent. . . . We appeal to South Koreans and South Korean government that they do not turn us into animals but instead treat us as humans and brothers.
>
> (1995-nyŏn 1-wŏl 9-il nongsŏng hosomun)

Wrapping their bodies with chains, Nepali workers marked their protests holding a sign that says, "Don't beat us. We are humans too. We are not slaves."

Migrant workers from China, Indonesia, Bangladesh, the Philippines, and other parts of Asia endured abusive conditions as follows[1]: extreme hours such as working continuously for ten to fifteen hours and working for thirty-two hours with only three hours of sleep; wages below minimum standards and unpaid wages that are attributed to their illegal status and real and feigned bankruptcy of employer; insufficient job training resulting in preventable workplace accidents, such as injury to fingers and hands and exposure to toxic chemicals, and discharge rather than medical care for accidents; prohibition of changing jobs, kidnapping, and forced labor, including confiscation of worker's passport and foreign worker's certificate; physical, verbal, and sexual assault in the workplace; forced monthly deposit to prohibit changing workplace; owners' report on migrant workers to the authorities when workers demand unpaid wages, compensation for accidents, and better treatment; and immigration raids. It is reported that the Indonesian government included military training, face slapping, and beating in its preparation of prospective workers for South Korea (JCMK 2001a). This violence against migrant workers is a ghostly reminder of the earlier oppression of domestic workers in the 1970s and 1980s. According to Chŏn T'aeil's report in the late 1960s, women coworkers operating sewing machines in garment factories were on average nineteen to twenty-three years old, and their assistants between fourteen and eighteen years old. In his words:

> The size of their workplace is usually 8 p'yŏng [26.4 square meters], in which tailors and other 14–15 pale workers are crammed together in seats. The height from bottom to ceiling is about 1.5 meter, as the 3-meter-high room is divided into two. Workers can't straighten their backs when they walked. If you watch from the overpass near Ch'ŏnggyech'ŏn 6-ka, these workplaces are like cages for swine or chickens. Locked into the closed chicken cage and with the ceaseless noise from the sewing machines, workers usually work the whole day without seeing any sunlight from 8:00 A.M. to 11:00 P.M. Beyond the repeated work of ironing, doing all kinds of errands, and removing lint from clothes, the most unbearable is the scolding from the owner or sewing machine operators several times a day which subjects them to all kinds of verbal abuse and, sometimes, beatings. A woman worker has tears and black mucus if she blows her nose because of the exposure to the odors of oil, sweat, and fabric, and dust from cutting and sewing fabric all day.
>
> (Chŏn T'aeil kinyŏm'gwan kŏllip wiwŏnhoe 1983:83–84)

Given the democratization since 1987 South Koreans are perplexed by the extent of the violence against migrant workers, for they have come to regard such workplace violence as a thing of the past. How do we explain the seeming return of this deadly violence that turns the bodies of migrant workers into absolute thing-ness? Does merely their illegal status invite exploitation and abuse? Or is there a primordial origin as labor activists and NGOs claim—namely, Korean ethnocentrism and xenophobic racism? Activists and scholars concerned with migrant workers focus on their migratory passage, labor relations, and racism. Social science studies of migrant workers especially attend to structural and network determinants, such as overseas investment, policies of host and home countries, brokers, and ethnic and familial ties. They also focus on the institutionalization of migrant workers as illegal and disposable labor, exploring cultural and political exclusion and NGOs' human rights advocacy (Sŏl 1999; JCMK 2001a). Distinct from studies of migrant workers, accounts of the labor struggle of South Korean workers focus on three shifts: from social unionism to economic unionism, a change from enterprise-level unionization to industry-level unionization, and the move toward creation of the Labor Party.[2] The failures of the labor movement result from various factors, ranging from its promoting interests of unionized workers in heavy-chemical factories owned by conglomerates, the failure of industry-based unionism, its leadership's bureaucratization and culture of compromise with capital, to its neglect of migrant workers, nonunionized workers and growing irregular (pijŏnggyujik) workers (Kim Tongch'un 1995; Goldner 2009; Son Mia 2009). In this critique, the consolidation of Fordism in South Korea after the 1987 Great Strikes becomes indistinguishable from the unions' compromise to maintain their members' own jobs and wages at the expense of those of more underprivileged workers, feeding the ideology that labor unions become "the labor aristocracy." The failure of the Labor Party stemming from enduring schisms among leftists and age-old localism going back to the 1980s is also well documented. These characteristics are noted as being responsible for the Labor Party in South Korea becoming empowered more slowly than those in Brazil and Chile, although democratization began at a similar time in all three places (Cho Tonmun 2004).

An analysis of the comparability of nonunionized domestic workers before 1987, unionized domestic workers since the 1990s, and migrant workers is warranted by the fidelity of the history and the logic of modern sovereignty. It not only helps us to comprehend their historicity beyond differences in work, organization, and politics but also reveals the specific linkage of democratization and capital accumulation. South Korean history underlines that migrant workers and unionized workers since the late 1980s are entwined by the bifurcated industrial structure of small- and medium-sized factories and conglomerate-owned large factories and their linked responses to the capitalist crisis. Since the 1990s, the South Korean economy confronted multiple challenges resulting from increasing production costs, intensified competition with cheaply priced goods from newly developing countries, and expanded export regulations of developed countries. Industries' responses to these challenges reflect their bifurcated structure. Cost-saving measures taken by conglomerates consist of outsourcing in developing countries, subcontracting with domestic factories, and adopting flexible employment programs (Paik Nakki et al. 1998; Yi Sangho 2007). The inequality between conglomerates and small- and medium-sized firms deepens with growing discrepancies in levels of technology, financial capacity, and unionization of workers (Kim Hyŏnggi 1994; Kim Yŏngmi and Han Chun 2008). Small- and

medium-sized factories increasingly rely on cheap labor rather than technological improvements, which is the context of the growing need for unskilled
foreign workers.[3]

The new culture of capital accumulation compounds labor shortages
in small- and medium-sized factories. In tandem with the economic panic
after the 1997 financial crisis and neoliberal reforms, South Korean society
has seen a rise in the speculative measures of wealth accumulation. A lure to
investment in venture capital firms, the explosion in stock market trading,
and fascination with the lottery are fantastical techniques of speculative accumulation. New desires for consumption combined with high unemployment
engender mounting debt among young adults and ordinary households,
with default on debt emerging as a vexing social problem. The new regime
of capital accumulation fans the ideology of postlabor society as if the manufacturing sector is withering away in South Korea, if it is not already dead.
Manual labor is fetishized, as hard labor is reduced to individual dedication
and ethics, especially of small shop owners and workers, thus erasing labor's
characteristics of objectification and abstraction. Weekly television programs
such as The Skilled in Everyday Life (Saenghwal ŭi tarin) and Extreme Jobs (Kŭkkan
chigŏp) are examples that eschew the social in favor of morality and ethics.
The ideology of postlabor society contributes to the declining appeal of labor
unions. This new regime of production and consumption underpins the conditions that attract migrant workers.

Associating the historical relationship of migrant workers and unionized
workers with the logic of modern sovereignty allows us to consider their
cotemporality with pre-1987 workers. I conceptualize military and democratic
rule as two specific moments of the state's exceptional sovereignty when
their conventional opposition fragments the three groups of workers from
one another. Whereas the military state monopolized the means of violence
and suspended law in the name of a national emergency, the democratic
state has resorted to violence in the name of defending the rule of law. Specifically, the military dictatorship constructed firms and factories as national
assets, likening each of them to an army as an expression of their role in the
competition with North Korea over national economic development. Docile
workers were hailed as national heroes, while workers waging protests and
labor struggle faced national security law. Accordingly, private companies
such as conglomerates were considered public and national property, having
been created with the state's financial subsidies and protected against market
fluctuation. For example, in 1994 the state approved Samsung Group's entry
into the automobile industry only after years of heated debate on its projected

effect on the use of national resources, including human capital, and on the global competitiveness of the South Korean automobile industry as a whole (Kim Panghee 1993; Chin Chŏngsun 2010). Since the 1990s, private property ownership has constituted the backbone of the democratic order of freedom and equality in the neoliberal era. Labor strikes by unionized workers have been ruled unlawful and cracked down by the police on the grounds that they damage the private property of their company. Striking workers fear not only arrest but also threats of court orders to pay for damage to buildings, machinery, and other company assets. Despite advances in political democratization, the rule of law simultaneously intensified a phantasmagoric process of commodification. I bring the discussion of the sovereignty of the modern state into the terrain of capital accumulation and the sovereignty of labor. I analyze the rule of law not just in terms of its content but also its form that abstracts social relations of production and defends them with the state's power.

POLITICS OF MIGRANT WORKERS: BETWEEN HUMAN RIGHTS AND LABOR RIGHTS

The life and work of migrant workers have become integral to South Korean democratic politics almost immediately after migrants first arrived in late 1980s. Ever since Catholic and Christian churches opened their doors to migrant workers in Seoul and its outskirts in 1992, many religious organizations, labor groups, and NGOs have offered shelter, medical care, and legal assistance, with more than 130 providers of services to migrant workers as of 2003 (Song Chongho 2006). Moreover, the rights of migrant workers quickly became a contentious sociocultural and political issue that challenged national culture and spurred major legal reforms. Here, the focus is on the Joint Committee for Migrant Workers in Korea (JCMK), the umbrella organization of advocacy groups for migrant workers, which was formed in July 1995 a few months after the Nepali workers' protests. The organization spearheaded the drive to legalize the migrant work program, organizing an alliance of political forces, mobilizing the media, experts, and citizens, and negotiating with branches of the government. According to migration studies in the United States, undocumented migrant workers and their advocates fruitfully contested their illegality by stressing their societal membership on the basis of their economic contributions and integration into the community (Coutin 2005; Hagan 2006; Basok and Carasco 2010). In a different move, JCMK pursued the legalization of migrant workers through two means:

cosmopolitanism and legalism. Its cosmopolitanism emphasized South Koreans' obligation to protect the human rights of migrant workers. Its practice of legalism shaped a new repertoire of politics, favoring appeals to the courts and legal reform over street protests, mobilizing citizens and experts, and negotiating with the state.

In a section called "Remembering Chŏn T'aeil Again" (Tasi Chŏn T'aeil ŭl ttŏollimyŏ), JCMK's report lists the aforementioned labor conditions of migrant workers under the despotic labor regime that mirrors that of the Chŏn T'aeil generation of the 1970s and 1980s. This overlay of the two groups of workers suggests a rare indication of their cotemporality, but its account stops there. A more thorough understanding of their relationship requires understanding the differences and similarities in their representations. Migrant workers and earlier domestic workers differ in their double representation. During the rapid industrialization Korean factory workers were simultaneously exalted as national heroes and denigrated for performing low-status manual work. From the late 1990s migrant workers are concurrently idealized as cosmopolitan subjects and criminalized as threats to the social order because most of them were undocumented until the mid-2000s. They are disparaged as ruthlessly economic creatures who would exchange life for money and target vulnerable South Korean women for marriage and are portrayed as violent and lawless in headline news of sporadic brawls and murders among them.[4] Their enclaves of ethnic restaurants, shops, and Hindu and other religious facilities are, however, reported as becoming emblematic of Korea's cosmopolitan multiethnic future. South Korean activists and media welcome their presence as a sign of the new multicultural mosaic of democratic society. They invite migrant workers to participate in holiday singing contests on television. Korean Chinese women appear in television soap operas as workers in restaurants, hotels, and private homes, providing realistic embellishment to the dramas.

The cotemporality of earlier domestic workers and recent migrant workers emerges from the state-capital nexus that authorizes the state's use of violence to sustain their labor conditions. In this regard, their comparability needs to be explored in terms of their representation in the democratic movement. I therefore investigate JCMK's activism and its response to the state-capital nexus. The organization straddled the old and the new democratic politics: It integrated its advocacy into the emergent civil society movement, while key leaders maintained some of the earlier principles, that is, the labor rights of workers. Comparing migrant workers' advocacy in South Korea and Japan, Yi Pyŏngha (2013) has argued that despite organizational weaknesses, the South Korean case exhibits political strengths that made successful legal reforms possible, whereas the Japanese case shows the opposite tendency. The uncanny relation JCMK has with the past further elucidates the historical specificity of its migrant workers advocacy.

Cosmopolitanism

A JCMK newsletter (2001b) stated that human rights "fill the river of freedom and equality breaking down all barriers of difference and discrimination." JCMK (2000) also characterized human rights as uninfringeable natural rights of all people and demanded political action to ensure the acquisition of these rights. In its observation, infringement on human rights begins with the failure to accept "differences and distinctions" (*ch'aiwa tarŭm*). To raise public interest in migrant workers' issues, JCMK launched a public campaign to change the name "skin color" (*salsaek*) to beige color. The name "skin color" was disapproved for making Asian skin color normative and dismissing the skin color of other racial groups. This campaign reflects that if not from China and Mongolia, most migrant workers came from southern parts of Asia, where skin color, religion, and diets differ from those in eastern parts of Asia, including Korea. The tension between nationalism and cosmopolitanism pervades JCMK's advocacy of human rights. Since the late 1980s nationalism has been a crucible for mixing democracy and globalization. A mixed sense of economic achievement, uncertainty about sustaining economic prosperity, and disenchantment with giving priority to development has fueled intense debates on Korean identity and culture. For some, the rediscovery and preservation of Korean cultures are necessary for maintaining Korean identity and even commodifying it for the multicultural global market. Others call to replace parochial, "inward-looking," or even xenophobic Korean national cultures with a cosmopolitan identity, cross-cultural education, and flexibility in order to adapt to intensifying global competition (Moon 2000).

Certainly JCMK politics signifies that human rights in South Korea constitute a new democratic order. Principles of pluralism, liberalism, and universalism articulate a new democratic subject, "you and me." Pluralistic universal human rights are devoid of history and social relations. The general claim of rights to difference and inclusion is an abstract form of human rights. Like money as a general equivalence, human rights establish migrant workers and others in a relationship of equivalence. That is, the notion of universal human rights imagines a multiplicity of social relationships in which difference is a condition of equal exchange. This equivalence places foreign workers on par with other groups—whether other minority or majority groups within and beyond South Korea—whose social status and experience differ. Pluralistic universalism binds migrant workers and other minority groups together despite their differences.

Democratic ideas permeate JCMK's discourse on minorities, which erases potentially antagonistic relations between citizens and illegal migrants, such as the fear of the latter's encroachment on jobs. The organization frames migrant workers as the most disadvantaged minority after women, homosexuals, and people with disabilities. While calling for a study of other countries' concepts of minority and policies of affirmative action, it maintains that the protection of migrant workers' rights is an interest or ideal of everyone in South Korea's new democratic society (Sŏk Wŏnjŏng 2003; Pak Kyŏngt'ae 2008). Its advocacy for minority rights imparts a vision of a multiethnic and cosmopolitan community years before the state began to promote it as a way to integrate the foreign brides of South Koreans and their children. Drawn from identity politics, JCMK's notion of minority differs from other radical references on minority. A post-Marxist, Yun Sujŏng (2005) has constructed minority as an alternative political subject, which, unlike minjung, recognizes social differences and includes new groups such as prostitutes, people with disabilities, homosexuals, prisoners, children, the homeless, and the unemployed, while, like minjung, addressing economic and social conflicts deepened by neoliberal capitalism.

The JCMK's appeal to cosmopolitanism attests to a cultural turn in post-1987 politics. The organization seeks to recognize the singularity of individuals and create solidarity across classes, nationalities, and identities by emphasizing culture, performance, and spontaneous participation. For Lefebvre (2008:204), cultural revolution in everyday life, like the revival of art, does not have a "cultural aim" but instead directs culture to transform everyday life beyond changes in the state and property system. Similarly, cultural practices during the 1980s minjung movement directed everyday activities, e.g., university students disguising their identities and working and living with workers, to forge solidarity between intellectuals and workers. In contrast, with its emphasis on multiplicity of identities, the cultural turn in the civil society movement since the 1990s makes culture autonomous of politics and economics.

Legalism

JCMK's advocacy separates human rights from labor rights, which is the signature of the civil society movement from the 1990s. Humanism and labor rights were conjoined in the minjung movement and the social formation debate of the 1980s. The utopian vision at that time regarded the workers' struggle for unionization as the basis for building solidarity with other social groups and creating a mass struggle against the military state and monopoly capital. In contrast, in JCMK's advocacy, the foundation of human rights is the rule of law that hinges on rationality and liberalism. The organization's politics benefits from the zealous legalism of democratic politics. Since the democratization of the late 1980s, social movement groups have called for transforming society through rational dialogue and negotiation. Consultation with experts and professionals has become standard practice for political groups, including the government, political parties, and NGOs, some of which have their own or affiliated research institutes. Public forums have become the usual channel for communication among these groups. Reflecting this trend, JCMK's advisory board includes professors, legislators, and lawyers, all vital to efforts to appeal to the courts and lobby the National Assembly and government ministries. The organization also follows the trend to professionalize activism, although it has not completely abandoned former political strategies such as street protests and hunger strikes.

The Industrial Training Program (ITP) became the center of the drive to legalize the migrant work program, particularly from the mid-1990s until 2003. Although industrial trainees composed a small proportion of the total foreign workforce, the program was the only legal channel for foreigners to come to work in South Korea. Introduced in October 1991, ITP allowed Korean firms to bring workers for training purposes from foreign countries where they had investments. Initial beneficiaries of this policy were those conglomerates that increased outsourcing to developing countries and investment in the United States and Europe after economic liberalization in South Korea from the late 1980s. The government agreed to requests from small- and medium-sized factories to expand the ITP to sectors including dyeing, shoemaking, glass-making, leather processing, and electronics. It extended the training period up to three years and increased the total number of ITP workers to 68,020 by the end of 1996 (Sŏl 1999:89–90). The program was primarily an expedient strategy for acquiring cheap and disposable labor. It put trainees to work after brief technical instruction despite the hazardous working conditions, including the use of dangerous machines and chemicals. Trainees were paid less than half as much as domestic workers because they were defined as trainees and their wage levels were based on pay scales in the trainee's home country. They were prohibited from leaving their assigned workplaces by punitive practices such as forfeiting their deposits and passports. Despite these penalties, low wages induced trainees to leave assigned workplaces for employment elsewhere and to thereby become undocumented. According to a report of the Ministry of Justice in July 2001, undocumented migrant workers comprised about 70 percent of the total 314,086 migrant workers. The actual number of the undocumented was much greater, with estimates of over a half million, given that this number for undocumented workers included only those who came as industrial trainees and excluded those who came with a fifteen-day tourist visa and a one-month family visitation visa (for ethnic Koreans from China) and overstayed to work for three to five years, if not eight to ten years (JCMK 2001a:99).

On February 13, 1995, shortly after the Nepali workers' protests, the Ministry of Labor announced its plan to introduce the Employment Permit Program (EPP) for migrant workers within that year (Pak Sŏkun 1995). After this aborted attempt, JCMK teamed up with the Ministry of Labor in the movement to replace ITP with EPP, although some of its leaders and labor organizations at the same time pursued the Labor Permit Program (LPP). The Employment Permit Program would legalize recruitment of migrant workers for three to five years with tight restrictions on changing workplace, whereas LPP would guarantee workers the freedom to choose and change their workplace. Debates on migrant work programs centered on ITP and EPP, largely discounting LPP. Defenders of ITP included the Ministry of Industry and Resources (formerly the Ministry of Commerce and Industry, which institutionalized ITP in 1991), the Committee on Industry and Resources of the National Assembly, the Ministry of Justice, and the Federation of Small- and Medium-Sized Factories (FSMF) in charge of managing ITP. The main issues under debate concerned the management of migrant workers, the administrative agency responsible for management, the length of their employment, and their rights. Contending groups framed their positions in terms of national competitiveness, development, and rational management of the labor market, all of which were in the idiom of capitalists. A renewed focus on development opened the back door for a return to nationalism by demanding a rational policy that would strengthen the competitiveness of South Korean firms in a fierce global marketplace.

Advocates of EPP underlined the importance of rationalizing and stabilizing the labor market in order to enhance the competitiveness of small- and medium-sized factories. In their observation, mistreatment of migrant workers under ITP had the potential to damage alliances and economic cooperation with Southeast Asian countries. They warned of the migrant workers' distrust of South Koreans and their potential boycotts of South Korean products after their return home, citing recent attacks on South Korean tourists. They also noted that most migrant workers were well educated and could become leaders in their own countries and that their experience of discrimination might make them hostile to South Korea. They pointed out that the lack of legal channels for employment fed rampant deception and corruption among recruiting agencies in sending countries that increased the cost of migration and encouraged migrant workers to frequently leave their workplace and endure abuse and exploitation to pay off the debt (Pak Sŏkun 2000; Ministry of Labor 2003b). In rebuttal, defenders of ITP projected that EPP would raise the wages of migrant workers and increase production costs, thus undermining flexibility in the labor market. In their assessment, EPP would also increase the administrative costs of managing migrant workers by splitting it into administration of their employment by the Ministry of Labor and administration of their visas and length of stay by the Ministry of Justice. Debates were seemingly at a stalemate when a dire labor shortage led smaller factory owners to publicly dissent from FSMF and call for speedy implementation of EPP in 2003 (FSMF 2000a, 2000b; Chŏn Yŏngp'yŏng and Han Sŭngju 2006).

The division of administration produced predicaments for the involved government offices. The illegal status of most migrant workers placed them under the jurisdiction of the Ministry of Justice's Office of Entry and Exit. The sheer volume of undocumented migrant workers became an embarrassment to the Ministry of Justice. Until EPP passed in 2003, the Ministry of Justice relied on seasonal or annual crackdowns on undocumented workers and occasional drives to register them by offering temporary work permits or repatriation with waived fines as incentives. Although leading some workers to despair and suicide, the crackdowns were largely symbolic. Having fewer than fifty officials, the Office of Entry and Exit lacked any real capacity to effectively track down illegal migrants even with police cooperation. The director of the Office of Entry and Exit told me that his team targeted illegal workers first in places of prostitution and bars, and then in restaurants and other service businesses, but they rarely raided factories. Many of his colleagues and even some officials in the Ministry of Justice were aware of the ineffective monitoring and even favored replacing ITP with EPP. However, they neither initiated nor openly supported any legal reforms that would end the Ministry of Justice's jurisdiction over migrant workers (Interview on June 29, 2002).

The Ministry of Labor also harbored contradictions by pursuing EPP as a means to stabilize the migrant workforce while simultaneously seeking to safeguard the labor market for domestic workers. Its Office of Employment Policy attracted criticism about the state's ineffective policies on migrant workers. Court rulings in 1996 and the 2000s recognized illegal workers and industrial trainees as eligible for compensation for job-related accidents and retirement benefits (JCMK 2001a:159–60). Backed by court rulings, activists' and workers' centers brought migrant workers' grievances to Ministry of Labor officials. The labor ministry, however, feared that if migrant workers were not regulated, they would take jobs away from unskilled domestic labor, especially women and the elderly. According to an official at the Office of Employment Policy, employing migrant labor to fill 30 to 40 percent of the labor shortage would be optimal to ensure flexibility in the labor market and safeguard the employment of domestic workers (Interview on July 31, 2002). Another Ministry of Labor official, who was deputed as an advisor to the Office of the President, expressed concern that the preference for cheap labor would eventually lead factories to replace domestic workers with migrant workers (Interview on July 25, 2002).

Compromise became synonymous with the culture of legalism. The Office of Government Policy Coordination within the Prime Minister's Office, which was in charge of supervision, mediation, assessment, and regulation of administration, mediated conflict among administrative units. The National Assembly emerged as another mediator between administrative units and social movement groups. Between 1996 and 2003, National Assembly members, the Democratic Party, and social organizations submitted at least nine bills on EPP and LPP. On July 31, 2003, the National Assembly finally passed the bill on EPP after striking a compromise. The deal not only maintained but also enlarged ITP with a provision allowing "trainees" to work as "workers" for one additional year after completing two years of "training." The EPP bill established three years as the maximum period of employment for foreign workers, requiring that the contract be renewed at least once per year and permitting workers to return to Korea six months after their departure. In January 2007 ITP was integrated into EPP and since then has been amended regularly to ease restrictions on hiring of migrant workers, to legislate a special program for Koreans from China, and to expand employment sectors to the livestock industry, fishery industry, automobile service centers, and saunas. The implementation of EPP since 2004 has significantly reduced the number of illegal migrant workers, except for those who remain and work illegally after the completion of their contract.

Capitalist Excesses: Labor Rights in the Transnational Age

What kinds of capitalist excesses exist in JCMK's politics that posit the rule of law as the foundation of human rights? Assessed from its movement to legislate EPP, JCMK ended up working as a disembodied state in reinforcing the capitalist and democratic order. It enabled illegal migrant workers to continue working and thus helped manage production relations by assisting job allocation, providing health care and shelters, and helping workers obtain unpaid wages. Their assistance to migrant workers in meeting their everyday needs helped stabilize social relations when changes resulting from their illegal status were causing instability. Moreover, when the state implemented new social categories of workers, JCMK and its membership centers reinforced them without challenging the social separation of domestic workers and migrant workers.

Human rights and labor rights were integrated into the nationalist and labor-centered people's struggle in the 1980s. Their split is a signature of the civil society movement since the 1990s. The difference in these approaches to humanism denotes the different social response to commodification of the people under old and new democratic politics in South Korea. During the military dictatorship, the state and the social movement sector produced diametrically opposite visions about nationalism and people's sovereignty. When the military state maintained its power by invoking the threats of North Korea and home-grown communists, the social movement sector merged the task of national unification with democratization. As the military state treated labor strikes as threats to national security, the social movement staged labor as the vanguard of mass struggle. While the military state suspended the rule of law in the name of national security, the social movement sector viewed law as an instrument of power. After the 1990s, these features of the minjung movement—nationalism, labor centrism, and mass struggle—were replaced by new hegemonic ideas, namely, cosmopolitanism, citizenship, and the rule of law. This shift enunciates the explosive growth of the civil society movement, which is touted as the fourth power next to the three components of state power—the judiciary and the legislative and executive branches. Devoid of historicity or connection with material conditions, this new idea of democracy forfeits an approach that linked democracy with the transformation of social relations. Pak Sŏkun (2002), a JCMK leader and long-time labor activist, has stated that JCMK's separation of human rights and labor rights was simply a strategic choice. It may well be a strategy for creating a movement to advance the rights of migrant workers and foster popular consciousness about human rights. This strategy seems sensible, since its membership has consisted of loosely networked religious and humanitarian organizations that aim to offer relief to migrant workers rather than change laws or society. However, JCMK's cosmopolitanism and legalism show that human rights and labor rights have become irreconcilable.

I characterize the defense of labor rights by JCMK leaders as a "non-contemporaneous contemporaneity," in Bloch's (2009) term, that is, the continued presence of earlier utopian politics in the present. The advocacy of labor rights establishes the people's sovereignty as labor. This legacy of the minjung movement provides a space to critique the neoliberal capitalist system, the civil society movement, and their symbiosis. Thus, the advocacy of labor rights exposes the decisive capitalist character of EPP, which treats the right of migrant workers to change workplace as an exception that in principle would be granted in cases of workplace shutdown, contract violation, and infringement on labor and human rights. Yi Nanju (2002), director of policy at JCMK, pleaded for the labor movement to lead the drive to realize the labor rights of migrant workers and create a labor union for migrant workers (see also Yi Kŭmyŏn 1999). Pak Sŏkun (1995) demanded that domestic labor laws be applied to foreign workers, citing two court rulings that recognized South Korean trainees, namely, high school student interns and medical interns, as workers whose rights were protected by the labor laws. Leaders of the JCMK persistently enlisted the support of the Association for Democratic Lawyers (ADL) and the Korean Confederation of Trade Union (KCTU), even when their support was routinely nominal.

The stance on the nation-state and the rule of law separates JCMK leaders' vision of labor rights from that of emergent activist migrant workers. Although illegal, the Seoul-Gyeonggi-Incheon Migrants' Trade Union (MTU) was formed in 2005 by migrant workers themselves as the first center of the migrant workers' movement. Masum, director of MTU, considers the identity of all migrant workers to be "trans-state," saying, "I am a Korean worker since I work in Korea, and I am a Korean worker though without Korean citizenship" (Joh 2007:145). Here nationality loses its universal appearance. Nationality, like other laws, is exposed as the foremost mechanism of regulating the movement of labor across borders. Masum's statement is contrasted to the JCMK leaders' appeal to the state and its legal protection. This "trans-state" identity repudiates the distinction between citizen and noncitizen that places both under the state's control in service of capital. According to Joh Won-kwang (2007), this claim of free mobility as a universal right of the people—with or without citizenship—establishes the people's sovereignty beyond the representative national or democratic system. Joh calls for a movement that declares, "We are all migrant workers." This avowal of universal politics revolves around the intrinsic right of people to mobility across any boundaries, including national borders. In this framework, EPP enables the state to manage foreign workers by producing docile subjects and surplus labor.

The expression "We are all migrant workers" in Joh's analysis refers to a new politics that exists outside of law and the social body. It does not advocate the inclusion of foreign workers within the given democratic order, as leaders of the JCMK demanded. Instead, it repudiates the state's legitimacy and its juridical relations with subjects. Joh's analytic framework resembles Ranciere's (1999) critique of the state's categorization of social relations and the consequent differential inclusion of citizens and foreign workers. The EPP's distinction between citizens and foreign workers is crucial not merely for efficient management of foreign workers but also for keeping citizens within the parameters of the law and the imagined social whole called the nation. The universal democratic subject expressed in "We are all migrant workers" is an alternative to the old and new political subjects—the working class and postmodern plural subjects.

UNIONIZED WORKERS AND PRIVATE PROPERTY RIGHTS

Coexisting with migrant workers' advocacy is the unionized domestic workers' struggle against "restructuring" (kujo chojŏng) that is implemented as a solution to capitalist crisis. When economists engage in animated debates on the sources of the latest capitalist crisis in South Korea, other experts such as consultants and accountants blur the distinction between real and fictive crisis. Their professional opinions and assessments produce speculative value by creating financial portfolios whose validity is backed by their professional status and readily accepted by courts, the state, and the media. I analyze the ways that the trinity of state, capital, and accounting consecrates private property rights as the sublime. By invoking restructuring as the necessary means to overcome the crisis, the three parties justify onslaughts against unionized workers, who are then replaced with lower paid, more vulnerable temporary and part-time workers. I also capture historical moments when the struggle of unionized workers against restructuring lays bare the democratic politics of consensus and illuminates a new political possibility. These historical moments emerge when workers and intellectuals recognize the cotemporality of state violence in the Chŏn T'aeil generation and in the generation of unionized workers thirty years later. The workers' struggles at the Yusŏng and Ssangyong factories demonstrate that Chŏn's hard-won lesson about the relationship of the state, law, and machinization of workers' bodies is still true in the putative era of democracy—and all the more necessary today for forging a viable democratic politics.

Chŏn T'aeil presented his self-immolation as the death sentence of the Labor Standards Act. On the day of his death, he planned to stand on the desk that he and his companions placed in the middle of the street, read the key articles of the Labor Standards Act, and then say, "What is the use of all these articles when they are not observed? Let's burn them" (Chŏn T'aeil kinyŏm'gwan kŏllip wiwŏnhoe 1983:214). In a deviation from this plan, he set his own body on fire, shouting, "Observe the Labor Standards Act!" And a member of his group threw the book on the Labor Standards Act into the fire. His political awakening involved the process of demystifying the law. In 1968 Chŏn T'aeil learned about the existence of the Labor Standards Act from his father, who participated in the labor strikes right after the 1945 liberation. Chŏn T'aeil's father vainly tried to dissuade him from organizing coworkers by talking about his own failed experience. Upon his repeated pleading, his mother borrowed money from neighbors to buy him *A Dictionary of the Labor Standards Act*. With only two years of elementary school and one year of middle school, Chŏn T'aeil could not understand legal concepts and terms in the text. Even if he could read only one page per night, he refused to set the book aside. He often said, "I wish I had one university student friend who could help me to understand the book," a statement that became a lightning rod for the university student movement of the 1980s. As he sought to improve working conditions for himself and his coworkers, the labor laws gave him tremendous hope. In his thinking, thorough observance of the labor laws would ensure that workers could live with human dignity. Chŏn organized a small group with his coworkers, surveyed working conditions in the Peace Market, visited government agencies to advocate for the investigation of labor law violations, and submitted his reports to newspapers. For over a year government officials disregarded his appeals, leaving him disillusioned about the law and the state's intention to enforce it. The book that was burned with his body was the book he cherished, carried in his bosom, and stared at through sleepless nights to decipher the meaning of its words and sentences.

His self-immolation spurred the labor movement and democracy struggle that led to a momentous shift in 1987 to popular election of the president. Given the history of radical politics during the 1980s, it is an extraordinary reversal that class compromise under the rule of law has become equated with democracy. This reversal in democratic politics is a result of the politics of crisis from the mid-1990s, which engenders negotiations between the state and labor leadership over labor laws. Immediately after the 1989 amendment to labor law that established the forty-four-hour-maximum work week, capitalists demanded that the state enact measures to facilitate flexible employment, namely, restructuring discharge, temporary employment, and other irregular employment. When the National Assembly rammed these laws through committee in December 1996, KCTU immediately launched national strikes until 1997. The 1997 financial crisis, however, forced KCTU to accept the flexible employment program and the multiple unions at a firm in return for its own legalization, unionization of public officials, and the right of unions to engage in political activities. A verdict as of 2014 is that capitalists won their class struggle and expanded the size of the flexible workforce to about 60 percent of the total workforce, while the political empowerment of workers failed with the disintegration of the Democratic Labor Party. Now KCTU is searching for an alternative labor strategy beyond its focus on unionized workers in conglomerate-owned firms and its neglect of flexible workers. The Yusŏng and Ssangyong struggles show capitalist strategies and workers' oppositions.

The Yusŏng Union's Struggle: Consulting Firms and Stock Prices

Founded in 1961, the Yusŏng union joined the 1987 Great Strikes and since then has negotiated with its company mainly over wages and working hours. On May 18, 2011, the Yusŏng union waged a four-hour partial strike at a factory in the city of Asan in Ch'ungch'ŏng Province, demanding that the management implement the agreed monthly wage system and two-shift program without night work. On that evening the company responded with indefinite closure of the factory and closed another factory as a preemptive measure. The Yusŏng case attracted nationwide attention, since its interrupted production of two small and cheap yet crucial parts (pistol rings and cylinder liner) of automobile engines nearly halted automobile production for all four automobile companies, especially Hyundai and Kia. The Yusŏng union began its sit-in strike inside the Asan factory. When police removed the strikers on May 24, the union moved its strike to a greenhouse near the factory to protest the workers' discharge and discipline by the company. The greenhouse strike lasted until August 22, but the leaders' protest continued as of June 2014.

The Yusŏng case discloses the new formula for union-busting that has become routine in South Korea. A company provokes a labor strike by refusing labor's demands, asserts that the strike is illegal, closes the plant in response to the allegedly unlawful strike, and mobilizes private security forces and police forces to crack down on striking workers in the name of protecting the company's property. Next the company fires the striking unionized workers and reopens the factory with a new labor union that is aligned with management. According to labor law, a company has the right to restart production as long as it hires workers who are not on strike. At Yusŏng, the steps and details of this process were devised by Ch'angjo Consulting, which from 2003 to 2012 served 186 client firms and broke labor unions at more than 20 leading firms and universities, including Korea Telecom, an information technology company, the Mando machinery factory, and a hospital at Tonga University. Before the strike, Ch'angjo installed hidden cameras to document potential damage to the factory by striking workers and requested the nearby police station to dispatch officers to protect the facilities in the event of a strike. When the original labor union decided to return to work on June 14, Ch'angjo executed its plan to organize a new labor union and inaugurate it on July 21, enlisting skilled technicians, foremen, and former workers, as well as clerical and white-collar workers. When the original labor union's members returned to work after August 22, the company began to fire or discipline the workers who had led the strike. After November 30 its newly created promanagement union became the primary negotiating body. It took about six months to complete the steps in this strategy of dismantling a labor union (Ch'angjo Consulting 2011; Kim Soyŏn 2012).

Rights of private property were cited to legitimate closing the plant and using force to end the strike. The company rationalized the plant's closure as the necessary response to prevent the labor union from interfering with its business and to protect its private properties, including buildings and machinery. From June 2011 to April 2014, the local and high courts at Taejŏn and Seoul continued to uphold the legality of the plant's closure even after the National Assembly's special inquiry in September 2012 declared Ch'angjo's role in union-busting illegal. The local court set a 5 million won penalty for each time a union member enters the factory, takes resources and products from the factory, or contacts clients of the company. The same court also sentenced Yusŏng union leaders to prison for their responsibility in the violence, unlawful entry into buildings, and property damage but placed them on probation, reasoning that their initial actions were not of the magnitude capable of disrupting business. The local court rejected the union's demand for wages during the plant's closure, while the high court upheld the ruling but ordered the company to pay wages to workers for the period after the labor union announced the decision to return to work. The local court in Seoul ordered the labor union to pay 45 million won for damages that it caused to state property (i.e., police equipment and vehicles), and for injuries sustained by police officers during the crackdown on the strikers, but the court remained silent about injuries sustained by workers during the same clash (Im Chŏnghwan 2013; Chŏng Chaeŭn 2014).

The sudden upsurge in Yusŏng's stock price during the strikes reveals the new nexus between the state, industrial capital, and finance capital. Its stock price jumped nearly 260 percent shortly after the initial strike. After a decline to 150 percent of its former price, it went back up to previous peak levels a month later, the day after another violent clash between the police and workers that injured more than one hundred people. The skyrocketing value of the stock during the strikes perplexed financial experts, some of whom attributed it to the public's discovery of Yusŏng's economic value (Kim Ch'anggyu 2011; Kim Wusŏng 2011). However, the simultaneity of the stock price increase and police suppression indicates that the company's stock price rose because the government decided to dispatch the police, justifying this decision as a step necessary to resolve the violent clash between the striking workers and the private security personnel hired by the company. That is, financial markets interpreted the plant's closure and the government's action as strategies to reduce production costs and increase profits, since factories would soon reopen with much less expensive subcontracted or irregular workers who are paid lower wages and have negligible employment security or labor rights. The enormous financial gains for the company and its shareholders of increased stock prices outweighed losses from months of lost production during the strike, not to mention the losses suffered by workers.

The Ssangyong Union Struggle: The Apparition of Capital

The speculative process of merger and acquisition forges a new relationship among the state, industrial capital, and financial service institutions. The Ssangyong automobile company illustrates that repeated transfer of ownership helps factory owners evade their liability for fired workers and interrupted production. The Ssangyong conglomerate bought the Tonga auto factory in 1986 and sold it to the Daewoo conglomerate in 1998 during the financial crisis. When Daewoo went bankrupt in 2000, the factory went into receivership and was named Ssangyong again. After record-breaking profits in 2003 resulting from government investment, Ssangyong Automobile was sold in 2004 to SAIC, the Shanghai Automotive Industry Corporation, owned by the Chinese state. In 2009, SAIC filed for bankruptcy of Ssangyong Automobile, which was once again placed under receivership and received a bailout from the South Korean government. Subsequently, the consortium created by government bailout sold the factory in 2010 to Mahindra and Mahindra, an Indian corporation. The firm's accounting record was instrumental for legitimating bankruptcy, plant closure, and the dismissal of workers in the name of regaining competitiveness. Even when the factory recovered from its purported losses and earned huge profits after the government's bailout, the government was lured by the idea of privatization and sold the factory to foreign firms. Given the prevalence of the strategy of fabricating losses, discharging workers, and selling the company, the Ssangyong case became paradigmatic of neoliberal restructuring. Under neoliberalism, capital takes on its ghostlike characteristics: it is inherently unstable, ungraspable, and superfluous through repeated bankruptcies and transfers of ownership. Companies stage their own material and physical death to raise capital by boosting the price of their stock. Capital becomes devilish because the repeated transfer of ownership makes it difficult for discharged workers to challenge layoffs legally; this process traumatizes workers and for some leads to suicide. Kong Jiyŏng (2012) succinctly calls the owners of Ssangyong Automobile an "apparition" (yuryŏng).

The speculative process of accumulating capital hinges on the rule of law and intensifies the effects of private property rights on labor. For Marx (1992), the falling rate of profit arises from the very process of competition and monopoly that increases investment in technology and production facilities to expand production and increase productivity; this process leads to reducing the number of workers, who themselves are the source of surplus value. Measures such as the devaluation of constant capital can temporarily circumvent this law of capital accumulation. This economics of crisis of capital accumulation is turned into a phantasm by Ssangyong capitalists and their agents. Financial service firms create the appearance of severe losses that justify plant closure, layoffs, government bailouts, and the factory's sale to foreign capital. The professional authority of accounting and finance discourse that uses numbers to conjure depreciation of fixed capital and associated losses makes it almost impossible for workers and the public to challenge the claims. For example, SAIC's filing for bankruptcy of Ssangyong was certified by Anjin, the accounting firm retained by Ssangyong, whose audit declared a 517 billion won decline in Ssangyong's assets on the basis of its valuation of tangible assets, including factories, structures, machines, tools, and appliances. In its audit, the loss soared from 2.3 billion in 2007 to 200 billion won in 2008: from 86 million to 37.5 billion won for buildings and from 800 million to 100 billion won for machines. Accordingly, the company's debt on paper increased from 168 percent of its assets to 561 percent, whereas its losses skyrocketed from 98 billion to 710 billion won in just three months from September to November 2008. Kong Jiyŏng and other critics have questioned the credibility of these figures, since no catastrophes such as earthquakes, fires, or wars occurred during that period. Then SAIC hired Samjong KPMG, another leading accounting firm that is well known for its key role in negotiating the sale of the Korean Exchange Bank to Lone Star Funds on terms extremely favorable to the US-based private equity fund. In 2009 Samjong KPMG recommended that SAIC lay off 2,646 Ssangyong workers, or 37 percent of the total workforce, as part of its bankruptcy, legal receivership, and recovery process. The court approved SAIC's bankruptcy despite challenges to Samjong KPMG's assessments by the official Korean Appraisal Board and KCTU lawyers (Kŭmsok nojo Ssangyong chadongch'a chibu nodongja yŏksa hannae 2010:18–31; Kong 2012:72–85; see also Han Hyŏngsŏng 2012).

The private property system renders profitability the sole grounds for legal decisions on the company's operation. It identifies profit loss rather than the needs and rights of workers as the overriding concern for both the company and the state. Invented and actual crises in the rate or size of profit are invoked to justify firing unionized workers, replacing them with low-paid, nonunionized, and precarious labor and intensifying the productivity of remaining workers. The real meaning of restructuring through layoffs is the abstraction of social relations by the private property system, which fixes social relations between capitalists and workers through their contract. The commodification, hidden in the form of contract, is the origin of the trauma, leading to an unprecedented high rate of suicide among Ssangyong workers. Apart from their protests, the suicide of twenty-two Ssangyong workers between April 8, 2009, and March 30, 2012, attracted extensive attention among activists and intellectuals. Most suicides came after the occupying strike that was conducted by 976 workers, who seized the P'yŏngt'aek plant for seventy-seven days from May 22 to August 5, 2009, and demanded an emergency bailout, the elimination of SAIC stocks, and the maintenance of jobs with job sharing. Although the suicides were primarily among the strikers, they also included workers who remained employed or opted for the buyout. According to psychologists, the fact that Ssangyong workers killed themselves without leaving a will signifies the severity of their trauma, which erased the difference between life and death and dispossessed them of their ties with the world (Kong 2012:35–38). Like those who were not laid off, the striking workers were in their forties and had worked an average of fifteen to twenty years at the Ssangyong factory. The job was far more than the wages and benefits; it was an embodiment of their life. The private property system strips this historical specificity away from social relations. Regardless of their needs or their contributions to the company's wealth and profits, they were treated as individuals whose contract with the company was subordinate to the company's profits. No inquiry about workers as bearers and producers of value was expected. During the occupying strike, the company turned the lives of the sit-in strikers into bare existence by cutting the supply of electricity and water to the buildings they occupied and even denying medical care to workers in urgent need. However, the workers decided to use their only available generator not to cool their quarters in heat over 100 degrees Fahrenheit but to keep painting materials from drying, since drying would stall the production process at least one month. The violation of their physical and emotional being by the company and the police indicates the reification that was a source of their trauma. Their trauma comprised more than shock, alienation, and exclusion, for it resulted from the reconstitution of social relations.

FIGURE 2.1 Ssangyong workers' strike in May 2006. Courtesy of the Ssangyong Automobile Labor Union.

Private property rights confer on capitalists the right to eliminate workers who challenge their power and authority. Private property rights are not simply the law but also an embodiment of social relations. The imagined construction of private property law as democracy originates in its appearance of the relationship between the individual and things.[5] Ambiguous criteria for restructuring and discharge of workers turned friends into enemies, tore apart their middle-class community, and ultimately blurred the distinction between the living and the dead. On the eve of discharge, some workers even borrowed money from relatives to buy a new car produced by the company because there was a rumor that doing so would save them from losing their job. Uncertainty was rife because no one knew if and when they would be laid off. The company repeatedly insisted that "without the state's bailout, whose likelihood is only ensured by the restructuring discharge, everyone will be destroyed" (Son Mia 2009:34). Workers who joined the strike were condemned as communists and terrorists for damaging property and disrupting social order. With this discursive strategy, the company mobilized the living (i.e., the still-employed) to damn the dead and shout at them, "We are going to all die soon [if the occupying strike doesn't end]. Leave [the factory]" (Kong 2012:152–53). Yet the living also joined the trail of the dead, as the fear of being discharged hung over them, compelling them to work even harder. Indeed, labor productivity at the Ssangyong factory after the suppression of the strike broke auto industry records, reducing production time for one car from 106 hours to 38 hours (Kong 2012:155). Under the neoliberal state and its laws, little separates the dead from the living who are working to death on production lines and are driven to join those who committed suicide.

Workers occupying the Ssangyong factory defended themselves with iron pipes and Molotov cocktails. The police deployed their entire panoply of arms against them, including tear gas, taser guns, rubber-bullet guns, and water canons. The police further menaced protesters with the terrorizing roar of hovering helicopters and even the incessant blare of dance music when striking workers were mourning their coworkers' suicides. Emblematic of the police brutality under the Lee Myong Bak regime (2008–2013) is the so-called container suppression, in which police officers were placed in big containers, hoisted above the building occupied by discharged workers, and lowered onto the roof to break the occupying strikes.[6] Police forces violently attacked protesters, beating them unconscious and dragging them away until the authorities declared the containment of violence. When the court ruled that the restructuring plan and firing of workers was legal (and thus the occupying strike was illegal), striking workers and their families feared the loss of their homes over the payment for damages done to the factory facilities. The court ordered Ssangyong union members and leaders to pay 17 million dollars in punitive damages, which led to seizure of their own properties (Goldner 2009; Im Sŏngji 2011).[7]

Recognition of the real face of the law, capital, and the state awakened unionized workers and led them to bridge the former divide with irregular workers and to unite in their common struggle. With the slogan "Let's Live Together" (Hamkkye salja), Ssangyong workers aspired to create a new universal movement that brings together all workers across the division of unionized workers and irregular workers. This embrace of a universal principle breaks with the KCTU-led labor movement's strategy since 2000s that centered on unionized workers and their pursuit of job security and better wages. Ssangyong workers chided the Metal Workers' Union of KCTU for trying to persuade the Ssangyong union to compromise with management and end the occupying strike and for becoming too bureaucratic to mobilize an industry-wide strike in support of the Ssangyong strike. The Metal Workers' Union vainly continued to promise an industry-wide strike if the government's forces were to suppress the Ssangyong strike (Son Mia 2009). Like E-Land and the KTX struggles, the Ssangyong struggle carved out a critical moment in the South Korean labor movement by advocating the solidarity of all workers beyond the social division of workers.

However, a critical limit to the Ssangyong struggle was its failure to reach an adequate understanding of the state and capital, as it appealed to the state to reinstate their employment. The South Korean state played a key role in SAIC's speculative acquisition and planned declaration of bankruptcy. It was the state that decided to sell Ssangyong Automobile to SAIC, which was suspected of being interested only in accessing Ssangyong's hybrid engine technology instead of having any long-term interest. Moreover, the official Korea Development Bank (Sanŏp ŭnhaeng) voided the SAIC agreement to make a long-term investment and stabilize employment at Ssangyong. Unlike in the United States and Germany, the state in South Korea neither enforced job sharing and transfer of workers before implementing restructuring discharge of workers nor sufficiently drew on funds set aside to assist workers discharged as a result of restructuring (Kim Namgŭn 2012; Yi Hogŭn 2012). The South Korean state continued its blinkered drive to privatization and right after it brutally ended the Ssangyong workers' occupying strike once again expressed the urgency of finding a buyer (Chŏng Chongnam 2006).

The uneven articulation of the state, industrial capital, and finance capital in constructing disparate labor regimes for migrant workers and unionized domestic workers signifies a fractured temporality of capitalism. South Korean democracy since the 1990s is Hegelian in the sense that leftists and activists elevate law as an expression of universality, while abstracting the state as the embodiment of such universal principles as equality, and freedom. At this juncture, the extreme violence committed by the democratic state against migrant workers and unionized workers signifies the law's intrinsic role in effecting commodity fetishism. Accordingly, capitalist exchange appears as the exchange between free and equal juridical subjects. Legal contract bestows on both migrant and unionized workers the formal characteristics of freedom and equality while removing all traces of labor as the source of profit. The rule of law is neither illusory nor does it simply conceal labor power as the source of value. Its relations with the state and capital are institutionalized in uneven ways.

CRISIS, HISTORICISM, AND REPETITION

The politics of migrant workers and discharged unionized workers bear on political disquiet about democracy, neoliberal reforms, and the relationship between the two in South Korea. The 1987 democratization was followed by increasing socioeconomic insecurity and inequality. In the 1990s and 2000s major popular protests developed over restructuring layoffs, violence against South Koreans by members of the US armed forces, the Free Trade Agreement with the United States, and the dispatch of South Korean troops to Iraq. At such a conjuncture, prominent political scientist Choi Jang Jip (2002) galvanized discussions on democracy when he characterized the state of democracy in South Korea as "democratization without democracy." He regarded the continued mass street protests even after the 1987 democratization as signs of a malaise that capitalized on expanded political and civil rights and pushed democracy beyond institutional limits. According to Goh Byeong-gwon (2011), Choi's antidemocratic sentiment is an example of the "hatred of democracy," Ranciere's (2009) term that expresses intolerance for demands and protests that challenge power and authority. For Choi, the mass protests denote the failure to create a genuine representative democracy because the political party system is deformed by hierarchy and localism. For Goh, they indicate disapproval of the system of representative democracy itself.

The aporia of democracy fosters historical disquiet. A bewildering sense of crisis permeates the heated debate on the temporalization of history, which distinguishes the present from the past. The debate pits the 1987 democratization against the 1997 financial crisis as the moment of rupture. The 1987 thesis (ch'ejeron) names the present as the phase of "consolidation" of democracy or simply "the era of democratization" (minjuhwa sidae) following the momentous move to popular election of the president in 1987. It represents democratic transition as an irreversible act in an attempt to defend it from conservatives' threats, while recognizing its clear limit. In its diagnosis, the current crisis of democracy originates in two features of democratization from its very beginning in 1987. On the one hand, the 1987 thesis notes that the compromise between democratic and antidemocratic forces in 1987 made both groups so uncertain about their success in popular presidential elections that they agreed to limit the president's political power by increasing juridical and legislative power. On the other hand, the 1987 thesis ascribes the lack of economic democratization since 1987 to the competition between capital and labor, both of which acquired power after 1987. Economic liberalization enabled private capital to create its own financial institutions and escape the state's long-standing control of lending and credit. Workers won the right to unionize and form their political party by making concessions to neoliberal restructuring and the flexible employment system. Based on this diagnosis, some advocates of the 1987 thesis call for the continuous broad national struggle between the rising middle class and the minjung in order to eliminate the antidemocratic military culture in society and engage with North Korea. Others see the 1987 struggle as the culmination of the minjung movement of the 1980s and call for renewing class struggle in order to expand social and welfare programs (Kim Chongyŏp 2009).

The competing 1997 thesis states that starting with the 1997 financial crisis, the era of democratization was replaced by the neoliberal capitalist system. It maintains that the same progressives who led the 1987 transition furthered economic deregulation and financial liberalization, defying their earlier promises for more equitable distribution of wealth and expansion of social welfare (Kim Chongyŏp 2009:12–138). Some advocates of the 1997 thesis consider the adoption of a Keynesian social compromise between capital and labor as the measure to advance democracy. The thesis reduces change in the capitalist system to financial crisis, without any serious analysis of capitalist crisis. The 1997 thesis remains detached from other leftists' debate on three key causes of the South Korean economic crisis. One cause is the rapid increase of short-term loans, which made the economy vulnerable to a sudden demand for the repayment of loans (Heo and Kim 2000; Cho Yongchŏl 2007). Another is the state's financial deregulation, leading to conglomerates' excessive borrowing from foreign capital, and the financial industry's lobbying, corruption, and nepotism (Crotty and Lee 2002). The third cause is the falling rate of profit and its resolution through the creation of alternative sectors for capital investment through privatization and the pursuit of short-term profits (Chŏng Sŏngjin 2006). Each of these three perspectives on the 1997 crisis and the turn to neoliberal capitalism since then underscores its own claims and cancels each other on statistical grounds.

The periodization of the two competing views, the 1987 thesis and the 1997 thesis, embodies an "epochal consciousness," in Koselleck's (2004) term. The contention of the two theses over the key event enunciates the modes of historical consciousness that conceptually separate democracy from the capitalist system: Democracy is transmuted to a mere political institution that grants rights to individual citizens and thus loses its intrinsic connection with capitalism. This conceptual separation is a contemporary form of the political unconscious. Whereas in the past Korean leftists envisaged the elimination of the capitalist system as a necessary means of democratization, they now contend with its shadows in the form of bewilderment or aporia concerning current democracy. The changed conceptualization of democracy is accompanied by a new approach to the social. During the democracy struggle of the 1980s and its social formation debate, the social was treated as commodified social relations under the domination of the state and capital. In the civil society movement since the 1990s, the social is regarded as society, an aggregate of political, economic, and cultural institutions. In social movement and leftist scholars' circles in the 1980s, the nature of the state's power and its relationship with capital and US imperialist power was at the center of the inquiry. In contrast, the debate on democracy since the late 1990s lacks a cogent analysis of the state, using vague terms such as "progressive" and "conservative" governments. The state is even said to have changed "from an exceptional state to a normal state," equating normalcy with liberal representative democracy (Kim Hogi 2009). The earlier Marxian critique of political economy is now replaced by a dichotomy of political and economic analysis that approaches the advance of democracy in terms of stages of transition and consolidation.

In 2008 Yi Jin-kyung (2008) at the Suyu Institute in Seoul, a center of the new commune movement of intellectuals, called to renew the social formation debate in order to theorize capitalist accumulation and its linkages with class relations and mass movement. This renewal is, he argues, demanded by the constellation of financialization, deregulation, and popular candlelight protests against US militarism and the Free Trade Agreements. In a journal,

AlteRevolution, he and other members of the Suyu Institute characterize South Korean capitalism since the 1990s in variant terms: a "flow system" with the increased mobility of labor and capital; a regime of the simulacrum with the valorization of speculation and images; a regime of social exclusion that turns citizens into refugees; and a regime of financialization and securitization with knowledge, information, and desire as immaterial commodities. My discussion here joins the renewed social formation debate and makes two interventions. One is to go beyond the delineation of new features of South Korean capitalism and instead return to the debate's original question, posed in the 1980s, concerning a quintessential issue for modern Korea—the articulation of national division and capitalism. This book, *The Capitalist Unconscious*, as a whole investigates the new transnational characteristic of contemporary South Korean capitalism: South Korean capital hierarchically integrates North Korea and the Korean diasporic community into its capitalist and democratic structure. The other intervention is to theorize the social formation debate of the 1980s and the two historicisms since the 2000s as *historical repetition*. I return to the social formation debate not to excavate instructions from past practices for today's problematics but to recognize the repeated pursuit of a political form capable of resolving a historically specific capitalist crisis, and discern the capitalist logic behind the repetition.

Two moments of the social formation debate of the 1980s and the historicisms of 2000s are repeated contemplations on new conjunctures. They share the task of defining the characteristics of South Korean society and formulating a new democratic politics. The fidelity of theory and history is at the center of recognizing this temporality of the debates. My accounts of their cotemporality reveal historical specificities of both eras while delineating the crises of capitalism that set off a repeated search for social action. Armed with the Marxist-Leninist theory of history and revolution, the social formation debate of the 1980s carried out a comprehensive theoretical investigation into the history of capitalist development that was entwined with imperialist domination in the Korean peninsula. Although politics and scholarship since the 1990s have denounced the social formation debate as dogmatic and pedantic, this debate originated in an urgent task to formulate a precise strategy of social movement in which theory was vital for teasing out the intricacy of the present. In other words, the dialectics of theory and praxis constituted the development of the social formation debate. This fidelity of theory and praxis is warranted now as much as before, as the age of cultural studies, identity politics, and poststructuralism emphasizes contingency, events, and indeterminacy and reduces neoliberal capitalism to the spread of markets, cultural ethos (e.g., self-management), and a form of state governmentality.

For nearly ten years from late 1984, the social formation debate provided the most significant platform for addressing twentieth-century capitalism in South Korea.[8] The social formation debate emerged from fluctuations in the capitalist crisis of the late 1970s to the unprecedented prosperity in the early 1980s and another deep crisis in the mid-1980s. The instability caused a sharp increase in consumer prices, trade deficits, and foreign debt and led the military state to introduce economic liberalization and reformist policies. The state began to grant more autonomy to industrial capital and advanced the privatization of banks and credit institutions. At the same time, the state consolidated the power of monopoly capital known as Chaebol and its ownership of financial institutions, thus increasing its autonomy from state control. While maintaining a despotic labor regime with low wages and prohibiting unionization, the military state enacted a series of reformist policies that softened political surveillance, permitted activities by the minority party, and introduced social policies such as minimum wage, national medical insurance, low-income housing, and the welfare pension system. These socioeconomic and political changes in South Korea coincided with the American project of pushing the Third World toward democracy, which included popular elections. Leftists saw these real and proposed reforms as attempts to contain the discontent of the middle class while separating them from workers. At this juncture, leftists tried to formulate a radical popular struggle capable of realizing the revolutionary and transformative power seen in the 1980 Kwangju uprising.

The central issue in the social formation debate was the nature of colonial conditions in South Korea and their constitutive relationship with capitalism, given the US role in dividing Korea in 1945 and consolidating the national division since then. Groups of activists and scholars diagnosed the historical nature of capitalism and its links with a fascist military dictatorship and US imperialism and prescribed courses of political action for South Korea. Although similar debates on capitalism, revolution, and imperialism took place in other parts of the world, including China, France, and Italy from the 1960s through the 1980s, the South Korean debate exclusively extrapolated the relevance for South Korea of Marx and Marxist theories of history in the early twentieth century and the Russian revolution in terms of the stages of development of capitalism and revolution.

The debate began around the issue of whether and how US imperialism blocked or facilitated the development of capitalism. The debate, in general, developed into the polemics of the National Liberation (NL) thesis and the People's Democracy (PD) thesis in the context of the ascendancy of the antiwar and antinuclear movement in and beyond South Korea that emboldened the critique of imperialism. For the NL thesis, colonialism produced capitalism's hybrid character, in which imperialist exploitative mechanisms reproduced and exacerbated the landlord-tenant relationship, fettering the development of productive forces. Colonial domination was considered the fundamental characteristic (ponjil) in South Korea. The basic (kibon) and primary (chuyo)— and thus more immediate—contradiction involved the opposition of imperialist landlords, dependent capitalists, and bureaucrats against the minjung. With this approach called the thesis of semifeudalism or semicapitalism, the NL view reiterated a task of national liberation for South Koreans that was similar to that of the 1917 Russian Revolution and ones adopted by the Comintern in the 1920s for colonized countries.

In contrast, the PD thesis continued to grapple with how South Korean capital developed into monopoly capital despite its low productive forces. It counterpoised Lenin's theory of monopoly capitalism with the question of whether South Korean monopoly capital embodied a distinctive characteristic when compared to that of advanced capitalist countries (including the United States and Japan). The PD approach was split between those who saw the intensification of the universal monopoly and those who defined the South Korean form as a higher stage of capitalism than the monopoly capital stage theorized by Lenin. For the PD thesis, the class conflict was the basic contradiction in South Korea, while the primary contradiction developed between a small number of monopoly capitalists and the minjung. A democratic revolution by the minjung was thus identified as the immanent task for defeating fascism and bringing the basic contradiction to the forefront as the foundation for subsequent socialist revolution.[9]

In this book, I make two shifts from the previous social formation debate: from the stage theory of history to the notion of repetition; and from analysis of class struggle to analysis of commodification. The renunciation of the social formation debate in the post–Cold War era is directed justifiably against its metatheory of history, economic determinism, and class analysis. Despite its own quest to bind theory and praxis, the more the social formation debate tried to assess the contradiction of capitalism, the more it became removed from reality. The polemics were caught in a dogmatic limbo of the seemingly insurmountable split into national and class contradictions despite all claiming to observe the dialectics of the universal and the particular. The social formation debate of the 1980s entailed and was constantly thrown back to the imperative of developing productive forces that was seen to decide the nature of capitalism and the agents of revolutionary struggle. The more "scientifically" they distinguished the "fundamental," "basic," and "primary" contradictions of South Korean capitalism, the more their aspirations fell back into the formalistic stage theory of history, if not recapitulating paradigmatic European cases. In contrast to the developmental law of history, I consider multiple temporalities in social relations not as an object for transcendence through class struggle prescribed by the law of history but as the process of historicity itself. I do not consider the temporality of capitalism in terms of the tendential development of productive forces and the corresponding growth of the working class. Nor do I take a region or event as the origin, presupposing an evolutionary process. My analysis of repetition seeks to capture the instantaneous acceleration of capitalism that produces accumulation and commodification.

Repetition does not mean the homogenization of capitalist temporality. Rather, it refers to the repeated production of crisis, which spurs a renewed search for a new political form capable of resolving the crisis. A question concerning the original inquiry of social relations is at stake here, i.e., the figure of labor that enables Marx to ground capital accumulation in the process of producing surplus value, not in an incremental increase of profits and savings. Commodification of labor is obscured by a valorization of capital that constitutes a democratic appearance of equality in the market exchange of labor and products. Interrupting the appearance of market equality requires questioning commodification in everyday life. The sphere of everyday life represents processes of commodification through language and other cultural and political mediations. With each new conjuncture in South Korea comes a new manifestation of capitalism's immanent crisis. In today's conjuncture, the crisis is managed and produced by new capitalist institutions, identity politics, and poststructuralism, which have emphasized singularity of experience irreducible to economics and class politics as well as multiple temporalities of historical change.

CONCLUSION

How do we understand the violence of the state and capital in the neoliberal democratic age and compare it with that of military rule? The inquiry belongs not only in the realm of the state's sovereignty and its monopoly of violence but also in its production of capitalist crisis and its responses that organize the life and death of workers. This is not to approach the state's violence in terms of its intrinsic capitalist character as is in orthodox Marxism, but rather to give attention to its production of crisis, both its staging and organizing the social experience of it. In specific, this study delves into the question of what the state's sanctification of private property right says about the state's sovereignty, labor's sovereignty, and the relationship between the two. It explores private property rights as a terrain of rethinking the transition to neoliberal capitalist system, linking this transition to the new aesthetics of democratic politics. The making of the private property system as the sublime is crucial for conceptualizing the violence of capital and the state, and their relationship in the neoliberal age. Courts, NGOs, and consulting and financial service firms operate as phantasmagoric means of capital accumulation in that their rationalism and expertise give a legal appearance to the new social regulation of labor in the neoliberal era. This study of neoliberal capitalist system is, thus, not limited to the hegemonic domination of finance capital. It also concerns the transformation of the labor process or the reconfiguration of socially necessary labor time so as to produce and appropriate more value. The processes of privatization, deregulation, and attack on labor union, which David Harvey (2005) identifies as key features of neoliberalism, are to be understood as "the trinity"—one and the same in their production of surplus value.

My notion of historical repetition debunks the transition thesis of history by attending to the performative services for capital accumulation by different political regimes. Recognition of the cotemporality of the democratic present and the military past emerged, for instance, among Ssangyong workers and their supporters in their unexpected remembrance of the 1980 Kwangju massacre. Citing Wu Hijong's column in the *Hangyoreh* newspaper, Kong Jiyŏng poignantly reports that the crackdown by police and private security personnel on the Ssangyong workers' protest in 2009 brought about flashbacks of the paramilitary's suppression of the Kwangju uprising in 1980s (Kong 2012:138). After all, the Kwangju massacre inspired Kong and other intellectuals to join the university student democracy movement, whose members worked in factories in solidarity with labor. In both events, protestors were "eliminated as enemies," revealing the state's lack of compunction. Whereas the military state suspended the law with its declaration of national emergency, the liberal democratic state resorts to the rule of law to authorize its use of violence. My analysis shows that this cotemporality of the two historical moments is more than a return of repressed memories. The return lies in the concrete materiality of the state–capital nexus that is common to both moments.

The awakening of the Ssangyong workers and leftists to this political reality enabled them to reject the fragmented social categories of workers and search for a new universal politics. The appeal to life brings JCMK's politics and the Ssangyong workers' struggle back full circle to Chŏn T'aeil. The JCMK leaders' insistence on migrant workers' labor rights is a leftover from the earlier minjung movement, which allowed the JCMK to distance itself from the civil society movement and its identity politics. The Ssangyong struggle broke the mantra of the 1990s labor movement, reclaiming community (kongdongch'e), or an "us," which is, according to Pak Sŭngok (2010), the ethos of Chŏn T'aeil's struggle. A rethinking of history and historical change enabled JCMK leaders and Ssangyong workers to envisage new democratic politics. The uneven experience of migrant workers and unionized workers signifies the fractured temporality of the capitalist system, in which crisis is produced and politicized through the invocation of past and future.

The urgency of understanding the present is expressed by the polemic debate on periodization, which pits the 1987 democratization against the 1997 financial crisis as the decisive moment that separates the present from the past. The minjung movement's social formation debate of the 1980s and the civil society movement's cultural turn since the 1990s both attempt to access the present, although through different approaches to the social. Both the social formation debate and the cultural turn share what Lefebvre (2008:204) calls "the transfiguration of everyday life," as they seek to metamorphosize the present into a new political moment, again through different means. The former prescribed the practice of "going to hyŏnjang" (literally, the present place), which refers to university students' sharing of work, food, lodging, and other aspects of daily life with workers and peasants. This practice was nothing other than the students "becoming" workers and minjung (people) through dialectical consciousness-raising. In contrast, the cultural turn reconstituted everyday culture with an emphasis on spontaneity, difference, and plurality. It blended protests with festivals to create a space for the expression of one's identity and individuality without the earlier ready-made political formula. The recognition of these common and different aesthetics of democratic politics is crucial for my thesis on the historical repetition of capitalist crisis and its attempted resolution in and through the new democratic imagination.

PART II
REPARATION

3
REPARATION:
ON COLONIAL RETURNEE

This chapter examines the intrinsic link between the formation of a deterritorialized Korean nation and capitalist integration of home and diaspora. Reparation politics in South Korea constitutes this immanent link and represents capitalist integration of Koreans across borders into a democratic process. South Korea has developed new affective engagements with diasporic Koreans of formerly socialist countries along the lines of Hungary, Greece, and other countries that have incorporated ethnic members migrating from the former Soviet Union since the 1990s. The migration of ethnic Koreans from China (Korean Chinese hereafter) in particular has become a testing ground for the emergent transnational Korea. Their migratory work becomes unexpectedly crucial for the production of the South Korean state's democratic sovereignty. Whereas the legitimacy of the South Korean state weakened during the Cold War by its ties with the Japanese colonial legacy and American imperialism, it now faces another challenge. Namely, neoliberal capitalist reforms call into question the state's promise to realize a welfare society in the democratic era. In this juncture, Korean Chinese fill the gap between democracy and the neoliberal capitalist system by enabling the state to outsource its promise to the market. That is, Korean Chinese supply cheap labor in the construction sector and services, such as food services and the care of children, the elderly, and sick, all of which concern the production of life.

Reparation politics for Korean Chinese establishes the issues of nationality and rights of Korean Chinese as a new fault line in the formation of transnational Korea. It performs the uncanny work of consolidating the sovereignty of the South Korean state. With dubious effects, its construction of Korean Chinese as colonial victims departs from the Cold War equation of Korean Chinese with North Korean allies. Reparation politics renews the importance of history in the putative era of the end of history, establishing reparation for colonial injustice as the urgent task of democratization. At the same time, it naturalizes the South Korean state and its exceptional sovereignty by reconfiguring the Cold War issue of decolonization into the moral responsibility of the (South Korean) state for colonial victims. As a key mode of democratic politics, reparation politics turns democracy into a universal history of ethics characterized by the mantra of nonviolence and the state's responsibility for its citizens. It is contrasted to democratic politics during the Cold War that bound democracy to the elimination of military dictatorship and capitalist exploitation. In this chapter, I investigate narratives and political practices of reparation politics.

Reparation politics is the capitalist unconscious. It envisages capitalist crisis as democratic crisis. This political inversion is embodied in the Overseas Korean Act, which pledges to integrate the Korean diaspora, but excludes Koreans from former socialist countries from the category of overseas Koreans (*tongp'o*). Reparation politics sparked animated debate on the act from 1999 to its amendment in 2004. Yet it does not address the capitalist integration of the Korean diaspora and South Korea, especially Korean Chinese migratory work. I uncover this capitalist excess that continues to haunt reparation politics. I inquire into the temporal structure of the subjectivities of activists and Korean Chinese migrants, as the repressed history of colonial migration and of the socialist Korean diaspora returned with the waning of the Cold War, democratization, and neoliberal capitalist system.

A Hierarchical Transnational Korea: Overseas Korean Act

During the Cold War era, the two Koreas regarded overseas Koreans as pawns in their rivalry. In the name of defending itself against North Korea, the South Korean military state territorialized its sovereignty by separating citizens within its border from overseas Koreans, who comprised both citizens living abroad and ethnic Koreans. With the pledge to eliminate North Korean spies and mobilize its citizens in the event of emergency, beginning in 1968 the military state issued each individual a resident registration number that records place and date of birth, gender, and place of registration. The resident registration system enabled the state to manage information about citizens and their political orientations (Kim Tongch'un 2000; Oka 2002). When citizens left Korea to reside in a foreign country, they lost their status as registered residents and were treated as outsiders like other overseas ethnic Koreans. The two Koreas competed for political loyalty and financial support from Korean Japanese and Korean Americans for economic development in the 1970s and 1980s. When North Korea launched the repatriation project in 1959, which brought about ninety thousand Koreans from Japan by the late 1970s, South Korea invited putative North Koreans in Japan to visit their hometown and ancestral graves in South Korea during the Autumn Thanksgiving holidays and created a cemetery for Korean Japanese in South Ch'ungch'ŏng Province in 1976.[1] To counter North Korea's influence on Koreans in Japan, South Korea spent about 65 percent of its budget for overseas Koreans on Koreans in Japan as of 1997 (Ryang 1997).

The economic crisis and the consequent global capitalist expansion transformed South Korean policy toward overseas Koreans in the post–Cold War era. The signature globalization policy (Segyehwa) of the Kim Yong Sam government (1993–1998) pursued economic liberalization in all sectors of finance, employment, and trade while also embracing overseas Koreans as human capital vital for strengthening the global competitiveness of the South Korean economy. Its deterritorialized and capitalist approach consisted of the "localization" (hyŏnjihwa) of the Korean diaspora and the mobilization of its economic assistance for the Korean economy. The vice minister of foreign relations, who chaired the Overseas Korean Policy Committee (Chaeoe tongp'o chŏngch'aek wiwŏnhoe) during the regime, has described the hyŏnjihwa policy:

> Lacking legitimacy for its rule, previous military governments provided a lot of financial support to, exerted unnecessary intervention in, and showed excessive interest in overseas Koreans in order to use them for security purposes. Since the legitimacy problem no longer pertains to the new democratic government, its new policy toward overseas Koreans is not to take an interest in them or associate with them.
>
> (Choe Wugil 2001:8)

According to Yi Kuhong, director of the Overseas Korean Relations Institute, this policy aimed to help overseas Koreans settle in their host countries [hyŏnjihwa], making it desirable for Korean Americans to become Americanized and Korean Japanese to become Japanized (Choe Wugil 2001:8). The Segyehwa policy designated overseas Koreans as "tongp'o" (compatriots) instead of the hitherto-used term "kyomin" or "kyop'o" (sojourners) (Cho Kwang-tong 1996). As an integrative and inclusive concept, tongp'o accentuates the fraternal ties of Koreans above the territorial divide.

After this turning point, transnational Korea in the post–Cold War era was formed through animated debates among officials, legislators, activists, and the Korean diaspora during the following two governments. Urgency about the economic recovery after the 1997 financial crisis opened an opportunity to establish a government agency and legislate the rights of overseas Koreans in South Korea, which had been promised in every South Korean presidential election from 1971 to 1992. The Overseas Korean Foundation was formed in March 1999 to foster cultural exchange with overseas Koreans. In September 1999 the Overseas Korean Act (Immigration and Legal Status of Overseas Korean Act) was legislated to "promote globalization among overseas Koreans [chaeoe tongp'o] . . . and facilitate their participation in reviving the economy of their mother country [South Korea] by easing restrictions on overseas Koreans and promoting their economic investment in their mother country" (Taehanmin'guk kwanbo 1999:8–9). The act endowed overseas Koreans holding the F-4 visa de facto dual citizenship without key obligations of citizens such as mandatory military service and taxation. It granted the right to a renewable two-year visitor permit, a residential card comparable to the citizen's registration card, health insurance for residence over ninety days, property ownership, employment, free financial transactions, and other economic activities that do not threaten social order and stability.

The Overseas Korean Act reflected the orientation of a growing chorus of policy makers, legislators, activists, and elites who defined overseas Koreans as economic assets comparable to ethnic Chinese for China and the Jewish diaspora for Israel. In a study commissioned by the South Korean government, the Institute for International Economy in Washington, DC, assessed the economic value of the Korean diaspora for the South Korean economy to be $120 billion, or 20 to 25 percent of South Korea's GDP. The Korean diaspora was estimated to influence 16 percent of South Korea's exports and 14 percent of its imports through remittances to South Korea and foreign currency reserves. Moreover, the potential contribution of the Korean diaspora to South Korea is projected to be as impactful as that of the Chinese diaspora to China because overseas Koreans are concentrated in four superpowers (the United States, Japan, Russia, and China) and dispersed across more than one hundred fifty countries. According to the National Security Agency (kukka anjŏn kihoekpu 1998), the successor of the Korean Central Intelligence Agency, the mobilization of overseas Koreans as "human capital" (injŏk chasan) was key for the development of the nation-state. It attributed the importance of the Korean diaspora to its size: the population of Koreans living outside the two Koreas is the fifth largest in the world, after the

Chinese, Jewish, Italian, and Indian diasporas; and it is second only to Israel as a proportion of the home country's citizens.[2] The erasure of major rights from the Overseas Korean Act highlighted the economic character of the act. The rights to vote and to run for government office, long-standing demands of Korean Americans, were included in the initial notice of legislation posted in August 1998 but were removed from the final version. A major privilege granted by the act is, thus, the freedom to make financial investments, a freedom that was, according to the Ministry of Labor, the main interest of Korean Americans, whereas Korean Chinese mainly were concerned about the right to work as manual laborers (Ministry of Labor 2003a). The act's stipulation on employment became the most controversial right, given that South Korea sought to tap into the human capital of Korean Americans while regulating the employment of Korean Chinese in labor-intensive sectors.

This capitalist characteristic of the Overseas Korean Act is overshadowed by the fierce controversy over its criteria for overseas Koreans. While the initial legislative notice defined overseas Koreans as individuals of Korean lineage (Hanminjok hyŏlt'ong), its revised version identified them as those who once held South Korean citizenship and their immediate children. The principle of past citizenship was adopted abruptly because the Ministry of Foreign Affairs claimed the lineage principle violated international conventions that prohibit discrimination on the basis of race, ethnicity, or any other factor (Ministry of Foreign Affairs 1999; Ministry of Justice 2001; Oka 2002). Supporters of the principle of past citizenship bolstered their position by mentioning the ruling of the European Union's court in Venice against Hungary's lineage-based law for its overseas ethnic groups and cited the examples of Italy, Greece, and Austria, which extended the right to settle and work only to their ethnic groups living in designated countries (Chŏng Insŏp 2004). In general, both the lineage principle and the past citizenship principle define national membership by birth and thus meet the criterion of the ethnic principle (jus sanguinis), which is contrasted to the principle of national membership on the basis of place of birth (jus soli). However, the past citizenship principle excludes more than one-half of the Korean diasporic population, who emigrated to Japan, China, and the former Soviet Union during Japanese colonization (1910–1945) and remained there even after liberation because of the tumultuous conflict in the Korean peninsula leading to the division of Korea. In recognition of the problem, the Judiciary Committee of the National Assembly recommended measures to address the issue of the exclusion of the Korean diaspora in these countries, especially Korean Chinese working illegally in South Korea.

In late 1999 the Ministry of Justice broadened the categories of people eligible for naturalization from only those who joined the independence struggle and their descendants to those with their family registration (hojŏk). However, few people benefited from this because many emigrated before the 1922 adoption of hojŏk and because many others were born in northern Korea and thus could not prove their hojŏk. The controversy over the exclusionary nature of the Overseas Korean Act led to its amendment in February 2004. The government's response to the controversy indicates that it was more interested in using Korean Chinese as precarious labor than in giving them equal rights. The amendment itself neither eliminated the principle of past citizenship nor legalized Korean Chinese employment. It simply inserted in parenthesis "the inclusion of those who emigrated prior to the foundation of the Republic of Korea." This did not, however, resolve the undocumented status of the absolute majority of illegal Korean Chinese workers in South Korea because the Ministry of Justice immediately adopted a measure requiring overseas Koreans to pledge not to engage in manual labor and to submit proof thereof. Items constituting proof included evidence of previous employment at a large firm in their home county, of permanent residency in and frequent visits to developed countries, and of income tax payment. Overseas Koreans also had to ascertain that they had no record of misdemeanor offenses in South Korea such as illegal work or overstay.

Instead, Korean Chinese become incorporated as migrant workers. The family visitation program was an expedient to keep Korean Chinese as undocumented labor, as the Industrial Training Program was for the whole migrant workforce, as explained in chapter 2. The family visitation program became a breeding ground for subsequent illegal work, given that the majority of Korean Chinese had lost contact with family members in South Korea. Even those who had family contacts still relied on brokers to buy a family invitation and overstay the few months allotted for an official family visit. An invitation for a family visit to South Korea sold for between 50,000 to 80,000 yuan ($6,500 to $10,000) in the early 2000s. From the mid-1990s to the mid-2000s, the most expensive means for visiting South Korea was for a Korean Chinese woman to marry a South Korean man, which cost between 70,000 and 80,000 yuan, though its price could go as high as 120,000 yuan. The cheapest and most risky means for the visit was clandestine entry without passport or documents for a visit, which usually cost about 40,000 to 60,000 yuan, though the cost could run up to 85,000 yuan. In these circumstances, family members, relatives, friends, and neighbors often became envoys as Korean Chinese accessed brokers using personal ties and word-of-mouth introductions. They also lent money for brokers' fees, as the purchase of counterfeit documents required borrowing money from three to five individuals or households at an annual interest rate of about 2 to 5 percent.[3] Risk in coming to South Korea is shared by family and village members. In this period, swindles were extensive and suicides were therefore not rare (Mun Hyŏngjin 2008). In fact, swindles and their effects on family and community in China drew the attention of South Korean activists and media to Korean Chinese migrant workers and their illegal status.

The family visit by the first generation of overseas Koreans (and thus those with family registration in Korea) has steadily increased ad hoc. Eligibility has been broadened from sixth-degree to eighth-degree relatives, and the duration of visit increased to one year with permission to work. The age for overseas Koreans' family visits steadily lowered to fifty years old and older in 1999, then to forty-five and older on July 1, 2002, forty and older on December 10, 2002, thirty and older on May 10, 2003, and twenty-five and older on January 10, 2006 (Ministry of Justice 2003; Sŏl Tonghun 2007). The quota for Korean Chinese in the Industrial Training Program also increased from 15 percent to 20 percent (Yi Kwangkyu 2001:15). Moreover, the Program to Manage Employment (Ch'wiŏp kwallije), which was introduced in November 2002 and managed under the Employment Permit Program starting in 2004 (see chapter 2), granted the H-2 visa to overseas Koreans without families or relatives in South Korea. In addition to being allowed to work at various jobs in the service sector, Korean Chinese were officially permitted in 2004 to work for two years in the construction sector—the work that was most popular among Korean Chinese men and unskilled South Korean men—and in 2006, in manufacturing, agriculture, livestock industry, and fisheries.

REPARATION: SOVEREIGNTY AND DECOLONIZATION

The capitalist character of the Overseas Korean Act is illustrated by the simultaneous exclusion of Korean Chinese from the act and the continuous expansion of Korean Chinese as precarious labor. Existing studies of the act focus on the principle of past citizenship and its discriminatory effect (Oka 2002; Chae Hant'ae 2005). Instead, I approach the movement to amend the act as reparation politics and its liberal and capitalist logic. I inquire into the democratic representation of Korean Chinese rights in the form of reparation, its paradoxical effect on the state's sovereignty, and capitalist excesses that escape discourses and practices of reparation. South Koreans come to rely on Korean Chinese women for domestic services, including housekeeping and caring for children, the elderly, and the sick; similarly, middle-class households in Canada rely on migrant labor from the Philippines and the Dominican Republic as domestic workers in the post–welfare era (Stasiulis and Bakan 1997). In South Korea, democratization has long been expected to bring about the welfare society. Instead, democratization coalesces with a mixture of rising unemployment, worsening income inequality, and rejection of manual labor. In that conjuncture, low-paid Korean Chinese workers ease deficiencies in welfare programs, thereby reducing the political liability of democratically elected governments. The social movement to amend the act from October 1999 to February 2004 had an important effect on consolidating the state's sovereignty. I locate this effect in its reparation form that framed the amendment of the act and the inclusion of Korean Chinese as the state's responsibility to resolve historical wrongs.

In the post–Cold War era decolonization is transformed into reparation. During the Cold War, national unification of the two Koreas was envisaged as decolonization. Upon the end of the World War II Korea was divided by superpowers that intervened in Koreans' struggle to create an independent nation-state. The United States incorporated South Korea and Japan into its Cold War bloc in East Asia. It thwarted South Koreans' efforts at decolonization from Japanese rule by helping to reinstate to key military and official positions those who had collaborated with the Japanese colonizers, large landlords, and anti-Communist nationalists. It also facilitated the normalization of official relations between South Korea and Japan by arbitrating the latter's one-time payment and loans as reparation for colonization. The democracy movement in South Korea painstakingly analyzed the relationship between US imperialism and capitalist development in order to determine an effective strategy. A new opportunity for decolonization came in 1987 with democratization, which was followed by the state's reparation for victims of massacres before and during the Korean War and for victims of the military dictatorship during the Cold War (Hŏ Sangsu 2009; Yi Yŏngjae 2010).

Given this emphasis in reparation politics for South Korean victims of the Cold War, those who advocated amending the Overseas Korean Act did not explicitly consider their cause as linked to reparation politics. However, their language and practices are consistent with those of reparation politics. In advocating the lineage principle for the act, they did not base their cause on the ethnic primordiality of the Korean community but instead inscribed it in the universal ethics of addressing past wrongs and seeking redress for victims. When opponents charged advocates of the amendment of the act with nationalism, they did not recognize that the advocacy of the amendment had translated nationalism into human rights advocacy. As a new modality of democratic politics, reparation politics reconfigures subjects and politics to frame the very concept of the political. The movement to amend the act enlisted a young generation of South Korean activists, such as those in the Korean International Network, which promoted the inclusion of all overseas Koreans and informed South Koreans of stateless Koreans in Japan, who had taken neither Japanese nor South Korean citizenship and thus by default were considered North Korean. But the movement was mainly spearheaded by three activist members of the clergy—the Reverends Kim Haesŏng, Lim Kwangbin, and Sŏ Kyŏngsŏk—who had participated in the democracy struggle against the military dictatorship. Their churches, like other organizations for non-Korean migrant workers, provided Korean Chinese with assistance in recovering unpaid wages, obtaining compensation for job-related accidents, accessing health care, and finding housing and jobs. Their different approaches to the movement to amend the act demonstrate the range of influences from the minjung movement.

Constitutionalism and Cosmopolitanism

The movement to amend the Overseas Korean Act began with the appeal to the Constitutional Court. On August 23, 1999, eleven days after the act was passed in the National Assembly, an appeal to the Court was submitted by three Korean Chinese, one whose husband committed suicide by setting himself on fire over the inhumane working conditions in South Korea. The appeal was organized by Rev. Kim Haesŏng, who in the early 1980s led the urban poor movement in the city of Sŏngnam, near Seoul, and starting in the mid-1990s pioneered human rights advocacy for migrant workers in the same city. At the beginning, his main task was to conduct funerals of migrant workers who died of accident or illness. Within a few years his center in Seoul became the largest center for migrant workers, serving several thousand migrant workers including Korean Chinese. It was equipped with a six-story building and a two-story building that housed a three-thousand-seat auditorium, small rooms, and floors designated as classrooms for theology lessons. It offered Sunday worship services for all migrant workers, regular gatherings by migrant workers grouped by their originating countries and regions, and lectures on the Bible. Participation in Sunday services was almost a prerequisite of membership, particularly for newcomers and the jobless and sick staying at the center. Kim's approach exemplified the new activism of the churches, which from the 1990s onward mixed evangelism and humanitarianism while providing relief to refugees and victims of famine and poverty elsewhere in the world. Kim came to lean toward moral and religious education for migrant workers. He considered moral education (insŏng kyoyuk) the prerequisite for addressing migrant workers' fundamental issues because he observed that they tended to waste hard-earned savings on personal desires such as taking additional wives after they returned to their home countries rather than supporting their family or investing in business (Interview with Rev. Kim Haesŏng on July 26, 1996).

The appeal to the Constitutional Court charged that the Overseas Korean Act violates the constitutional rights of Korean Chinese to equality and happiness. It called on the South Korean state to protect the constitutional rights of all Koreans, including Korean Chinese, on the grounds that the Republic of Korea inherited the 1919 independence movement and the legal authority of the Provisional government exiled in Shanghai during the Japanese colonization. The Ministry of Justice dismissed the appeal, referring to their status as foreigners, which gave them no constitutional rights in South Korea. However, the Constitutional Court affirmed the validity of their petition, stating that the Constitution protects the human rights of foreigners and that their petition concerns intraethnic equality among overseas Koreans. After two years of deliberation, the Court ruled in November 2001 that the act was unconstitutional, drawing on abstract notions of equality, humanitarianism, and individual choice on which the meaning of ethnic homogeneity was premised. According to the ruling, the abrupt adoption of the principle of past citizenship would not resolve the government's concerns about diplomatic conflict, the threat to the domestic labor market posed by the migration of overseas Koreans, or security issues. Nor would it be justifiable because the timing of Korean emigration is "not fundamental enough to revoke the homogeneity" (tongjilsŏng) of those who emigrated before and after 1948. The ruling stated that such discrimination of overseas Koreans cannot be considered "rational equality," since it is not necessary for accomplishing the act's goal of enhancing the national identity, localization, and cultural homogeneity of overseas Koreans (Hŏnbŏp chaep'anso 2001). Here, the legitimacy of the (South) Korean state is reduced to the historical timing of its foundation in 1948. This jettisons the Cold War history of the rivalry between the two Koreas for legitimacy and the long-standing critique of the South Korean state as the heir of Japan's colonial legacy and collaborator with American imperialism.

The Court's majority opinion stated that those who emigrated before the foundation of the Republic of Korea were forced to leave Korea in order to join the exiled anti-Japanese independence movement or to escape oppression and war mobilization by the colonizers. It reasoned that the exclusion of these Koreans from the act was indefensible on "humanitarian grounds, even setting aside the national standpoint." The majority opinion found that these Koreans were deprived of the "equal opportunity" to acquire South Korean citizenship because there was no South Korean embassy or consulate in socialist countries during the Cold War. A special opinion of the ruling reasoned that the unavailability of overseas offices of the South Korean government constituted "regional discrimination" against Koreans in former socialist countries and that this was "more inhumane than racial discrimination, posing an obstacle to social integration, national integration, and the free and creative development of individuals." This construction of Cold War history as a regional factor or a matter of individual choice decisively dehistoricizes the past. Chapter 5 looks at greater depth into the tumultuous relationship between Korean Chinese and the Chinese socialist state in the context of their process of becoming an ethnic minority from the 1940s to the present. The matter of their Korean identity was too embedded in the history of colonialism and socialist revolution to be interpreted in terms of geography or timing.

The Court's opinions on national history are framed in the language of human rights, sitting ambiguously between cosmopolitanism and ethnic nationalism that was an axis of the debates on the act. The conservative Grand National Party proposed a bill supporting the principle of lineage while completely eliminating the act's stipulation on freedom of employment. The majority Democratic Party's alternative bill omitted the principle of lineage while abolishing the date of emigration as a criterion for overseas Koreans and accepting those individuals who emigrated as ethnic Koreans before 1948. The Ministry of Foreign Affairs and Trade rejected both bills for their reverse discrimination against non-Korean foreigners and violation of international conventions against all forms of discrimination. Similarly, the National Human Rights Commission alleged that adopting the principle of lineage to define overseas Koreans is a form of "favoritism based on race" and that the rights of overseas Koreans as foreigners must be assigned by treaties between the involved states and international conventions on human rights. The opponents of the principle of lineage remained oblivious to the fact that the Overseas Korean Act had already granted de facto citizenship to Korean Americans. The Ministry of Labor opposed the principle of lineage on the grounds that from the Korean Chinese community alone it would bring approximately three hundred seventy thousand workers, who would take jobs away from unskilled low-income South Koreans. It proposed treating Korean Chinese as any other migrant worker group and managing them under the Employment Permit Program (Chaeoe kungmin yŏngsaguk 2001; National Human Rights Commission 2001; Ministry of Labor 2003a; Yŏllin wuridang t'ongil oegyo t'ongsang wiwŏnhoe 2004).

The Court's ruling on the Overseas Korean Act as unconstitutional legitimated the movement to amend the act. The appeal to the Constitutional Court and the responses to the Court's decision reflected a growing trend of democratic activism in South Korea and the world, which equates the rule of law with democracy. The rule of law is "a silent revolution toward participatory democracy," a legal scholar declared triumphantly, interpreting skyrocketing lawsuits since the late 1990s as a sign of Koreans' awakening to their rights (Ahn 1998). The Constitutional Court was established in 1988 to amend the Constitution and introduce direct presidential elections. At first it drew little attention because of the long-standing deprecation of constitutional rights under South Korea's military regimes. It quickly came to wield the highest judicial authority, however, and became perhaps the most sublime institution in democratized South Korea. That is, the Constitutional Court has come to be imbued with a religious character that assumes a priori existence outside sociopolitical reality. As Marx (1977) notes in his critique of Hegel, the Constitution was confounded with the sovereignty of the people and became a substitute for the voice of the people. However, constitutionalism also created an unexpected moment for rethinking about national history. When history disappeared in the advance of cosmopolitanism, the Constitutional Court and the movement to amend the act summoned the forgotten national history to the political front by blending it with universal ethics. The Court's language and the social movement's responses to its decision thus carved out the state's responsibility to resolve historical wrongs as the primary discourses of the movement.

The Right to Free Travel

Formed in December 2001, the Committee for Amending the Overseas Korean Act (Chaeoe tongp'obŏp kaejŏng taech'aek hyŏbŭihoe, hereafter the Committee) counteracted the economic instrumentalization of Korean Chinese by constructing Korean Chinese as "colonial returnees." Though Reverends Kim and Sŏ joined the efforts, Reverend Lim emerged as the central figure in representing the Committee's positions. Lim had engaged in the democracy movement in the 1980s as director of the Human Rights Committee of the National

Council of Churches in Korea, participated in official and civic processes of reparation in the 1990s, and continues to lead the progressive church movement. From 2000 he directed the Korean Welfare Mission Center founded by twenty-five clergy activists, progressive pastors, and theologians who held regular seminars and published books on the church's role in the causes of migrant labor, unification, and North Korean refugees. According to the Committee, Korean Chinese were the metonym of the colonized nation, for they symbolized the colonial suffering of all Koreans, including South Koreans. The Committee broke the Cold War perception of Korean Chinese as North Korean allies by voicing the double victimization of Korean Chinese: first by the Japanese, who forced them to emigrate to China during the colonial era; and again by the home country (South Korea) because they were forced to stay in China and become Chinese nationals through South Korea's indifference and failure to arrange their return home. The Committee argued that Korean Chinese also engaged in the anti-Japanese struggle in the area of northeast China known as Manchuria. According to the Committee, if the South Korean state claims to be the legitimate heir of the Korean nation, it must fulfill its responsibility to embrace Korean Chinese. Lim Kwangbin observed:

The meaning of amending the Overseas Korean Act is to care for those who left their hometown to join the anti-Japanese independence movement and escape poverty, and for their descendants, when their nation-state had failed to take care of them. . . . Now they are returning to their hometown again in economic difficulty. Who dares to say they can or cannot work? There is no justification for preventing Koreans and their descendants from returning. . . .

They are overwhelmed by persimmon trees still standing at the homes in Korea where they grew up before their emigration. Their brothers and sisters still live in the houses left by their parents. Grandparents who had raised them are still laid in mountains near their houses.

They have the right to visit, live, and work in this land. Who dares to say that they do not have the right to work in this country? It is disgraceful to deny them the rights in the name of equality of all migrant laborers under the UN declaration of human rights, and that it deters the unity of the national community. The Committee for Amending the Overseas Korean Act rejects the approach that regards overseas Koreans as objects of management and control and, moreover, as cheap foreign migrant laborers.

(Lim Kwangbin 2002)

Lim likened Korean Chinese to family members who leave home during a family crisis to go abroad to earn money, or to a daughter who is married to a poor family and now wishes to return to her natal family to earn money necessary for survival. The "home country" (*koguk*) must be the place where overseas Koreans can freely visit or return, as in Germany and Israel, which accepted their ethnic kin from the former Soviet Union. The common expression of "rich home family and poor returnees" was used to bolster the moral claim of the right of Korean Chinese and other Koreans of the colonial diaspora.

When proponents of the principle of past citizenship drew on cosmopolitanism, Lim charged them with a lack of historical consciousness. Preferential treatment in recognition of past suffering, like affirmative action in the United States, was not to be confused with reverse racial discrimination, argued Lim. In his words,

> What is equality? Is it equality to regard as the same foreign migrant laborers and tongp'o who engaged in anti-Japanese struggle and survived in their host countries even when the home state could not protect their lives? It is not. On the contrary, treating tongp'o as any other foreign migrant worker constitutes discrimination against tongp'o. . . . As an act of rewriting history, the Overseas Korean Act must perform *ssikkimgut* [a shaman's cleansing dance], capable of fully cleansing [national history of] the perturbed relationship between tongp'o and our [South Korean] society.
>
> (Lim Kwangbin 2002)

The Committee presented the right of Korean Chinese to travel freely (*chayu wangrae*) between South Korea and China as a solution to Koreans' illegal status in South Korea. The right to travel freely was expected to establish the equality of Korean Americans and Korean Chinese in South Korea. It would allow Korean Chinese to dispense with brokers, their high fees, and swindling. Although Korean Chinese employment was the most contentious issue, the Committee did not identify it as a goal of the campaign to amend the act. In fact, Lim projected that even if the state were to accept the right of Korean Chinese to visit freely, it would restrict the number and length of visits per year. In his reasoning, the right to travel freely would reduce the length of stay in Korea from five to ten years to two to three years, eliminating the period to pay back their broker's fee and assuring their revisit to South Korea, and thus solve problems resulting from long years of family separation and the loss of human capital in the Korean Chinese community in China (Interview on July 15, 2002). The right to travel freely would not, however, ensure the right to work, especially because political parties and the government administration officially separated visitation from employment.

Lim's approach to mobilizing Korean Chinese for the movement followed the practice of the minjung movement of the 1980s. Intellectuals and college students in the minjung movement assisted workers and peasants to organize themselves by raising their consciousness, for instance, by establishing night schools. Similarly, Lim helped to form the Korean Chinese Coalition (Chosŏnjok yŏnhaphoe) in May 2000, the first organization established by Korean Chinese themselves. After studying with Lim the history of South Korean policies and laws on overseas Koreans, including the Overseas Korean Act, six founding members of the coalition produced their own proposal that affirmed advocacy of the right to travel freely and added to it the rights to work, vote, and freely engage in financial transactions (Chosŏnjok yŏnhaphoe 2000). The Korean Chinese Coalition comprised about three hundred members as of 2003. During the intense campaign to amend the act from 2001 to 2003, about fifty active members of the Korean Chinese Coalition congregated on Sundays in Lim's church to learn about the act and Korean history and to discuss ways to mobilize other members and acquaintances to attend rallies and sit-in protests. As Lim framed the campaign to amend the act in terms of rewriting history, members of the Korean Chinese Coalition called their cause an effort to "write one page in history [yŏksa ŭi han p'eiji ssŭgi] and become protagonists [chuin'gong] of history" (Interview on June 14, 2004, in Seoul). About one hundred members of the Korean Chinese Coalition gave up their jobs in order to lead the sit-in protests for eight months in 2003, despite the fact their earnings were essential for paying debts and supporting families in China. Many of them saw the sit-in protests in 2003 as a life-altering experience because learning about Korean colonial history enabled them to recognize their rights in South Korea as "returnees" (Interviews on June 12, June 14, and June 20, 2004, in Seoul).

Korean Chinese in the coalition represented themselves as ethnic Koreans, victims of Japanese colonization, and casualties of shallow South Korean policy. The president of the Korean Chinese Coalition, Yoo Pongsun, in her mid-forties, was a farmer in China and worked as a street vendor of Chinese medicine at T'apkol Park in downtown Seoul, where she was mocked by South Korean vendors as "a Chinese beggar." She became the most articulate and charismatic leader of the Korean Chinese Coalition and was routinely invited to speak about the Overseas Korean Act at political gatherings. Nam Sŏngch'il

(2004), who was in his late sixties and one of few intellectuals in the coalition group of Korean Chinese, spoke about the exclusion of Korean Chinese from the category of overseas Koreans in terms of a form of national division comparable to the quintessential national division of the two Koreas. The division of the two Koreas was called "the 38 division" because the Thirty-eighth Parallel North separated the two. Nam called the division of Korean Chinese and Korean Americans "the 48 division" and "the 22 division" for the exclusion of Koreans who emigrated before the 1948 foundation of South Korea and before the 1922 adoption of hojŏk. The appeal written by members of the Korean Chinese Coalition during the last sit-in protest in late 2003 replicates the familiar trope of reparation:

> Our minjok [ethnic nation] is a sacred ethnic nation with tens of thousands of years of history. Its descendants were afflicted by Japanese colonization during which we lost our country and land, emigrated to other countries in search of a new livelihood, and became separated from our parents, brothers, and sisters. However, our minjok as a courageous and wise nation risked their lives to recover the country fighting the Japanese in China, Manchuria, and Russia. The present existence of the Republic of Korea is a product of this bloody struggle to liberate minjok. However, this minjok [Korean Chinese] couldn't return to Korea due to the Korean War and the consequent division of Korea. How many of our ancestors yearned to return to their hometown? As changing international politics has opened the border [of South Korea and China], Korean Chinese have come to South Korea with the Korean dream.[4]

Another participant invoked a similar discourse of Korean national history, claiming undocumented Korean Chinese to be descendants of those who took refuge in Manchuria during the colonial period and maintained ethnic homogeneity and identity (Yi Wŏnsŏk 2003).

Except for a few dozen non-Korean migrant workers supported by the Korean Confederation of Trade Union, the Korean Chinese Coalition and Lim's Korean Chinese Welfare Mission Center were the only organizations that rejected the state's voluntary registration drive from March 25 to May 25, 2002. Though carried out periodically before, the registration drive this time became perhaps the biggest spectacle in the history of migrant labor in South Korea. Predicting that the imminent World Cup tournament in South Korea would bring at least one hundred thousand illegal migrant workers in the guise of tourists, the government promised those who registered one year of employment as a preparation period before departure. This incentive led undocumented migrant workers to respond with such zeal that government officials were left unprepared when they opened only four sites as reporting facilities in greater Seoul with more than two hundred sixty thousand undocumented workers, or about 70 percent of the total foreign workforce. The facility in Yŏngdŭngp'o-ku in Seoul, where Korean Chinese were concentrated, turned away about one thousand of six thousand people who waited in line each day. The undocumented lined up in the early evening and waited overnight in order to register the next day. Observers and the media reported on their refugee-like appearance as they slept or rested on mats on the ground and ate overpriced instant noodles and cups of coffee sold by peddlers or bread and milk donated by neighboring churches. The police treated them like jailed criminals as soon as they entered the facilities, subjecting them to stand-up and sit-down drills and sending anyone who failed to obey commands to the end of line. Standing in line meant missing work and losing wages, with one day's wages equal to a month's at home; and if they were unable to register one day, they had to return to wait in line and lose another day of wages. Overwhelmed officials sent people to the end of the line for making the slightest mistake, such as using an incorrect letter when romanizing their name in English, an easy mistake for many who do not know English well.

Among about two hundred fifty thousand of the registered, very few intended to leave after one year, except for long-time migrant workers with more than ten years of work in South Korea, whose return to home had been discouraged by the hefty fine for illegal residency on their leaving South Korea. The absolute majority of those registering readily paid the fee and purchased a one-way plane ticket—the proof required by the state of their intended return, which cost about half a month's income in South Korea—as the security to work legally for one year. Given that South Korean and foreign airlines were incapable of handling the departure of that many people during the two-month period in the following year (since most of the people were expected to leave at the last minute if they would indeed leave), the registered people derided the campaign as a strategy to generate revenue for the state, airlines, and travel agencies. Despite its unprecedented success in registering undocumented migrant workers, the campaign failed to reduce their number or resolve the issue of their illegality (Ministry of Justice 2002). Leaders of the Korean Chinese Coalition visited the registration sites and vainly tried to dissuade people from registering and instead tried to recruit them to the struggle to amend the Overseas Korean Act. About fifty to seventy of its members refused to register, though the exact number was unknown because of controversy even among the members.

An irrepressible historical past and present underlined the tensions among members of the Korean Chinese Coalition and between the coalition and South Korean activists. On the one hand, leaders of the coalition confronted Korean Chinese history while mobilizing its members to the struggle to amend the act. Directed by its devoted secretary Chin Pokcha, recruiting one hundred to two hundred persons for the street protests took several days of outreach to members and involved leaving telephone messages and making personal calls and visits to workplaces and homes. Many members condemned coalition leaders for abandoning paid employment and family responsibilities for political activity, saying they had gone crazy or sold out to the church. Nam Sŏngch'il attributed such response to fear and apathy about politics and the law, which resulted from their suffering during the Chinese Cultural Revolution. According to Nam, they were recently reminded of their vulnerability as a minority when the Chinese government was suspicious of their loyalty during disputes between South Korea and China over the archeological remains of the ancient kingdom of Koguryŏ (Interview on June 25, 2004).

FIGURE 3.1 Korean Chinese joining the march on the anniversary of South Korean democratization in 2004 in Seoul. Photo by Hyun Ok Park.

On the other hand, a schism developed between Korean Chinese and South Korean activists over history and politics. Despite the life-changing effect of learning about Korean national history, Korean Chinese learned a version of South Korean national history that treated Manchuria as a site of the anti-Japanese independence movement. This representation did not leave much room to reflect their tumultuous experience during the colonial era and the Chinese revolution.[5] Moreover, notwithstanding appreciation for the selfless devotion of South Korean activists to the Korean Chinese cause, leaders of the Korean Chinese Coalition complained about their lack of power to direct the course of the movement, let alone formulating specific goals of their struggle against the South Korean state. Even when the coalition's president Yoo Pongsun joined the executive committee of the Committee for Amending the Overseas Korean Act, she did not have full authority to express the actual interests of Korean Chinese. Lim Kwanbin justified this on the grounds that as foreigners, Korean Chinese did not have power equal to that of South Koreans on the South Korean legal and political matters (Interview on June 22, 2004). This hierarchy contributed to the sidelining of Korean Chinese interest in the freedom of work. Their tension found little outlet in South Korean politics beyond backstage complaints and gossip among Korean Chinese.

FIGURE 3.2 After the march, members of the Korean Chinese Coalition washing t-shirts in 2004. Photo by Hyun Ok Park.

The Right to Return

When the deadline to amend the Overseas Korean Act was looming in 2003, Rev. Sŏ Kyŏngsŏk asserted that Korean Chinese were dual citizens and promoted their rights to "restore" their South Korean citizenship. He was a founder of the Citizens' Coalition for Economic Justice (Kyŏngsillyŏn), which as the first liberal NGO was established in 1989 to promote freedom and justice in market activities and secure private property rights. He is also a founder of the Korean Sharing Movement (Uri minjok sŏro topki), created in 1996 to offer humanitarian assistance to North Korea and support to the Korean diaspora, especially those in the former Soviet Union. Sŏ ran the Korean Chinese Church (Chosŏnjok kyohoe) in Seoul and participated in the movement to amend the act. Like Korean Chinese in other large centers, its members usually kept their passports in a safe place and carried their membership cards issued by the church. Police tended not to arrest them when they presented their membership cards. Sŏ's Korean Chinese Church brochures advertised itself as helping members obtain a release from police custody to the extent that the Ministry of Justice launched a special crackdown in the church's vicinity. Like Rev. Kim Haesŏng's church for Korean Chinese and migrant workers in Seoul, the Korean Chinese Church mobilized only 50 to 120 people for a rally to amend the act though its total membership numbered several thousand.

In 2003, Sŏ increasingly distanced himself from the other two leaders in the drive to amend the act. Although Kim and Lim insisted on distinguishing between ethnicity and nationality and constructing overseas Koreans as tongp'o, Sŏ conflated them in his drive to restore Korean nationality to Korean Chinese. On November 13, 2003, Rev. Sŏ's Korean Chinese Church in Seoul submitted to the Ministry of Justice applications of 5,525 members and their acquaintances for restoration of their Korean citizenship. The next day, they submitted the appeal to the Constitutional Court, charging that the government failed in its responsibility to resolve their dual citizenship after normalizing the diplomatic relationship with China in 1992 and that the Ministry of Justice's 2001 Instruction on Issuing Citizenship to Korean Chinese restricted the restoration of citizenship to Korean Chinese, violating the principle of equality. The appeal maintained that Koreans in China and Russia were denied the right of return to the home country and thus were reduced to the status of victims, similar to that of so-called Korean comfort women and forced laborers struck by the atomic bomb in Japan. The appeal based its claim on the long-forgotten Provisional Law on Nationality adopted under US military rule in 1948, which used the principle of lineage to define Korean citizenship. The Provisional Law declared as Korean nationals those whose father was Chosŏnin (Korean) and those who were referred to as Chosŏn minjŏk of Taehanjeguk (Korea from 1897 to 1910) and enlisted later on hojŏk from 1922. In addition, it ruled the loss of Korean citizenship to be contingent on both "voluntary" acquisition of foreign citizenship and permission from the Korean state to renounce Korean citizenship. According to the appeal, Korean Chinese never voluntarily gave up Korean nationality; they were forced to take Chinese nationality when the People's Republic of China was established and therefore held dual citizenship all along. To bolster the South Korean state's responsibility for Korean Chinese, the appeal cited the Constitutional Court's minority opinion in a reparation case that named the state responsible to victims of civilian massacres by the South Korean military during the Korean War. The appeal maintained that the constitutional right to "human respect" (ingan chonŏmsŏng) of Korean Chinese—not just their rights to equality, pursuit of happiness, change in residence, change in employment, and conscience—was violated (Kwak 2013).

The appeal by Korean Chinese drew a linear narrative of the South Korean state's legitimacy that extends from Taehanjeguk through the colonial period to the Republic of Korea. It neither recognized the history of the family registration system as a colonial system dating to 1922 nor addressed Koreans in China whose families emigrated before 1922 and thus lacked family registration. It did not register struggles among Koreans in pursuing national independence and creating a sovereign nation-state, struggles that were exacerbated by the superpowers and led to the national division and the Korean War. In March 2006, the Court ruled against the appeal. It noted that the 2001 Instruction was abolished in 2004. The Court affirmed the opinions of the Ministry of Justice and the National Assembly speaker that the 1997 Nationality Law stipulates the criteria and procedures to be used in deciding dual citizens' nationality and that the inability to choose nationality because there was no diplomatic relationship between the two countries during the Cold War does not make Korean Chinese dual citizens. However, its minority opinion largely affirmed the appellants' claims to dual citizenship and the South Korean state's responsibility to them as victims. Accepting the validity of the 1948 Provisional National Law, it closely reiterated that the South Korean state legitimately succeeded Taehanjeguk and the spirit of the 1919 independence movement. The minority opinion added a restriction on dual citizenship, limiting it to Korean Chinese born before the October 1949 foundation of the People's Republic of China.

Although the Court's ruling came years after the deadline to amend the Overseas Korean Act, the assertion of dual citizenship of Korean Chinese itself threatened to derail the movement to amend the act. When about one hundred fifty Korean Chinese mobilized by the Committee for Amending the Overseas Korean Act and the Korean Chinese Coalition began an eighty-four-day sit-in demonstration on November 15, 2003, about twenty-three hundred of those who had applied for restoration of South Korean citizenship and submitted the appeal to the Constitutional Court also started hunger strikes on the same day in eight churches. Some of them stood dramatically for hours with their hands on the ground to protest the overturning of their status. During the hunger strike, Kim Chayŏn said, "I have my grandfather's grave in this land/country, my own hojŏk, and my relatives in South Korea. Why should I be forced to be repatriated? The hunger strike is the only option for us on the brink of being expelled. . . . Since we left the country not because we loathed it but because of our victimization by its painful history, please do not bind us with the yoke of undocumented status" (Yoo and Yoo 2003). Here, she connected her desire to work freely in South Korea with the narrative of South Korean reparation politics. Having lost $30,000, her savings of six years, in a swindle in South Korea, Kim was clear about her purpose—to work and earn money in South Korea. Approaching the deadline set by the Constitutional Court for the amendment of the act, media reports of hunger strikes and petitions quickly brought attention to Sŏ's proposal rather than to the issue of the act itself. Reflecting the public's growing interest, President Roh Moo Hyun visited the hunger strikers to pledge his support in writing: "Chinese tongp'o [Korean Chinese]. Be strong. Even if the border and legal system fetters our freedom, our people [kŭngmin] support you. Our government will do its best in various ways. Please take care of your health" (Shin Sŭnggun et al. 2003). The next day the minister of justice explained that the president's pledge was not promising any specific resolution but offering moral support (Cho Hojin 2003). Regardless, the president's pledge of support provided justification for ending the hunger strikes on December 29, 2003, when criticism against Sŏ's campaign to restore citizenship began to increase after the response of the Chinese state.

The Chinese government began to sanction Korean Chinese who returned to China at that time, detaining them for interrogation over application for South Korean citizenship and threatening them with up to three years of imprisonment and 100,000 yuan in fines, an amount a fully employed Korean Chinese could earn in South Korea in one year. Public criticism faulted Sŏ for endangering the welfare of Korean Chinese. Sŏ's campaign was further scandalized by the charge that he misused revenue from the filing fee, totaling 570 million won, which his organization collected from about five thousand applicants seeking to restore their citizenship. Faced with rapidly fading support, he altered the drive to restore citizenship to "the drive to regain the right to return and live in one's hometown" (kohyang e torawa sal kwŏlli ch'atki undong). As the deadline for amending the Overseas Korean Act approached, Sŏ officially withdrew his support for amending the act and instead sided with the Ministry of Labor, which sought to enlist Korean Chinese in its proposed Employment Permit Program for all migrant workers. He also expressed support for the Ministry of Justice, which insisted on maintaining the act's principle of past citizenship by revising the act's Enforcement Ordinance to accept Korean Chinese as overseas Koreans and yet prohibit their employment in South Korea. Sŏ also supported the act's controversial clause on the right to freedom of employment on the grounds that its elimination would compromise the interests of Korean Americans (Sŏ Kyŏngsŏk 2002; Yi Pyŏnghye 2003). His seemingly variable positions reflect his view that nationality policy is not a legal matter but a political, historical, and institutional one.

The right of freedom of employment was an ultimate concern even for those who applied to restore their South Korean nationality and waged the hunger strikes. In their official letter to the Chinese government, some of them stated: "All that we wanted is to visit and work freely in South Korea. . . . Although we have applied for South Korean citizenship, not all of us want South Korean citizenship. In fact, most of us want to return to China. What we really want is to possess the right to choose Chinese or Korean citizenship at our will."[6] Some also angrily confessed that they joined the drive to restore South Korean citizenship because of assurances from Sŏ's church that the application itself would ensure at least the three-year period of residence and work during the review of their application even if the application was to be rejected (Yi Chinsŏk 2003; Kang Kukchin 2003a). Nothing more clearly illustrates the disparate politics and subjectivities of Sŏ and Korean Chinese applicants than the words they used to describe their efforts. Sŏ's drive was to "restore" (hoebok) South Korean citizenship, whereas Korean Chinese joining the drive used the word "acquire" (ch'widŭk), which connotes coming into possession of something not previously one's own. For most Korean Chinese, acquiring Korean nationality was a means to work legally in South Korea ("Sarye" 2003).

Preoccupied with their economic goals, many applicants did not expect anything to be of consequence to their Chinese nationality. Many of them were not interested in giving up Chinese citizenship. A Korean Chinese pleaded that he joined the hunger strikes as a last resort to obtain work. Others spoke of their intention to live in South Korea as almost nil, even if they were to "acquire" South Korean citizenship (Kang Kukchin 2003b). According to Kim Sŭngch'ŏl, "The reason for our participation in the hunger strike was less the acquisition of South Korean citizenship than the request to allow us to go freely between China and South Korea and work in South Korea" (Shin Sŭnggun et al. 2003). According to Mr. Choi, who came to South Korea eight years before, "My 16-day hunger strike did not yield anything. . . . More than 90 percent of those who participated in the hunger strike felt deceived by the Chosŏnjok church" (Kang Kukchin 2003c). Chinese officials visited Mr. Choi's household in China and asked many questions, including the timing of his visit to Seoul, the payment of his dues to the Chinese Communist Party, and verification of his participation in the drive to restore South Korean citizenship. Most Korean Chinese wrongly assumed that they could regain Chinese citizenship once they finished working in South Korea—if they even thought about losing Chinese citizenship. When they learned that the Chinese state imposed a fine on those who applied to restore their South Korean citizenship and even imprisoned them on return to China, they accused Sŏ of pushing them into the fire of hell and of turning them into international criminals ("Sarye" 2003). A sixty-five-year-old man, who stayed in Korea for eight years and applied to restore his citizenship, thought that Chinese citizenship could be obtained again later (*Chaeoe tongp'o sinmun* October issue 2003). On hearing reports of the Chinese government's sanctions and mockery by the Han Chinese, Korean Chinese feared that if they came to be perceived as opportunistic, they would be welcome nowhere.

THE HISTORICAL UNCONSCIOUS:
CAPITALIST EXCESS AND STATE CENTRISM

All parties involved in amending the Overseas Korean Act implicitly or emphatically shunned the right of ethnic Koreans from developing countries to work. The responses of Korean Chinese to the drive to amend the act, however, demonstrated their experience as migrant workers whose crucial concern was the right to freedom of work in South Korea. Their simultaneous participation and distancing from two main strands of the movement—the promotion of the rights to travel freely and restore South Korean nationality—shed light on their subjectivities and politics as migrant labor. The right to freedom of travel might tacitly imply the right to freedom of work, given that Korean Chinese work in South Korea under the pretense of visiting family or visiting for other purposes. However, in principle the rights to freedom of travel and to freedom of work authorize different sovereign subjects. The goal of freedom of travel concerns ethnic national membership of Korean Chinese in South Korea that would open South Korean borders for them. It inscribes sovereignty on the South Korean state by authorizing its responsibility for the suffering of Korean Chinese. In contrast, the right to freedom of work as a concrete interest of Korean Chinese shifts sovereignty from the home state to diasporic laborers. The capacity of workers' consciousness to redefine the terms of their commodification is harbored in claims of the right to freedom of work. The rights to freedom of travel and work also denote different temporalizations of Korean Chinese experience. The former links Korean Chinese to reparation of colonial and Cold War history; the latter concerns capitalist relations with South Koreans in the present. South Korean reparation politics effaced the history of Korean Chinese, including their history of becoming an ethnic minority in China and the historical meanings of their current migratory work. Representation of their current capitalist relations within the nation–diaspora dyad obscures the hierarchical form of their capitalist integration. Whether as South Korean citizens or overseas ethnic Koreans, Korean Chinese membership in a deterritorialized Korean nation evokes a serialized linear history that moves to the future through resolution of the past in the present. This linear historical perspective inhibited South Korean activists from recognizing the specific conditions of Korean Chinese as migrant laborers whose biggest concern was improving their working conditions.

What does this impossibility of addressing Korean Chinese as migrant workers say about reparation politics? What is the relationship between reparation politics and neoliberal capitalism? The former represents the latter in terms of universal moralism and state centrism. This form of democratic politics embodies a historical unconscious about the present as historical progress. It represses the neoliberal reality, in which the appearance of a welfare society in South Korea is founded on the appropriation of Korean Chinese labor. Waged from the victor's standpoint, reparation politics in South Korea develops a consensus or identification with the state. This means that reparation politics exceeds the liberal logic that turns the relationship between the state and its citizens into the relationship between the sovereign power and its victims. Its capitalist logic becomes evident when we conceptualize reparation politics as the capitalist unconscious and discern the haunting presence of capitalist reality hovering over reparation politics. The inquiry into historical unconscious warrants the problematization of historical periodization inherent in reparation politics and an analysis of the new temporal subjectivity of activists since the 1990s.

State centrism equates the democratically elected state with being representative of the people. Although old and new activists shared the pledge to fight against neoliberal capitalism, they also developed consensus on neoliberal capitalism. Reparation politics is at the heart of this paradox of the democratic activism, and it turns the people into sublime victims of the state's violence. When advocates for the rights of Korean Chinese present Korean Chinese as victims, they abstract the capitalist relationship between South Koreans and Korean Chinese into a dyadic relationship between a violent state and diasporic victims. The politics of overcoming the past translates the unequal capitalist exchange between South Korean employers and Korean Chinese into a liberal framework of individual diasporic victims and the current South Korean state's responsibility to protect them. Democracy becomes a utopian space where the state is expected to seamlessly suture and heal past conflicts and ruptures, as a shaman reconciles the dead with the living. Reparation approaches the resolution of Korean Chinese status as surrogates of South Korea's own colonization. The narrative of reparation as democracy figures the wish to heal wounds of the past and to imagine a new homogeneous whole as a timeless expression of ethnic homogeneity. The representation of Korean Chinese as embodying the nation's suffering empties out their experiences of colonial emigration and their history as an ethnic minority in China. Nothing demonstrates this historical amnesia more effectively than the naturalization of the South Korean state as their home nation-state. More than anything else democratization in South Korea justifies South Korea as the legitimate nation-state, especially when North Korea's economic crisis at the same time prompts South Koreans to regard the north as an object of ethnic and national compassion.

Reparation politics involves the activists gazing at current forms of democratization through the lens of the past. It recognizes the present as "democratic" through what Žižek (1989:65, 95) calls retroactive causality. The state's legitimacy is grounded in its symbolic meaning, which for former activists signifies the triumph of the former minjung democracy movement. Their identification with the current state is wedded to activists' memories of the past primarily in terms of terror, loss, and repression. With this view of the past, the present signifies the political progress indisputably achieved by the heroic revolution of the minjung. The project of overcoming history offers a post hoc interpretation of democratic rupture. It searches for factors that guarantee historical transition from oppression to democracy, such as the mythic power of minjung. This mode of memory and the gaze from the past make it difficult for activists to recognize the continued violence of the state. Official commemoration reduces the uprising in the city of Kwangju on May 18, 1980, to a priori universality such as the desire for freedom and justice. Memory of the people's mythic power preordains the people as the collectivity that is destined to create the present order. Such historical memories may be formulated as a defense against challenges from conservatives in the present. Yet they inevitably entail ideological effects that legitimize the present order. Epic memories of the Kwangju revolt erase historical contingencies of the insurgency's tumultuous process and the singular experiences of diverse participants—children, social outcasts, students, parents, white-collar workers, and officials. Official commemorations forget persistent conflicts between groups of minjung, particularly laborers and peasants, as well as between minjung and educated activists during the minjung movement of the 1980s (see Abelmann 1996; Namhee Lee 2009). Usual irregularities of politics, ranging from unforeseeable effects of action, divisions within the movement, and tactical mistakes to frustration about the formidable power of the social order, are effaced in accounts that pit the unified "people" against the violent state.

Mun Pusik (2002) discerns from the politics of overcoming the past the paradoxical coexistence of state centrism (kukkajuǔi) and the ethos of the post-state (t'algukka). A former theology student, Mun served six years in prison after his sentence was reduced from the death sentence for setting fire to the American Cultural Center in the city of Pusan in 1982—a decisive event that became a lightning rod to anti-Americanism during the 1980s. The Special Law on the 5.18 Democracy Movement legislated in December 1995 cleared the Kwangju uprising of previous charges of antinational violence with the aim to punish those responsible for the massacre and to exonerate the victims. The stated objective of the special law was to "rectify the spirit of the state [kukka kigang], consolidate democratization, and foster the essence of nationality [minjok chŏnggi]." According to Mun, it is deeply ironic that both the Kwangju massacre and the special law condemning the massacre were undertaken with the same goal, namely, serving the nation and the state. He argues that the very idea of modernity makes overcoming the past an impossible task. That is, the democratically elected government continues to inflict brutal violence on striking laborers in the name of overcoming economic crisis and defending the social order while simultaneously apologizing for the previous state's aggression against its people. For Mun, violence is not simply a property of the state but deeply ingrained in the interior subjectivity of the people who, whether explicitly or unconsciously, condone the state's violence because of the desire for modernization and development. The fanatical zeal of Korean soldiers in the Kwangju massacre is, according to Mun, the twin not only of ordinary people's indifference to the democracy movement or even their condemnation of it during the military rule but also of their tolerance of state violence as a measure for resolving the present socioeconomic crisis. Lim Jie-hyun (2000) and Mun Pusik call this collective zeal for progress the "fascism in us," which is the twin of modern sensibility. They call for self-referentiality through which we continuously scrutinize ourselves for symptoms and traits of fascism.

The notion of "fascism in us" signifies a new humanism in the postmodern and post-politics era. If modern politics posits an opposition between structural oppression and voluntary revolt, postmodern politics denies such distinctions. If modern politics embraces divine violence, that is, the violent nature of revolution and radical egalitarianism, post-politics rejects violence regardless of its end and contexts. The self-referentiality that critiques the "fascism in us" therefore denounces even the violence innate in the democratic struggle, namely, the minjung democracy movement. The liberal opposition of democracy and violence runs through both reparation politics and the fascism-in-us critique. This liberal approach to history partners with the capitalist order in the present. Reparation politics rejects the violence committed by the former state against its own citizens, whereas the postmodern critique of interiority faults both aggressors and victims for their fleeting desire for modernity. In the politics of overcoming the past violence, the notion of unavoidability of the people's revolt and their eventual triumph, which the minjung movement came to symbolize, asserts the truth about the present regime of democracy. In the postmodern politics of self-referentiality, fixation on individualistic morality fosters disregard for the historical specificity of the socioeconomic and political order in the present. The opposition of democracy to violence in South Korea aligns with the global trend in recent years away from radicalism. The collapse of socialist countries followed by the current global war on terrorism provides a new occasion for rethinking democracy, violence, and collectivity. The war on terrorism since the 2000s opposes democracy to terror and equates democracy with procedural equality.

The concept of legal fetishism turns the dichotomy of violence and democracy on its head. Legal fetishism helps us to comprehend the rule of law under capitalism, which inverts the appropriation of surplus labor by capitalists into exchange between free and equal subjects. Pashukanis (1924) is faulted for conceptualizing legal fetishism in terms of commodity exchange rather than commodity production as Marx does. Yet this concept allows us to focus on the formal role of the law in the abstraction of social relations. I use the concept of legal fetishism to map the capitalist logic of reparation onto the abstraction of social relations under capitalism beyond its routine characterization as liberal politics. The debates on identities and rights of Korean Chinese among activists, the Constitutional Court, and government authorities address the *content* of legal abstraction: The rights of Korean Chinese depend on the substance of law and vary from one law to another. Yet the *form* of legal abstraction demands us to explore the constitutive role of law in creating and reproducing the capitalist system, especially the production of "free and equal" subjects. In the reparation politics concerning the Overseas Korean Act, the relationship between South Koreans and Korean Chinese developed in the form of a contract between free and equal subjects, that is, between owners of capital and of labor. This legal form laid the foundation for their capitalist exchanges, obscuring their unequal relations and the production of value, and disguising the enforcement of socially necessary labor. In this case, kinship and national relations naturalized the regime of labor. Installing socially necessary labor time, the debate on the Overseas Korean Act inverted social relations between Korean Chinese and South Koreans from work to the exclusion of Korean Chinese from the category of overseas Koreans through debates on their rights as ethnic and/or national returnees. The debate on the act abstracted rather than overcame the fundamental inequality between them. The argument for the right of freedom to work for Korean Chinese was lost when their ethnic and national rights were defined within South Korea's democratic process of reparation.

The controversy on the right of Korean Chinese to work concerns the issue of whether their labor is equivalent to South Korean labor regardless of difference in nationality and history. It is a question that would be determined only by reference to private property rights under the South Korean legal system because the legal construction of identities and rights render Korean Chinese private owners of their labor power. The utilization of Korean Chinese labor facilitates the government's outsourcing of social welfare services to the neoliberal market. In this way Korean Chinese migrant labor assists the South Korean state in managing both a legitimacy crisis and an economic crisis. Legal debates divest Korean Chinese of this historical present and the specific social conditions of their migratory work, that is, the simultaneous socioeconomic crises of Korean Chinese and South Koreans that have spawned their capitalist integration. The law as a social form of power instead turns Korean Chinese into individuals—in this instance as victims in reparation narratives. Advocacy for legal rights becomes a fetishized form of social relations resulting from the shared temporality of an aging populism and new human rights activism.

CONCLUSION

The socioeconomic crises unexpectedly beckon colonial and Cold War history in democratic politics. The exchange of capital and labor across borders, in response to the crises in South Korea and the Korean Chinese community, gives rise to a reconciliation after their decades-long enmity during the Cold War. From the mid-1990s onward South Korea's policy toward the diaspora has changed from mobilizing it in the rivalry against North Korea to using it for global capitalist expansion. Debate on the criteria for the Korean diaspora and its rights denotes a hierarchy in the emergent transnational Korea that bears on the global capitalist network of South Korea and its various diasporic groups. Reparation politics as a new mode of democratic politics transforms the advocacy of discriminated diasporic groups into a new moment of decolonization. It transforms colonial and Cold War history into the grounds for interpreting meanings and solutions to the capitalist crisis.

Reparation politics constitutes the ethnic and national body as a site of constructing an alternative community in a transnational form. Involving groups of activists, reparation politics generates new contested narratives of national history. The crises become an occasion to reconstitute the state's sovereignty by representing the crisis and crisis resolution as a democratic moment. Adopting idioms of constitutionalism, universalism, and the liberal state, reparation politics reconstitutes democracy in the post–Cold War era. If the twentieth-century mode of democracy hinged on ideas of historical progress, reparation politics espouses a universal ethics of nonviolence, justice, and human rights. The living conditions of Korean Chinese workers in South Korea are addressed by a social movement that loosens its earlier radical critique of the global capitalist system and instead assumes the position of victor in the post–Cold War era. In turning Korean Chinese into surrogates for decolonization in South Korea, South Korean activists establish colonial history as the ur-form of Korean ethnic experience in the present. They construct Korean Chinese as emblematic victims of Japanese colonization and, more important, as a metonym of universal subjects under neoliberal humanitarianism, that is, as victims of the state's violence. New memories of colonial history perform cultural work for democratization and decolonization by various groups ranging from capitalists, the state, legislators, and experts, to activists and migrant workers. Contending constructions of colonial history within strands of reparation politics, including Korean Chinese responses, retemporalize the transnational capitalist moment in the present.

The rule of law is deeply implicated in the process of capital accumulation, for it establishes and upholds the state's role in protecting private property rights. I therefore inquire into the ways that reparation politics abstracts the social relations of South Koreans and Korean Chinese arising from their new capitalist network. By transforming the repressed history of colonial migration into the ur-history of the present, reparation politics sidelines the problem of capital accumulation and its national mediation, which came to manifest itself as a haunting excess. Reparation politics fails to address the interests of Korean Chinese in their migratory work and their right to work in South Korea. Their capitalist social relationship occupies a shadowy existence in the transnational Korean community during the era of neoliberal democracy.

4

SOCIALIST REPARATION:
ON LIVING LABOR

Reparation of the socialist revolution in China takes the form of deregulated economic development and the subsequent overseas migratory work of Korean Chinese in the Yanbian Korean Autonomous Prefecture and other autonomous villages in northeast China. I explore the intrinsic linkage of this migratory work, the mode of capital accumulation, and the diasporic politics of ethnic nationality. I characterize the capitalist regime in Korean Chinese communities as "capitalist devolution," because their migratory work in South Korea provides income for purchasing what was once promised by the socialist revolution. That is, the process of privatization commodifies earlier socialist goals—health care, housing, and education—through the new small-business service sector supported by remittances from South Korea. The Chinese state considers the privatization and deregulation that began in the 1980s reparation for the socialist revolution. Yet this reparation is a continuation by other means of capital accumulation, which the state and the Chinese Communist Party were pursuing all along throughout the era of socialist construction, as will be explored in chapter 5. This chapter concerns the temporalization of history by Korean Chinese migratory workers during the formative period of capitalist devolution, especially from the mid-1990s to the mid-2000s. Their everyday experience of migratory work and their construction of a dual nationality as Koreans and Chinese are juxtaposed with the narrative of transition or crisis put forth by the state and Korean Chinese intellectuals.

An assemblage of linguistic and somatic experiences permeates the everyday existence of migrant workers, who have no determination other than the production of life. The concept of labor's sovereignty looks into political consciousness and organized activism as exemplified by South Korean activists was explored in chapter 3. This chapter locates the sovereignty of Korean Chinese in their amorphous and discordant expressions of everyday experience, as well as in their politics of dual nationality. Corporeal and sensorial manifestations, such as weight loss, skin disorders, anemia, ignominy, and confusion, as well as suppressed emotions released in crying and singing, reveal the repressed death drive in their migratory work, which they narrate as the process of becoming modern. The loss of one's mind, body, and senses as a unitary whole renders everyday life as confounding as hieroglyphics. In this conjuncture, migratory work becomes a monumental subject for historical inquiry by Korean Chinese as they enact their social body in the form of the ethnic nation. The transference of their capitalist experiences onto ethnic and national identity, whether Korean or Chinese, is not merely an act of transcendence but also a performative act. It distills the complex and disparate experiences of migratory work into the seemingly durable category of community. Their narrative of dual nationality repeats an earlier trope of reason and affect, although within it transposing the places of Korea and China. It is less the enjoyment of belonging to both the Korean and Chinese nations than their investiture and divesture of either or both nations that constitute their historical sensibility as diasporic subjects.

PRIVATIZATION AS REPARATION

Reparation for the Cultural Revolution in China came in 1978 with the policy of "reform and opening up." Although reparation routinely followed a series of political campaigns in the 1950s and 1960s, the 1978 reform aimed at correcting not simply the wrongs of the Cultural Revolution but rather all of the wrongs committed during the making of the socialist revolution dating back to the 1940s. Key to this wholesale reparation was a repudiation of Mao's permanent revolution that supplied the stage-by-stage map for undergoing socialist revolution. As will be elaborated in chapter 5, Mao called for continuing the socialist revolution even after the completion of collectivization and engaging in political and ideological rectification campaigns in order to advance the development of productive forces and catch up with English capitalism without bureaucratizing the state (Schram 1989:130–31). The 1978 policy of opening and reforming the Chinese economy rejects a basic principle of its earlier permanent revolution by replacing collective property ownership with "diverse" property ownership as the foundation of socialism. This change was justified by distinguishing the socialist concept of ownership from the historical process of "actualizing" (silhyŏn) it. Diverse property ownership, which encompasses state ownership and private property ownership, is taken as a transitional form of socialist collective ownership (Hyŏn et al. 2000:1–6). However, the urgency placed on the development of productive forces remains the same before and after the 1978 reparation. In fact, reparation was and remains a means of removing barriers to rapid capital accumulation.

The continued elevation of the development of productive forces as the highest goal raises the temporality of history as a key question. Recent discussion posits the Chinese revolution as a failure in which state power debilitates popular initiatives (Badiou 2005; Russo 2005). Marxist economists saw the socialist economy as the twin of state capitalism (Cliff 1974; Harman 2010). Privatization is neither a rupture from the socialist economy nor simply a renewal of previous socioeconomic development. Instead, it entails both continuity and change. The language of reparation throughout the history of the Chinese socialist revolution attests to contentious and continuous debates and practices concerning socialism, capitalism, and their distinction in China. The 1978 reparation in the form of privatization and deregulation was another, yet new, instance. The 1978 reparation in the form of liberalization and privatization lays bare the imperative to develop productive forces, an imperative wrapped in the language of political and ideological struggle against counterrevolutionaries. Economic liberalization and privatization since 1978 engender the paradoxical development of the continued economic domination and deregulation by the state. The central state seized profitable local factories and businesses while enforcing deregulation. The new 1994 tax law increased the central state's revenue from an average annual increase of 17 percent for more than a decade to 70.3 percent in 1997 (Hyŏn et al. 2000:18–26).

Economic liberalization and privatization began in the Korean Chinese community (Chosŏnjok in Korean or chaoxianzu in Chinese) of northeast China in 1983, a few years later than in China proper.[1] Since then the Korean Chinese community has come to rely on migratory work, first as small-bag traders (pottari changsa) in China proper, Russia, and North Korea, and then as migratory workers in South Korea. Once known as the most productive heavy-chemical industrial area in China, cities in northeast China experienced plant closures with the termination of the state subsidies for production and allocation of their products. The mandatory retirement age of forty-five for women and fifty-five for men in the surviving factories also intensified the search for alternative ways to earn income. After the distribution of the right to land to individual households momentarily raised agricultural productivity, farmers began to abandon farming because of the rising cost of chemical fertilizers and the uncertainty of the market (Chŏng Sinch'ol 1999:47–90). Under such conditions, Korean Chinese ventured into rudimentary forms of trade in cities and neighboring countries. Married women were the first to embark on small-bag trade, traveling by train with bags of goods to the cities and countryside of China, to Russia, and then to North Korea to sell easily portable everyday items such as socks, towels, underwear, and clothes. Men soon joined this small-bag trade in Russia and North Korea. Women were also selling clothes, fruits, vegetables, and pickles in street stalls and marketplaces in their own neighborhoods. Other common jobs for former farmers, laid-off workers, and low-income white-color workers were taxi-driving, money changing on the street, construction work, and running small cafés (Pak Minja 2000; Kim Insŏn 2004). According to interviews with about sixty Korean Chinese migrant workers in Seoul and Yanbian, China, they commonly held more than five different jobs in China over an approximately ten-year period since the beginning of marketization. The exception was high-ranking local administrators, prosecutors, and doctors, whose salaries kept pace with rising prices and inflation.

Deregulated border-crossing migratory work has become a quintessential feature of the participation of Korean Chinese in the global capitalist economy. This contrasts with the regulated migratory work from countryside to cities that captivates scholars of Chinese studies and neoliberal capitalism, prompting them to explore the emerging regime of private property rights, citizenship, and the rule of law (Lee 2007; Loyalka 2013). The migration of Korean Chinese to South Korea exceeds their migration to cities in China proper and foreign countries such as Japan, Australia, and the United States. At first, in the late 1980s and early 1990s, Korean Chinese sold Chinese medicine and herbs on the streets in downtown Seoul and in front of the Seoul Railway Station during short family visits of usually one to three months. This was the brief period when Korean Chinese were welcomed by South Koreans as ethnic kin. Yet from the mid-1990s they began to engage illegally in manual work, typically for three to seven years. This migratory work in South Korea fed South Koreans' negative attitudes about Korean Chinese; it expanded hand in hand with South Korean investment and tourism in China, as well as the need for low-paid manual labor in South Korea in the construction and service sectors. After its initial exploration in Yanbian, South Korean capital moved to other parts of China. South Korean capital involved in small-scale manufacturing favors locating its overseas production in Shandong with its easy access to the sea. South Korean conglomerates concentrate their investment in major cities such as Beijing and Shanghai. In 2005, direct investment in China was one-third of South Korea's total direct foreign investment. The migratory workforce of Korean Chinese made up about 21 percent of employees hired by 529 South Korean companies in China in 2004 and numbered around seventy thousand in Shandong alone (Yi Tuwŏn 2006; Ye Tonggŭn 2010; Ku Chiyŏng 2013). Korean Chinese university graduates and other elites worked as managers and clerical workers in South Korean–owned factories and firms, also working as translators, real estate agents, travel agents, and Chinese language tutors for South Koreans. In Yanbian, South Korean tourists supplied capital to Yanbian with their visits to historic sites in northeast China and Paektu (Changbai) Mountain bordering North Korea.

At the same time, Korean Chinese migratory work in South Korea has become commonplace among farmers in and beyond Yanbian, though it also includes the educated elite. Migratory work in South Korea is somewhat more pronounced among Koreans in the Yanbian Autonomous Prefecture in Jilin Province—where most had originated from adjacent northern Korea (presently North Korea)—because of their Korean fluency and their new economic and cultural ties with South Koreans in trade and tourism. According to Chŏng Kŭnjae's (2005) ethnographic report of twenty-two Korean villages across northeast China, on average one to three persons in each Korean household either currently work or had worked in South Korea since the mid-2000s, while also having many relatives and friends working there as well. Those who remain in villages, usually children, the elderly, or adults waiting for their turn to go to South Korea, depend on remittances. Most returnees from South Korea abandon farming and move to cities. Some hire Han Chinese for rice farming on their land. Throughout the twentieth century in northeast China rice farming was considered a primordial element of Korean ethnic culture and community. Korean Chinese migratory work has come to be celebrated as exemplifying individuals' novelty and productivity. Entrepreneurs and migrant workers are reminiscent of the labor heroes of the 1950s and 1960s (Chungguk Chosŏn minjok palchach'wi ch'ongsŏ wiwŏnhoe 1994).

FIGURE 4.1 Hŭngan market in Yanji in 1998. Photo by Hyun Ok Park.

Socialist Promises as Commodities

Beginning in the mid-1990s, privatization is marked by South Korean influence in all aspects of labor migration, capital investment, culture, consumption, and politics in Korean Chinese communities. Since the normalization of South Korea and China in 1992, Yanji (Yŏn'gil) quickly became a hub for South Korean economic and scholarly interaction with North Korea, as well as for its archeological study of the ancient Korean kingdom of Koguryŏ. When I arrived in Yanji in the summer of 1998, this initial phase of interaction between Korean Chinese and South Koreans was coming to a close. The thrill of the initial exchanges of Koreans of the two Koreas was visible largely in accounts told to new visitors, which were dramatized with stories about bloody scuffles between South Korean and North Korean secret security agents in Yanji. Notable changes were hard to miss during my subsequent visits. Yanji was being transformed rapidly with overflowing consumer goods, freshly paved roads, high-rise apartments, and neon signs lighting the night sky. Clothing imported from South Korea came to be considered the best on the market in Yanji. In both the streets and mass media, Korean Chinese began to pick up South Korean accents and idioms, ditching North Korean styles. With steady outmigration of Korean Chinese, their abandoned houses and land increasingly were sold to or illegally occupied by Han Chinese migrants from neighboring regions. Leisure and entertainment in Yanji were dominated by restaurants serving South Korean dishes, coffeehouses, and features of South Korean street culture such as karaoke places (noraebang), beer halls, and massage parlors. South Korean television programs, including soap operas, were popular. Speaking Korean with tourists in hotels, restaurants, taxis, and local businesses was expected and even favored in Yanbian during this period. It signified the pride of Korean Chinese in their minority culture. From the mid-2000s, however, changes in South Korea and China reconfigured South Korean hegemony in economics and culture in and beyond Yanbian. The legalization of Korean Chinese employment in South Korea especially from the mid-2004 made it easier for them to migrate, at the same time subjecting them to more political scrutiny from the Chinese state. The Chinese state began to invest in Yanbian's infrastructure, while Han Chinese investors and tourists from China proper became prominent in the service and real estate sectors. Local Han Chinese and migrants from northern China have increasingly come to replace Korean Chinese workers in taxi service and big businesses like hotels, and speaking Mandarin has become routine in and beyond Yanji.

Two features of capitalist devolution characterize the regime of capital accumulation in Korean Chinese society under South Korean hegemony: the commodification of socialist dreams and self-employed small business in the flourishing service sector. Capitalist devolution fuses socialist dynamics with capitalist dynamics into renewed utopian aspirations. Korean Chinese use remittances from their work in South Korea to purchase deferred socialist dreams, namely, modern housing, health care, and education. Privatization commodifies fundamental human needs that the socialist system previously provided for or promised to fulfill. Capitalist devolution does not mean that the former socialist era completely failed to meet such goals, especially when the universal provision of such needs is perhaps the most visible accomplishment of the socialist system despite disputes over quality. It is, rather, that capitalist forces have commodified these critical socialist goals, making them diverse and ubiquitous and creating unequal access to them.

The purchase of a spacious modern apartment in the city of Yanji, for instance, became a capitalist dream. From the mid-1990s, new five- or six-story apartment buildings began to replace crumbling apartments and old brick structures known as "single-story houses" (tanch'ŭngjip) that were distributed to individuals through their work units. In 2002, a small three-bedroom condominium in downtown Yanji cost between 130,000 and 150,000 yuan. High-rise condominiums along rivers and on hills are the most prized locations, with prices in 2006 between 200,000 and 250,000 yuan for a three-bedroom unit. Starting in the late 2000s, Han Chinese investors began to dominate the high-rise condominium market. Korean Chinese either are mere consumers or at best provide interior design services and sell furnishings to new buyers. Moreover, paying for medical care of sick family members is a primary cause of Korean Chinese migratory work. Access to modernized medical care since marketization has resulted in rising costs for such care, including expensive medical tests such as CT scans and MRIs.

Under privatization, education is a diversified commodity, as the market offers choice in the quality and expense. That is, the child's academic ability and its family's financial means determine the family's expenditure on education. It is said that it takes at least one parent working in South Korea to pay for one child's school fees. For instance, a woman in her thirties worked in South Korea to pay for her son to attend art school, which costs more than 100,000 yuan, or the equivalent of what a professor in Yanji would earn in ten years (Interview on January 22, 2002, in Seoul). A forty-five-year-old former white-collar worker who was working in construction in South Korea when we met in 2002 and 2003 also said that major universities in China not only require higher test scores but also charge higher fees than do local universities. He explains the financing of children's education as a basic parental responsibility:

It would be unacceptable if one can't send his or her own child to a university for financial reasons. If one lacks financial ability, he or she should not get married or have children. Once one is married and has children, he or she has not just the responsibility as a parent but also financial responsibility. Since my wife runs a small restaurant and cares for our children in Jilin, I came to South Korea to earn money [for my son's education] before getting old.

(Interview on January 24, 2002, in Seoul)

A forty-one-year-old woman who went to South Korea five times between 1991 and 2001 said that she and her family can live well without working in China with savings she earned in South Korea. However, she plans to return to work in South Korea to finance her only daughter's education. According to her, to be successful in the highly competitive job market in Yanbian demands higher education such as study abroad. Her daughter's private extracurricular lessons cost more than 300 yuan per month, half of her husband's monthly salary. It would cost about 100,000 yuan just to buy a visa from a broker for her daughter, not to mention other expenses for her university education in Japan, Canada, or New Zealand. She said that it would be impossible to

FIGURE 4.2 A Korean house in Helong (Hwaryong) County in Yanbian. Courtesy of Cho Ch'ŏnhyŏn.

FIGURE 4.3 An apartment building of the socialist era in the city of Longjing (Ryongjŏng) in Yanbian. Courtesy of Cho Ch'ŏnhyŏn.

support her daughter's education with her husband's salary, as the cost of university education even in China is more than six times her husband's annual salary (Interview on May 17, 2002, in Yanji).

The new pursuit of former socialist dreams has become entangled with petit bourgeois ventures in the rapidly growing service sector. Korean Chinese dream of opening a business for themselves or for their grown-up children with earnings from South Korea. They prefer to be self-employed driving a taxi or running a small restaurant, coffeehouse, sauna, noraebang, hair salon, massage parlor, or store selling comic books or renting movies. Korean Chinese businesses tend to have fewer than three employees and serve a Korean Chinese clientele (Yi Changsŏp et al. 2007). Their investments are restricted to these petit bourgeois ventures, not only because of the limited savings left after expenditure on higher priorities, but also because they learned how to operate these types of businesses when working in South Korea's service sector. When speaking of their work experiences in South Korea, Korean Chinese often point out the virtues of capitalist principles, namely, hard work, competition, and rationalization, referring to them as modern ethics that they learned or need to learn from South Koreans.

Many Korean Chinese manage to open small businesses. Others return to work in South Korea after depleting what they had saved from previously working there. It is common for returnees not to work for wages in China. Their work ethic seems to evaporate on their return to China. This occurs because the value of wages in China is substantially lower than in South Korea. For example, the income from working in a restaurant, store, or factory or in construction work for one month in China equals one day of wages in South Korea. This subsistence-oriented living or petit bourgeois business might be seen as a sign of a "lack" of entrepreneurial spirit or of a retreat from the uncertainty and incomprehensibility of the market's sudden changes. Characterizing subsistence-oriented living as a lack, however, paradoxically invokes the idea of "delay" in the complete marketization of social life. Such a lack or delay assumes a linear process of change from the socialist life to capitalist life, with a decisive break between the two. Rather, near-subsistence-oriented living and business is a feature of capitalist devolution in China as a historically specific form of the regime of capital accumulation.

Capitalist devolution signifies a new phantasmagoria of capital. The regime of capital accumulation hinges on an exchange value of migratory work that increases with the comparatively higher value of their wages in South Korea and the high exchange rate for South Korean currency. However, this exchange value of migratory work loses meaning over time. The fetish character of migratory work in South Korea can be inferred from the two approaches to commodity fetishism that are distinguished in Buck-Morss' (1989:81) reading of Benjamin's *Passagen-Werk* (*Arcades Project*): "The *Passagen-Werk* entries cite . . . from [Marx's] *Capital* on the fetish character of commodities, describing how exchange value obfuscates the source of the value of commodities in productive labor. But for Benjamin . . . the key to the new urban phantasmagoria was not so much the commodity-in-the market as the commodity-on-display, where exchange value no less than use value lost practical meaning, and purely representation value came to the fore." In Marx's sense, South Korea obfuscates unequal and uneven social relations within South Korea. For Korean Chinese, South Korea embodies mere exchange value, where they earn less than their South Korean counterparts but more than they can in China. Savings are expected to make possible the dream of enjoying economic security in China.

At the same time, the Benjaminian phantasmagoria becomes evident in the Korean Chinese community under the regime of capitalist devolution. The exchange value of wages and savings in South Korea has lost meaning because the speed of capitalist transformation has exceeded the ability of Korean Chinese to calculate the exchange value of their labor in South Korea in terms of their future expenses in China. The increased value of Chinese currency also devalues their South Korean earnings, causing their dreams to slip away during their migratory work in South Korea. In 2003, Korean Chinese migrants calculated 200,000 to 300,000 yuan as an optimal goal for savings from their employment in South Korea. Yet because of the fast pace of change in China, it is difficult for Korean Chinese migrant workers in South Korea to identify a potentially profitable type of business to open on their return home. It is also difficult to estimate accurately the amount of savings required for starting such a business. Furthermore, the market for the small businesses they plan also saturates quickly. The exchange value of their work in South Korea after returning to China is uncertain. That is, savings and remittances from Korean Chinese migrant workers in South Korea do not necessarily translate into wealth or capital accumulation in China. As illegal workers in South Korea, they can be victimized by swindlers, threatened with deportation, and cheated of wages, among other abuses. After the legalization of their migratory work in South Korea, their work has become a revolving cycle of migration, return, and repeated migration. For example, a Jilin newspaper reported on December 6, 2012:

A Korean Chinese in her mid-forties returned to Yanji in late 2012 after about five years of working in South Korea. She was shocked after she spent 100 yuan to buy just a little bit of beef and vegetables. Although eating beef had never been a big burden in the past when she was not living well, she now hesitated to buy beef. "The reality in South Korea, where beef is too expensive for people to eat without feeling burdened, is also the case in China," she states. Spending on gifts at banquets, birthdays, or other social occasions is becoming a challenge. Whereas 100 yuan was reasonable to save face in the past, she now felt shame when giving as much as 200 yuan to someone close.

When she tried to buy a condominium, she was again shocked because the price had soared. Whereas a condo was valued about 200,000 yuan [in downtown] when she went to South Korea in 2007, the same-sized condo even on the outskirts of the city now cost about 280,000–320,000 yuan. She managed to save about 50 million won in South Korea, . . . but that is worth less than 300,000 yuan in China and doesn't fetch even a small condo [in Yanji] because the exchange rate plunged recently. Because she is not working and is spending her savings from South Korea in this era of high prices, she feels apprehensive about daily life, as if sitting on a pin cushion.[2]

FIGURE 4.4 Housing development in the city of Longjing (Ryongjŏng) in Yanbian in 1998. Photo by Hyun Ok Park.

WORDS AND SENSES
IN EVERYDAY WORK

In Koselleck's term (2004), migratory work in South Korea leads Korean Chinese to distinguish the past from the future and to temporalize history. Given that Korean Chinese maintained close ethnic and political ties with North Korea during the Cold War, their new relationship with South Korea demands a reordering of their historical sensibility. Temporalizing their past, present, and future involves abstraction of the everyday experience of their migratory work. In the Korean Chinese community in northeast China, the capitalist present is construed through two forms of temporalization contrasting instances of life and death of Korean Chinese: the historical justice resulting from a new economic wealth; and the breakdown of the Korean minority community through displacement, family separation, and moral decay.

In Chŏng Kŭnjae's (2005) report, Korean Chinese elderly call migratory work in South Korea the "South Korean wind" (Han'guk param), which reverses the earlier "Manchurian wind" of the colonial period. When the harvest ran out in Korea during the winter, they rode on the Manchuria wind, inspired by adages that Manchuria was so fertile that a potato grows to a size of child's head and a radish fills a whole harvest basket. Moreover, when the colonial Korean government launched the program of collective migration in the late 1930s, Japanese colonizers promised sizable plots of land and financial support. After arrival in Manchuria the Koreans were, however, dismayed to find instead barren grassland, bone-chilling winds, and icy waters. The Japanese promised rice but provided millet as the staple food and forced them to construct high defensive walls around their villages against Korean guerrillas and communists. While backbreaking work and perseverance of Koreans turned wasteland into fertile rice fields, before the Chinese revolution the Han Chinese rapaciously appropriated their crops as rent and taxes—if not their land itself. Beginning in the late 1990s the tables have turned, and conditions for Korean Chinese have become markedly different and improved. Korean Chinese, including the first generation that had emigrated to China, began returning as migrant workers, not to North Korea, which was considered the home nation-state of Korean Chinese under socialism, but rather to South Korea. Korean Chinese now have the upper hand with their earnings in South Korea. While under Japanese colonialism Korean Chinese were beaten by the Japanese for speaking Korean and attacked by Han Chinese for speaking Japanese, Han Chinese now come to envy them. Whereas in the past Korean Chinese sought land in Manchuria, Han Chinese now aspire to settle in Korean

Chinese villages, which have a higher standard of living as a result of rice farming. Korean Chinese now mobilize administrative and coercive power to block settlement of Han Chinese in their villages, whereas in the past Korean Chinese were subject to eviction by Han Chinese. The gratification associated with the wealth generated by migratory work in South Korea is pronounced among the elderly, who also express uneasiness about the abandonment of agriculture and migration to cities by Korean Chinese.

This melancholic narrative of their current migratory work is diametrically opposed to the narrative of crisis formulated by Korean Chinese intellectuals that depicts the South Korean wind as threatening ethnic self-rule in China. According to Korean Chinese elites, the combination of low birthrates and migration to other cities in China and abroad reduced the proportion of the Korean population in the Yanbian Korean Autonomous Prefecture from 62 percent in 1952 to 46 percent in 1965, 41 percent in 1976, and 39.8 percent in 1995 (Kim Chongguk 2000; Hyŏn et al. 2000). Brain drain, declining enrollments in Korean schools, and waning usage of the Korean language are said to have undermined the institutional rationale for the Yanbian Korean Autonomous Prefecture and Korean autonomous villages throughout northeast China. Moreover, the corruption of Korean Chinese culture by the South Korean wind deepens this institutional crisis and imperils the survival of Korean Chinese ethnicity itself (Chŏng Sinch'ŏl 1999; Kim Chongguk 1999; Pak Minja 2000; Kim and Hŏ 2001). Published in conjunction with Yŏnbyŏn nyŏsŏng (Yanbian Women), a major magazine in Yanbian, an edited book entitled The Sorrow of Family Separation: What Is Called Money compiled forty nonfiction episodes about the destructive effects of the migratory work on family life and morality (Yi Sŏnhi 2001). Its motifs include children's feelings of abandonment, overconsumption, and delinquency; the trauma caused by the sudden and unexplained death of family members working in South Korea and Japan; and the sexual promiscuity of married men and women working in South Korea or left behind in China. Members of the Korean Chinese elite blame South Korean society for the decadent trends of overconsumption, excessive greed, and hedonism for instant gratification, all of which undermine family ties, morality, ethnic solidarity, and the interest in Korean Chinese history. To counter these trends they uniformly prescribe consolidating (Chinese) national consciousness (kongmin ŭisik or chogukkwan) by increasing instruction in the Korean language and Korean Chinese history and culture. This appeal to the nation and national consciousness among Korean Chinese mirrors the approaches of South Korean activists, examined in chapter 3, that tamed capitalist relations by means of national politics.

Unlike these two contrasted characterizations of the present as historical justice and epochal crisis, Korean Chinese migrants' daily experiences remain fractured. The loss of totality is evident when narratives of their will to life are juxtaposed with their corporeal and sensory experiences. An exploration of their felt senses conveys the larger scope of their experiences that surpasses language, desire, and the will to survive (see Seremetakis 1994). If linguistic construction brackets death from the everyday experience of migratory work, attention to the senses adds dimensions to the analytic plane of everyday experience and subjectivity. Korean Chinese construct migratory work as learning the modalities of modern life, such as competition, hygiene, the work ethic, and its associated culture of frugality, saving, and renunciation of self-indulgence and vice. Their somatic experiences entail the haunting effects of death that are eviscerated from the zone of life and at the same time interrupt narratives that rationalize their work. Their physical experiences include skin ailments, weight loss, internal bleeding, insomnia, ulcers, emotional distress over one's vulnerability and inhumane treatment, and emotional catharsis through crying and singing. If their will to life represses the moments of death, the scattered assemblage of emotions, psychoses, diseased skin, and bodily organs manifests the complexity of their existence.

Korean Chinese workers construe their social relations with South Korean employers by constructing South Korea as the modern. A narrative trope of reason and affect constructs South Korean culture as blending competition and cold-heartedness, modern "beauty" and inhumanity, and the work ethic and abuse of others. This narrative structure enables Korean Chinese to maintain their identification with South Korea despite exploitation and dehumanization and to adhere to their capitalist future. Korean Chinese confound their backbreaking and sometimes lethal work routines with obtaining privileged access to modern life. Their impression of South Korea is characterized by its clean air, efficient transportation, convenient shopping, commitment to children's education, restraint from smoking and wild drinking, and public etiquette such as no spitting on the streets. In this act of associating South Korea with modernity, the commodification of their labor metamorphoses into a universal history of human development.

Cold-Heartedness

Korean Chinese rarely complain about their long and difficult work routines. They accept these difficulties as a prerequisite to their future life and displace their complaints about work onto the realm of emotion. A woman in her forties who came to South Korea in July 2000 from a village near Tudo in Yanbian told me that in South Korea she worked as a cook at a construction site for about $1,000 per month, with the backbreaking hours of 4:30 A.M. to 9:30 P.M., with at most a one-hour break after lunch. After ten days she changed to a thirteen-hour night shift in a restaurant for $800 per month. Like many others from the countryside of China, she maintains that she can easily work like this since she was used to working in the fields in China from 5:00 A.M. until 8:00 or 9:00 P.M. during growing season, only taking a break during the hottest hours of the afternoon. After China's economic reforms, she farmed during the summer and worked at a restaurant in a nearby town during winter. Our conversation about stress led her to discuss her goals, which consisted of educating her two sons, especially her adopted younger son who was sixteen years old and attending art school, the construction of a new house, and saving as much as possible for retirement. She went on to describe her impression of modern South Korea:

South Korea is a developed country, whether in economic or other areas. First of all, raising children here is very different from China. Since we lived in the countryside in China and were poor, we couldn't do all the things that we wanted to do for our children. Here South Koreans show enormous attention to their children and provide them with a lot of support. . . . Secondly, if our country [China] is a socialist country and this [South Korea] is a capitalist country, we have to learn from South Korea. South Koreans have superior etiquette, such as the honorific usage of Korean language toward the elderly. I realized that we are really behind South Koreans when it comes to manners. . . . Moreover South Koreans help their neighbors more than we do. Although the rich help others in our country, they are not as committed as here.

(Interview on January 22, 2002, in Seoul)

Korean Chinese most commonly characterize South Korean employers as "cold-hearted" or "lacking compassion" (injŏng i ŏpsŭm). A middle-aged woman came to South Korea by legally leaving her sick Korean Chinese husband and marrying a South Korean, and in South Korea she worked as a street vendor, a dishwasher at restaurants, and a housekeeper. She attained the resident registration card and then South Korean citizenship, sent money to her original husband and children in China, and eventually brought her two sons to South Korea. She sums up her work experience in terms of her distress over South Koreans' cold-heartedness and contrasts it with the altruism she attributes to the socialist Chinese:

South Koreans gaze at us as Chinese, don't they? We share the same blood. I am really frustrated. They don't treat us as the same ethnic kin [minjok], regarding only North Koreans as their own. . . . Yet, my father was born and raised here [before migrating to Manchuria during the colonial era]. This is also my mother country as well. Although some South Koreans have chŏng [affection], they are usually very cold-hearted [naengjŏng haeyŏ]. . . . I feel they are cold, when they suddenly change after being so nice. . . .

South Koreans change quickly because they act according to their interests. . . . Our kyop'o [overseas Korean and here Korean Chinese] have been contaminated by South Korean culture. Only money matters now. In the past we didn't live like that in China. We were taught to live for others, to do good things for others. Chairman Mao told us to model ourselves after the heroes who sacrificed and died for others. When I was young around 1962 or 1965, we used to go to school early to clean up the place and fix broken chairs before others came so as not to brag about such things to others.

(Interview on January 10, 2002, in Seoul)

A forty-year-old, second-generation woman who came to South Korea to support her family after her husband's illness left them in debt ties cold-heartedness to the logic of capitalist competition that makes employees disposable. In China, she worked from 1982 to 1992 as an inspector in a liquor factory, monitoring fermentation and sanitation with a microscope, and then she ran a corner store and a small cafe attached to her apartment. In South Korea, she worked in restaurants as an assistant cook, server, and dishwasher. During our conversation in Seoul about marketization in China, she shifted to talking about capitalism in South Korea:

What can I say about [my impression] here [South Korea]? People don't have compassion [injŏng i ŏpta], aren't they? [In China] we encourage others to do better, if they make mistakes. Here it isn't like that. People [employers] just dismiss employees [who make errors] right away.

I think people are cold-hearted here because of competition [emphasis added]. They must be thinking why they should bother to have the headaches of an inept worker, when they can hire a better one for no more money. In China it isn't like that. They teach you at least three or four times. If a worker can't do a good job even then, they recommend a transfer to a different job in the same work unit. Even when the manager in the restaurant [in South Korea] treated me really well, for instance, buying me and other employees bread and other things when we didn't have time to eat dinner, he behaved like any other employer. He taught the employees what to do only once. If one can't do well the second time, he would say, "Don't come. Don't come back tomorrow. Come back in a few days to get paid."

(Interview on January 20, 2002, in Seoul)

For her, market competition in South Korea is not all bad but actually fair, given that "those who work hard receive material payoffs" (noryŏk han saram ŭn kŭ mank'ŭm chabon i toego). She thinks that since liberalization China has become similar to South Korea: "Before economic reform, making an effort [noryŏk] was unnecessary in China, since people ate in the same pot with others [in the collective system]. My mother and dad earned the same monthly wage as others for more than ten years, 62.80 yuan for him and 48.60 yuan for her."

This temporal construction of South Korean and Chinese culture envelops her daily life, which is yoked to long hours of work and bottled-up stress. In China, her workday as a liquor factory inspector lasted for six to eight hours, from 7:30 A.M. to 4:30 P.M., including a two-hour lunch break. In South Korea, to earn $800 per month she worked in a buffet restaurant from 8:00 A.M. to 3:00 A.M. next day with a break of one or two hours after lunch; and from 9:00 A.M. until 10:00 P.M. at a barbecue restaurant, where she was well treated. As a result of such demanding hours her weight went from 64 kg to 47 kg during the first few months of work in South Korea and she suffered from uterine bleeding. When working at the buffet restaurant, she relieved her stress on her two days off per month by sitting overnight in a park or by going to a noraebang that charged $6 (7,000 won) for thirty minutes, where she usually cried for the first fifteen minutes and then sang loudly for the next fifteen. Her weight loss and poor health, tears, and emotional displays separate her body and soul from the seemingly continuous routine of deadly yet life-promising work.

In fact, it is common for Korean Chinese workers to experience significant weight loss after just a few months in South Korea and to develop chronic illnesses associated with malnutrition, inadequate sleep, anxiety, and exhaustion. A forty-nine-year-old woman lost 20 kg over four and one-half months during her first job as a live-in housekeeper, and she suffered from uterine bleeding, mental disorder, heart disease, ulcer, ear infection, and anemia from her different jobs. She said that these illnesses signified the "animal-like" life she endured to earn $800 to $1,000 a month for cleaning motel rooms and doing other housekeeping (Interview on January 27 in 2002, in Seoul). A man in his late forties who had worked in China as a driver on a collective farm before privatization and then as a boiler mechanic also lost 20 kg after working for five months at his first job in South Korea on a pig farm; during this time his hair turned white and his teeth loosened. Although the pig farm owner never withheld his wages, the employer verbally terrorized him. Despite teaching the pig farm owner basic math and how to write in Korean, the employee was abused with vulgar insults (Interview on January 14, 2002, in Seoul).

Insults

The emotional disturbance caused by verbal abuse brings to the surface the repressed experience of migratory workers. In fact, the notion that such abuse is worse than the harsh work routines is a commonplace narrative among Korean Chinese migrant workers in South Korea. A migrant worker in her forties from Tudo village in China expressed it like this:

> I think that the seasoning of the food can vary from time to time. However, the owner of a restaurant turned the kitchen upside down when customers complained about the food. The owner shouted insults at me, throwing away food when I tried to explain. . . . I think it is unacceptable for us to hear such verbal abuse from South Koreans who are our ethnic kin. . . . Their insults are really vulgar. . . . When I tried to quit, the owner threatened to report me to the police.
>
> (Interview on January 22, 2002, in Seoul)

In her observation, South Koreans employers lash out only at Korean Chinese workers, not at South Korean workers. This suggests that the mediation of the ethnic nation allows employers to transfer their abusive class-based relations with Korean Chinese workers to the domain of culture and emotion.

A forty-year-old former farmer in China similarly accepts the difficulties of migratory work as price of passage to modern life, also identifying his supervisors' insults as the worst source of stress. After economic reforms in

China, he had a range of jobs, such as tobacco farming, electrical work, and merchandise sales. He went to South Korea with a fake visa for a one-month business trip. Like many others, he said that his work in tobacco farming in China was as physically demanding as construction work in South Korea. Tobacco farming required only three months of working in the fields, but once leaves were gathered, they were steamed, dried, and roasted. The process of curing the tobacco required that his wife and he tended a wood fire for at least three days straight. Despite the physical demands, Korean Chinese men prefer construction work because it pays a high daily wage. He spoke of the stress associated with the verbal abuse:

> I have a lot of stress at the construction job. How can I figure out the name of supplies and tools? They have either English or Japanese names, if not a blend of the two. When I was told to bring this and that, I couldn't understand and then get lots of insults. I was getting angry at the insults. I was getting angry, because I came here thinking that this is the home country [koguk]. Why don't they use the home language [kogugŏ] instead of a fusion language. . . . They do tell us the name of things, but only once. I, however, forgot them easily, since they are not what I am used to calling them [in China]. . . . I haven't heard such insults at home. When I am agitated, I stare at them, making my eyes as sharp as the blade of a knife.
>
> (Interview on January 21, 2012, in Seoul)

He must not let such incidents develop into fights, since doing so could lead to a police report. Like many others, he displaces such humiliating experiences by speaking about qualities of South Korea that he describes as "beautiful" (arŭmdawŏyo). These qualities include good customer service, a convenient system of transportation, and clean, well-ventilated restrooms. He elevates South Korea's beauty to general characteristics of Korean ethnic traits whereby he harmonizes Korean Chinese and South Koreans:

> Transportation like the subway is convenient. Restrooms are clean with fresh air. We Koreans have the custom of living cleanly, don't we? We [Chosŏnjok] also have a clean life in China, clean inside and outside of the house. I also feel the same here [South Korea]. Whenever I go to a restaurant, the waitresses are very nice. They wear bright uniforms. I feel like even tasteless food would be delicious. . . . We ask each other which restaurant has better service. . . . I feel I came home,

when waitresses are asking nicely whether we need more food. . . . It is very different with Han Chinese. Han Chinese are brusque, while Koreans are affable. . . . Since I have been in South Korea I realized that people should live like they do in South Korea. Why should we live arguing and fighting?

(Interview on January 21, 2012, in Seoul)

Capitalist Ethics

The cold-heartedness of South Koreans is fetishized as an expression of capitalist ethics. An owner of a sauna in Yanji, a woman in her sixties, ascribes cold-heartedness to rational time management. During her work in restaurants and motels in South Korea, she suffered from cardiac pain and debilitating physical exhaustion because of demanding work and long hours, from 7:00 or 8:00 A.M. to midnight as a maid in motels, or from 5:30 A.M. to midnight as a dishwasher in a restaurant. In her words:

It is true that work in South Korea is demanding. But it is also because we don't understand [the capitalist system]. Korean Chinese think that South Koreans . . . force them to work harder without any compassion [injŏng sajŏng ŏpsi]. But I came to think differently, as I run my own business here [in Yanji]. People here are so slow in everything. Chinese people [including Korean Chinese] like chatting [at work]. Nothing is urgent for them. They work slowly but eat quickly. But South Koreans are not like that. They finish their given tasks no matter what happens. . . . South Koreans finish today's work today . . . even if it requires working until midnight or 1:00 A.M. . . . As it has been almost four years since I came back from South Korea, the old custom slowly returns, making me think that if I can't finish today, I will do it tomorrow. . . . It is not like that in South Korea. . . . It is because of competition. In this era of competition, every business will close if it is run like in China. . . . To excel others by working harder is the secret of survival in [the era of] competition.

(Interview on May 2, 2002, in Yanji)

She blamed the foolishness of Korean Chinese for being swindled by South Koreans. Demonstrating her acquired business acumen, she shared that since her sauna was neither the largest nor located in downtown, she charged half as much as other facilities and kept her sauna as clean as possible to beat the competition.

The comparison of work ethics in the two countries is also effectively described by a thirty-nine-year-old man who came to South Korea in 1994 as an industrial trainee and was working as a construction worker when I met him in 2002. In his view, "People in China just fill up their required work hours, taking a long lunch break and a nap in the afternoon, and excusing themselves from work when the weather is too hot. But in South Korea one can go home early after finishing the day's work" (Interview on January 16, 2002, in Seoul). For him, the capitalist work system is not about long hours of work but about the rational management of time. This is echoed by a forty-nine-year-old woman who carried bricks at a construction site in South Korea and later worked at a dining facility there. Her first impression of South Korea was the lack of *injŏng* (compassion), as her own aunt in Seoul invited her and six other visiting family members to South Korea but only provided them with a small room for about ten days. Humiliation and harsh treatment notwithstanding, South Korea taught her the discipline of hard work, which she said became "a guiding principle" for running her restaurant in Yanji (Interview on May 6, 2002, in Yanji).

Embracing hard work, freedom, and prosperity, a sixty-year-old man defends the capitalist system and South Korea over the socialist system and North Korea, even when the North Korean government treats Korean Chinese better. After his retirement in 1993 from well-paid work in the mines, he engaged in small trade with North Korea and Russia and then worked at construction sites in South Korea. After his return to China he was working as a security guard at an apartment complex when I interviewed him in Yanji in 2002. During his work in South Korea, he paid back his broker's fee within six months and saved about $15,000, with which he bought an apartment in Yanji and helped his daughter and son to open a small café and a store. He recalled that the insults and despicable treatment of South Koreans made his first year in South Korea unbearable:

South Koreans differ from Korean Chinese. We [Chosŏnjok] do not speak Korean like South Koreans. We are not complaining about our wages being lower than those of South Koreans and back pay. . . . There are many occasions that we can't understand Korean vocabulary, since Koreans use Japanese and English. We can understand colloquial Korean about 95 percent. But either English or Japanese words are used for tools and materials. What we call *pangmok* here in China is called *namu mokchae* [wooden pieces] there. *Tarikki* means "small"; and *orikki* means "big" here. Metal wire usually known as *ch'ŏlsa* even in South

Korea is called *pansang* on construction sites. . . . Supervisors rebuked us for not understanding these terms, using derogatory words, even when we were much older than them, a behavior unacceptable in China.

(Interview on May 1, 2002, in Yanji)

Yet he is reluctant to dismiss South Korea. In his observation, since the 1980s the North Korean government has permitted Korean Chinese to engage in small-scale trading under the pretense of visiting relatives. Moreover, his parents were born in northern Korea. However, he shows more attachment to South Korea because North Korea retains an outdated political and economic system and is yet to embark on market reform. He compares socialism and capitalism in the following terms:

Everyone was all the same before [during the socialist era], whether poor or living well at times. Now [during the capitalist era] people live according to their ability. If they have competence [*nŭngnyŏk*], they can live well. . . . It [capitalism] isn't good for those with low competence. Some people say things were better in the past. Since I can earn and save money, I think it is better now. . . . There are people who can't return to China even after five to seven or seven to eight or even ten years of work in South Korea [because they couldn't save enough money] after wasting money on amusements and gambling. They should be reminded of the reason they went to South Korea. . . . The success rate [for saving enough money] is less than 50 percent. . . . I beg them one more time. Don't waste money. Spend money on worthy causes.

(Interview on May 1, 2002, in Yanji)

The word "service" is in vogue among Korean Chinese workers when they compare notes about their work experience in South Korea. The virtue of giving good service to customers was described by a forty-two-year-old man when I met him in early 2002. He had come to South Korea under the alias of Yi Kyŏngho in the mid-1990s in pretense of purchasing an ice cream maker. He was given less than a day to memorize the personal information of Yi Kyŏngho, such as family history, occupation, and details of his business. After four months of paid training in South Korea, he worked as a scrubber in a sauna for five years and paid back the debt incurred from the broker's fee within half a year, and he also had sent about $20,000 to his mother as of early 2002. He speaks of his determination to earn and save money, even it means he drops dead from working:

I will work hard until I collapse. With this determination and mindset, there is nothing I can't do. I even quit smoking for my customers, after one of my customers complained about the smell. I even offer other free services such as massage. . . . If there is any good thing [about the socialist past], it would be that no people died of hunger during the Mao era. . . . But I think the socialist era was no good. . . . In retrospect, people envied others with good cigarettes or good clothes. . . . They also envied those who earned good money and lived well, even though there wasn't much to do with money back then. Now it is better as we can earn money. It is worth working hard. . . . At first I thought money would roll on the streets or lie at my footsteps in South Korea. . . . I learned that money is coming to me only with my effort, blood, and sweat. I didn't know it is so hard to earn money.

(Interview on January 11, 2002, in Seoul)

Saving is naturalized by a cultural logic that turns forbearance of exploitative relations and hard work into a joy of daily life. According to Yi Kyŏngho:

Since I came to earn money anyway, I told myself to keep focusing on it. The old saying about the virtue of digging one hole is right. A mouse finds out nothing at the end, if it digs up many holes. . . . I thought initially that I would go back to China after paying my debt [since life in South Korea was unbearable]. But after I paid back all the debt within half a year, all the money I earned became my own. After paying the debt, saving money becomes very enjoyable. It gives me energy to go on every day. So I keep working. I go to the bank every three days to deposit about $400 to $500 every time. . . . When I return to China, I plan to open a sauna. Isn't it that nothing is impossible if you do it with the will to complete the work even if you might die?

(Interview on January 11, 2002, in Seoul)

In 2008 I heard that Yi returned to China, lost a lot of money after investing in Hunchun near North Korea and the Rajin-Sonbong special economic zone in North Korea, and was frequently visiting North Korea for trade.

Feeling like "a bird in a cage" defines a migratory worker's daily existence in South Korea, as Yi portrays. He neither went to movies nor took time off to be with friends, not to mention traveling anywhere for fun. He shuttled between a rented basement room and his workplace. The constant exposure at work to water caused a skin ailment on his toes, which made him walk with a limp. Like his exposure to the black mold on walls in his damp room, his skin ailment and limp signify the discontinuity of the present and the future. A woman in her late forties also spoke of "a prisonlike" life in South Korea without time to rest or go out. In South Korea she worked from 6:00 A.M. to midnight to clean thirty-eight rooms in five-story motel; then she worked in a restaurant from 9:00 A.M. to 5:00 P.M.; and later as cook's assistant and dishwasher from 5:00 A.M. to 10:00 P.M. in a dining facility on a construction site. In her first job as a cleaner, she ran up and down stairs the entire day to the point that she could not walk properly and had to drag her legs as she walked— a common story among Korean Chinese women working as cleaners in South Korea. She endured it by thinking that her wages in South Korea for one or two days equaled her monthly income in China. She gave her work experience a positive face, saying it taught her the virtues of frugality and saving:

> When I went to South Korea, I thought of earning money and looking around [South Korea] to learn from it, because South Korea is more developed [than China]. I learned a lot from it. It provides an important lesson for us to live in China. Frankly speaking, while Korean Chinese say they live well and happily, they fall behind South Korean, when it comes to saving and frugality. . . .
>
> At first I didn't understand South Korean culture. South Korea is far more advanced than us, but it falls behind when it comes to eating. When I worked in a restaurant for the first time, I was surprised to see that we have to make soup with the outer leaves of cabbages that we wouldn't even gather from the field in China except during the famine of the 1960s.
>
> (Interview on May 5, 2002, in Yanji)

She was also shocked to find out that [with the trend to healthier lifestyles] South Koreans eat all kinds of mountain vegetables that Korean Chinese in China would not even look at and that the owner of a restaurant made a soup with sour kimchi that Korean Chinese in China would have thrown away. For her, Korean Chinese must learn from the frugality of South Koreans. Her appreciation of South Korean culture is superimposed on her experience of excruciating work to create an apparently seamless embrace of the capitalist system. For her, North Korea must introduce economic reforms as China did in the late 1970s, which spurred economic development in China and enabled Korean Chinese to visit and work in South Korea. The value of learning capitalist ethics outweighs the chronic physical ailments and pain—such as ulcers, diarrhea, and muscle numbness—incurred from migratory work.

Reclaiming mobility denotes the sovereign power of Korean Chinese when they turn their bodies into machines to work the long, socially necessary hours established by capital. As illegal and migratory labor, they are pitted against South Korean workers in terms of wages and working conditions. Korean Chinese claim that the demands of their work are fine because they resemble the long hours and hard work of farming back in China. When the valorization of capital relies on the reproduction of labor power, Korean Chinese work under conditions that threaten their labor power. Sending remittances and saving for future dreams become key ways to contend with uncertainty in the market and to create a new life in China through migratory work. Turning death into life in this way, Korean Chinese workers fulfill capital's quest for accumulation and obscure its logic of crisis-ridden accumulation. Yet, death creates excesses. Paradoxically their illegal status made them assert their sovereign power over their own bodies by frequently changing jobs. My interviewees usually held four to six jobs within two to three years in South Korea, each job lasting from a few weeks or months to less than a year. The physical demands of work and low and unpaid wages are the main reasons for changing jobs, although psychological stress and isolation also play important roles. Their illegal status in fact makes it easier to switch, and some even consider it to be a means of protecting their identity and securing their position. For South Korean employers, this high turnover in the labor market threatens the stability of the valorization of capital accumulation. They face a limit in valorizing their capital, as much as the state faces its own limit in eliminating death. The latest presumption of the real or total subsumption of labor in postindustrial society (Hardt and Negri 2001, 2011) is an overstatement.

The subjectivities that Korean Chinese repress in the production of their future lives are visible in their physical symptoms and sensibilities.[3] Illness, skin ailments, weight loss, and pulmonary diseases caused by inhalation of mold bear the corporeal memory of the present. Singing and crying release knotted emotions arising from loneliness, family separation, humiliation, and physical and mental exhaustion. Verbal violence creates a sensorial experience of time and memory. It disrupts the temporal construction of South Korean life as the future. Verbal abuse breaks affective identification with South Korea. Denunciation of insults suggests a crack in the determination of Korean Chinese to make a future life and marks their commodification with this perceptive unconscious. The montage of bodily senses and language interrupts the continuity of past, present, and future. It is not synthesized into a whole but highlights the multiplicity and contradiction in everyday experience. The montage indicates performative acts on the part of Korean Chinese migrant workers who repress the death drive in everyday life and yet bear its marks on their bodies and emotions. Their everyday existence becomes ciphers in the simultaneous construction of living in the present and future and the experience of death's somatic imprint in everyday life. Their experience is fractured by the disembodiment of mind, emotion, body surfaces, and the senses. The discordant experience of time in narratives and conscious and unconscious senses signifies the very impossibility of the real subsumption of labor under capital.

The Historical Unconscious: Dual Nationality in Repetition

Capitalist ventures lead Korean Chinese to reconfigure their ethnic identities as a foreground for their sovereignty as diasporic subjects. Their ethnicity and nationality are commodified as being inseparable from their experience as illegal migratory workers. When Korean Chinese routinely resorted to using counterfeit documents to pursue migratory work in South Korea, until their employment began to be legalized gradually starting in 2004 with the implementation of the Employment Management System for Overseas Koreans, they constructed a new spatiotemporality of ethnic nationality that revealed their historical consciousness. Their diasporic identity entails the dual nationality that they construct in terms of a totality of reason and affect that repeats in their history. They tend not to choose one nation over the other but to order their ties with both nations in terms of reason and affect. As will be explored in chapter 5, becoming Chinese nationals in the 1950s and 1960s was a rational decision, whereas loyalty to Korea was bestowed with an emotional quality. In a reversal of reason and affect in the 2000s their Chinese-ness becomes the affective quality and Korean-ness becomes the rational quality. Identification with or renunciation of one nation rather than the other is neither complete nor fixed. Simultaneous attachment with both nations makes their ethnic national identities into signs of the unfulfilled desire for community. The changing order of the two nations in the trope of dual nationality bespeaks a diasporic agency that refuses rupture with one's life while adapting to momentous changes.

Primordializing South Korea

Envisioning South Korea as the home country inverts the commodification of Korean Chinese into an ethnic nation. From the 1940s until the end of the 1980s, Korean Chinese considered North Korea the home country not only because the majority of Koreans in the Yanbian Autonomous Prefecture migrated from northern Korea but also because the People's Republic of China recognized North Korea as the only legitimate nation-state in the Korean peninsula until it signed a treaty with South Korea in 1992. Since the 1990s Korean Chinese have come to regard North Korea as fossilized in its socialist past. Although they express keen interest in transnational developmental projects that link the border region with North Korean ports, Korean Chinese have come to identify with South Koreans. According to Comaroff and Comaroff (2009), commerce produces an ethnic group, not the other way around. In their study, economic interests in operating casinos and claiming intellectual property rights to natural resources and cultural practices produce a new dialectics of sovereignty for indigenous peoples in the United States and Africa. Capitalist ventures have led indigenous peoples to essentialize their ethnic identity and enclose their cultures into stereotypical forms. Notwithstanding this reification, profit enables, the Comaroffs argue, Native Americans to consolidate ethnic identity among young generations through education and increase sovereign power through lobbying and litigation against the state. Similarly, capitalist aspirations of Korean Chinese fashion a view of South Korea as the home country, and not the other way around. The primordialization of South Korea as "koguk" (home country) and the association of ineffable feelings with it take place under capitalist devolution in their community that commodifies the promises of socialism. Primordialization paradoxically makes the present of Korean Chinese futuristic and uncertain.

Blood ties themselves do not automatically produce affective attachment toward South Korea, even for first-generation Korean Chinese. Reflecting the decades-long separation during the Cold War era, locating relatives or family members in South Korea does not lead immediately to rekindling identification and belongingness. For instance, a first-generation elderly Korean Chinese came to hear about her brother in South Korea and exchanged letters in the late 1980s. Initially it was enough for her to know that he was alive. Only after several years did she accept an invitation from his children to visit South Korea, and with the help of a broker later returned to work (Interview on May 2, 2002, in Yanji). For many Korean Chinese, South Korea is merely a country where they go to work and earn money. *The Diary of an Undocumented Woman* (Lim Tŏksil 2000), the account of a former schoolteacher's experience of migratory work, is devoid of any impression of South Korea as her home country. The diary records her difficulties as a migrant laborer in a foreign country, ranging from homesickness, lack of familiarity with South Korea's vernacular Korean, and fear of arrest and deportation to "slavelike" working conditions.

South Korea becomes a phantasmagoria when it is fastened to the desire for capital accumulation. It is imagined as a place where one's life suddenly improves like the sun's appearance on a gloomy day. Money is thought to be ubiquitous and freely available as if falling from the sky or rolling like stones on the streets of South Korea. Goods of all kinds are thought to be piled up on the streets just waiting to be grabbed (Interview on January 20, 2002, in Seoul). Media coverage of the 1988 Seoul Olympics was the first time that Korean Chinese saw the glittering images of South Korea. A forty-two-year-old, second-generation Korean Chinese woman recollects her impressions after watching a videotape from Hong Kong on the Olympics: "The stage decorations in the Olympic ceremonies captured on the videotape were beautiful. It made me wonder how capitalist South Korea became developed like that. It aroused my curiosity" (Interview on January 17, 2002, in Seoul). A forty-five-year-old, second-generation Korean Chinese man who was a white-collar worker in China speaks of his changed impression of South Korea during his short visit there in 1990 with his father and aunts:

At first I didn't feel much about South Korea [as a nation or home country]. . . . Frankly speaking, I didn't have any special feeling toward South Korea, since I was born in China. . . . Once I saw South Korea, I realized how different my classroom knowledge about South Korea was from the reality. I felt that South Korea has a higher standard in all aspects. . . . I came to feel what blood relations would be like. . . . After I returned from the home country, I felt restless by a new thought about life. I thought it would be too much in vain to live as I did at that time. I begin to think about how to do business, earn money, and help my children to become famous and rich.

(Interview on January 18, 2002, in Seoul)

The inspiration from seeing South Korea led him to work in Malaysia, run restaurants in Yanji, and work in South Korea so as to provide a better education for his two sons. He sums up the discrimination he faced at work, when he believed South Korea to be koguk:

> After I got used to the life and language here [in South Korea], South Koreans usually didn't notice me as Korean Chinese, unless I told them. Employers asked for identification such as a copy of the resident registration card, when they pay our salary. Such a situation forces me to reveal that I am Korean Chinese. As soon as they hear that I am an overseas Korean [kyop'o] from China, their treatment changes immediately. . . . South Korean workers even pass the hard work to us. . . . When South Korean workers are paid on time, our wages are delayed a month. . . . At work I do the physically demanding work. On my way home, I am worried and nervous in fear of being caught by the police. . . . I realized how hard it is to live as an illegal. Once I arrived home, I made a meager dinner before going to sleep. . . . Didn't I come to the home country [koguk ttang]? This is the home country where my grandfather and father lived. The persimmon trees planted by them are still alive in my hometown [in South Korea]. Why should I live with the label of an illegal resident on my back, when I came to the home country where my grandfather and father lived? Am I a criminal? What crime did I commit?
>
> (Interview on January 18, 2002, in Seoul)

He worked in a factory along with about a dozen foreign workers, including two or three Korean Chinese, where he melted and molded aluminum to make auto parts, during which sparks from molten metal routinely burned his face and arms. He invoked the notion of South Korea as the birth mother and China as the adopted mother who raised Korean Chinese—a commonplace trope for both South Koreans and Korean Chinese. For him, it is wrong for the birth mother to refuse to recognize her children who had to leave for another family because of poverty. As a leading member of the Korean Chinese Coalition, he speaks of his rights:

> We [Korean Chinese] must reclaim our rights. We know how difficult it must have been for the South Korean government and people to develop South Korea this far. We didn't help them when they tightened their belts and worked very hard . . . because we [Korean Chinese and South Koreans] lived in different systems—democratic capitalist and

socialist systems. . . . However, we [Korean Chinese] share the same blood, don't we? Is it a crime for us to earn money with our own blood and sweat in the home country to which we returned? Isn't it that the work we do with blood and sweat creates a new wealth here?

(Interview on January 18, 2002, in Seoul)

As Korean Chinese begin to imagine South Korea as their capitalist frontier, the Cold War history of their enmity evaporates. A second-generation Korean Chinese woman attributed her anxious yearning to work in South Korea to her envy of the seemingly instant enrichment of those who returned from working there (Interview on January 20, 2002, in Seoul). Capitalist desire suffuses the decision of a sixty-four-year-old woman from Heilongjiang Province to come to work in South Korea:

After marketization began, I ran a hair salon and a restaurant for twelve years and sold clothes in Khabarovsk. I have always wanted to have a business of my own that I would really like. As Korean Chinese increasingly went to South Korea to work, I saw their living standard was getting much higher than mine. So I came to South Korea because I wanted to come to my home town and because I wanted to earn more money. . . . At first I really wanted to return to China because of the feeling of foreignness here and the language difference [especially given South Koreans' frequent use of English vocabulary]. However, after two to three years of learning the everyday customs here, I don't want to go back to China, even if someone reports me to the police. I would resist deportation, saying that I came to my own country, my own house, my own hometown. Why would they deport me?

(Interview on January 16, 2002, in Seoul)

Despite initial indifference toward South Korea at the time of their arrival in South Korea, Korean Chinese became passionate advocates of their ethnic and national membership in South Korea. She protests South Koreans' perception of Korean Chinese as Chinese [nationals], instead calling herself Han'gugin (South Korean):

When I worked as a housekeeper in Seoul, I was asked how I came to speak Han'gungmal (Korean) so well. I told them I am not Chinese but kyop'o. We are the children of ancestors who emigrated from Han'guk [South Korea]. . . . Whenever I am asked the same question, it struck me that they think of us as Chinese. . . . I told them I am Han'guksaram and my father and mother are both Han'gukpun.

(Interview on January 16, 2002, in Seoul)

A forty-seven-year-old farmer who came to South Korea in the late 1990s through marriage to a South Korean after legally divorcing her ailing husband recollects:

After my bad investment in a coalmine incurred a serious debt, coming to South Korea [via marriage] and staying in China [with my husband] was a choice between life and death. It is better to live than die. *Anyway* [emphasis added] we can earn lots of money [here in South Korea]. . . . I chose a fake marriage to come here, although the false marriage [with a South Korean] at that time was very rare [unlike now] and was considered a shameful act.

(Interview on June 14, 2004, in Seoul)

Note her use of "anyway," with the connotation of indifference toward ethnic sentiment or psychological detachment. She earned her living as a street vendor and dishwasher and became the president of the Korean Chinese Coalition in South Korea.

The reification of South Korea points to the desire of Korean Chinese for recognition as ethnic kin. This desire runs through their narrative that verbal abuse is more unbearable than hard work. It makes verbal abuse from South Koreans far more traumatic than otherwise, since it breaks down the unconscious objectification of South Korea by Korean Chinese. This reification also explains the seemingly confounding identification with South Korea, as their participation in the campaigns to amend the Overseas Korean Act and to restore South Korean nationality created tension with South Korean activists.

Primordializing China

Rejection by South Koreans reconfigures the imagined dual nationality of Korean Chinese, transposing South Korea and China in the matrix of reason and affect. The reordering once again displaces onto the realm of ethnic nation the present temporality, that is, the new global capitalist network that involves Korean migratory work. South Korea and China in their dual national narrative constitute a familiar trope of modernity that posits rationality against emotion. Korean Chinese migrant workers consider South Korean employers to be modern and thus lacking in compassion (*injŏng*), at the same time embracing China as the embodiment of compassion. A thirty-eight-year-old, second-generation woman identifies China as her home country because of the continued presence of compassion in China, although she does so with pronounced ambivalence. In South Korea she worked in restaurants as a dishwasher for two shifts covering thirteen hours to earn as much as $70 per day. When I asked her what she thought of China and South Korea, she replied:

> Although we have rights in China since we were born and lived there, as an ethnic minority it doesn't mean that we have the full rights. Isn't it so that we live in China, the country of somebody else? It is.
>
> [Me: Do you feel that way despite having been born there?]
>
> Yes, I feel I am living in a foreign country.
>
> [Me: Which do you think is your country?]
>
> I don't know.
>
> [Me: Do you think it is South Korea?]
>
> Well. I want to consider South Korea as my home country since my grandfather was born in southern Korea. But I was raised in China, learning and growing up like this. I wonder sometimes which country to choose.
>
> [Me: Do you think you can live here, South Korea?]
>
> Yes, I can live here.
>
> [Me: What do you like about South Korea? What do you think of problems here?]
>
> I don't know. Everything is great in everyday living. When you go to a house, there is an automatic gas stove and heating. However, children are more liberalized [kaebang] than in China. Even teenagers smoke cigarettes here [South Korea]. . . . [But] I like it here, since life is convenient. . . . If we can visit South Korea freely, I hope to get a house and money here, going back and forth between here and China. But I don't want to live here. For China is my hometown [kohyang]. There is injŏng there.
>
> (Interview on January 17, 2002, in Seoul)

Similarly, a Korean Chinese woman in her sixties who worked in South Korea and became a successful businesswoman in Yanji contrasts South Koreans as stingy and Chinese as "warm-hearted" (*maŭm i ttattŭt'ada*), taking as an example an affluent elderly South Korean woman who met a decades-long-separated sister in North Korea and gave her only $300 for the arrangement (Interview on May 6, 2002, in Yanji). For a forty-nine-year-old, second-generation Korean Chinese woman from Hebei Province, hardship at work and slavelike treatment in South Korea erased her feeling for South Korea as her home country and led her to identify China as her home, where Korean Chinese are free and share "*jŏng*" with Han Chinese. She recounts:

> When I landed in South Korea, I felt that this was my home town [*kohyang*]. However, the hardship here left me nothing. . . . We underwent hardship in China too in order to live well, but we didn't have to go through this kind of emotional anxiety [*maŭm kŏkchŏng*]. Since we are the same ethnic group and speak the same language as South Koreans, I didn't expect to be despised. No one discriminates against Korean Chinese like this [in China]. . . . I miss China a lot. Since I came to earn money, I will earn as much as possible here. But I will return to China and live there.

> [Me: What do you like about China? Is it because you were born there?]

> True, I was born there. But most of all, I live freely there. If I have enough money after some years of earning here, I can live freely [in China].
> (Interview on January 27 in 2002, in Seoul)

Her shift to embrace China over South Korea maintains her capitalist future. The new China with which she identifies is a country with the prospect of rapid economic growth. She expresses her understanding of South Korea and China as capitalist doubles:

> I like the open door policy [*kaebang*]. South Korea has developed a lot since then, hasn't it? But just wait, China will be developed and has a lot of treasure [natural resources] to make it possible. We [China] can develop many times faster than South Korea did. I think we have to make China known to the world soon, developing [its economy] quickly. I really feel great that our country [China] is being developed. . . . I feel great when I think that Chinese development will exceed

South Korean development. I feel great when I think that my children and grandchildren will live in a developed country. There are a lot of places under development in our country. There are also a lot of places suitable for development.

(Interview on January 27 in 2002, in Seoul)

In the dual nationality narrative, the trope of reason and affect turns South Korea and China into mere signs of becoming modern. South Korea and China are just different names of the community that one invokes to tame an uncertain and dream-filled life. It is through this imagination of belonging that one maintains hope and becomes sovereign. Ethnic and national belonging gives one a place when drifting from job to job. It creates a life and history for migrant laborers whose troubled names are "Chosŏnjok." In China, the name Chosŏnjok refers to their institutional status in socialist Chinese history as an ethnic minority. In South Korea, it is derogatory word with no meaning other than "foreignness." A thirty-six-year-old woman who came from Jilin Province to South Korea in 1998 and worked as a cleaner in a motel in 2002 explains her changing national and ethnic identity:

I used to live in China as a Korean with a feeling of superiority [that Korean Chinese are better educated and more prosperous than Han Chinese and other minorities]. . . . In the past I thought of North Korea and South Korea as my home country, yet I now feel this [South Korea] is a foreign land [t'ahyang]. . . . Where are our roots? I feel we [Korean Chinese] are E.T. [extraterrestrial]. . . . I don't want my kid to live in South Korea. . . . No one greeted me here. People regard Korean Chinese with indifference, suspicion, and icy looks. I don't need a home country. I would live in a place that treats me well. If we were to live in China, it is better to speak Chinese rather than our Chosŏnjok language. Korean Chinese used to admire South Koreans. Now they call South Koreans bastards [Han'gungnom]. In China we have rights as a minority. . . . Do you think South Korea will live well forever, for a thousand or ten thousand years? Korean Chinese can support South Koreans [when China becomes more prosperous than South Korea].

(Interview on January 16, 2002, in Seoul)

Despite her husband's objections, she sent their child to a Chinese school.

In his book *There Is No South Korea* (Han'guk ŭn ŏpta), Kim Chaeguk (1998), a professor of literature in Jilin, reembraces China after his lengthy stay in

South Korea. His visits and graduate studies demystified his initial belief in South Korea as an emblem of "beauty, purity, cleanliness, desirability, and generosity." He declares, "I can't help but love China, where I was born and raised. I am more familiar with Chinese mountains than the Sŏrak and Halla Mountains of South Korea." He describes this sensibility:

> Until they learn about South Korea, Korean Chinese lived as nationals [kongmin] in China, a loving land which our ancestors cultivated with sweat and blood. . . . With sweat and blood our ancestors reclaimed the land on which we live right now and protected it by sacrificing their lives. . . . We know that our ancestors fought against the Japanese with blood and sweat and turned wasteland into fertile farm land, and that Korean Chinese is the most excellent and brightest among fifty-six ethnic groups.
>
> (Kim Chaeguk 1998:80–81)

In his binary logic, South Koreans suffer from narrow-minded patriotism and an inferiority complex, whereas Korean Chinese belong to the great nation of China; South Koreans' obsession with "hurriedness" or efficiency results from the high stress and anxiety of living in a small country, whereas Chinese "slowness" and stress-free living reflect the scale of life and outlook of a big and powerful country. If South Korea has built a system of modern education with an enlightened mentality, China embraces its "dumb" culture in which pretending to be ignorant is a survival strategy. The "don't do it culture" of South Korea indicates a small and ethnically homogeneous country that is intolerant of difference, whereas the "can do it culture" of China, such as in smoking in front of the elderly and men walking bare-chested in public space, attests to a large and multiethnic country that is open to difference. According to the Korean Chinese critic Kim Howung, Kim Chaeguk's opposition of South Korean and Chinese cultures is a "double consciousness" that "drifts aimlessly and endlessly between the two cultures" and works at best as an emotional retort (Kim Chaeguk 1998:283–93). If Korean Chinese were to have a genuine understanding of South Korea, according to Kim Howung, they must respect the South Korean capitalist system and its culture and philosophy of life. Kim Howung urges Korean Chinese not to reclaim backwardness as more compassionate and cultured but to outcompete South Koreans and enter mainstream South Korean society. Here Kim Howung inadvertently recognizes capitalism as the kernel of double consciousness experienced by Korean Chinese.

Switching from South Korea to China, or from China to South Korea, as one's national community reveals the ambivalence pervading the everyday life of Korean Chinese. This ambivalence is capable of interrupting the futuristic time of the present. The trope of rationality and emotion distills this ambivalence into capitalist aspiration. Whether Korean Chinese migrants identify with South Korea or switch to China, their capitalist aspiration is preserved. Simultaneous identification and disidentification with a nation signifies the commodification of Korean Chinese and attests to their vulnerability as illegal workers in capitalist conditions deregulated by both the South Korean and the Chinese state.

Neitherness

In contrast to the competing identifications with South Korea and China, the espousal of neither national identity discloses an interruption in their commodification. When excluded from the Overseas Korean Act (see chapter 3) in South Korea, Korean Chinese migrant workers have encapsulated their diasporic existence in terms of "the people without place to go [to settle]" (kalgot ŏpnŭn saramdŭl) or "living in sorrow whether coming to South Korea or going to China" (odogado sŏrŭm). The unresolved status of Korean Chinese throughout Chinese socialist history offers a clue to their present condition, according to a sixty-six-year-old, second-generation man from Jilin Province whose employers in South Korea paid him wages for only two and one-half years of work despite his having worked for seven years at a fishery farm, a factory that handles asbestos, a rice cake factory, and an agency that cleans the streets:

The mother country that gave birth to us is Chosŏn [Korea], whether it means South Korea or North Korea. The mother country that embraced and raised us during hardship and suffering is China. . . . Many Korean Chinese in China proper are pitiful, as they don't know their roots, their own [Korean] language, customs, and habits. . . . We [Koreans in northeast China] used to be regarded as overseas Koreans in China [who had residential permit, not Chinese nationality]. Suddenly sometime between 1952 and 1953, we were categorized as Chinese nationals [following the pact between China and North Korea]. This sudden change of status left unresolved the most important matter, namely, the notion of home country. . . . When we are discriminated against in China, we tend to accept it because China is not the mother country that gave birth to us. Even here [South Korea] we feel awkward since we left a long time ago.

(Interview on January 22, 2002, in Seoul)

A man in his late forties, the aforementioned white-collar worker and successful entrepreneur in China before coming to work in South Korea, speaks of the neitherness of Korean Chinese identity, which he thinks can be changed only by advocating for their rights in South Korea:

> Frankly speaking, we Korean Chinese are miserable. The Chinese state recognizes us as an ethnic minority. However, it is hard to say that there is no ethnic discrimination. Therefore we sometimes feel distressed, thinking this is because we are living not in our own country but in a foreign country. For instance, Han Chinese are preferred to Korean Chinese for government positions, even when Korean Chinese are more qualified. . . . Therefore we Korean Chinese must get organized to build our power. We can build power only when we are organized together. We can change policy only when we have power. Korean Chinese are miserable. . . . We are miserable whether we go to China or come to South Korea. What did we do wrong, when we were forced under the Japanese rule to migrate to Manchuria to survive and settled for two generations? We didn't abandon South Korea [Han'guk]. We had no choice but to go to China in that situation. . . . People say that it is a foreign land [t'ahyang] whether we go [to China] or come [to South Korea].

(Interview on January 18, 2002, in Seoul)

Simultaneous investiture and divestiture in the South Korean and Chinese nations embodies the historical unconscious of the present. Through this performative act Korean Chinese experience their capitalist present by temporalizing it in reference to the past and the future. The processes of identifying, renouncing, and identifying anew with an imagined nation offer respite from the restlessness and numbness of a future-driven present. This performative act engenders new memories of the past and experiences of the present, which provide the appearance of historical sensibility, when capitalist social relations turn Korean Chinese into commodities without origins. The insertion into colonial and socialist history allows Korean Chinese unconsciously to find the cotemporality of their downtrodden existence in South Korea and China and simultaneously criticize and tolerate their present conditions. In the next chapter, the analysis of their socialist history in China addresses further the repetition of the narrative of dual nationality.

CONCLUSION

The epochal shift from a socialist economy to privatization and deregulation does not have a fixed meaning or experience. The state reifies it as reparation for all the violence committed by the state and party throughout socialist history. Korean Chinese intellectuals consider these changes as portents of the looming extinction of the Korean Chinese minority in China. However, socialist promises have not died. Instead, they have been transmuted into commodities in the mode of the capitalist accumulation, which I describe as capitalist devolution. The lives and dreams of Korean Chinese migratory workers suggest that privatization and deregulation do not bring about a historical rupture but instead create multifaceted temporalities for their past, present, and history. Rapid industrialization was pursued in the name of developing productive forces throughout Chinese socialist history, and it still continues in a futuristic present marked by Korean Chinese migratory work. In other words, privatization and deregulation are other means for pursuing capital accumulation.

Until early 2004, Korean Chinese were driven to work illegally in South Korea under the pretense of family visits in order to obtain health care, housing, and education—socialism's promises. They continue to endure daily demanding work routines and debilitating discrimination, describing their existence as a workshop of modern life involving rational time management, the discipline of hard work, the law of competition, an ethic of service, and the virtues of frugality and saving. The cultural politics of modernity inverts capitalist discipline into learning to become modern. Their chronic crisis is palpable in their somatic experiences, in their crying, singing, and illness that are characteristic symptoms of the torments of their daily life. Narrative and somatic experiences need to be considered together in order to understand the historical disquiet in their everyday life, in which their will to make a future living continuously faces interruption and breakdown.

The invocation of ethnic national community becomes a privileged mode of representation that is deployed to make sense of the changes in their daily life. In their strenuous living and working conditions, Korean Chinese illegal workers have sought to carve out their sovereignty by establishing their social body in the form of an ethnic nation. This performative act of transferring capitalist experiences into ethnic and national relations and identities distills complex and diverse experiences into the hope for another day or even a foreseeable future. This act is an affective transfer, whether to the South Korean or Chinese community, as it attempts to preserve a sense of wholeness and make meaning of the present. The pains are at least numbed, and restlessness is stilled in their composition of community. Various temporalities of the present are assimilated into a familiar organic whole via this new construction of community. When the present immediately becomes the past in the race toward the future, the evocation of community inadvertently creates a residue of past history. The historical unconscious is located in this simultaneous identification and disidentification of national identity, whether Korean or Chinese, as well as in the renunciation of both national identities. Historical temporalization of everyday life is affective because it allows one to imagine being in the company of others or being the other. When the nation-state, either Korea or China, becomes the passageway to the future, historical continuity seemingly pervades everyday life.

The narrative of dual nationality, of reason and affect, surprisingly harks back to a time decades ago. The affective embrace of natural landscape and culture as the source of primordial identity is a haunting repetition of the dual nationality expressed by Korean Chinese in the 1950s, which the next chapter investigates. The binary narrative of reason and affect crystallizes the past and present into comparable historical moments.

5

CHINESE REVOLUTION IN REPETITION: THE MINORITY QUESTION

The displacement of Korean Chinese to South Korea returns them to the era of socialist revolution in China. Their two prominent anamneses are the narrative of dual nationality during the 1950s and the narrative of intraethnocide during the Cultural Revolution. These ethnic national recollections are allegorical rather than symbolic. The ethnic national form in these reminiscences conveys the irreconcilable tension between the socialist principle and the historical and material conditions of its actualization, which was repressed in the repeated efforts to resolve it. Like efforts at industrialization in the USSR, China's pursuit of rapid industrialization contradicted the axiom of socialism, namely, elimination of the exchange value of labor or the law of value. The imperative to develop productive forces imposed homogeneous agricultural and industrial polices on the society at different moments of the socialist era. Nonsocialist elements in social relations became "noncontemporaneous contemporaneity," in Bloch's term (2009), which the Chinese socialist regime called feudal and colonial remnants, capitalists, or simply "mixed demons" (*chapkwisin*).[1] The putative historical past was encapsulated in an ethnic national mode that is counterposed to socialist universalism. The Korean Chinese became these others whose containment is necessary for the realization of true socialism or to use a Hegelian term, the world-spirit.

The tension between Chinese socialism and Korean ethnic nationalism results from the contradiction between socialism and capital accumulation. Chinese revolutionaries confounded proletarian sovereignty with Chinese national sovereignty as early as the 1930s, even when they espoused proletarian internationalism and incorporated Korean revolutionaries in Manchuria into the Chinese Communist Party.[2] Hidden behind the facade of socialist universalism, the national character of Chinese socialism shaped the formation of a Korean ethnic minority. In this chapter, making an analytic shift from the language of nationalism to the problematic of capital accumulation enables us to articulate the seemingly primordial dynamics of ethnic nationalism with historicity of socialist economics. It also moves the analysis of the sovereignty of the socialist state from the realm of the political to the realm of the social, where social relations of production are also a space for the sovereignty of labor. Marxist economists characterize the Soviet economy as "state capitalism," a twin of twentieth-century Western state capitalism (Cliff 1974; Binns, Cliff, and Harman 1987; Harman 2010). Buck-Morss (2002) interprets this twin character as a contradiction between the Soviet state's sovereignty and its material conditions, whose visual representation is the focus of her study. I approach the contradiction as a repressed imperative that governed the process of actualizing socialism through the 1950s and 1960s in China. Situating Koreans' memory of intraethnocide in this continued contradiction, I interpret that memory as an inverted mode of their social existence.

The repeated and repressed contradiction between the socialist ideal and its material conditions raises history as a philosophical category. The depiction of socialism as a unitary whole prevails in contemporary scholarship and the popular imagination and gives the Cultural Revolution its present popularity. Historians and philosophers declare the Cultural Revolution a failure because factional struggle and its obscene collective passions and senseless violence caused the Cultural Revolution's initial utopian intentions to degenerate (Badiou 2005; Russo 2005). In China's era of deregulation and privatization, memories of the Cultural Revolution's violence coexist with popular nostalgia for the collectivism of that era (Lu Xiuyan 1994–1995; Yang 2003; Dutton 2005; MacFarquhar and Schoenhals 2006; Gao 2008). Whether historical failure or nostalgic transcendence of the present, reminiscences of the Cultural Revolution are the latest examples of simultaneously exceptionalizing it and considering it emblematic of Chinese socialism. However, the Cultural Revolution needs to be understood as but one moment of socialist history, albeit a particularly important and violent one. Indeed, its historical character is comprehensible only within the entire process of the Chinese revolution that wrestled with historical contradiction in distinct and yet repeated instances. The repetition arises from a process of representation that puts the principles of socialism into practice under concrete historical conditions. The fidelity of logic and history reveals that each approach sought to realize

socialism in different ways: collectivization and the 1958 national rectification movement with its goal to homogenize society, the Great Leap Forward
to intensify industrialization, and the Cultural Revolution against the bureaucratization of the state. Each of these different responses to the contradiction
between socialist ideals and material conditions turned the idea of socialism
into concrete praxis. Socialism acquired a singularity in each instance. Like
Deleuze's (1994) concept of simulacra,[3] socialism does not possess an original form other than as an idea, whether the idea is mass sovereignty, collective property, or use value of labor; and socialism is "communicated through
differences," in which each instance is differentiated from another through
representation. Socialist history is to be considered as "constellations" of
historical realization rather than a totalized reality.[4]

METAMEMORY OF THE NATIONAL MINORITY

The involuntary memory of the Cultural Revolution as the era of the intraethnocide is a philosophical incursion into the history of the Chinese revolution.
That "Koreans killed each other" is not a true memory in the sense that intraethnocide is a truthful rendition of what took place and was repressed from
conscious experience. Instead, recollection takes place through the bodily
dislocation of Korean Chinese to South Korea, where they became illegal
migratory workers. This is significant because the nostalgia for and commodification of the Cultural Revolution seen across China during the first decade
of the 2000s are largely absent among the Korean Chinese community in
China. Not every Korean Chinese worker with whom I spoke in South Korea
recalled the Cultural Revolution as being relevant to their present life or even
mentioned it. For some, the Cultural Revolution is dead history, as its atrocity
was corrected by the state's exoneration of the wrongly accused and its material compensation of victims. A Korean Chinese woman in her late thirties
when we met in 2002 in Seoul, for instance, saw the Chinese government's
compensation as reparation for her family's victimization. She spoke of her
father's persecution during the Cultural Revolution when he was accused of
being a spy (tŭkmu) from South Korea, and his vindication in the late 1970s:

When I was in the first grade in elementary school, I wasn't allowed
to wear the red tie that denoted membership in the children's group
because of my father's persecution. . . . But after his name was cleared,
our family benefited from the state's compensation. . . . Even when

rice rationing was not sufficient . . . my father received more than three times that of others. When the normal monthly rationing of grain amounted to 18 kŭn[5] including rice and other grains, my dad received 50 kŭn for his own individual share, which was sufficient for all the members of my family.

(Interview on January 17, 2002, in Seoul)

But the Cultural Revolution continues to haunt others. It holds the key to the present conditions of life for some of those working illegally without South Korea's validation of their Korean-ness. When I asked what prompted her decision to come to South Korea, the unexpected reply of a fifty-five-year-old woman, who came to South Korea in 1997 and was working in a restaurant in 2002, began with a reference to the Cultural Revolution:

The Cultural Revolution still [emphasis added] brings out bloody tears from me. My parents died from the sufferings of the Cultural Revolution after being accused of being spies. My father died in a hospital after torture broke his ribs. My mother died from the traumatic wound to her heart. In the end, the state [kukka] resolved the torments inflicted by the Cultural Revolution. He was vindicated as an honorable comrade. But my mother died of cancer in the late 1970s.

With the death of my parents, I had to raise my siblings. I can't even begin to explain the hardship. During the Cultural Revolution, I survived doing the worst kind of work that no one wanted to do, such as cleaning human waste. . . . The state asked me what I wished to have as reparation for the torment caused by the Cultural Revolution. I wanted new housing, although my husband was given housing by his factory that made trucks. For four years, the state refused to accept my wish on the grounds that I was a married-out daughter, while granting me a new job in an electronic store. I kept pressing the government and finally won the housing.

(Interview on January 10, 2002, in Seoul)

Koreans' intraethnocide relates to the issue of Korean ethnic national character (minjoksŏng). According to her, the Cultural Revolution was more ferocious in the Yanbian Korean Autonomous Prefecture (Yanbian hereafter) than other places because of Koreans' ethnic character:

Korean Chinese fought against themselves. . . . Isn't the ethnic nature of Korean Chinese that they are jealous about the other's success?

Koreans can't be united among themselves. If a Chinese and a Korean fight on the street, Koreans would ignore it as if this Korean were a stranger, while Chinese would join the fight to save the Chinese. . . . [During the Cultural Revolution] people even built up more cases against their own relatives by spreading ridiculous charges. . . . When I was rebuked for not shouting "overthrow" at my mother during her public condemnation, my relatives were at the forefront in attacking her.

(Interview on January 10, 2002, in Seoul)

In 2002 a man in his fifties who served as a leader in the Korean Chinese Coalition in South Korea similarly pointed out that Korean Chinese probably suffered more persecution and death from the Cultural Revolution than any other ethnic group because of the Korean tendency to attack one another. For him, intraethnic violence resulted from Korean Chinese using any means to survive. His father was persecuted during the Cultural Revolution when accused of having worked for the Japanese during the colonial period and harboring a bourgeois mentality about earning a high income, while his mother avoided harassment because of her official status as an overseas North Korean (chokyo).

In their memories Korean Chinese juxtapose the capitalist present with the era of the Cultural Revolution. Gone from their consciousness are the historical global conditions for continuous or permanent revolution in the form of the Cultural Revolution (Dirlik 2003). They narrate the Cultural Revolution as a harrowing event that delayed the arrival of the capitalist present in China. A construction worker in his late forties in Seoul refers to the Cultural Revolution when speaking of the ascendancy of capitalism over socialism:

I thought cities in a capitalist society like South Korea must be dark and gloomy. But once I saw it, I realized how wrong I was. Anyway, capitalism is the way to go. For instance, there are many volunteers here [who help the unfortunate], while they are absent in China. It is clean everywhere here. Everyone is civil, greeting others unlike in China. I feel like everything in China is more or less outdated.

[Me: Do you think that the way people think is also different in South Korea and China?]

What is different is not just culture but also history. Firstly, though we are the Korean Chinese minority [Chosŏnjok], we don't know about our ancestors and family history.

Even some people from northern Korea [with which Korean Chinese maintained close contacts] don't know which generation of Korean Chinese they are. There is neither education about it nor family pedigree [chokpo]. I think at least one generation is forgotten.

[Me: Why do you think it is forgotten like that?]

Do you know our Cultural Revolution? . . . When I got married at the age of twenty-six in 1979, my dad told me that he burnt his Korean family registration document and all of family photos out of fear during the Cultural Revolution. At the outbreak of the Cultural Revolution, our neighbors planned the public interrogation of my dad on the grounds that he served in the Japanese Army. . . .

[Me: Were people persecuted during the Cultural Revolution for their deeds back during Japanese colonial rule?]

Right, people severely beat the accused.

[Me: Aren't they all Korean?]

Yes, Koreans assaulted one another. For ten years.

[Me: Are you saying that history was put on hold at least for a generation because of the Cultural Revolution?]

My dad's generation knows the family's history, while our generation doesn't.

(Interview on January 24, 2002, in Seoul)

This conversation was followed by my question about how his experience in South Korea has changed his thoughts about capitalism. Through his transference of history onto culture, he constructs and embraces capitalism as the antithesis of the Cultural Revolution. While affirming capitalism despite his subjection to exploitative capitalist relations in South Korea, he reasoned that the Cultural Revolution suspended history. As a second-generation Korean Chinese whose parents were born in Kyŏngsang Province in southern Korea, he came to South Korea in 2000 from near Yanji, capital of the Yanbian Autonomous Prefecture, under the alias of a man visiting his married daughter. His migratory work experience in South Korea failed to weaken his faith in capitalism despite his rapid weight loss and other signs of his rapidly deteriorating health. His understanding of capitalism is contrasted with the irrationality and absurdity that are thought to epitomize the Cultural Revolution. Although his father worked for the Japanese army during the colonial period, he saved the lives of revolutionaries by turning a blind eye to communists on trains or by hiding them in his compartment when on duty on the South Manchuria Railway. After the 1949 revolution his father became a hero when one of the men he saved told the government about his courageous behavior. Yet during the Cultural Revolution fellow villagers tried to persecute his father, which he regards as intraethnic violence.

Involuntary recollection of intraethnocide is an excess of the national politics of South Korea and China. In Halbwachs' terms (1992), the memory of intraethnocide among Koreans offers Korean Chinese migrant workers a new collective language, one with which they understand their past and the present. The memory disrupts the South Korean temporalization of history that either denies them their overseas Korean status or assimilates them via reparation for colonial wrongs. At the same time, the very notion of intraethnocide creates cracks in the model minority consciousness into which Korean Chinese flee in order to moderate South Koreans' discrimination against them. Korean Chinese often give South Koreans a ready-made narrative that they are one of the best-educated ethnic minorities in China and enjoy special benefits such as a larger allocation of rice than Han Chinese and the right to speak Korean. Their model minority consciousness reflects their participation in the anti-Japanese struggle and the liberation struggle, unlike other minorities such as Mongolians and Tibetans. However, their history in China involved their routine subjection to charges of being counterrevolutionaries, local nationalists, and spies, as they were purged as early as 1932 and exonerated as late as 1978.

In 2005 the Yanbian government authorized a study of Korean Chinese history to clarify the issue of Korean Chinese minority status. From May 2003 to April 2005, a group of seven Korean Chinese scholars attempted to resolve the controversy over the formation of the Korean Chinese minority and the nature of their revolutionary struggle (Chŏnmun munje chŏjak sojo 2005). Historical accounts had variously traced the formation of the Korean Chinese minority to the late nineteenth century, the early twentieth century, the 1928 incorporation of Koreans in China into the Chinese Communist Party, or the post-1949 period. The role of the Korean Chinese community in modern Chinese history was also disputed. Some claimed that its participation in the anti-Japanese struggle in China supported the cause of independence in both

China and Korea. Others claimed that Korean Chinese pursued the liberation of Korea until 1931 and began to concentrate on the liberation of China from 1932. However, the group's monthly meetings, workshops, and regular communication with the Yanbian government and Jilin provincial government for two years produced yet more inconclusive findings. It determined that the Korean Chinese minority first formed in 1885, when the Qing government accepted the legal immigration of Koreans, and that Koreans became a national minority in China after the Qing government not only enacted the 1909 nationality law granting nationality to foreigners with at least ten years of residency but also granted Koreans rights to cultivate and own land. This conclusion means that Koreans became Chinese nationals and a national minority decades before the Japanese domination of Manchuria. It also means that as a Korean Chinese minority, they fought against Japanese imperialists as part of the Chinese anti-Japanese struggle to liberate China. In his dissenting opinion, Pak Ch'angwuk, the most highly revered historian at Yanbian University, wrote that their political struggle from 1905 to 1945 entailed the dual goal of liberating Korea and China. In his elaboration, this dual goal reflected their "historically specific conditions": The Qing and warlord governments considered Korean settlers to be Japanese and thus simultaneously coerced and prevented their naturalization as Chinese; and Koreans escaping Japanese rule engaged in anti-Japanese and antifeudal struggles to liberate both Korea and China under the leadership of Korean nationalists (including communists) and Chinese communists.

Adequate historical accounts of Koreans' nationality, their politics, and their memory warrant consideration of the socialist revolution in relation to global capitalism. From the very moment of Korean settlement in Manchuria to the Cultural Revolution, the history of Koreans in China demonstrates that their nationality and politics were embedded in their cultivation and ownership of land. That is, they were farmers who came with their families in search of land. The Japanese empire integrated Manchuria into the global capitalist circuit and lured Korean migrants with financial credits to settle and collaborate with the Japanese, turning soybeans into a leading export. In its postcolonial moments, socialist China sought to make a transition to socialism to communism. Mao's vision of continuous revolution envisaged this transition in terms of stages. His linear vision of continuous revolution conflicted with the putative remnants of the old society, which repeatedly were targets of official campaigns in the 1950s and 1960s. I ground the unstable relations between Korean Chinese and the Chinese socialist state in this gap between the vision of socialism and its historical process. The memory of intraethnocide connects the past and the present in terms of the violence against and among Koreans in China and South Korea. But I situate this mnemonic representation of the past and present in the historical process of actualizing socialism through contradiction and repetition. This perspective allows us to consider socialism as a utopian vision whose historical actualization was never free from capitalist principles. The Chinese regime repeatedly sought to reconcile its socialist principles with pursuit of rapid industrialization by continuously shuffling the relationship between production and distribution. Koreans became signs of various "others" of socialism through the instability and flux of social relations. The contradiction between the state's sovereignty and its material conditions highlights the problem of recognizing the historical present in socialist history. The question of Korean nationality sits on the fault line of the problematic of representation and recognition.

DUAL NATIONALITY AS A SOCIAL QUESTION

The Chinese Communist Party (CCP) incorporated Korean communists in Manchuria beginning in 1928 under the Comintern's principle of one party in one country. The CCP's anti-Japanese struggle in Manchuria depended on Korean communists and peasants in eastern Manchuria who were the backbone of the struggle. The study by Kim Pyŏngho and Kang Kiju (2001) shows that the CCP at first saw Koreans in Manchuria as "Chosŏnin" or "Koryŏin," both of which meant Korean, but soon began to classify them as "Chosŏnjok," meaning the Korean national minority. In "The Statement to Koreans in Manchuria" in 1928, the CCP's Manchuria Committee defined its relationship with Koreans (in Manchuria) as a coalition (yŏnhap), recognizing their common struggle against the Japanese through their shared suffering and goal. In "The Korean Peasant Question in Manchuria" in the same year, the Manchuria Committee noted Korean peasants as both allies of the anti-Japanese struggle and constitutive parts of the peasant revolutionaries in Manchuria. From 1930, however, the Manchuria Committee began to call Koreans a national minority like any other national minorities inside Chinese territory. In a letter to the Central Committee in 1930, the Manchuria Committee defined Koreans' revolutionary activities in Manchuria as the Chinese nationalist movement in Manchuria. In "The Resolution on National Minorities in China" and "The Constitution of the Chinese Soviet Republic" adopted in November 1931, the CCP included Koreans in the category of national minorities and stated that Koreans (Koryŏin), like Mongolians, Tibetans, and other national minorities, held "the right to self-determination [chagyŏlkwŏn] and thus had the choice to join the Chinese Soviet Republic, leave it, or create their own self-rule area." In its preparation for the establishment of the Northeast People's Revolutionary government in 1934, the Manchuria Committee of the CCP declared that all people in northeast China, including Koreans and Taiwanese, were nationals of the People's Revolutionary Government. Despite these references to Koreans as a national minority, Kim Pyŏngho and Kang Kiju emphasize, the CCP accepted Koreans' dual nationality as a national minority in China and as nationals of Chosŏn, especially in the late 1940s. In fact, after the CCP's purge of Korean communists in the anti-Minsaengdan incident from 1932 to 1936 nearly eliminated revolutionary forces in Manchuria, Korean and Chinese communists reconstituted their relationship as a coalition by forming the Anti-Japanese Northeast United Army (Park 2005).

Upon liberation from Japanese rule, the Chinese Communist Party sought to consolidate Koreans in the region as a national minority through a dual strategy: purging Korean communists in the region and linking land ownership to national membership in China. Yi Chinryŏng's (2002) study offers rare clarity into this dual strategy. After Japan's defeat, Korean communists in the Anti-Japanese Northeast United Army who had fled to the Soviet Union in the early 1940s returned to Yanbian. They founded the Yanbian Committee of the CCP and mass organizations. Dispatched by the central CCP from Yenan, a group of thirty-three Han Chinese communists quickly dissolved these organizations on November 12, 1945. The dispatched group established the CCP's Northeast Department, which carried out land reforms in 1946 and purged Korean communists from February 1947 to March 1948. Distributing land to 116,681 Korean households in eastern Manchuria (Yanbian) out of a total of 154,243, the CCP used land reform to garner support from Korean peasants. Koreans became Chinese nationals through land ownership, although some land distributed to Koreans was not suitable for rice farming (Ch'ae Chaebong and Kim Ch'ŏllyong 1993:93). Korean peasants quickly joined agricultural cooperatives, increasing the percentage of Korean households in cooperatives in Yanbian from 52.64 percent in 1950, to 76.48 percent in 1952, to 90 percent by late 1955. These cooperatives were reconstituted into advanced cooperatives starting in 1956. Koreans were also lauded for surpassing their quota for grain production.

The purge of Korean communists was carried out by the Jilin Provincial Committee of the CCP, which moved its party, military, and administrative organizations to Yanbian in February 1947 to defeat the allied forces of bandits and the Kuomintang Party (KMT) in eastern Manchuria. Until it returned to the city of Jilin in March 1948, the Jilin Provincial Committee cancelled the party membership of seventy-one out of a total of ninety-three Korean party members and suspended forty-two Korean officials from the party's mass organizations in a campaign to restore purity and unification to the party's organization and ideology. The CCP filled vacancies created by the purge with Korean and Chinese recruits from China proper, placing Koreans in middle- and lower-level positions and Chinese in high-ranking positions. Korean recruits were former members of the Chosŏn Ŭiyonggun, an anti-Japanese military force of Koreans in China proper that supported the KMT and joined the second united front of the KMT and CCP from 1936 to 1945. Chu Tŏkhae, who had joined Chinese communists in Yenan and in the Anti-Japanese Northeast United Army, emerged as the top Korean leader in Yanbian to become the secretary in the CCP's Yanbian committee in March 1949, president of Yanbian University in April 1949, and the first governor of the Yanbian Korean Autonomous Region formed in 1952. He was the only Korean on the CCP Central Committee when the Cultural Revolution broke out. As membership of Korean Chinese in the CCP increased, their representatives made up about 60 percent of officials in the Yanbian Autonomous Prefecture in 1959, though mostly in administrative and cultural sectors rather than military and political sectors (Yi Chinryŏng 2002).[6]

The formation of the Korean Chinese national minority in China entailed disputes and negotiations over its nationality. In December 1948, the Northeast Department of the CCP convened the debate on Korean nationality and Yanbian's future in Jilin. Some Chinese regarded Koreans who became Chinese nationals as foreigners and demanded cancelation of their residency. Many Koreans advocated for multiple national membership: as ethnic Koreans in Chosŏn, as Chinese nationals in China, and as members of the world proletariat in the Soviet Union.[7] Some Koreans under the USSR's influence also advocated the formation of an independent republic for Koreans. Former Korean members of the Northeast United Army vainly pursued the independence of Yanbian from China and integration into North Korea on the grounds that the CCP promised self-determination to Koreans during their joint anti-Japanese struggle. In that conjuncture, Chu Tŏkhae promoted the self-rule of Koreans in China with Chinese officials' welcoming support. Chu defined the Korean nationality question as a social question, embedding the Chinese state's sovereignty into social relations. Chu Tŏkhae appealed to Koreans to choose Chinese nationality in order to enjoy self-rule in China and safeguard the decades of labor they had invested in their land and livelihood in China. Koreans' entitlement to socioeconomic and political rights in

China, he argued, was earned through their agricultural work and participation in the revolutionary struggle.

For Chu Tŏkhae (*Chu Tŏkhae ŭi ilsaeng* 1987:228–9), the multiple nationality approach denied this historical character of Korean nationality. In his view, "*choguk* [literally fatherland] comes to be considered a concept with very strong historical and political characteristics. While in the unenlightened era, *minjok* [ethnic nation] was about being loyal to the king and worshipping ancestors, it overcomes its narrow and closed character in this current era of imperialism and proletarian class revolution by moving across borders with new means of transportation and communication and develops political, economic, and cultural links with other national groups. It is thus already common that various minjok live in one *nara* [country] and that one minjok lives in various nara." Arguing that each person has only one nation-state, Chu Tŏkhae conflated choguk and *kukchŏk* (nationality). For him, "choguk and kukchŏk are directly entwined so that an individual has only one choguk and one kukchŏk." In this way Chu conceptualized choguk as the modern nation-state. After the debate, the CCP's gerrymandering reduced the proportion of the Korean population in Yanbian by excluding the Mudanjiang (Mokdan'gang) area with its Korean concentration from Yanbian, placing it in Heilongjiang Province, and incorporating Tonhwa County, with its Han Chinese concentration, into Yanbian (Yi Chinryŏng 2002). Self-rule for Koreans in Yanbian was postponed to 1952 as a result of the Korean War. Under the framework of self-rule, Koreans were allowed to practice their ethnic culture and operate Korean schools abolished during Japanese colonization, founding Yanbian (Korean) University and creating newspapers and broadcast agencies (Yŏnbyŏn tangsa hakhoe 1989:1–106).

The popularity of dual nationality as Koreans and Chinese, however, continued throughout the 1950s. The CCP pursued its nationalist move while forging socialist internationalism with North Korea during the Korean War (1950–1953) and the period of postwar reconstruction. This ambiguity was fertile ground for Koreans to explore their double attachment to two nation-states leading up to the national rectification movement in 1958. North Korea offered strategic assistance to the CCP during the 1945–1949 period, allowing tens of thousands of Chinese revolutionary forces and strategic materials to move from southern to northern Manchuria through North Korea, operating Chinese weapons factories relocated from Manchuria to North Korea and providing shelter to the wounded and families of the armies. While integrating Koreans as Chinese nationals, the CCP mobilized Korean Chinese to fight in the Korean War, to increase production and donate resources to assist North

Koreans, and even to move to North Korea.[8] When China and the Soviet Union disputed the principles of socialist development in the 1960s, North Korea sided with China until the mid-1960s. In a matched partnership, China blamed the Soviet Union for threatening both Chinese and North Korean socialist revolutions (Yŏnbyŏn tangsa hakhoe 1989:34–51). Even in June 1959, about one thousand representatives of nationals and sectors in the city of Yanji gathered to show support for the peaceful unification of Korea and demanded withdrawal of US forces from South Korea. In 1962, Koreans in Yanbian opposed the South Korea–Japan summit and affirmed their support for North Korea (Chu Tŏkhae ŭi ilsaeng 1987:148, 191).

The issue of dual nationality of Koreans became a constitutive element of permanent or continuous revolution in China.[9] The vision of continuous revolution centered on the "people's democratic dictatorship," in which social relations were no longer defined by antagonistic class relations, since private property relations were abolished, but instead involved various contradictions among the people. In the 1957 speech "On the Correct Handling of Contradictions among the People," Mao Tse-tung attended separately to the issues of cooperatives, the bourgeoisie, industrialists, intellectuals, and national minorities. For Mao, overcoming Han chauvinism and local nationalist chauvinism was necessary to resolve contradictions between Han Chinese and ethnic national minorities. The national rectification movement in the Korean Chinese community, from spring 1958 to early 1960, however, shows the entwinement of socioeconomic, political, and minority issues. Succeeding the 1942 campaign during the Yenan period, the 1957 anti-Rightist campaign censured Korean intellectuals for local nationalism, though these individuals were subsequently exonerated in 1962 and again in 1978. The 1958 rectification movement pledged to fight three problems within the Chinese Communist Party—bureaucratism, factionalism, and subjectivism. Its key target in the Korean Chinese community was the national exceptionalism of Koreans, which referred to Koreans' multiple nationalities, their slow assimilation, and their demand for Korean self-determination (Chungguk Chosŏn minjok palchach'wi ch'ongsŏ wiwŏnhoe 1993:111–16). Self-critique forums led by Yanbian University and the Yanbian newspaper invited intellectuals including university faculty, broadcasters, publishers, and literary scholars to "open the inner mind" (sokmaŭm) before the party and expose their deep-seated bourgeois tendencies and reactionary perspectives. Criticism addressed the reluctance to take Chinese nationality, refusal to learn Chinese, discontent over the size and administrative status of self-rule areas, and disapproval of the appointment of Han Chinese officials to administrative positions in self-rule areas. From March 1 to June 29, 1958, about 206,800 big-character posters of self-critique were displayed, and nine hundred officials were sent to factories and farms as forced labor (O T'aeho 1993:129). Although the method of resolving contradictions among people was purportedly through self-critique, the national rectification campaign exposed counterrevolutionary tendencies among Koreans and led to the arrest and persecution of Koreans who were later exonerated (O T'aeho 1993).

The trope of the totality of reason and affect, displayed in the posters at Yanbian University, epitomizes variant forms of subjectivization that emerged from the tension between territorialization and displacement (Minjok munje "ttajŭbo" hoejip 1958). In this trope, Chinese nationality was rational, materialistic, and class specific because acquiring Chinese nationality allowed Koreans to own land; Korean nationality was affective, ethnic national (minjokchŏk), and heartfelt because Korean ethnic nationality remained associated with ancestral and family ties, language, customs, and natural environment. This trope of dual nationality enabled Koreans to challenge their own suspect status as a minority group in China by disparaging Chinese culture as inferior and primitive. Mockery of Chinese culture targeted the inferiority of Chinese dry farming compared to Korean rice farming, the crude nature of Chinese attire, Chinese valuing money over children's education in contrast to Koreans' devotion to education, the deficiency of emotional resonance in the Chinese language, the lack of refinement in dance and musical instruments, backward marriage customs, and China's harsh and barren landscape compared to Korea's beautiful and verdant landscape. One confessed that even if he pledged the PRC as his nation-state, in his heart he considered the DPRK (Democratic People's Republic of Korea) his nation-state because it was the nation-state of his family members and relatives. A Yanbian University student confided about his longing for Chosŏn, given that he was born in Chosŏn and had grandparents and relatives living there. Another student professed thinking of Chosŏn as the nation-state for all Koreans throughout the world, whereas China and other countries are their nation-state merely in a political sense. When the socialist state sought to domesticate Koreans as a minority, Koreans responded by attempting to reconcile their social and political rights by unifying rationality and emotion.

Koreans' discursive construction of their double (or triple) nationality is a postcolonial discourse of vanishing. Exaltation of Koreans' rice farming as their ancestral culture in the process of becoming a national minority suppressed the social and political meaning of their rice farming during the Japanese colonial era. Japan used Koreans' migration, landownership, and nationality in Manchuria as mechanisms for claiming de facto sovereignty in northeast China and for making Manchuria into Japan's imperial gateway to the West. The Chinese warlord governments shared with the Japanese an interest in developing agriculture in the region and utilizing Koreans' expertise in rice farming, and thus they oscillated between prohibiting Koreans from becoming Chinese nationals and imposing Chinese nationality on Koreans (Park 2005). This colonial past became an excess that the narrative of dual nationality could not contain. A self-critique of nationality by a Yanbian University student expressed this excess by doubting the difference between current rule by China and past colonial rule by Japan:

Let's say China is our choguk. Then it should be alright to call Chosŏn *minjokchŏk* (ethnic) choguk. If it isn't, would siblings belong to different countries? Would father and son belong to different countries? This [the state's policy on Korean nationality] is an act of making Koreans into Chinese. Then what's the difference from the Japanese era [when Koreans were coerced to become assimilated by being prevented from speaking their language and forced to choose either Japanese or Chinese nationality]? If China is our nation-state, it is the nation-state where we get leftovers by begging [ŏdŏ mŏkta]. When we lack any commonality with China whether in national sentiment, language, or customs, what else would make China our nation-state? I wrongly used to think this way and say that we cultivate land here so that we eat rice [earn our living here], and that's all.

(*Minjok munje "ttajŭbo" hoejip* 1958:1–2)

The sense of oppression deepened when they observed the undeniable inequality between China and Chosŏn (North Korea). A Yanbian University student confessed to shedding tears and being choked up with emotion on hearing the slogan "Long live the unity of people in China and Chosŏn," wondering "why people of the two countries are not called brothers but friends, when Koreans in Chosŏn and in China were in fact the same minjok. We just have a river between us, and that's all." The seeming indifference of the North Korean state toward Koreans in China did not mitigate this fantasy of Korean ethnic national identity. The North Korean state did not consult with Koreans in China when it agreed to China's naturalization of Koreans as Chinese nationals, nor did it seem to have equal power with the Chinese state. Korean Chinese complained that they were not allowed to live as overseas North Koreans, when Han Chinese in other parts of Asia often lived as overseas Chinese (*hwagyo*). One saw that having multiple choguk was equivalent to having none:

> I used to think of Chosŏnjok [Korean Chinese] as miserable. Why do we live in a foreign country when Chosŏn is minjok for Koreans? When Han Chinese children assaulted Korean children and when Han Chinese pushed Koreans behind and cut in the waiting line in cooperatives to receive goods, it struck me that we are living in a foreign country. We could live freely only if we return to live in Chosŏn. I agree with late Kim Il Sung's will that "those without choguk are like a dog at a funeral."
>
> (*Minjok munje "ttajŭbo" hoejip* 1958:4)

Though Kim's statement referred to Koreans during the colonial era, Korean Chinese related it to their current condition in the late 1950s in China. During their self-critique, they expressed discontent over compulsory collection of their rice and distribution of kaoliang that was the staple for Chinese, the unequal subsidy for Korean schools, and the inadequate infrastructure and resources in Yanji, the capital of the Yanbian Autonomous Prefecture.

SOVEREIGNTY AND DIFFERENCE: THE GREAT LEAP FORWARD

During the Great Leap Forward, the national sovereignty of the Chinese state acquired a universal character in the narrative of history's linear development. The state established its sovereignty not just in the realm of law but in the realm of the social. It envisaged collectivization and industrialization as the means of developing productive forces necessary to make the transition to communism, given that the socialist revolution took place in conditions of underdevelopment. The task of mass production in both agriculture and industries embedded the state's sovereignty in the social sphere. It also created an intrinsic tension in the state's sovereignty itself, as the imperative of developing productive forces countered its pledged proletarian sovereignty in independence from capitalism. Taken as a progressive measure, the strategy of mass production standardized labor processes and homogenized the relationship of the state and the social. Rice farming and other Korean Chinese agricultural practices stood on the fault line of this contradiction in the making of socialism. Through the practice of different labor process and culture Korean Chinese pursued and completed the production goals set by the state.

During the Great Leap Forward, Mao Tse-tung characterized the three stages of the great socialist transition: first, the transformation of the ownership of the means of production that was declared to have been completed in 1956 with collectivization[10]; then, political and ideological transformation over a fairly long period in accordance with the rectification movement's formula of "unity-critique-unity"; and finally technical revolution with the 1958 Great Leap Forward. Pledging to "catch up with and overtake England in fifteen years or a bit longer," the Leap was a utopian project that pursued mass production in agriculture and rapid industrialization (Schram 1989:130–31). Enabled by a mixture of the state's central planning and increased discretionary power and responsibility of the local administration, mass production was expected to develop mechanization and productive forces. According to a *People's Daily* editorial on May 2, 1957, "The principal contradiction in China was no longer between hostile classes, but the contradiction between 'the demand to build an advanced industrial country and the reality of a backward agrarian country,' and others of a similar nature" (Schram 1989:124). The Leap shifted economic policy from its earlier emulation of the Soviet model to moderation through decentralized production and political incentives. While Stalinist practices led to the forced deportation and liquidation of rich peasants, Chinese policy did not consider the relationship between rich and poor peasants as inherently antagonistic. The move toward decentralization and the reformist move in the USSR and Eastern Europe in the mid-1950s encouraged Chinese policy makers to reassess their own historical conditions. Namely, peasants constituted a much larger proportion of the population in China than in the USSR, whereas their per capita output in China was only half that of the USSR in its collectivization period of 1928. To boost production and increase material incentives for peasants, the Chinese state sought to increase investment in light industry that produced consumer goods; it eased control on private markets and expanded discretionary power to provincial and local governments. At the same time the state emphasized the superhuman power of collectives and political zeal in mass mobilization to overcome material and technological constraints. These changes constituted a revision rather than a departure from the Soviet model. They continued until the failure of the Great Leap Forward led to a return to centralized planning that was made to align with the expansion of the market and private initiatives (Perkins 1991; Schram 1991).

By late 1955 Mao had already proclaimed the superiority of big cooperatives, stating that "some places can have one co-op for every township. In a few places, one cooperative can embrace several townships. In many places, of course, one township will contain several co-ops" (Schram 1989:127). In April 1958 the party's Central Committee issued a directive that small cooperatives must be combined into large-scale cooperatives. Communal society was conceived in terms of larger-scale organization so as to create a more effective infrastructure in the countryside, including irrigation works. The Leap accordingly produced huge, machinelike social organizations that were conceivable only because of the state's extensive and coercive apparatus for planning and implementation. In the Korean community the Great Leap Forward began with slogans and fanfare: "To realize in five years what was set to complete in ten years . . . with determination clenching one's teeth," and "double the harvest in five years" (Chungguk Chosŏn minjok palchach'wi ch'ongsŏ wiwŏnhoe 1993:178). Korean Chinese transformed advanced cooperatives into giant people's cooperatives that were called "golden bridges to communism." Between August 20 and September 30, 1958, across the entire Korean Yanbian Autonomous Prefecture 172,388 peasant households transformed 921 advanced cooperatives into 78 people's cooperatives, with an average size of 2,021 households and 10,855 households as the largest. According to a Korean Chinese official history, this reorganization created a military-like organization of production processes, with agricultural production collectivizing everyday life and becoming like warfare (Chungguk Chosŏn minjok palchach'wi ch'ongsŏ wiwŏnhoe 1993:181–2; Choi Sangch'ŏl 1997).

It did not take long, however, for the failure of collectivized agricultural production to become obvious. For example, in 1957 the state increased one co-op's target by 1,193 kg while its production decreased by 7,738 kg, causing the co-op to reduce its per capita grain allocation to 188 kg. Catastrophic famine and floods in 1960 aggravated this food crisis. Speaking of the failure of the Great Leap Forward, Mao stated that when the state set production quotas, it was concerned only with meeting the need for resources, such as steel, without realistically assessing the costs of meeting this need. The Leap's failure called for a more realistic timeline for achieving economic development. In late 1959 the state eased the push for collectivization. It ordered people's cooperatives to return savings to banks and credit unions, give seized assets back to previous individual owners, and allow peasants to own fruit trees around their houses, raise livestock, and engage in activities that would generate secondary income. The drive to produce economic and technical miracles continued during the Cultural Revolution (Schram 1989:133).

In the Leap, the labor process was homogenized through mass production and collective zeal. Competition among collectives intensified to meet harvest quotas and earn the title of "heroes." For instance, during the summer of 1958, Antu County in Yanbian pledged to harvest more than 50,000 kg per hectare because other areas in Jilin Province pledged 25,000 kg to 50,000 kg. As reports to the government inflated the size of the harvest, larger amounts had to be handed over. Staples were reduced to a bare minimum, and in the end there was nothing left to feed oxen (Chu Tŏkhae ŭi ilsaeng 1987:281). In November 1958 the Yanbian government ordered that 60 percent of all agricultural land be plowed to a depth of 60 cm to 90 cm. Soon people throughout Yanbian began to plow their agricultural fields even before completing the harvest. Lower-level authorities emphasized early and fast completion and mobilized the people to plow the fields before the land froze. This rush to plow the land in preparation for spring planting interrupted the autumn harvest. The push to plow early and deeply at first increased production but later led to unharvested crops being lost to snow and ice. Detonators used to loosen soil in frozen fields created holes a meter deep and the size of a house. The following spring when water was let in to prepare the fields for rice seedlings, the fields became like reservoirs with water engulfing oxen and people. It was reported that oxen drowned in water-filled fields, and people nearly lost their lives (Chu Tŏkhae ŭi ilsaeng 1987:281; Choi Sangch'ŏl 1997:284). Moreover, in September 1958 when the state began a drive to increase steel production, provinces competed against one another, pledging to meet twelve-year production targets in seven or nine years. On September 9, 1958, an editorial in the Yanbian Daily promoted small-scale steel production and encouraged households to fulfill their duty by melting their iron pots. Soon all organizations in Yanbian, from administrative units, factories, mining enterprises, firms, farms, and schools to military corps, were caught up by the frenzy of smelting iron to produce steel. Even a paper mill collected iron pots from workers' households and neighborhoods and built a furnace to melt them. In one county, nine thousand people formed "iron corps," and many people's cooperatives organized several thousands of iron corps to build hundreds of makeshift furnaces. However, lacking the necessary facilities and expertise, such furnaces could not smelt the quality of iron needed to make steel. Nevertheless, they reported to the authorities that they were producing "steel" (Choi Sangch'ŏl 1997:269, 282–84).

Chu Tŏkhae, the head of the Yanbian government, criticized as "fanaticism" the tendency of the people to comply with the state's orders without regard to their merit and even to compete with one another in their eagerness to comply. Instead, Chu based the development of the Korean Chinese community on the principle of "equal but different," distancing it from the party's uniform approach to agricultural production and consumption. The revolutionary past of Koreans, as well as his stellar record as a revolutionary, likely emboldened him to make such a strong critique of state policies (*Chu Tŏkhae ŭi ilsaeng* 1987). Speaking of equality but difference between ethnic and national groups, he stated, "We shouldn't speak of equality only in a political sense, but in actuality [*sasilsang*]." Accordingly, he simultaneously consolidated Koreans' self-rule, which led to accusations during the Cultural Revolution that he was a local nationalist and was attempting to create an "independent kingdom" of Koreans. During the Leap, he expanded the self-rule area for Koreans based on CCP instructions that counties and districts adjacent to an existing self-rule area could be incorporated into it.[11] In an effort to improve facilities for Korean education and culture, he expanded Korean educational institutions at all levels and created Korean newspapers, broadcast media, and publishers. He also expanded Korean national industries in Yanbian, for example, bringing a factory from Shenyang to Tumen to produce rubber shoes for Koreans. Chu also arranged to make it easier for Koreans to visit North Korea and for small-scale trade between the two countries such as the import of seafood from North Korea.

Chu also implemented a production system that reflected Korean styles and customs in production. He emphasized production of rice and fruit, staples of Koreans, and constructed water reservoirs to increase production. He also built a factory to produce farm implements that Koreans had invented for cultivating steep mountainous areas. When he observed that the health of oxen deteriorated from 1958 to 1961 with a 50 percent mortality rate for newborn oxen, Chu urged a return to traditional Korean ways of raising them, namely, giving them boiled grass and warm water and keeping them warm. When this was criticized as local nationalism, he responded by asking whether oxen themselves should be subject to the national question (*minjok munje*). Chu was later called "the king of oxen" during the Cultural Revolution, when raising female oxen was condemned as an act of spreading the seeds of capitalism.

The critique of collectivization was central to Chu's reforms in Yanbian. In the late 1950s, Chu censured the collective dining hall system, pointing out lessons from the USSR's experience and emphasizing a realistic approach instead of uniform application of the principle. Chu argued that collective dining removed individual accountability and responsibility. In his critique, when collective dining halls were first set up, people ate and played as if every day were a feast, eating rice three times a day, killing cows and pigs for meals, and making drinks every other day. Singing and dancing of drunken people disrupted life in the countryside. It was not long before a collective dining hall ran out of resources—even grain and porridge. Moreover, collective meals did not suit all individuals' taste, so Koreans tended to bring cooked rice and other dishes from a collective dining hall to eat at home with Korean dishes prepared at home. While Koreans usually raised pigs and dogs by feeding them leftovers, collective preparation and dining meant few leftovers for domestic animals. This in turn affected households' ability to earn money on the side (puŏp). In addition, even when eating in the dining halls, they still had to make fires in the kitchen to warm up the house for at least five months during winter, because Koreans typically heated their home by passing heats from the kitchen fireplace to the floors throughout the house (ontol). Chu invoked the principle of realism (silsagusi), saying that "no matter what others do, we have to act on the basis of actual conditions in our region." Under his leadership, collective dining halls disappeared in the Yanbian countryside.

Chu was not the first leader to oppose the state's policy of centralized and homogenized production. In October 1957, Pak Kyŏngok, the twenty-year-old director of the National Affairs Committee in Lioniang Province, was accused of being Rightist and demoted to working in an automobile factory in Shenyang after proposing to delay the integration of Han Chinese and Korean agricultural cooperatives. On observing that Korean peasants' income declined after integration, he concluded in an official report that the united cooperatives of Koreans and Han Chinese were detrimental to the development of productive forces because of differences between Koreans and Han Chinese in their production methods and life habits. But Chu offered a more systematic critique of the social reforms. He criticized as fanaticism the competition to realize communism "in one breath" (tansume) through the homogenization of farming and lifestyles. According to his critique, fanaticism coexisted with people's avoidance of labor and accountability. In his observation, people in cooperatives worked as if roaming in a group or like herded sheep. When a bell rang, people came out and went to the fields walking in single file. The practices of collective labor did not, according to Chu, register any differences in an individual's strength and skill, making everyone do the same work and distributing an equal portion to each person. Accordingly, cooperatives fed lazy people, destroyed agriculture, and turned productive agricultural fields into wastelands, where rice seedlings were overgrown with grasses. He reported that people left lamps on in the field at night in fear of criticism and punishment, while sleeping at home. When people could not harvest their quota, they reported that the unharvested crop was run down by people and eaten up by livestock. Chu refuted such practices as "the principle of averaging," which ignored the different inputs of individuals.

He instead employed a policy of wage differentials that reflected the labor inputs and interests of the cooperative's members. He implemented a cooperative system of production in Wangqing County that divided rice fields into small plots and assigned the responsibility for each plot to a household, with directives on the type and quality of work, quota for the harvest, and amount of time for labor and compensation. Wages were based on an assessment of their labor. This change led each member of the household to work in the fields voluntarily from early morning until late evening. Even those who had not participated in the cooperative's labor force, such as the elderly and students, assisted other household members to complete their assigned tasks (Chu Tŏkhae ŭi ilsaeng 1987:319–21; Kim Tonghwa 1993).

The socialist revolution pledged to abolish the law of value, or the extraction of surplus value of labor for capital accumulation. This socialist ideal, however, contradicted the goal of rapid economic development that required the extraction of surplus on a massive scale by homogenizing the labor process. When the Leap confronted a decline in production, wasted resources and labor power, and lack of individual motivation, Chu redeemed the law of value in the Korean community by applying the principle of "equal but different" as the rule of distribution by labor. Chu's coordination of production and distribution imposed a more precise socially necessary labor time on Korean peasants. The paradox is that by abandoning the homogenization of production and distribution, Chu's reforms expedited the production process in yielding the desired increase of production. The Korean question during the process of making the socialist revolution starkly exposes the spectrality of the social: the imposition of homogeneous socialist reforms did not help the state attain its goal of rapid industrial development, and the difference and unevenness of social relations did not disappear. Under Chu's leadership, which later was condemned as counterrevolutionary, agricultural production and animal husbandry in Yanbian were kept at a distance from the universal approach of socialism, and economic development was pursued by recognizing differences in production and distribution.

The framing of Koreans as counterrevolutionary is more than an inversion in the Lacanian sense of transferring the impossibility of making socialist revolution onto an external enemy (see Žižek 2005). That is, Koreans were more than scapegoats who were blamed for interfering with or blocking the Chinese revolution. Instead, Koreans were symptomatic of the heterogeneity in social relations. In the drive for mass production, the state subordinated diverse farming and economic practices to a homogenized production and distribution system. The actualization of socialism was tumultuous, not necessarily because revolution came "too early," but rather because revolutionaries and policy makers were unable to recognize multiple temporalities in production and social life. Their inability arose from the state's class-based categorization of social relations that was as inoperative in China as it was in the USSR. In the 1960s the Chinese state sought to rethink class categories by taking into account family origin and political behavior (White 1976). Despite such efforts, an axiomatic class approach to social relations made it difficult to comprehend reality in this locus of socialist transformation. When Trotsky found state power to be necessary for establishing the material conditions of socialist society, the class-based approach to history ill-served this effort in China. Chu's adoption of the principle of distribution according to one's contribution of labor demonstrated the predicament confronting the task of permanent revolution. Koreans responded to the homogenizing forces of the socialist state with an epochal transformation of their ethnicity and nationality; they constructed their social differences and unevenness in farming and labor as national and ethnic distinctions.

The Great Leap Forward reconstituted democracy in the pledged transition to socialism. The Leap elevated mass production with an invocation of collectivity and homogeneity. Its politics of democracy rooted in the reorganization of the production shows that the discussion of democracy in socialist society is not to be completely subscribed to the state's bureaucracy and the rise of the new ruling class, as was debated in the USSR. Trotsky recognized the necessary power of the state to enforce revolutionary reforms, while counting on proletariat politics to protect the class nature of the state. Trotsky (2007:39, 130–31) rejected the Mensheviks' assertion that compulsory labor was always unproductive labor and that democracy was opposed to terrorism. According to Trotsky, violence is not a necessary characteristic of revolution but often accompanies it because revolution entails a radical transformation of society. Trotsky considered universal suffrage and the parliamentary system to be "the metaphysics" of democracy that sanctifies them as "unalterable and sacred things-in-themselves" and detaches democracy from historical meaning, which I think he conveys the importance of the social. Social relations of production and distribution in China, as in the USSR, were pulled in diametrically opposite directions: on the one hand was the imperative of developing productive forces through an increase of surplus value and its reinvestment in technology and the means of production; and on the other, the fundamental task of equality in production and distribution through the abolition of the law of value. This repressed yet commanding imperative to overcome underdevelopment refused to disappear but continued to contradict the socialist ethos of democracy. In response the Chinese state resorted to two disciplinary techniques: purges and mass appeals to ethics and honor. During the Leap compulsory labor was given a democratic character by mass appeals to political honor and superhuman power in overcoming material constraints. One's moral duty was to comply with the state's policies, given that the state was the agent of a truly democratic society. In this way, ethics replaced politics during China's socialist construction. Ethics and violence were the two conjunctural instances in the state's politics of democracy that bore on the contradiction between the imperatives of developing productive forces and establishing equality in social relations. Mobilization of political submission through enforcement of honor and purges was intended to fill this gap between the change in property ownership and the birth of a new democratic society.

The debate over the state, labor, and democracy concerns the dialectics of the universal and the particular, given that the debate was an effort to reconcile an axiom of socialism with historical conditions. Korean Chinese turned democracy into performative politics under its historical conditions, namely, the postcoloniality of their existence and the state's drive for rapid development. Invoking the principle of equality with difference, Koreans used the politics of identity to define new social relations that did not conform to the forceful norms of the Chinese state. Whereas the state sought to normalize the moral concept of peoplehood and the idea of belongingness by invoking absolute equality and superhuman zeal, Koreans in China diverged from state-prescribed norms by claiming their rice farming and animal husbandry as ethnic practices and invoking the principle of equal but different. Such representations simultaneously displaced their troubled colonial history of farming in China linked to Japanese imperialism, as happened during the national rectification movement. Yet, the primordialization of Koreans' ethnic national character came full circle. The struggle during the Cultural Revolution closed this performative space of critique when Koreans' present identity was fixed to their earlier colonial ties with the Japanese and when Chinese nationalism essentialized Koreans' ethnic nationality and presumed their exclusive allegiance to North Korea. Stripped of its historical specificities, Koreans' past and present were divested of the political and economic processes of their colonial and anticolonial politics, not to mention their participation in the Chinese civil war on the side of the communists; and Koreans were portrayed as a menace to the Chinese revolution. Even the self-rule of Koreans was threatened at the zenith of the Cultural Revolution.

VIOLENCE AND REPETITION:
THE CULTURAL REVOLUTION

Upon the failure of the Great Leap Forward and the five-year drought in northeast China, a compounded sense of crisis laid the ground for rethinking the place of the socialist present in history. The Cultural Revolution was another moment in which the contradiction between the state's sovereignty and its material conditions once again raised questions about the development of history. During the Cultural Revolution, the revolutionary vision of the transition to socialism and communism confronted the issues of putatively feudal, colonial, and capitalist elements in society. The corresponding gap between the society and the state was to be overcome through the regeneration of a genuine politics to end bureaucratization of the state. Its struggle soon swirled into the reformation of social relations in the renewed pledge to move history forward. This conjuncture of history and power is inscribed on the Korean Chinese, who were condemned as local nationalist separatists like any other ethnic minority, although from the colonial period to the Cultural Revolution they zealously participated in the communist movement.[12] An adequate analysis of their experience needs to shift from the problematic of Chinese nationalism and ethnic separatism, which is the framework of the current scholarship on the experience of national minorities in the Cultural Revolution (Shakya 1999; Brown 2006; Goldstein, Jiao, and Lhundrup 2009), to the problematic of the state's power and the historical transition. Korean Chinese acquired "nonidentity" through which the revolution itself was interpreted. Constructed as the antithesis of revolution, Korean Chinese were decried as feudal remnants, underground Kuomintang elements, colonial turncoats, capitalists, and Soviet and North Korean spies. Remembering as an intraethnocide, Korean Chinese struggled among themselves against amorphous ghosts, which fed paranoia and obscene violence in everyday life in Yanbian. Korean Chinese signified noncontemporaneous elements in the present social relations that contradicted the purportedly linear time of revolutionary history.

According to a compiled history of Korean Chinese in China, the Cultural Revolution was advanced on the basis of the theory of continuous revolution under the dictatorship of the proletariat (Chungguk Chosŏn minjok palchach'wi ch'ongsŏ wiwŏnhoe 1993:290). According to Mao Tse-tung, many in power sought to restore capitalism and had followers in organizations throughout the country. In his assessment, at least one-third of the leadership was not under the control of the proletariat class, and despite many political movements since 1949, problems were not resolved because those in power continued with their bourgeois thinking. The Cultural Revolution was a mass struggle aimed at wresting power from those who had it. In the reparation language of the 1980s, the compiled history of Korean Chinese states that the leaders and officials framed as capitalists during the Cultural Revolution were in fact heroes of the socialist revolution who had dedicated their lives to the Chinese revolution. This compiled history of Korean Chinese in China traces the social cause of the Cultural Revolution to the law of development of socialist society. In its declaration, the principles of distribution by labor and the provision of material interest of individuals, which were condemned outright to be capitalist during the Cultural Revolution, were in fact in agreement with Marxist and Leninist principles and socialist principles. It concludes that such gruesome errors were made because of the short history of the socialist movement (Chungguk Chosŏn minjok palchach'wi ch'ongsŏ wiwŏnhoe 1993:279–91).

The Cultural Revolution began in Yanbian with editorials on June 2, 1966, in the *Yanbian Daily* and the *People's Daily* in support of students at Beijing University. On June 16, students, mostly Korean Chinese, at Yanbian University and Yanbian Agricultural Institute declared their support for students at Nanjing University, posting two hundred big-character posters in just half a day. Students in the city tore down store signboards written in Korean and with motifs of Korean culture, attacked women wearing short skirts, and burned Korean cultural artifacts such as the traditional sedan chair. During the ferocious period of struggle from this initial moment until 1968, four major organizations of the Red Guards engaged in a power struggle, contending over two issues: the linkage with students from China proper and the protection of Chu Tŏkhae and other key Korean Chinese officials. On June 12, 1966, Red Guards from Beijing began to arrive in Yanji to make the link. Citing the central government's call to engage in the struggle in one's own place, Chu Tŏkhae, the head of the Yanbian Prefecture, directed students from Beijing to return and instructed local students not to link themselves with students from outside. Cho Namgi, who was the highest-ranking Korean Chinese in the northeast military division and became a crucial protector of Chu, also supported Chu's directive, citing a security issue because Yanbian was a border region. In opposition to this directive, the 8.27 Red Rebels was formed by students in various schools, including Yanbian University, Yanbian Agricultural Institute, Yanbian Medical Institute, the Art Institute, and middle schools. The 8.27 Red Rebels launched a wholesale critique of officials in the government, educational institutions, and all other important official and public institutions in their struggle against capitalist reformers and "the Four Olds" in customs, culture, habits, and ideas. Formed by former and retired soldiers in Yanji on January 8, 1967, the Red Flag Military Alliance challenged the 8.27 Red Rebels, resulting in a series of violent clashes (Chŏng P'anryong 1993).

The alleged struggle against ethnic local nationalism in Yanbian intensified with the arrival of Mao Yuanhsin, Mao Tse-tung's nephew, from Beijing and Red Guards from Harbin on January 25, 1967. The struggle against local nationalists staged the purge of Chu Tŏkhae and other key officials as a central issue. Accordingly, some in the 8.27 and Red Flag groups created new organizations: the Red Revolutionary Committee, called the New 8.27 Group under Mao Yuanhsin's leadership, which enacted the purge of Korean Chinese officials and intellectuals; and the Peasant and Workers Revolutionary Committee, which was called the Protectionist Group (pohwangp'a) against the purge. The four groups competed to control administrative offices and key organizations, seize accused leaders for interrogation, and mobilize the masses in the process. The groups sought the army's support and stole its weapons, as they maneuvered through what was soon called a civil war. After the organizations wrested Chu Tŏkhae from each other, in April 1967 the central government ordered the military in Yanbian to secure Chu and placed him in a safe house in Beijing, where he was subject to an investigation of all his revolutionary activities until his death in 1972 (*Chu Tŏkhae ŭi ilsaeng* 1987; Kok and Chung 2004; Ryu Eun Kyu 2007). The charges against Chu Tŏkhae during the Cultural Revolution and his complete vindication in 1978 focus on whether his practice of increasing production and distributing according to labor inputs was capitalist or socialist. Chu Tŏkhae was renounced for practicing capitalist revisionism that "placed the emphasis on production over the study of Mao Tse-tung." He was accused of saying in 1957 that socialism was accomplished, that class struggle had ended, and that landlords and an absolute majority of bourgeois intellectuals were already reformed, all of which contradicted Mao's continuous struggle to realize socialism.[13] He was persecuted for suspicion of having collaborated with the Japanese; he was also condemned for supporting the thesis of Koreans having multiple nationalities and for promoting the independence of Koreans from China, though he, on the contrary, appealed to Koreans to adopt Chinese nationality and created self-rule in China.[14]

A decisive moment in the Cultural Revolution was the armed clash occurring August 2 through 4, 1967, between the New 8.27 Group and the Protectionist Group in the city of Yanji. During this fighting the New 8.27 Group

FIGURE 5.1 Struggle against Chu Tŏkhae in 1967. Photo by Hwang Yŏngrim. Courtesy of Ryu Eun Kyu.

killed thirty members of the Protectionist Group and attacked a group of Koreans on an island adjacent to North Korea, forcing them across the border into North Korea. As the 1978 official investigation concluded, this clash was the backdrop of a fabricated report about the outbreak of civil war in Yanbian, which the 8.27 group under Mao Yuanhsin's instructions spread throughout Yanbian and the rest of the country on August 9, 1967.[15] According to an instigator who confessed in 1978 in an official investigation, a flier with the headline "Fire, Fire, and Fire, and Blood, Blood, and Blood" was instrumental in spreading the rumor of the civil war in Yanbian. Including fake photographs, it concocted the story that Koreans under instructions from North Korea engaged in rebellion, had set fire to buildings and houses in Yanji, and armed with the bats and knives had killed and kidnapped hundreds of people.[16]

The falsified reports on the Korean rebellion appealed to the people to pro-tect the revolution from counterrevolutionary attempts spreading in Yanbian as throughout Eastern Europe. In 1968 the struggle added more charges against Koreans, namely, those of being spies and traitors. Twenty espionage rings were claimed to have been discovered, including the Chosŏn Unifica-tion Construction Committee, the underground labor party, and an under-ground national army. In this incident, about three thousand were accused of being spies (from both Koreas); two hundred died from beatings or suicide; eight hundred were crippled from torture; forty were formally charged; and two hundred were reprimanded at the administrative- or party-level. Also identified during that year throughout Yanbian were 1,453 members of the underground Kuomintang Party; 14 among them were either stoned to death or committed suicide, and 181 were crippled and 294 injured from torture. In a cooperative in Antu County alone, 264 people were charged as class enemies of the proletariat, and 29 of those charged died from beatings. In a coopera-tive in Yanji County 170 people were identified as class enemies within a few days, and 20 of them either died or committed suicide during interrogation (Chungguk Chosŏn minjok palchach'wi ch'ongsŏ wiwŏnhoe 1993:306–7). In April 1968 alone, 175 Korean Chinese officials—or about 70 percent of Korean Chinese in security offices, prosecutors' offices, and courts in Yanbian—were indicted as foreign spies (Choi Sangch'ŏl 1997:330–31). During the Cultural Revolution in Yanbian, tens of thousands were identified as spies, traitors, or underground North Korean party members, and two thousand died of beatings, were crippled from torture, and/or imprisoned. From 1969 to 1973, the campaign to study Mao's thought and to go to the countryside continued. After 1970, agricultural and industrial production was given some emphasis as the violence diminished (Yŏnbyŏn tangsa hakhoe 1989).

The obscene violence during the Cultural Revolution denotes that the rev-olution lost its positive attributes beyond the pledge of mass struggle against bureaucracy. Scholarship on the Cultural Revolution attributes the intensity and banality of the violence to factionalism and collective zeal. I shift the anal-ysis to the relationship between violence and identity. The compiled history of Korean Chinese is filled with details of systematic and ritualistic violence against Korean Chinese (Chungguk Chosŏn minjok palchach'wi ch'ongsŏ wiwŏnhoe 1993:354–405). The accused were made to stand on platforms erected in the street so that they would be visible to far-flung crowds. They wore big triangular hats made of steel. Their heads were shaved and their faces painted black. To make them objects of further ridicule, they were forced to bend over 90 degrees during their public interrogation and display. They were

FIGURE 5.2 Big-character posters in 1967 that criticize the Peasant and Workers Revolutionary Committee. Photo by Hwang Yŏngrim. Courtesy of Ryu Eun Kyu.

kicked in the knees and thighs. The force of the blows knocked them off the platform. According to Appadurai (1998), ritualized and repeated violence produces ethnic identity, not vice versa: The inscription of violence on bodies of neighbors and women in cases of ethnic genocide, such as in Rwanda in the 1970s, produces certainty in the form of ethnic identities, when globalization dispossesses existing social and official group categories of concrete meanings and feeds uncertainty. However, the Korean Chinese experience was different. Violence repressed their experience and identity rather than making it concrete. Deleuze (1994) theorizes that one represses because one repeats, not vice versa. Similarly, Korean Chinese experience denotes repression through repetition. Their different experiences in rice farming and other social practices of labor and customs were interpreted as threatening to

FIGURE 5.3 Big-character posters in 1967 that criticize the Peasant and Workers Revolutionary Committee. Photo by Hwang Yŏngrim. Courtesy of Ryu Eun Kyu.

the socialist project; indeed, revolutionaries (both Chinese and Koreans) throughout the socialist revolution, including the Cultural Revolution, refused to acknowledge the contradiction between the imperative of pursuing rapid industrialization in the name of developing productive forces and the socialist axiom of democracy. The revolutionaries resorted to repeated violence through which they repressed the contradiction and were unable to recognize heterogeneity or noncontemporaneous contemporaneity in social relations arising from the contradiction.

The repeated violence against Korean Chinese entwined each singular moment into historical repetition. In the anti-Minsaengdan incident of 1932–1936, Koreans were singled out as pro-Japanese infiltrators into Chinese revolutionary organizations. Even minor deviations from norms were regarded as signs of the influence of Minsaengdan, the pro-Japanese organization formed by Koreans. The slightest hint of criticism of the party and random events such as an accidental firing of a gun, misspelled words in reports, and oversight in cooking a meal were treated as signs of support for the Minsaengdan (Park 2005:222). During the anti-Rightist campaign of 1957, Korean students, schoolteachers, actors, and party officials were charged with being remnants of pro-Japanese colonizers and bourgeoisie on the basis of such minor mishaps. A similar paranoia pervaded everyday life during the Cultural Revolution. The absurdity of the violence can still spark animated and emotional debate among Korean Chinese in China today, even though most of them remain averse to speaking about the Cultural Revolution. During my visit to Yanji in June 2007, dinner guests recounted various incidents: being prosecuted for accidentally writing "Overthrow Long Live Chairman Mao" in the midst of writing repeatedly "Overthrow Revisionism, Long Live Chairman Mao"; committing suicide or self-chastisement over mistakenly shouting "Overthrow Chairman Mao" after long hours of chanting "Long Live Chairman Mao"; being accused of disrespect for referring to Mao's photo on a picket as a thing; and being tortured for inadvertently putting out a cigarette through Mao's eye in a newspaper photo. P'ungnang, a volume of the compiled history of Korean Chinese, records other examples: On the streets the Red Guards cut the long hair of women and removed high heels from women's shoes. Thousands of shoes in a Changchun factory were burned after being condemned as antirevolutionary signs on the grounds that their soles were shaped like the Chinese character for "people" (ren) and thus an insult to the people. In both the popular memory and official history, the obscenity of violence is often likened to the anti-Minsaengdan incident (Chŏng P'anryong 1993).

Korean Chinese were given various names during the Chinese Revolution: local (ethnic) nationalists, capitalists, feudal remnants, underground Kuomintang elements, traitors, foreign spies, or chapkwisin. These charges illustrate that Korean Chinese were suspected and condemned as enemies at all times in the past and present. They suggest that Korean Chinese ethnic nationality was not fixed but contested over again. At first glance, the charge of local nationalism pronounced Korean Chinese as ethnic Koreans. For instance, in its booklet on one hundred sins of bourgeois intellectuals, the Yanbian University's Revolutionary Committee, formed in December 1968 with its top three posts held by Han Chinese, charged Korean Chinese intellectuals with ethnic nationalism. Korean intellectuals were incriminated for opposing Mao Tse-tung's orders, by insisting on classroom studies over learning from labor and political struggles, discriminating against students from poor and working-class backgrounds, and refusing to study Mao's thought and display his portrait. In addition, they also were condemned for promoting Korean language and culture over those of Han Chinese, as well as expanding the study of Korean history and Korean Chinese history modeled after the Kim Il Sung University's curriculum. The long-standing controversy over Korean self-determination was brought to the fore once again. Chu Tŏkhae and Lim Manho, respectively president and vice president of Yanbian University, were accused of following instructions from Kim Il Sung to build an independent Korean kingdom and become foreign spies (Yanbian daxue geming weiyuan hui jiaoyu geming zu 1969).

However, despite the appearance that Korean Chinese identity had returned to its ethnic roots, the very struggle over and among Korean Chinese demonstrated that the issue of their dual nationality had not been resolved. Repeated contestation of their dual nationality, though new each time, results not from clashes between Chinese and ethnic nationalisms per se but from concrete historical conditions. During the land reform, the anti-Rightist struggle, and the rectification movement, Koreans bound their ethnic nationality with their social life by narrating their Chinese and Korean identities in terms of the unity of reason and affect. During the Great Leap Forward, they reworked the socialist notion of community through the construction of their ethnic social life. The Cultural Revolution laid bare the tension in these forms of dual nationality. Moreover it brought their repressed colonial history to the forefront of politics in the present. During the Japanese occupation, Yanbian (eastern Manchuria) was the stronghold of both Japanese imperialist power and anti-Japanese resistance by Koreans in the 1920s, which laid the ground for a purge of Korean communists in the CCP in the anti-Minsaengdan incident. This tumultuous colonial history was repressed by the earnest participation of Koreans in the CCP's liberation struggle and the PRC's foundational period, only to resurface during the Cultural Revolution. In addition, the emerging Cold War, and particularly China's growing tension with the USSR and North Korea, framed Korean Chinese as traitors and counterrevolutionaries.

The repeated construction of Korean Chinese as counterrevolutionaries is a political and historical question rather than an ethnic and national question. The charges against Korean Chinese signify the disrupted order of historical time set by the vision of continuous revolution in China. Notwithstanding—or perhaps because of—their ethnic nationality, Korean Chinese became a hieroglyph for the disorderly present that diverged from a linear projection of the transition from capitalism to socialism to communism. In Koselleck's terms (2004), the Cultural Revolution was a moment of "crisis," which authorized an interpretation of the present through a new ordering of its relationship with the past and the present. As inferred from their superfluous label as counter-revolutionaries, Korean Chinese acquired "nonidentity," that is, anything and everything that is not revolutionary. Given that Korean Chinese represent phantoms of the old and new history, their repression enabled the Chinese revolution to construct the totality of history in the stage-by-stage historical transition. Korean Chinese constituted an intrinsic link between the present condition and the aspired historical totality in China.

The imperative of historical repetition has a social origin in the Chinese revolution. Socialism was treated as if it were an ossified ideology or objectified as a homogenizing project. This totalizing view of the social became an uncanny social imperative when the historical actualization of socialism contradicted the idea of socialism by sustaining the extraction and accumulation of surplus labor. Collectivization and standardized large-scale production under the state's control imposed socially necessary labor by invoking the utopian notion of equality and freedom. Revolutionary reforms equated social homogenization with the universal path toward the socialist transition to communism. This contradiction of the ideal and reality denotes the contradiction between the state's sovereignty and its material conditions in social relations. Mao's permanent revolution was not equipped to recognize the multiple temporalities of everyday life. When ethnic differences in farming, commodity production, and material incentives were considered instances of noncontemporaneous contemporaneity and thus treated as threats to socialist transition, they were simply called "mixed demons." Heterogeneity in social relations acquired the status of mischievous ghosts from the past that haunted the revolution. The memory of the Cultural Revolution as intraethnocide is comprehensible within the repeated political process: uncertainty and terror spread especially among Koreans, intensifying conflict and violence in the act of negating their recurrent political rejection by the socialist state. My analysis maps this logic of the political—the sovereignty and its violence—onto the philosophical question on the historical present, arising from the tumultuous historical process of realizing the socialist mode of production and transforming social relations accordingly.

CONCLUSION

This chapter has approached the violence of the Cultural Revolution and its current memory of intraethnocide among Koreans as a crticial issue involving history and power. Despite its scale and intensity of violence, the Cultural Revolution was not a single, exceptional event. Instead, it was a new instance of the repeated violence throughout the Chinese revolution. In socialist China the continuous pursuit of rapid industrialization became a key and yet repressed imperative in the social. Each phase in Chinese socialist history, from collectivization to the national rectification movement, to the Great Leap Forward, to the Cultural Revolution, enacted a different strategy to resolve the contradiction of the socialist ideal and its historical actualization. Violence marks the Korean experience of the Chinese revolution at different historical moments. If considered separately, violence in each historical moment points out political theology that turns the state's sovereignty into the sublime. In my analysis, the repetition of violence points to the imperative of the political (the state's sovereignty) that represses in and through repetition the contradiction between the socialist ideal and its historical actualization. The repeated attempt did not resolve the contradiction but instead enabled the regime to maintain and manage it. When the existence of nonsocialist social relations clashed with the state's espoused linear historical transition, the state sought to homogenize the social by mobilizing the utopian ideal, collective zeal, and violence. In this repetition, socialism loses totality in its historical actualization. Socialism is a political form whose historical actualization involves representation, interpretation, identification, and recognition as such in order to be implemented in each historical moment. Repetition of the representation in a new way made socialist actualization too strenuous and unpredictable to be denounced as a failure or a twin of state capitalism, as has been argued in the scholarship on socialist economy. Rather, what is noted as failure or similarity with capitalist economies of the twentieth century is itself "the real." This real imperative was graspable only in the shadows of repeated measures to overcome it and in its continued repression through violence.

In the social, the real manifests as heterogeneity or multiple temporalities arising from the coexistence of different relations of production and social life. Such elements of noncontemporaneous contemporaneity in the social were named capitalist, feudal, colonial, counterrevolutionary, the old, or chapkwisin. The staged struggles against all of these putatively nonrevolutionary elements did not bring a dialectical overcoming into a genuine socialism. Instead, the repeated struggle hid the real imperative of Chinese socialist history. Given that socialism was represented and repressed as such, Korean Chinese acquired "nonidentity" as others whose reification helped the regime maintain the appearance of a new social whole and of historical progress. The continuous objectification of and violence against Korean Chinese are not reducible to an ethnic national clash with Chinese nationalism, as depicted in official history; rather they are inscribed to the impossible task of homogenizing the social without the use of violence. Violence against Korean Chinese did not turn the uncertainty of realizing socialism into concrete identities. It instead helped to obscure the real.

As individuals remember the Cultural Revolution as intraethnocide, the social origins of the Cultural Revolution evaporate in their recollections. Instead, the memory of violence, especially the memory of the rituals of violence, comes to the fore. The official language of reparation links the "heinous errors" of the socialist past to an incorrect understanding of the law of socialist development. However, both individual recollections and official history routinely focus on details of violence without sufficient contextualization, let alone linking the Cultural Revolution to earlier moments of the Chinese revolution when similar charges were made against Koreans. Whether in China proper or other parts of the world, the politics of reparation represents those who were wrongly accused and killed as victims. But Korean Chinese even seem unable to represent themselves as victims of their putative nation-state. Instead biographies of the wrongly accused exalt them as "heroic martyrs," who remained devoted to the revolution despite being forsaken by it. For Korean Chinese, the Cultural Revolution remains a repressed history rather than an object of nostalgia.

The deeply repressed memory of the Cultural Revolution surfaces in unexpected ways as an irreplaceable mode for conveying the experiences of Korean Chinese as undocumented migrant laborers in South Korea. Remembering the past becomes a mode of living—both for making sense of mediated experience and for registering the effects of forces beyond one's control. The official narrative of reparation of the Cultural Revolution is more Hegelian: overcoming past errors in order to foster reconciliation and social unity. In contrast, the Korean Chinese recollection expressed in South Korea unconsciously exists more like Benjamin's montage of unreconciled meanings and desires. It is an act of making sense of the present rather than an act of resolving past history. It is also an embodiment of commodification, which involves discursive construction of identity, representation, and other symbolic performances. It offers a template and reference with which Korean Chinese temporalize their reified relations with South Koreans.

The memory of the Cultural Revolution as intraethnocide among Korean Chinese is an inverted trauma of the impossibility of becoming a national minority in socialist China, whether by participating in the liberation struggle, constructing a dual nationality in totality, surpassing production quotas, or driving out phantoms. The experience of Korean Chinese exposes an insurmountable tension between socialist internationalism and the nation-state's sovereignty. In the present historical moment, their recollection of intraethnocide captures another trauma, namely, the rejection and violence they experience in South Korea. In this narrative the lapsed time between previous moments of the Chinese revolution and the current moment disappears. The recollection is an unconscious interruption of historical temporalities evoked by China's official language of privatization as reparation of socialist wrongs and by South Korea's language of reparation of colonial wrongs. Just as a rupture between past capitalism and present socialism was unattainable during the socialist revolutionary period, the relationship of past socialism and present capitalism must not be considered a rupture, whether in terms of reparation or the transition to capitalism.

PART III
PEACE AND HUMAN RIGHTS

6

KOREAN UNIFICATION AS
CAPITALIST HEGEMONY

Unification politics in South Korea (and the United States) during the post–Cold War era invents North Korea as a space of capitalist hegemony. When socialism and fascism reigned over Europe in the first half of the twentieth century, Hayek (1944) unflinchingly moralized about the liberal economic system being the road to peace. Liberalism returned decades later, this time after socialism lost its appeal. Privatization and deregulation were introduced in former socialist economies in Russia and Europe in the 1990s as the shock therapy necessary to create market and other new economic institutions (Burawoy and Krotov 1992; Sachs 1992; Burawoy 1997; Gerber and Hout 1998). North Korea similarly becomes a workshop of neoliberal capitalism especially from the late 1990s. The dual politics of national unification in South Korea prescribes neoliberal capitalism as a means of creating democracy in North Korea: the policy of economic engagement (kyŏnghyŏp) aims to induce gradual changes through trade between the two Koreas; and North Korean human rights advocacy, combined with the US war on terrorism, advocates decisive regime change in North Korea to establish political freedom, the market system, and the rule of law. Although the two visions of unification are heatedly opposed in South Korea, they undeniably evoke neoliberal capitalism as a utopian force of peace and liberty.

Within this moral approach to North Korea, Korean unification politics in the post–Cold War era performs ideological work for capitalist hegemony. It turns the decades-old task of national unification into a space of consensus among state, capital, and the social movement concerning the necessity of neoliberal capitalism. This consensus is the capitalist unconscious: it consists of utopian narratives of the capitalist system as democracy, and it entails a historical unconscious that inverts the crisis of South Korea into the crisis of North Korea and legitimizes neoliberal capitalist rule by putatively progressive governments in South Korea. Leftists gained power in South Korea from 1998 to 2007 and enforced neoliberal capitalist measures despite their promises for equal distribution and social welfare. It is conventional wisdom that in this bewildering process of democratization, their policy of economic engagement with North Korea redeemed their claims to progressiveness. However, this signature unification policy of the progressive governments is in fact their technique for constructing capitalist rule as democratic rule. The opposition of conservative forces to the economic engagement policy became a spectacle that only further concealed the capitalist nature of the progressive governments.

I embed the dual unification politics in a larger scholarly discussion on capitalism, especially historical ideas of capitalism. Social science research on peace and conflict resolution considers trade and economic interdependence as a crucial mechanism of peace by finding two kinds of statistical correlation: one between peaceful international relations among countries and their levels of economic exchange (Gartzke, Li, and Boehmer 2001; Gartzke 2007; de Soysa and Fjelde 2010), and another between a reduction in armed conflict and economic relations of antagonistic countries, for instance, Israel and Palestine, China and Taiwan, and the two Koreas (Tait 2003; Friedman 2005; Cho Min 2006; Kahler and Kastner 2006; Rusko and Sasikumar 2007). This capitalist peace thesis is contrasted with the democracy peace thesis that "democracies are less conflict prone, if only with other democracies" (Oneal and Russett 1997; Choi 2011). Seen from Hirschman's (1997) analysis of historical ideas of capitalism, the two theses are, however, intrinsically related, as capitalism was imagined as embodying the spirit of peace and liberty. More important, Hirschman's study demonstrates the importance of history and power, a consideration noticeably missing in the peace research discussed above. In his analysis, European philosophers of the seventeenth and eighteenth centuries variously construed that commerce and manufacturing production imparted interests capable of taming wicked passions of despotic rule and individuals' interests in private gain. Bound to medieval ideas of honor and glory, interests were defined broadly as the "totality of human aspiration" for conscience, health, wealth, reflection, and calculation, until its meaning was reduced to economic interest, most notably by Adam Smith. Philosophers also expected economic relations to directly impact the development of international peace and prosperity under a virtually permanent state of war in Europe, which they attributed to rulers' passion for conquest. This extension of the idea of capitalism onto international relations denotes, according to Hirschman, an underdeveloped understanding of international relations. The capitalist peace thesis and democracy peace thesis turn the ideas of capitalism into testable facts about international relations without any discussion of the origins and dynamics of modern wars. They also fail to register conditions under which the ideas developed and changed, not to mention the dark side of the modern economy about which Adam Smith cautioned.[1] Instead, I explore the politics of history and the history of the state–capital nexus in Korean unification politics in reference to the spirits of capitalism.

This chapter begins and ends with accounts of two different modes of union for families separated by the national division, both of which fall through the cracks of all modes of unification politics since the division. In the main section, I investigate dual unification politics as the capitalist unconscious, which treats capitalism as the basis for producing democratic life in North Korea; then I explain the historicity of dual unification politics by inscribing it onto two competing visions of the northeast capitalist bloc and contrasting its market utopia with the national utopia of the 1980s democracy movement.

Family Union

Family union of those separated across the demilitarized zone is a metonym of national unification.[2] As of late 2000, the first generation of the separated in the South amounted to 1.23 million, more than half of whom were sixty years old or older (Ch'ae 2001:546). For the first time since 1985 the two Koreas in 2000 and 2001 hosted family unions for two hundred people from both sides in each of three events. Although the Koreas agreed to regularize family unions, since then the unions were sporadic because of their conflicts; 127,547 South Koreans among those registered for family union were on the waiting list as of 2008.[3] T'albuk (escape from North Korea) is a form of family union in the post–Cold War era, in which Korean Chinese arrangers and South Korean human rights activists clandestinely assist North Koreans in going to South Korea through China and Southeast Asia. Different standpoints about t'albuk in *The Choice of Three South Korean Political Prisoners of the Korean War*, the documentary film by Cho Ch'ŏnhyŏn, bear witness to the weighty history of national division which refuses resolution.[4] The film follows three Korean War prisoners from 2001 to 2003, two of whom made momentary unions in China with siblings from South Korea for the first time in nearly fifty years. All of them had been captured in Kŭmhwa, one of the fiercest battlegrounds during the Korean War (1950–1953), and forced to remain in North Korea. They were among those who were unreported by the North Korean state during the 1953 exchanges of prisoners of war, which involved 110,723 North Korean, 21,374 Chinese, 8,668 South Korean, and 5,148 UN prisoners of war, when the number of South Koreans fell far short of the 88,000 estimated by South Korea (O Kyŏngsŏp, Yun, and Hŏ 2008). Because of political suspicion during the Cold War, South Koreans registered family members as deceased if they were missing or displaced to North Korea during the war, whether through voluntary migration or abduction. From the 1990s Korean Chinese began to broker covert unions of separated family members in China for compassion or for a fee, as they could visit North Korea and develop contact with South Koreans. In the film, a South Korean brother of a prisoner of war received a letter from China that contained information about his brother, whom he thought was dead. His brother's handwritten letter was accompanied by his photos and information, such as his childhood name, with the broker's message that he could meet his brother for about $30,000. Often implied in such an arrangement is that a family member can be brought to South Korea for an additional fee. The fee is higher for a prisoner of war, given that the South Korean government pays him five- to six-hundred thousand dollars in compensation.

The film affirms two powerful tropes of the memory of national division and the Korean War: blood ties and the state's violence.[5] Preparing for his trip to China with his younger brother to meet their eldest brother from North Korea, Kim T'aehyŏng, in his late sixties, reflects that "nothing would be more desired than our parents being alive to see him. I am going to China to allow the spirits of our deceased parents to go in peace." On his second visit to China six months after the aborted union, he utters, "We are one blood [p'itchul] after all . . . and I go to China to see my brother so I won't have han [unresolved resentment] [over not being able to see him]." Despite disbelief at first, siblings of Kim Kijong, another prisoner of war, split the broker's fee, thinking that "my parents wouldn't just sit there and do nothing if they were alive. That's the first thing that occurred to me. We should share the money. We are of the same blood." If the families ever hesitated to finance the visit even with a loan, invoking blood ties erased any equivocation. Brokers could not locate family members of Choi Chinyong, the third prisoner of war, which might well indicate their disagreement with the brokers' terms.

The prisoners of war from North Korea in the film enunciate their victimization by the state's violence. The linkage of the Korean War and the colonial struggle is found in literary depictions of the war in South Korea in the 1950s and 1960s (Han Suyŏng 2011). But such attention to history and to key characteristics of the conflict, namely, that it was at once a global and civil war, is largely absent in memories of the war since then.[6] Similarly, Kim Chaehyŏng recollects the war as a meaningless rivalry between the two Korean states, as he was forced to serve the North Korean People's Army shortly after being captured. Kim Kijong also remembered his participation in the war merely as "doing what he was forced to do" (kŭjŏ sik'inŭn taero haetsŭl ppun), whether he served on the side of the South or the North. After his capture, Choi Chinyong stayed in prison for three years before being sent to a coal mine with a 20,000 won subsidy for settlement. Devoid of the historical meaning of the war, their recollections highlight the war's universal and dehumanizing effects that tore apart families and individuals' lives. The film further accentuates the dehumanizing effects of national division by emphasizing the geographic proximity of their separated lives, as Kim T'aehyŏng laments that North Korea across the Tuman River is as close as a corner store from his home in South Korea and is also close enough for him to talk to children playing across the river in North Korea.

The importance of this film, however, is its representation of the experience of the national division, in which different choices about t'albuk challenge the dominant t'albuk narrative of human rights advocacy. As the only one seeking t'albuk among the three war prisoners, Choi Chinyong joined his son and daughter-in-law, who themselves had been living in China illegally for two years in order to escape to South Korea. Choi attributes his decision neither to his national identity nor to a search for freedom, as asserted in unification politics, but instead to the intractable wish to return to his home town to visit his parents' tomb and meet once more with the woman who loved him before he left for war. His tender longing to see his first love—a love that his poverty and lack of education prevented him from initiating—renders the lofty discourse of t'albuk (as escape from the totalitarian regime) rather pale. Choi Chinyong and his son are, however, arrested by Chinese police on the charge of illegal border crossing and residence. Things that bear his unfulfilled wish in the film include a large movable closet where Choi Chinyong was hiding at the time of his arrest, his magnifying eyeglasses, and bundles of dried goods hidden under the floor's wooden planks that must have been saved for sale in the market or as gifts for his yet-to-be found family in South Korea. Kim Kijong and his siblings from South Korea are also arrested a few hours after their union by Chinese security agents for Kim's illegal entry into China and his siblings' complicity with it. After being expelled from China, the siblings successfully pleaded to the South Korean government and media to bring their brother to South Korea, although he originally planned to return to North Korea. The impossibility of resolving the past is accentuated by his separation from his family in North Korea, as well as his brother's estrangement, which according to the filmmaker arose from their dispute over sharing the government's compensation.

Kim Chaehyŏng's happy reunion with his brothers from South Korea is soon turned into anything but a complete resolution of the national division. Kim Chaehyŏng told his brothers of his wish to return to North Korea despite their offer to bring him to South Korea. Their meeting came after a separation of fifty years, but within a few hours when preparing for another farewell they told each other that they no longer had any han. Instead of any resolution or more direct communication among the brothers, songs are sung to express their feelings of sadness that if it were not for the national division, they could visit their brother's home as easily as crossing the shallow river. "The Tuman River" sung by a brother from the South and "Welcome" sung by a brother from the North encapsulate the historical excesses

FIGURE 6.1 Reunion of brothers in 2010. Courtesy of Ohmynews, Nam So-Youn.

FIGURE 6.2 Reunion of a mother and a daughter in 2010. Courtesy of Ohmynews, Nam So-Youn.

that momentarily appear to be contained by things and shared emotions. The brothers promise to stay in touch and to perform together the annual memorial service for their parents, with Kim Chaehyŏng bowing toward the south at the same time his brother performs the service in the South. At that moment, the viewers hear the filmmaker's reflection that they might have been happier in the past when they thought each other dead, as it might be more unbearable for them not to be able to meet when they now know each other is alive. Family unions in the film are anything but a return to an undivided whole. Their disparate choices about t'albuk and their divergent fates suggest a historical present that is largely absent in the politics of unification. The brokering by Korean Chinese implies deterritorialization of the Korean nation in the post–Cold War era.

KOREAN UNIFICATION AND SPIRITS OF CAPITALISM

The dual politics of Korean unification since the late 1990s seizes the national body, producing new discourses of peace and liberty as the basis of envisaging democracy in the Korean peninsula. Of particular interest is the capitalist crisis in South Korea upon which the reconfigured unification politics establishes the power of capital. Despite being diametrically opposed, the two unification politics share a vision of the neoliberal capitalist system as the force necessary to democratize North Korea. Their common politics of morality transposes the South Korean crisis onto the North Korean crisis while divesting the envisioned national unification of history.

Korean Economic Engagement (Kyŏnghyŏp) for Peace

The Kim Dae Jung government (1998–2003) in South Korea established economic engagement between the two Koreas as a new principle of the national unification policy. Whereas groundbreaking economic exchanges between the two Koreas began in the late 1980s, the Kim government's policy of economic engagement formulated economic exchange between the two Koreas as the principal mechanism for achieving a gradual and peaceful unification. In an earlier approach, followed after the 1948 division, both Koreas vied for a total reunification of territories, economies, and ethnic cultures, which would have been possible only by one Korea subsuming the other. In contrast, the economic engagement policy rests on the principle of reconciliation first and reunification later. Whereas the earlier policy had conflated the state and the nation by assuming a unified state as the prerequisite for a homogeneous nation, the economic engagement policy aims at creating national unity through economic integration as a step toward union into a single state. Trade and economic exchange are envisaged as the means of bridging the divided state and society and circumventing opposition to Korean unification by neighboring superpowers, namely, China, Russia, and Japan. The economic engagement policy officially emulates the German unification experience on the grounds that West Germany's economic aid and exchange with East Germany and the USSR from the 1970s cultivated peaceable relations that ultimately led to unification (Kim Dae Jung 1997).

Three liberal principles in the economic engagement policy translated the ethos of the market as a maker of peace into viable policies: the separation of politics and the economy, peace through trade, and rationalization. The principle of separating politics from the economy releases the economic exchange between the two Koreas from political and military gridlock. Until the late 1990s, any remarkable gestures of reconciliation between the two Koreas following their agreement on mutual recognition in 1971, 1988, and 1992 were superseded by their military and political conflicts. In its Nordpolitik, the Roh Tae Woo government (1988–1993) began economic engagement with North Korea and the USSR through Hong Kong and China, to offset his military background and adapt to changes in the global capitalist system during the post–Cold War period. The Kim Young Sam government (1993–1998) integrated economic exchange with North Korea into Segyehwa, its signature policy of globalization (Kim Kyuryun 1999). These economic efforts were regularly suspended by political and military tensions in the Korean peninsula, ranging from persistent anticommunism in South Korea, sporadic yet alarming skirmishes between the two Koreas, North Korea's test of long-range missiles, and North Korea's demand for the removal of nuclear weapons and US forces from South Korea, to the US call for North Korea to end its nuclear weapons development. In a significant departure, the economic engagement policy's principle of separating politics and the economy has enabled the two Koreas, despite continued tensions, to sustain economic changes and expand South Korea's direct trade, economic aid, tourism, and direct investment.

The language of peace through trade in the economic engagement policy aims to create gradual change in North Korea. This objectification of North Korea is evinced by the well-known fact that the Kim Dae Jung government called the engagement policy the Sunshine Policy, which refers to the Aesop fable, "The North Wind and the Sun." In the fable, the wind and the sun compete to determine which one is more powerful by trying to make a man take off his coat. The wind's bluster and gusts make the man wrap his coat around himself more tightly, whereas the sun's heat induces him to remove his coat. The story shows the superiority of persuasion over threats and the effectiveness of voluntary over forced change. The sun's heat is comparable to the rational role of the market in the Sunshine Policy, while the howling wind is military force. The goal of producing change through trade and investment persisted even after the Sunshine Policy was renamed the Policy to Embrace North Korea (Taebuk p'oyong chŏngch'aek). Kim Dae Jung asserted that the absence of any reference to peace was a critical flaw in earlier policies of economic exchange between the two Koreas. The Sunshine Policy was expected to engender the trust required on both sides to end military and political conflicts, since trade requires only minimal trust between parties but builds trust over time.

The notion of peace through trade in the Korean economic engagement policy evokes Enlightenment ideas of capitalism that Hirschman traces back to the seventeenth- and eighteenth-century Europe. For Montesquieu, "commerce . . . polishes and softens barbarian ways" by concocting men's "gentle" behaviors and giving predictability and constancy to the world (Hirschman 1997:60). For Steuart, the modern economy is the most effectual bridle against the folly of despotism because the complex modern economy induces the ruler not to intervene in the economy but instead follow the law of the economy. This Montesquieu-Steuart position focuses, for Hirschman, on inhibiting the sovereign's power. Later physiocrats observed the direct contribution of the economy to the nation's prosperity. According to Hirschman (1997:31–100), these ideas during the early development of the capitalist system did not replace medieval ideas of honor and glory with new bourgeois virtue but, rather, involve complex formulations about human nature, the relationship between private interest and public welfare, and theories of the modern state. Whereas Hirschman expounds historically constituted and shifting ideas about capitalism, South Korean policy approaches capitalism as a universal truth capable of fixing a historical problem.

The transposition of a historical idea into a universal model dispossesses Korean unification politics of history and power. It obscures the fact that the policy of economic engagement emerged primarily from South Korea's own economic crisis. According to Kim Dae Jung (1997), the "politico-military wars" of the Cold War era have been replaced by today's "economic hot wars," in which economic powers are armed with free trade policies and economic regionalism. Economic cooperation with North Korea is considered an absolute necessity for South Korea's quest to maintain its global economic power; furthermore, Korean unification is not only feasible but also required for South Korea to survive in the economic hot wars, Kim reasons. The idea of North Korea as a capitalist frontier for South Korean capital is echoed by economists and unification activists, who call the economic engagement policy a "win-win" solution for both Koreas (Hong Sunjik 2004). The policy was welcomed as a means to facilitate industrial restructuring at home in South Korea, first moving labor-intensive and old industries to North Korea and later transferring heavy chemical, electronic, and technology-intensive industries. This projection expected a revived North Korean economy to serve as a new market for South Korean companies (Hong Ilp'yo 2004). It was hoped that dependency on foreign trade and the power of monopoly capital in the South Korean market would be curbed by establishing an "organic" linkage between the two Korean economies (Yŏksa munje yŏn'guso 1995).

Economic instrumentalism pervades economic engagement between the two Koreas, whereas early European philosophers saw the new "totality of human aspiration" as the spirit of capitalism (Hirschman 1997:32). The economic engagement policy reflects Weberian rationalization, although without any recognition of its iron-cage effects. The Korean policy construes the exchange between South Korean capital and energy and North Korean labor and resources as a division of labor within the same society. This exchange is expected to allow South Korean investors to export goods that are produced cheaply using North Korean labor as South Korean products while enabling North Korea to use South Korea's well-established global trading networks to export its products. With about ten thousand small- and medium-sized factories going bankrupt each year in South Korea, economic engagement with North Korea is desired as a way to protect these industries from decline by gaining access to less expensive labor and resources. South Korea would also invest in free trade zones in North Korea and jointly develop tourism and agriculture. As a singular national unit, the two Koreas would invest jointly in foreign countries, especially in the forestry industry in Siberia and fishing operations in the Far East. Kim Dae Jung (1997:129–51) formulated all of these plans before becoming president and initiated them while in office, with the exception of joint investment in foreign countries and international (American) recognition of trade between the two Koreas as internal trade.

The economic engagement policy narrowly defines the spirit of capitalism as economic interest. It resonates with the Hegelian argument about the modern economy made by Adam Smith (1976), although without registering Smith's ambivalence. Just as Hegel (1977:213) saw that "the individual in his individual work already unconsciously performs a universal work," Adam Smith argued that the very pursuit of individual interest leads to the betterment of the whole society, which consists of the division of labor and cooperation (Montag 2013:194). In parallel providential thinking, the pursuit of one Korea's own economic interest satisfies the other Korea's interest and serves their universal interest, that is, peace and national community. The economic engagement policy remains a utopian model devoid of the dark sides of the liberal economy that Smith himself recognized. Conflating rationalization of the market with its self-regulation, Smith opposed any intervention in the economy, such as lowering prices even during a famine, by citing the potentially grave consequences that would worsen the situation, including merchants withdrawing from trade. In Montag's (2013) reading, letting people die to maintain market equilibrium means that Smith's theory of the production of life in the modern economy intrinsically entails the necessity of death. In Hirschman's reading (1997:105–8), Smith was also concerned that there would be other unfortunate effects of the free pursuit of private gain, such as the contraction of the mind, devaluation of education, and decay of heroic spirit. The Korean engagement policy seems unswervingly more sanguine than liberal forefathers in crafting the life out of the economy, for it pledges to transform "the apparent cost of the national division into an important resource for improving economic production and enhancing the welfare of people" (Kim Dae Jung 1997:124).

The liberal utopian language of market exchange performs ideological work for capitalist hegemony in South Korea. The economic engagement policy has helped to establish neoliberal capitalist rule in South Korea by reconfiguring the state-capital network. During the military dictatorship, the state tightly regulated capital and labor by staging economic development as a way to build its national power and defeat the North Korean enemy. The military state monopolized the discussion and policy of national unification, permitting only authorized individuals and agencies to analyze North Korea and the unification policy. It owned banks and disciplined capital with loans and business licensing in the name of effectively using national resources. At the same time it outlawed labor unions and treated labor strikes as matters of national security. Since the 1990s, progressive governments have pursued neoliberal capitalist reforms to advance economic liberalization as the solution to capitalist crisis. In that conjuncture, the unification policy has contributed to South Korean capital consolidating its power over the state and society. Among myriad South Korean studies of the economic engagement policy, Kim Hakno's (2005) study is particularly notable because it recognizes the importance of the hegemonic power of capital. Kim's study notes that even when the South Korean government tried to impede economic exchange in response to North Korea's development of nuclear weapons, it could not diminish the zeal of South Korean capital for North Korea. Even before the Kim Dae Jung government came to power, the conglomerates had planned to use North Korea as an economic outpost, using railways to connect Asia and Europe. While agreeing with Kim on capitalist hegemony in South Korea's economic engagement with North Korea, I also extrapolate the utopian construction of capitalism as a force for peace, its constitutive effect on democratic politics, and its affinity with North Korean human rights advocacy.

The economic engagement policy created a broad consensus among the state, capital, media, academics, and the public about the current capitalist system. Economic institutes, including those run by the government and corporations, praised the economic benefits of the policy. New associations were founded through concerted efforts of corporate leaders, industrial associations, the media, universities, lawyers, and economists to advise the business community and educate the general public about economic engagement with North Korea. The National Movement for South-North Economic Engagement (Nambuk kyŏnghyŏp kungmin undong ponbu) collaborated with the Korean Industrial Complex Association (Han'guk sanŏp tanji kongdan) to sponsor public seminars on economic engagement and educational workshops for the business community. The Far East Institute of Kyŏngnam University and the *Hankyoreh* newspaper established the Academy of South-North Economic Engagement (Nambuk kyŏnghyŏp Academy). The Citizens' League for Inter-Korean Economic Engagement (Nambuk kyŏnghyŏp simin yŏndae) linked NGOs, scholarly institutes, and economic organizations to provide information and assistance to companies interested in investing in North Korea.

South Korean studies of the economic engagement policy concentrate on the progress of and barriers to economic exchange, including conservatives' opposition, uncertainty in North Korea, and the lack of support from the United States (Cho Min 2003; Yi Sŏngro 2013). Comparison with German unification was commonly invoked to justify the policy: the volume of the two Koreas' trade and investment was compared with that of the two Germanys as a measure of the progress of unification (Kim Unghi 2004); the economic engagement policy was justified as a rational approach since the German style of unification through absorption of North Korea would require an annual expenditure of 10 percent of GDP, which would exhaust the financial means of South Korea in less than five years (Yi Sŏngro 2013). By 2010, a total of 121 South Korean firms operated in the Kaesŏng industrial complex that had opened in 2004. They employed about forty thousand North Korean workers in 2008 and produced products ranging from kitchen goods to wrist watches, textiles, cosmetic containers, and shoes. The North Korean government shut down the industrial complex in April 2013, but four months later North and South Korea agreed to reopen it. Beyond its economic and national value, the significance of the economic engagement policy, however, lies in the ideological work it performs for capitalist hegemony. The economic engagement policy decouples nation and state. It does not reduce the state's power per se but instead authorizes the state to support the hegemonic power of capital. The neoliberal capitalist system dons its national mask, presenting its deregulated accumulation on a global scale as the truth of the post–Cold War era. Capital has replaced the state as the subject of national unification.

Politics of North Korean Human Rights

The issue of human rights in North Korea galvanized into a political force with the migration of North Koreans to China since the food crisis of 1995–1998. Reports estimated that 6.4 million North Koreans, or one-fourth of the population, suffered from starvation, with approximately 60 percent of children under five affected by malnutrition; 15 to 20 percent of the total population, that is, up to three million people died from starvation (Choi Ch'angdong 2000; Gong 2004). Testimonies and pictures of North Koreans drifting from North Korea to China filled the media in and beyond South Korea. Images showed displaced North Korean children (kkotchebi[7]) surviving by begging and sleeping on the street, eating food from the trash, or taking shelter in mountain huts in China. Their hunger-stricken appearance was particularly distressing because malnourishment stunted growth and made young adults looked like children. The famine aroused concern that malnutrition not only would adversely affect the health of the Korean gene pool but also would permanently differentiate the two Koreas and create a new barrier to genuine national unification. Widely circulated were heartbreaking photos such as those of a mother with her ravenous toddler crying and clinging to her naked and skeletal torso or of corpses floating in the Tuman River between China and North Korea. News about the abduction and trafficking of North Korean women, each sold for 3,000 to 5,000 yuan ($500 to $800), amplified attention to the plight of North Korean refugees (Choŭn pŏttŭl 1999; Paterniti 2003; Yi Kŭmsun 2005).

The issue of human rights in North Korea has bolstered a new conservatism in South Korea. It has united converted former radicals, evangelical churches, and other conservative forces against what they call the leftist turn (chwagyŏnghwa). In close collaboration with the US war on terrorism, conservative forces in South Korea constructed North Korea as an evil state threatening the global peace. Arendt (1951) delineated the modern paradox of refugees fleeing totalitarian oppression in the first half of the twentieth century. Their inalienable rights as humans are untenable under the nation-state system that confers rights only on citizens of a nation-state. For Agamben (1998), the distinction between refugees and citizens disappears, as the modern state bases its sovereignty on the production of life, yet holds the exceptional power to deny its citizens life and rights in conditions of prolonged emergency. The issue of North Korean human rights turns the paradox of the nation-state system into the issue of global democracy. The global democracy project authorizes putative supranational powers to invade a sovereign nation-state to protect not just the freedom of citizens within a given country but also a supposed global peace. North Korean refugees are taken as the sign of a failed state that abuses the human rights of its own citizens and defends its power with weapons of mass destruction that threaten global peace. While the aforementioned political science research tests the empirical association of democracy and peace, advocates of North Korean human rights turn it into a prescription to create democracy in North Korea and establish global peace. The head-on contention between the economic engagement policy and North Korean human rights advocacy revolves around the opposition between North Korea's sovereignty and global democracy. Human rights activists define North Korean migrants as political refugees in search of freedom, appealing to the international community to create refugee camps in Mongolia and places neighboring the two Koreas. In contrast, defenders of the economic engagement policy regard North Korean refugees as temporary migrants escaping a momentary crisis that resulted from a constellation of extraneous conditions, including natural disasters, the abrupt end of oil subsidies from the Soviet Union and China, the economic embargo imposed by the United States, and increased military spending following the clash with the United States over nuclear weapons. Taking the North Korean state as the legitimate state and partner in national reconciliation, advocates of economic engagement expect that North Korean displacement onto China would gradually decrease and eventually end as economic cooperation between the two Koreas improves conditions in North Korea.

North Korean human rights advocacy has developed in close conjunction with the US policy on North Korea. An exception to this trend is Good Friends (Choǔn pŏttŭl), which has become the most powerful Buddhist NGO through its work with and fundraising on behalf of North Korean refugees. Good Friends surveyed and interviewed North Koreans who were displaced to China and obtained information about their conditions in China as well as the living conditions in North Korea. After its members were arrested by the Chinese government in 2001 and released on the condition that the organization would no longer conduct research on displaced North Koreans, Good Friends shifted its primary activities to humanitarian aid in other parts of Asia. On the opposite end of the political spectrum, Citizens' Alliance for North Korean Human Rights and NKNET, in tune with the United States and its war on terrorism, spearheaded publicity about the North Korean state's human rights violations and the need for outside intervention to bring about regime change. Headed by a former director of Amnesty International in South Korea, Citizens' Alliance collaborated with the National Endowment for Democracy (NED), a US NGO, to host international conferences that discussed human rights violations in North Korea; discussion ranged across topics such as political and labor camps in North Korea resembling the Soviet gulag and Nazi camps, the treacherous conditions of North Korean refugees in China and Russia, and the political indoctrination and brutal punishment of refugees deported from China.[8]

As a think tank of the New Right Network, the Network for North Korean Democracy and Human Rights (NKNET) theorizes that protecting human rights in North Korea is the task of establishing global democracy. According to Kim Soo Young (2004) on its leadership,

> Under the concept of human rights, neither sovereignty nor interference can exist. Since the modern nation states emerged, national sovereignty seemed to be the highest priority of a nation in setting the international order. . . . After the Cold War, when the conflicts of Socialism vs. Capitalism had disappeared, there has been an increase of a new consensus on how the international community must handle the matter of human rights violations. The consensus is that . . . these values [human rights and democracy] are above the national sovereignty.

According to Kim Young Hwan (2005), a founding leader of NKNET, ignoring the extreme suffering in North Korea betrays South Korea's moral obligation, for North Korea is unlikely to pursue Chinese-style liberalization and reformation. Those who incorrectly predicted the imminent collapse of the North Korean state during the 1990s did not, Kim argues, understand the paradoxical effect of the rise of military power. Namely, the military's control over the state and the Workers' Party eroded Juche ideology, weakened the people's allegiance to the party and national leaders, and increased corruption. Thus, Kim asserts, only a small crack in any part of North Korean society with the outsider's covert intervention could break down the regime's safety net. Hwang Jang Yŏp, the highest-ranking defector and an architect of North Korea's Juche ideology, became the honorary president of NKNET and head of the North Korean government-in-exile. He justifies the use of force to defeat the North Korean state in the name of bringing democracy to North Korea. Publishing information on the North Korean state and society based on refugees' testimony, NKNET established the issue of North Korean human rights as a wedge that the new right-wing group used to separate itself from the so-called old right-wing politics; the new right-wing group pledged its support for market liberalism and small government, whereas the old right-wing group pursued state-led economic development founded on statism (kukka chuŭi), nationalism, and authoritarianism.[9]

After the United States declared the North Korean regime to be an axis of evil in 2001, the US Congress passed the North Korean Freedom Act of 2003 and the North Korean Human Rights Act of 2004. Both acts aim at supporting Korean unification under a democratic government and improving North

Korean human rights by installing the rule of law and the market system. The North Korean Freedom Act adds the elimination of weapons of mass destruction to its list of goals. The North Korean Human Rights Act enumerates twenty-five findings of human rights violations by the North Korean state that closely matched the human rights violations in North Korea that were discussed at the aforementioned international conferences. The two laws authorized US government funding to individuals, organizations, and government agencies so as to provide assistance to refugees, disseminate information, and bring economic liberalization to North Korea. They also support the exodus of North Koreans, reflecting a sentiment among conservative NGOs that the North Korean regime would collapse if one-tenth of its population would flee, as happened in the Vietnam War, though the US government denied asylum to North Korean refugees in its own territory except for a few cases (Kim Sunam 2004). The US legislation stirred up fear in the Korean peninsula of a US invasion of North Korea, given that the US Congress passed the Iraq Liberation Act before the US attacked Iraq. Accordingly, North Korea saw the North Korean Human Rights Act as a declaration of war (Yi Kŭmsun 2004). Defenders of the economic engagement policy denounced the North Korean Human Rights Act as a threat to peace in Korea.[10] They criticized both acts for their exclusive focus on political and civil rights without consideration of socioeconomic rights and the right to livelihood (saengjon'gwŏn); they also claimed that the acts are based on the Western concept of human rights that privilege legal freedom over other rights regardless of historical context.

Calling its approach quiet diplomacy, the governments of Kim Dae Jung and Roh Moo Hyun focused on union of separated families and humanitarian aid rather than confronting North Korea's human rights issues. The Roh government abstained from voting on the resolution on North Korean human rights at the fifty-ninth and sixtieth sessions of the UN Commission on Human Rights in 2003 and 2004, stating that the dialogue and cooperation between the two Koreas will eventually improve human rights in North Korea and that North Koreans must exert their own will to bring about improvements to their human rights. In a letter to the US ambassador in South Korea, dated September 2, 2006, legislators of the Uri majority party and the Millennium Democratic Party criticized the North Korean Human Rights Act for increasing tension in the Korean peninsula, while the conservative Grand National Party supported the act (Yi Kŭmsun 2004). In February 2014, the Citizens' Alliance for North Korean Human Rights organized a three-day demonstration with about sixty people in downtown Seoul. The demonstration called for the South Korean National Assembly to pass South Korea's own North Korean Human Rights Act, which was proposed a decade earlier and remained stuck in legislative process (Ku Jun Hoe 2014).

Any contradictions between the national power and the supranational authority of the United States or between South Korean conservatives' espousals of nationalism and global peace were repressed by two spectacles of North Korean "escape" to South Korea (t'albuk): one was a staged entry into foreign embassies and consulates in China; the other, a clandestine escape through a third country. In addition to the aforementioned organizations, the Association for Families of South Korean Abductees and the Christian Council of Korea (Han'gich'ong) played a key role in bringing North Koreans to South Korea. Staged entry became a strategy for politicizing the issue of North Korean human rights after seven North Koreans, including the Chang Kilsu family, entered the office of the United Nations High Commissioner for Refugees on June 26, 2001, and were immediately deported to South Korea by China, inciting global media publicity on North Korean refugees. The first staged entry involved 25 North Koreans trying to enter the Spanish embassy in China on March 14, 2002. The footage of a mother pushing her daughter inside the embassy's gate as guards apprehended her became an ultimate image of North Koreans' search for freedom. The number of forced entries peaked in September and October of 2004, coinciding with passage in the United States of the North Korean Human Rights Act on September 28.[11] Scenes from other forced entries and interviews with those who succeeded or failed to enter became a staple of media reports and documentaries on human rights in North Korea and were crucial in mobilizing college students and activists in the United States throughout the 2000s. However, viewers did not know that the forced entries were being orchestrated by NGOs. The entry into the Spanish embassy was planned by more than ten NGOs from South Korea, the United States, Japan, and Europe for several months; the twenty-five North Koreans were carefully chosen to meet international criteria for refugees, such as loss of family members through starvation, at-risk for trafficking, and political oppression in North Korea and China. Timed for an EU meeting slated to discuss North Korean issues, the entry was modeled on similar events that had taken place in Czechoslovakia and Hungary in 1989. Informed by organizers, journalists from media networks, including CNN and AP, waited at the Spanish embassy's gate to film the entry.[12]

Clandestine escapes are organized by local NGOs and conservative churches affiliated with the Christian Council of Korea. North Korean refugees in China and increasingly North Koreans directly from North Korea are smuggled to South Korea by train, by bus, and on foot through a third country such as Mongolia, Cambodia, Thailand, Laos, or Vietnam, where South Korean consulates evaluate them and arrange their passage to South Korea. Clandestine escape capitalizes on the South Korean Constitution, which states that South Korea is the only legitimate nation-state for Koreans and thus deems North Koreans to be citizens of South Korea. The Constitution provides a legal framework for the South Korean government to offer arriving North Korans financial assistance, including cash, permanent housing, monthly cash subsidy, job training, and education subsidy, which decreased by the mid-2000s but still exceeds the dreams of the South Korean poor. Clandestine escape is also arranged by brokers, missionaries, and other human right activists, often for a fee of $2,500 to $4,500 per escapee. Payment is typically made either in advance by a family member in South Korea or by the escapee on arrival with the cash subsidy from the South Korean government. Although less common, nonstop air travel from China to South Korea using falsified documents can be arranged for a higher fee. Media reports of escape routes through deserts and rivers and escapee's perilous ordeals in evading border guards and hoodlums not only incited interest in North Korean refugees and helped to retain it but also led to increased financial support for churches and other organizations involved in t'albuk and North Korean human rights issues.

Both staged entry and clandestine escape are controversial even among human rights activists. Framed in moral terms, critiques further reinforce North Korean human rights issue as spectacle. Staged entry is endorsed by NKNET, the Christian Council of Korea, and the Association for Families of South Korean Abductees, whereas Good Friends and the Citizens' Alliance denounce it. According to critics, staged entry instrumentalizes North Korean refugees, endangers the lives of North Korean migrants in China, and jeopardizes the operation of NGOs in China. Publicity about the entries, as well as about smuggled escapes, provoked the Chinese government to retaliate against illegal North Koreans, announcing a 10,000 yuan reward for each report of illegal North Korean migrants in order to preempt attention to China's own human rights violation. The controversy was aggravated by reports that North Koreans in China not only paid for staged entry after being recruited but also were abused in shelters during the period of planning and training for the staged entry. When organizing an entry into a foreign facility in China, those who paid the fee in advance were placed in the middle of the group so they would avoid direct confrontation with guards, whereas those who contracted to pay the fee after arrival in South Korea were placed in the front and at the end of the group (Cho Ch'ŏnhyŏn 2004b). Clandestine escape has also been criticized on moral grounds, as it exposes hideouts and secret migration routes of North Koreans. To fit the description of refugee, North Korean migrants in China or even Korean Chinese disguised as North Koreans were placed on display in mountain huts or caves for visitors from South Korea and other countries. In media reports and migrants' own accounts, human rights activists become indistinguishable from brokers who recruit North Koreans, collect fees from them and the public if not their families in South Korea, swindle them with promises of going to South Korea, and deprive them of their freedom during the operation (Cho Ch'ŏnhyŏn 2004a, 2006). The moral critique of t'albuk eclipses sufficient interrogation of the nature of North Korean migration, human rights activism, and the changing conditions of North Korean society.

North Korean human rights advocacy signifies a Kantian transcendence of democracy into an a priori universal value. In Bloch's (1987:161–62) critique of bourgeois consolidation of democracy, Kant's formula posits freedom as the thing-in-itself that takes flight from historical experience (reality) toward an a priori source—spontaneity—that unites theory with morality. For Bloch, Kant's thesis lacks a concept of history that could overcome the dualism between experience and postulate, between the "realm of necessity" and the "realm of freedom." Modern bourgeois democracy entails, according to Bloch, an intrinsic tension among its tricolor principles—freedom, equality, and fraternity—because freedom is associated with private property ownership. The distinction between freedom of choice and freedom of action under bourgeois democracy is important, since the struggle for democracy involves not just "freedom from something" but also "freedom toward" equality through the establishment of mass sovereignty. North Korean human rights advocacy sutures this original tension of modern democracy with its appeal to ethics. Espousal of liberty, global democracy, and integrity depletes the North Korean regime of its historicity. The prescription of capitalism as the panacea for the crisis of the regime obscures that the capitalist system's own crisis around the world deepens and restructures socioeconomic inequality, unemployment, social insecurity, and debt. Repressed in this capitalist unconscious are colonial origins and the Cold War history of national division.

FROM NATIONAL UTOPIA TO MARKET UTOPIA

With its goal of democratizing North Korea in the post–Cold War era, the dual politics of national unification shifts the democracy movement from the politics of national utopia to the politics of market utopia. I explicate market utopia as the democratic politics of the post–Cold War era in two steps: first I ascribe the economic engagement policy and North Korean human rights advocacy to the formation of global capitalist networks, and then I elaborate their shared ideological work in the production of market utopia. The dual politics of national unification offers competing visions of a new capitalist order in Asia during the post–Cold War era. The economic engagement policy is constitutive of South Korea's vision for a Northeast Asia economic bloc that includes China and North Korea as key economic allies. North Korean human rights advocacy is integral to a reconfigured vision for Asia by the United States. The Nordpolitik and Segyehwa policies of the late 1980s and 1990s attempted to create South Korea as a center of the Asian and global economic order. In the aftermath of the 1997 financial crisis, the economic engagement policy of the progressive governments constituted the vision for a new North-east Asia economic bloc capable of competing against US hegemony in Asia. With intensified neoliberal reforms, the Roh Moo Hyun government envis-aged South Korea as the heart of trade, finance, and research and develop-ment in its envisioned Northeast Asia hub. Deregulation and liberalization of foreign currencies were to make Seoul a financial center competing against Hong Kong and Singapore. Economic engagement with North Korea was to strengthen the South Korean economy and consequently secure its leader-ship position in Asia. Here, cooperation with China was considered impera-tive. Anticipating that China would become a global economic superpower, South Korea planned to link itself with China through its economic network with North Korea. If engagement with the North Korean economy was not upgraded to direct investment in the North, South Korea feared that China, Japan, and even the United States would dominate investment in the North. The imagined Northeast Asia hub shaped domestic policies, including reloca-tion of administrative offices out of Seoul and turning Seoul into an economic center of the hub (Kim Kyuryun 2004).

North Korea constitutes the last link in the envisioned Northeast Asia economic bloc. China and Russia steadily expanded their economic relations with South Korea and maintained close relations with North Korea, notably through China's offers of economic aid and political support. In the early 2000s, Japan and North Korea also attained a milestone in their move toward normalization by reaching an agreement on compensation for Japan's colo-nial occupation of Korea, which has since then stalled over the issue of North Korea's abduction of Japanese nationals decades ago. The imagined North-east Asia economic bloc foresaw the trans-Siberian freight route linking the natural resources and labor power of Russia and North Korea with the capital, technology, and surplus production of South Korea, Japan, and even China, while seeking to expand into Europe and Southeast Asia. The capitalist crises in Asian countries have invigorated the aspiration for unity, though its actualization has been constrained by their territorial disputes, competition for hegemony, and disagreement about the US war against Iraq. These countries tend to consider US aggression against North Korea as a threat to their common interests. Moreover, beneath the surface of cooperation and reconciliation, the policy of economic engagement with North Korea entails an intense struggle between the two Koreas for hegemony. South Korea has taken its leadership in economic engagement with North Korea for granted and forged the free trade agreement with the United States. North Korea has pursued economic cooperation with China to constrain South Korean hegemony over its marketization. The two Koreas' economic engagement has aligned the fetishized desire for national unity with the pursuit of capitalist growth. It has transcended their ideological antagonism only by spawning new unevenness and competition within and between the two Koreas.

North Korean human rights advocacy has merged with the US strategy of reconfiguring East Asia in the post–Cold War era. The United States has revamped its old alliance with Japan and South Korea to counter the emergent power of China in East Asia while creating new allies like India and Pakistan. During Bill Clinton's presidency, the guiding principle was the centrality of state-political action in economic affairs, binding tightly its military security and economic security (Gowan 1999:77–8). The newly created National Economic Council, comparable to the National Security Council, buttressed the power of Wall Street finance capital as the agent for strengthening American capitalism across the globe while consolidating the state's partnership with US businesses invested in Asia. Under the George W. Bush government (2001–2009), the alliance between the defense industry and neoconservatives became dominant political and economic interests. According to the Project for the New American Century, the neoconservative charter for foreign policy in 1997, American leadership required military strength, diplomatic energy, and commitment to moral principles (Harvey 2005:190–92). The American claim to protect universal values of human rights from rogue states dovetailed with its propagation of neoliberalism's free markets and free trade. Contemplating a preemptive war against North Korea helped the United States reconfigure its security and economic relations with Japan and South Korea. Promoting outsourcing and strategic flexibility, the United States relocated its reduced infantry forces to South Korea's west coast facing

China while transferring financial responsibility and military authority to South Korean armies. The critique of North Korea's human rights record and its nuclear weapons and missile development enabled the United States to reconstitute its hegemony in Asia.

While pursuing the economic engagement policy with North Korea, the Roh Moo Hyun government also strengthened its ties with the United States. Against resistance from leftists, farmers, and workers, it promoted the Free Trade Agreement (FTA) with the United States, which would open the South Korean service sector to US investment, services such as communications, law, health care, real estate, and education. The Roh government legitimated this as a move to soften the US stance on the two Koreas' economic engagement and to push the United States to officially recognize products made in North Korea as South Korean. The FTA between South Korea and the United States strategically countered the idea of the Northeast Asia hub that the Roh government pursued as its key economic development policy. The drive for the FTA with the United States defined China as an economic threat, whereas his envisioned Northeast Asia bloc regarded China as a source of opportunity. A close relationship with China was considered essential for South Korea's vision for the Northeast Asia hub, while the FTA with the United States was regarded as essential for strengthening South Korea's service sector and improving South Korean economic competitiveness (Yi and Goh 2006).

Despite their different visions of the global capitalist network, the dual politics of Korean unification fastens democracy onto a capitalist system. The conventional understanding of the engagement policy as "building peace through trade" and North Korean human rights advocacy as "propagating freedom through regime change" underplays their shared ideological character. Their ideological work is located within their construction of democracy as market utopia. The imagination of capitalism as spirits of peace and freedom detaches democratic politics from the emancipatory mass politics of the 1980s that aimed at overcoming foreign domination and class exploitation. The two rival approaches characterized the minjung democracy movement of the 1980s, discussed in chapter 2: the People's Democracy (PD) thesis and the National Liberation (NL) thesis. The PD thesis prioritized the class struggle against the fascism of the military state and the monopoly power of the bourgeoisie, whereas the NL thesis authorized the nationalist liberation struggle against US imperialism and military dictatorship and, especially for its most radical faction (Jusap'a), construed North Korea as the model of anti-imperialist revolutionary struggle. Both theses rejected the two Koreas'

economic exchange of the 1980s and 1990s: The PD group saw it as a means
for monopoly capital to expand its market in former socialist countries and
consolidate the national division if not absorb North Korea; the NL group
regarded it as intensifying US colonization of the entire Korean peninsula
and demanded a full withdrawal of US forces from South Korea as a precondi-
tion for the dialogue between the two Koreas (Cho Hiyŏn and Pak Hyŏnch'ae
1989a, 1989b, 1991, 1992).

From the late 1990s onward the PD and the NL groups diverged further
on unification politics and the collapse of their respective ideals: socialism
and North Korea. The economic engagement policy was led and endorsed
by leftists and activists, who in general sided with the PD approach. North
Korean human rights advocacy was spearheaded by former NL members
who underwent divergent changes upon the collapse of its utopian understanding of North Korea. With the formation of progressive governments
beginning in 1998, the state and social movement were no longer in opposition. Their personnel and ideas fused, as former activists served in key government positions and expanded their participation in political parties and
the National Assembly. In these circumstances, the social movement for
national unification fostered cooperation between the state and society for
economic engagement between the two Koreas via two new organizations:
the Korean Council for Reconciliation and Cooperation (Minhwahyŏp
or Minjok hwahoe hyŏmnyŏk pŏm kungmin hyŏbŭihoe, Korean Council
hereafter), and the Federation for National Unification (T'ongil yŏndae
or The 6.15 nambuk kongdong sŏnŏn silhyŏn kwa hanbando p'yŏnghwa
t'ongil ŭl wihan yŏndae). Founded in 1998 as a semiofficial organization
with 171 groups, including political parties and civil organizations, the
Korean Council aimed at creating national reconciliation "within" South
Korea (*namnam hwahae*) among diverse social and political sectors. Formed
in 2001, the Federation for National Unification consisted of forty-six organizations, most of whose members, including moderate NL members, had
participated in the minjung movement. The Federation for National Unification often critiqued the progressive governments' policy despite its support
for the economic engagement policy, while the Korean Council served an
auxiliary role for the state by hosting events such as joint-unification festivals, marathons, and public forums and by conducting a joint excavation
of sites of Koguryŏ, an ancient Korean kingdom whose history and culture
were claimed by China.

The NL group made the unification movement a crucial benchmark
of democratization. After the Great Strikes of 1987, the unification

movement and other social movements increasingly became dissociated from labor struggle, as explored in chapter 2. Labor unions adopted economic unionism to tackle shop-floor issues in response to neoliberal policies on labor. Breaking from the labor-centered social movement, various new local NGOs focused on cultural identity and social differences. The NL group, especially the Jusa faction, launched the Campaign to Know North Korea Properly (Pukhan paro algi undong). It successfully generated public interest in North Korean society and politics by reprinting books published in North Korea on topics including revolution, Juche ideology, and unification. The Jusa group's movement also electrified the whole country by organizing visits to North Korea during which its student representatives and opposition leaders walked across the demilitarized zone; it also arranged meetings abroad between representatives of both Koreas—all without the permission from the South Korean state. The Jusa group's unreserved embrace of North Korea, however, provided the state with an opportunity to crack down not just on unification movement organizations but also on other democratic demands, once again charging them with being masterminded by the North.

Confronting in that juncture the food crisis in North Korea and the consequent illegal migration of North Koreans to China transformed the NL group in at least three ways: the creation of the Democratic Labor Party, the move toward humanitarianism, and the conversion to anti–North Korea politics, especially by the Jusa group. As explained in chapter 2, the Democratic Labor Party formed in 2000 signifies the political empowerment of the labor movement. National Liberation members involved in its leadership made the party a spokesperson to demand complete withdrawal of US forces and to oppose the FTA with the United States. Some NL members traded their national liberation struggle for humanitarian activism. According to Yi Sŭngyong, director of Good Friends, he and his colleagues had been involved in the Buddhist Student Association during the democratic struggle of the 1970s and 1980s with an NL orientation. Their turning point was their shock over the grim conditions of North Korean refugees that they witnessed during their 1996 trip intended to explore traces of the anticolonial Korean struggle in northeast China. It led them to abandon their earlier emphasis on structural change and ideological disputation and instead adopt the principle of realism (silsagusi) to document concrete reality and everyday practice.[13] This change led to the birth of the Korean Buddhist Sharing movement, which simultaneously supported economic engagement between the two Koreas and provided North Korean compatriots with humanitarian aid, including food, clothing, and medical supplies. After being renamed Good Friends in 1999 and becoming the largest Buddhist NGO, the movement concentrated on surveying and reporting on the living conditions of North Korean refugees in China, documenting their stories, and appealing to the public to transcend ideological differences and help the refugees. The poststructuralist credo of difference and plurality binds the unification movement, peace movement, and human rights advocacy in Good Friends. Its president, Monk Pŏmryun (2001), stated that recognizing genuine difference is the source of peace:

> Contradictory thoughts of difference and homogenization exist in all sources of conflict, tension, struggle, and war. . . . The two Koreas fight because they think they should be one [by annihilating each other]. . . . All antagonisms and conflicts can be resolved by the recognition of difference since they arise from the inability to acknowledge diversity of things and humans. . . .
>
> Peace cannot exist with the violation of human rights. . . . What can the peace movement be in Korea? First of all, it must abolish ideological conflicts between the two Koreas. . . . Peace would be possible first by military reduction [of South Korea and the United States], and then must be followed by North Korea's halting of missile development and joining the Nuclear Non-Proliferation Treaty. . . . The peace movement expands from individuals to all around the globe. The privileged must give up their privileges, and victims must overcome the sense of victimization in order for them to cooperate, reconcile, and establish harmony.

The renunciation of the past is even more striking for some prominent NL theorists. Some staunch leaders of the Jusa group announced their conversion via the mass media and encouraged their colleagues to do the same. Becoming the architect of NKNET, Kim Young Hwan, whose legendary 1986 manifesto (kangch'ol sŏsin) elevated North Korea as the model of revolution and national independence, made his public conversion in 1995 and reaffirmed it four years later in the leading conservative Chosun Daily. Kim attributed his conversion to the reality of the socioeconomic and political suffering of North Koreans under their totalitarian state. He allied with other conservatives such as Chayuyŏndae (Liberalists United) led by Shin Chiho, who converted from PD in the late 1980s to form the New Right Network. For NKNET, the urgent task was to use any means necessary to realize freedom in North Korea.[14] For Kim Young Hwan (2005), the form of the state rather than the people's own action constitutes democracy, regardless of how such a democratic state comes into being:

> The North Korean regime stands not with the people but in opposition to them. Since we are revolutionaries, we have to fight on the side of the people. What is most urgent now is the revolution in North Korea to abolish the regime that represses and starves its people. . . . Resistance against the regime is unlikely to be widespread in North Korea. The North Korean society has very little possibility of overthrowing the regime through the gradual spread of an anti-regime movement.

An Pyŏngjik, an iconic figure in the social formation debate of the 1980s and another spectacular convert who became president of the New Right Foundation in 2006, also denounced North Korea's self-reliance principle. He advocated the FTA with the United States and scandalized the whole country by saying that Japanese and American colonization was necessary for capitalist development in South Korea.

The politics of national unification signifies a flight from history to idealism. With its advocacy of peace through trade and liberty through regime change, the dual politics of national unification appeals to the belief that the rule of law is an essential element of democracy, under which individuals are juridical subjects engaging in market exchange. The notion of market exchange as the foundation of peace and freedom obscures the historical present. That is, it obscures not only the crisis of industrial capitalism and its consequent development of a new relationship between the state, finance capital, and industrial capital in South Korea but also changes in North Korea. The dual politics of national unification produces consensus on capitalism through what Žižek (1989, 2007) calls "jouissance," the enjoyment of one's symptoms of domination by capitalism. Market utopia is enabled by a fantasy that keeps one's desire intact even at the moment of crisis by telling oneself, "We haven't fulfilled it . . . because someone stole the enjoyment from us" (Dean 2009:58). In South Korea, this someone is North Korea being putatively stuck in the Cold War as well as anticommunist institutions maintained in South Korea. The National Security Law and the state's use of anti–North Korean sentiment to repress freedom are blamed for draining resources and averting foreign investment that would have otherwise boosted economic investment. Instead of recognizing the problem of the current neoliberal form of capitalism as threatening democracy, Korean unification politics extends capitalism to North Korea. South Koreans displace their own capitalist debacle with this utopian inversion of capitalist expansion into national unification and attribute it to the North Korean other. This disidentification with North Korea enables South Koreans to maintain their identification with neoliberal capitalism. Peace in the form of free trade between the two Koreas is the enjoyment of the deferred promises of industrial modernity and mass democracy. The effect of unification politics is not about democratization of North Korea per se; rather, it is about affirming the neoliberal capitalist order.

Market utopia is a dialectical reversal. It turns sources of national division into mechanisms for its resolution. In South Korea, sources of national division and its reproduction include the state, monopoly capital, and American domination, whose complex interrelationship was the focus of the social formation debate and the minjung movement of the 1980s. The dual politics of national unification imparts a form of historicism that constructs the post–Cold War era as a stage of historical progress. This obscures the fact that neoliberal capitalism transforms realms of social life with deregulation, privatization, unemployment, flexible and precarious employment, and an ethos of self-cultivation. All of these neoliberal vices are loudly criticized but simultaneously muffled by a faux sense of ideological victory over North Korea. In his seminal investigation of liberalism, Polanyi (1944) observed that "peace through trade" is a quintessential liberal principle that commodifies land, money, and people respectively as private property, capital, and labor. He examined various social responses to commodification that envisioned new collectives and terms of equality. Similarly the dual politics of national unification is a social response to the tripartite commodification. Yet it entails a collective unconscious with an unspoken consensus about commodification under neoliberal capitalism.

The collective unconscious of capitalism offers some explanation of the seeming paradox in the politics of national unification. The economic engagement policy is belittled as no more than discarding South Korea's leftovers in North Korea, whether rice, oranges, clothing, or fertilizer. South Korean activists self-mockingly lament that their movement has been reduced to an annual commemoration of the two Koreas' 2000 declaration for mutual recognition, as well as to hosting youth, athletes, and delegates visiting from the North. Moreover, the broad consensus on the economic engagement policy is mixed with deep doubt and misgiving among South Koreans about national unification. In the era of globalization and cosmopolitanism, South Koreans question the homogeneity of the nation in both theory and reality, not to mention their widespread skepticism over the genuine feasibility of territorial and sociocultural integration of the two Koreas. Benjamin saw "megalomania" in a monument that represented capitalist and imperialist expansion as progressive forces of history (Buck-Morss 1989:92). A similar megalomania is found in the economic engagement policy that construes market expansion as a force of democratization. The economic engagement policy does not guarantee resolution of social antagonisms sown during and after the Cold War in South and North Korea. The animated opposition from North Korean human rights advocacy obscures this enervated nature of the economic engagement policy.

ANOTHER FAMILY UNION

The dual politics of national unification refuses to acknowledge the looming presence of colonial and Cold War histories. This historicity of unification politics is revealed by the family unions of North Korean escapees of the 1960s whose experiences exceed the language of both old and new unification politics. These escapees are, in Arendt's term, "stateless" subjects, as they escaped from political oppression in North Korea, were persecuted in China as North Korean spies, remained in China as overseas North Koreans despite their renunciation of the North Korean state, and then came to South Korea through epic struggles only to be denied recognition as citizens or escapees. In current terms, they are transnational subjects who live between nation-states, yet neither enjoy dual or multiple belongingness nor find any one place to belong.

Chang Chŏngsun and O Sunbok were born in P'yŏngan Province respectively in 1938 and 1936 into families of the landlord class.[15] Thus, they were categorized as belonging to an enemy group, which numbered about 3 million and, under Decree 149 in 1958, and were sent away to coal mines, collective farms, and mountainous areas far from major cities and the border with South Korea (Sŏ Chaejin 1995). Their families were relocated in Hamgyŏng Province, a mountainous area bordering China known for long, freezing winters. Their family members soon dispersed, as some siblings went to South Korea before and during the Korean War and their remaining brothers in North Korea were taken to mining camps, apprehended by authorities, or persecuted for espionage and other charges. Chang Chŏngsun's family status forced her to break her engagement and abandon her dream of becoming a writer. This led to deep resentment and abusive behavior toward her father, which left her with a lifetime of remorse. O Sunbok and her family suffered further because her older brother served the South Korean army and for decades gave anticommunist lectures in the South Korean army. Chang Chŏngsun and O Sunbok escaped to China in February 1966 and December 1966, respectively. Chang's escape was helped by a Korean Chinese who was returning to China after participating in the Korean War and postwar reconstruction efforts.

Upon their arrival in China during the heated moments of the Cultural Revolution, which were explored in chapter 5, they were immediately accused of espionage and suffered abuse and violence for four to six months. Chang used her knowledge of Marxist-Leninist theory to overpower her uneducated accusers, invoking socialist internationalism and claiming her commitment to join the revolution in China. After interrogation, O settled in Yanji in the Yanbian Korean Autonomous Prefecture, while Chang remained in Shangzhi in Heilongjiang Province after reluctantly marrying the Korean Chinese who brought her out of North Korea, as she had no one else to help her. Both Chang and O became well off by making clothes for neighbors and lived as overseas North Koreans instead of becoming Chinese citizens. Chang explained why she kept her North Korean citizenship despite her rejection of the North Korean state:

North Korean citizenship is the proof of my life ordeals. . . . I had undergone nothing but excruciating pain in North Korea, left North Korea facing unspeakable personal sacrifices and deep resentments, and suffered from the Cultural Revolution. I therefore wanted to go to South Korea and return to North Korea after the nation is unified. That's why I tightly held onto North Korean citizenship. . . . I carried *kongminjŭng* [certificate of North Korean citizenship] with me in China and brought it with me to South Korea.

Their North Korean overseas status was renewed by the North Korean government every five years. To hide her class origin and political status, Chang became active in the affairs of overseas North Koreans, who numbered 168 in her county, treating them with rice cakes at monthly meetings and showering officials visiting from North Korea with meals and gifts. When she and others were invited to North Korea by the government in recognition of their work in China, she did not go for fear of exposing her past. During her secret visit to North Korea in 1975, she saw her married younger sister but failed to meet her mother and learned that her father had died on the street in despair and madness after his two remaining sons were abruptly taken away (to be put to death).

With the 1979 Open Door Policy in China, Chang and O located their siblings in South Korea through a South Korean broadcast company and acquaintance, respectively. In the 1980s South Korean radio programs began to connect families scattered in South Korea, China, Sakhalin, and the former Soviet Union. The most remarkable program enabled by the spread of television in households was *Searching for Separated Families* (*Isan kajok ŭl ch'atsŭmnida*), a 138-day-long television program launched by the Korean Broadcasting System in 1983. Originally planed as a live broadcast over four consecutive days to promote anti-North Korea sentiment and enhance the military government's legitimacy, it registered 100,952 requests, featured 53,536 participants and their stories of separation, and televised the extraordinary events surrounding reunions of 10,189 people living in South Korea (Yang Kŏnmo; Cho Chŏnghun 2014). O Sunbok wrote to a South Korean broadcast company for help; it found her brother in South Korea, who then invited her to South Korea. But she was denied a visa because of her North Korean citizenship. Between 1980 and 1989 she made several attempts and was swindled when trying to go to South Korea via Hong Kong. Finally in 1989 she and her four-year-old son succeeded in reaching Burma after walking, taking a bus, and traveling by boat. However, a Korean intelligence agency officer at the South Korean embassy in Rangoon rejected her defection. She and her son were arrested in Burma for illegal entry and imprisoned for five months. They were released and brought to South Korea only after her brother, a retired general in the South Korean army, pleaded their case with the authorities. As for Chang Chŏngsun, a lucky break in her attempt to find her siblings in South Korea came through an acquaintance in China who found a contact with her hometown association in South Korea. Her father's friends in the association invited her to South Korea. However, the South Korean government refused to issue her visa because of her North Korean citizenship. In 1993 she came to South Korea after purchasing a certificate of Chinese citizenship from someone fifteen years younger than herself. After her arrival, she learned that her brother had died and was buried in the national cemetery for veterans, but she met her sister in a meeting of their hometown association. Chang Chŏngsun and her sister remained estranged. Her sister refused to believe that their family in North Korea suffered because of the rumor that she spied for South Korea in the 1950s during her stay in North Korea. Her sister also suspected Chang Chŏngsun of spying for North Korea.

Chang Chŏngsun and O Sunbok remained stateless in South Korea for years. The South Korean state neither recognized their North Korean citizenship nor granted South Korean citizenship (kukchŏk). Only after many failed appeals to the Ministry of Justice over more than three years, they acquired South Korean citizenship out of the compassion of individual officials.

Chang's cousin disapproved of her efforts to acquire South Korean citizenship and rebuked her, asking what right she had to demand citizenship after not having paid taxes for all those years. Chang told him that she and her family suffered under the national division and that the South Korean government must accept her as an escapee from the other Korea. In one of her visits to an office at the Ministry of Justice to appeal for citizenship, she threw papers from a desk out of anger and frustration. She sat on the floor wailing and shouting, "I am a victim of history. Why do you refuse to accept me?" A middle-aged official consoled her and asked her to wait about a week. In fact, she received her citizenship a week later, in 1996. O Sunbok received South Korean citizenship as a favor from a local city official in Seoul in 1993 after national security agency officials continued to threaten her about applying for citizenship—perhaps in fear of being reprimanded for denying her defection from Burma. O reconciled with her brother. To repent actions lecturing on anticommunism that caused suffering for his family in North Korea, he committed himself to writing about her life experiences. After writing day and night for several months, he died of a heart attack. Her brother's widow blamed O for the death and refused to give her the manuscript.

Their membership in the South Korean nation-state remains largely incomplete even after their acquisition of citizenship, because the South Korean government refuses to recognize them as *kwisunja* (defectors) or *t'albukcha* (escapees). In their minds, acknowledgment of their torment in North Korea and China must come from the South Korean state, for they suffered under the national division and waited decades to come to South Korea. After Kim Dae Jung became president, Chang Chŏngsun visited the Blue House and submitted petitions, but to no avail. In her emotionally charged argument, she is a true t'albukcha for having suffered from political oppression in North Korea, while many current escapees do not seem to suffer in North Korea and even enjoyed benefits and privileges as in cases of high-profile escapees. She describes the importance of being recognized as an escapee:

> The South Korean government does not believe that people like me exist. Those recognized as t'albukcha received money and a house from the South Korean government. I have been neither accepted as t'albukcha nor given a house. I am living in a rented place. Yet I don't feel grief over my financial situation. I just want to be recognized that I escaped political oppression in North Korea. . . . Undergoing social and political oppression is far more painful than having no money and

being starved. Although I don't have a house and am poor [in South Korea], I like that I can talk freely about my life.

While working as a housekeeper or in a restaurant for sixteen hours a day from 7:00 A.M. to 11:00 P.M., Chang continues to prepare her petitions at night, write her life history, and talk to anyone, including me, interested in her life experience. Carrying a photo of her brother's tomb in the national cemetery, she also appeals to the media. O Sunbok sums up her seventeen years of futile pleading to the government for acceptance as kwisunja, the period from 1989 until 2006:

> I went to China only to come to South Korea. I stayed there only because the border was closed during the Cultural Revolution. . . . I stayed there only because I would be put to death if return to North Korea. I got married to a Korean Chinese only to survive, and gave birth to three children only because I continued to live there. It is nonsense that I cannot be recognized as kwisunja only because of that. My resentment will be resolved only by being granted defector status . . .
>
> How could my koguk [home country], to which I came risking my life, treat me this harshly. I have been so resentful that I cursed this place and cried with every footstep over the last seventeen years.

Determined to be recognized as t'albukcha by the US government if not the South Korean government, she even went to Los Angeles. After declining to take her case, Kim Young Hwan of NKNET advised her to go to the United States and seek asylum as a refugee from North Korea. She pleaded her case to Korean American churches and the media for a month and then returned to South Korea after her health deteriorated.

The life experiences of Chang Chŏngsun and O Sunbok are a portmanteau definition of North Korean refugee life spanning the history of the Cold War and the post–Cold War eras: kwisunja (defector) and t'albukcha (escapee). While O identifies herself as kwisunja, in the post–Cold War era refugees from North Korea are called t'albukcha. Although Chang regards herself as t'albukcha, this term is reserved for post–Cold War refugees, and specifically in association with North Korean human rights advocacy. Chang's escape does not conform with that of t'albukcha because she left North Korea during the Cold War's ideological showdown between the two Koreas, when escaping from one Korea to the other was called kwisun (defection), and she stayed in China for decades. Even if they were to acknowledge the existence of people like Chang and O, neither the South Korean government nor social movement organizations would know how to place their migratory experiences within current models of unification. Their migration is the excess of national history both during and after the Cold War. Cold War history is too nation-state bound to accommodate their transnational status in failing to choose either South Korea or North Korea. Post–Cold War politics is globalized to the extent that their life histories appear bound to the putatively old era of the nation-state. Filled with class struggle, purges, and revolutions, their life histories seem a thing of the past with no place in the prevailing unification politics that espouses peace and global democracy. Trying to transcend the Cold War ideology, South Koreans do not understand that this determination to become recognized as kwisunja or t'albukcha is irreducible to possible economic gain. For South Koreans, Chang and O are indistinguishable in attire and accent from Korean Chinese who come from China to work. Given these historical conjunctures, their stateless experience is too transnational during the Cold War era, and too national in the post–Cold War era.

Conclusion

The economic engagement policy projected linear historical change from coexistence of the two Koreas to the construction of peace for a gradual national unification; its projected linear time hides the time of capitalist repetition that engenders uneven integration and crisis-embedded expansion. The peace movement risks becoming a new fetish by conjuring capitalism as the spirits of peace and liberty. Despite its flaws, the minjung movement of the 1980s recognized the importance of embedding the utopian unification ideal in the task of transforming the capitalist system and imperialist structure. On the contrary, the democracy movement since the 1990s, including the popular national unification movement, has been entrapped by an ideology that pits the movement for structural change against issue-oriented, fragmented politics and severs national unification from social and global issues. Under the dual politics of national unification, national unification becomes a pawn for translating capitalism into market utopia. Whereas the democratic politics of the 1980s contested the nation as a site of the mass liberation struggle, democratic politics since the 1990s constructs the nation as a space of consensus about capitalism. Whereas national utopia of the 1980s saw peace as a total structural liberation, market utopia equates peace with capitalist expansion. Market utopia inverts the utopian dream of liberation from inequality, alienation, and injustice into a dream of peace and liberty.

Dual unification politics epitomizes a politics of ethics that dissociates democracy from its original vocation of critique, or what Abensour (2011) simply calls "action." In an effort to rescue everyday experience and spontaneity from the earlier teleological mass struggle, dual unification politics sterilizes democratic politics by subscribing to an ethics of peace and liberty. Accordingly, it hides the source and mechanism of national division. As in reparation politics, the politics of peace and human rights enables the state and its legal apparatus to base their legitimacy on the need to resolve the unresolved national history of violence and protecting the people from further excesses of the autocratic nation-state. Dual unification politics is neither just about the clash between engagement with and hostility toward North Korea nor just about the opposition between state sovereignty and global democracy. More important, it concerns the clash between two spectacles of democracy, which advocating peace and liberty, establish capitalism as a universal value—a neoliberal dictum that dispossesses the present of history and politics. At the center of democracy's spectacle-making is a dual consensus on national unification and neoliberal capitalism. Dual unification politics substitutes altruistic ethics for the original task of national unification to establish decolonization and popular sovereignty.

7

NORTH KOREAN REVOLUTION IN REPETITION: CRISIS AND VALUE

The breakdown of socialism across the globe since the late 1980s has led to mixed forecasts of North Korea's imminent future. Studies on North Korea flourish in South Korea and the United States and focus on its marketization since the economic crisis of the mid-1990s. The debates over marketization in North Korea largely mirror those on postsocialist transitions in Russia, Eastern Europe, and China. The key questions in the postsocialist transition debates are whether marketization involves a "bottom-up process" that benefits direct producers or reconstitutes the power of old cadres and technocrats (Nee 1989; Szelenyi and Kostello 1996), whether the transition involves the duality of a market economy and bureaucratic intervention or provides pluralistic pathways to capitalism (Kornai 1986; Walder 1996; Szelenyi 2008), and how new institutional networks arise from and contribute to the transition (Stark and Bruzst 1998). Similarly, as will be explained shortly, experts in North Korean studies espouse marketization as the force for income redistribution and political democracy, examine the coexistence of economic planning and marketization, and identify barriers to full marketization.

This debate repeats the inquiry into the transition to capitalism that concerned sociology's founders, Marx, Durkheim, and Weber, then under the haunting presence of socialism. This neoclassical sociology, according to Burawoy (2001a), lacks sociology's critical power, as it largely focuses on superstructural elements of capitalism such as elite formation, property forms, and political democracy. In its place, Burawoy (2001b) calls for "the excavation of embedded socialism" and ethnographic accounts of the everyday experience of producers (see also Verdery 1999; Zbierski-Salameh, 2013). A decade later, his critique and prescription still offer a powerful alternative to the current debate on the North Korean transition. This chapter provides an assessment of North Korea's putative transition to capitalism within the history of its arduous transition to socialism, leaving the analysis of everyday politics of North Korean migration for chapter 8. Socialist construction in North Korea—like that in the USSR and China—developed an unruly tension between realizing socialist ideals of equality and pursuing swift industrialization. The North Korean version of permanent revolution based on Juche (self-reliance) ideology involved a variety of institutional measures for reconciling the planned economy with capitalist principles of commodity production and appropriation of surplus value. The state's seemingly capricious swing between expansion and contraction of marketization maintains the contradiction and crisis that were built into its socialist economy from the start. Any prediction about North Korea's future must take account of this history, within which the meaning of the marketizing reforms arises.

This chapter begins with tales of everyday marketization, which posit socialism against marketization in North Korea. The Group Struggle Against Anti-Socialist Phenomena (pi-sahoejuŭi hyŏnsang kwaŭi kŭruppa t'ujaeng) since the 1990s is an allegory of the status of socialism in putatively popular discourse in North Korea. The recent marketization is a contested feature in North Korean studies in South Korea and the United States. Next explored is the history of socialist construction in North Korea, with attention to its interpretation of colonial and postcolonial conditions, national division, and global conditions of the reformist trend in the USSR. Its socioeconomic and political structure developed from the 1950s under these conditions and despite important changes has continued to the present. Its socialist construction was inflicted with contradiction and crisis, making it difficult to sustain a common periodization of the consolidation phase of the 1970s and 1980s and the crisis from the 1990s. The analysis draws on the writings of Kim Il Sung and Kim Jong Il, which I regard as administrative, political, and scholarly texts rather than as expressing their personal opinions. Whether written by them or by scholars and practitioners on their behalf, their writings address major issues and debates confronting the North Korean society.

SOCIALISM AS SPECTACLE

Formed in 1992 under Kim Jong Il's instruction, the Group Struggle Against Anti-Socialist Phenomena (the Struggle hereafter) aims to eliminate market activities said to be a hotbed of antisocialism. Under the time-honored principle of realizing "our socialist style" (*wurisik sahoejuŭi*), the Struggle seeks to manage the economic crisis using a small group dispatched by state institutions rather than by relying on judicial and bureaucratic operations. The Struggle is a new moment of exceptional sovereignty. Institutional hierarchy is suspended by an investigating group consisting of about thirty people for a firm to three hundred people in a border city such as Sinŭiju; they are dispatched from five politico-administrative organizations, the Prosecutor's Office, Social Security Office, Party Committee, Youth Federation, and Occupational Federation (Sŏ Chaejin 1995). Kim Jong Il defined antisocialist phenomena in terms of "bad behaviors that disrupt social order, abuse and waste state and social properties, and commit illegal and fraudulent market exchange." According to Kim, "The people's government must create terror not among the people but among the recalcitrant," and "the exercise of dictatorship is an act of protecting human rights when it is used to eradicate forces and elements that threaten the interests of the people" (Kim Chinhwan 2010:101–2). The Struggle fosters terror throughout society by charging that market activities are antisocialist and are being perpetrated by South Korean spies, when such activities are ubiquitous and essential. This dispatched group is granted the authority to conduct swift inspections, make arrests and indictments without warrants, prosecute and try antisocialist elements, swiftly conclude military court or public hearings, and oversee public executions.

Imjin'gang, a journal that pledges to publish news and accounts by ordinary people smuggled out of North Korea, reported on the Struggle in Hyesan in 2000 and in Sunch'ŏn in 2007. On hearing that "Hyesan became a bourgeois society," Kim Jong Il dispatched an investigating group to Hyesan called Libya (euphemism for prosperity), a border city of Yanggang Province on the Apnok River. The journal reported that a three-month investigation led to the arrest of more than one hundred people, mostly party officials and entrepreneurs apart from a few drug dealers and users, and the execution of several dozen. Party secretaries and prosperous owners of shoe, paper, and food factories were accused of "threatening, under orders of the South Korean National Intelligence Service, the people's life and property, seeking to overthrow the regime, and accumulating personal wealth by embezzling the state's property." Among the group was a leading businesswoman who imported bulky bags of baking soda disguised as flour from China and repackaged the baking soda in small bags in Hyesan. This enabled her to sell it at much lower prices than charged by other merchants, who imported individually packaged soda. She thus became known to locals as a pioneer who understood the secret of reducing costs—purchasing wholesale and employing cheaper labor—to make larger profits. She also engaged in the lucrative but risky business of finding relatives in North Korea for South Koreans and overseas Koreans. *Imjin'gang* reports that on hearing the results of the investigation, Kim Jong Il exclaimed in shock, "With whom do I make a revolution [if all of the accused party officials and elites are to be executed]?" This shock led to an official declaration of the prosecution in Hyesan as "a [political] error" (Lim Kŭnho 2010).

Pak Kiwŏn was at the center of the Sunch'ŏn incident in 2007 (Son Hyemin 2009). He ran an export-centered stone-carving factory, a construction and real estate company, and a service industry offering recreational and leisure activities for elites.[1] Called "the lifeline of the country," the Sunch'ŏn Combined Enterprise housed factories that produced fertilizer, machines, medicine, textiles, shoes, cigarettes, and cement. It was the home of the Sunch'ŏn Vinalon Factory; throughout the 1980s Kim Il Sung urged for its completion in order to solve the shortage of cloth once for all. Though the factory was completed in 1989, a design flaw prevented its opening. After decades of the factory being looted, the state ordered the factory's official liquidation in 2005, including the sale of its equipment and materials to other factories and the export of recovered metals. Pak was executed in front of about one hundred thousand local people on the charge of "destroying the history of the Kim Il Sung's revolutionary struggle" by acquiring a large transformer from the factory under the pretense of installing it in his factory and then selling it on the black market. To express the absurdity of the charge against Pak, local observers equated the antisocialist struggle to the anti-Minsaengdan struggle of 1932–1936, namely, the Chinese communists' purge of Korean communists as Japanese spies (Park 2005).

According to reports on the two incidents in *Imjin'gang*, the real secret of the Struggle is the state's desire to transfer its own failure to outsiders and label them as threats to the community. According to a local witness cited in the report, the Hyesan incident attests to the current era of "the emperor with no clothes": only the state fails to recognize the meaninglessness of socialism and the fact that the state is already dead. The witness adds that "the indictment of putative South Korean spies substitutes for an indictment of the bourgeois management style and private business, either because it would affirm the ubiquity of capitalism in reality and thus an already collapsed socialism or because it would show that the court is ludicrous for making ubiquitous reality into the supreme crime." Local witnesses of the Sunch'ŏn incident note that "this state subcontracts to the market" (Son Hyemin 2009).

The state's economy and administration all collapsed except organizations that collect revenue and reconfigure class struggle into a struggle between those who pay large amounts of money to the state (including bribery) and those who do not. State-owned factories and the state's planned economy depend on household and small-scale production units that supply resources. For example, shoe soles are produced at home using the kitchen stove and then collected and brought to state-run shoe factories, or microorganisms are cultivated at home for state-owned pharmaceutical companies (Son Hyemin 2009). According to *Imjin'gang*'s reports, the ubiquity of markets and corruption often led investigators to cover up findings that market activities are too omnipresent and entrenched in the political establishment to be eliminated without destroying the system itself.

Imjin'gang's reports insinuate that the state's misrecognition leads it to concede the violent nature of its own sovereign power. When Kim Jong Il burst out with his remark, "With whom do I make revolution?" he confronted the paradox that he can save the regime only by not defending it—only by not disturbing what was condemned as bourgeois phenomena. It exposes the truth that the regime may well remain alive only because it forgot that it was already dead, to paraphrase the Freudian dictum of recognizing truth by failing to repress it. The state momentarily waved aside its delusion by declaring the struggle against antisocialism an error. In the reports, putative insiders understand the prosecution of entrepreneurs as the repression of an emergent democracy. The state is condemned for prosecuting enlightened national leaders who created jobs, invented a new leadership style, and spearheaded economic growth. Reported as the everyday experience of ordinary North Koreans, this construction of the crisis in *Imjin'gang* strips marketization of its history and construes individuals as liberal subjects who consider state sovereignty as the threat to their freedom. The socialist state is considered a predestined site where individuals place the blame for the exploitation, monopoly, and competition that arise and grow with privatization and marketization. The liberal metalanguage of the state's innate violence in such a representation in *Imjin'gang* naturalizes intersubjective exchanges of belief and desire for privatization. Turning socialism into a spectacle, subjects release perverse surplus enjoyment in Žižek's sense by externalizing one's own contradictions onto the other—here, the state.

The North Korean state may well be the emperor without clothes. Not so much because it is the only one unaware of the death of socialism as because of the contradiction built into its socialist construction. As I will elaborate, the North Korean state has continuously integrated what are known as capitalist

FIGURE 7.1 An evening market in Hyesan, North Korea, in 2014. Courtesy of Cho Ch'ŏnhyŏn.

principles of production and exchange into its socialist construction. The exchange between the socialist state and individuals reported in *Imjin'gang* illustrates their latest performative politics. Depending on one's perspective, the state's outsourcing to the market can be interpreted as a continuity that maintains the institutions and ideology of the socialist state by means of the state's licensing of businesses and regulation of exchange and taxation.[2] Both the state and individuals construct their identity and power in reference to the most recent economic, political, and social changes. By depicting socialism as belonging to the past, putative ordinary North Koreans represent themselves as victims of state violence. Representation by individuals of their own victimization is ideological in that it legitimates their belief in capitalism in the face of increasing social inequality and antagonism.

Marketization as Spectacle

The seeming oscillation between the alluring pace of privatization and the state's reclamation of socialism in North Korea fascinates scholars, policy makers, and investors in South Korea who keep their eyes on this capitalist frontier. Studies estimate the scale of marketization in North Korea to range from 20 to 90 percent of total economic activity based on information from interviews with t'albukcha (escapees) (Pak Sŏksam 2002; Yi Sŏk et al. 2009; Kim Pyŏngyŏn and Yang Munsu 2012). Despite their various assessments of the scale of marketization, scholars conjecture a range of meanings of marketization in North Korea. The progression of marketization in North Korea is assessed to be much higher than that in Russia and much lower than in Hungary on the eve of their capitalist transition (Kim Pyŏngyŏn 2009; Yang Munsu 2010:109–24; Lankov 2013a:37). Questions about the regime's volatility and stability, which are central to the debates in North Korean studies, revolve around the issue of whether the current pace and nature of marketization and privatization lead to a capitalist economy and democratization.

Three perspectives reflect a representative spectrum of the current assessment of marketization and privatization. Firstly, experts observe a momentous shift from the totalitarian system of supreme leadership (suryŏng) to the market system. The expansion of the market economy throughout society and daily life is considered to have threatened the state's planned economy (Ch'a Munsŏk 2007; Kim Chongok 2008; Lankov 2013b). Firms and their managers are seen to have increased their authority in relation to the party on matters of production, consumption, and pricing, while voluntary market activities have already introduced the freedom of market exchange. The vast secondary (market) economy drains resources from the planned economy. Furthermore, the state increasingly depends on fees and taxes from market activities such as from the sale of market stands and the leasing of state firms and factories to individuals. The market is seen as fostering civil society and an emergent affluent middle-class at the same time as dissolving the old socialist system (Kim Pyŏngyŏn and Yang Munsu 2012).

Secondly, others caution against such expectations about swift regime change in North Korea. They argue that marketization leads to capitalism and thus regime change only under conditions that are not yet established in North Korea: a free market pricing system, free market exchange, ownership of profits and surplus by producers and consumers, freedom of financial transaction, and free juridical individuals (Chŏng Sejin 2000; Choi Wangyu 2006; Yi Wuyŏng 2008; Yun Yŏnggwan and Yang Unch'ŏl 2009). At present North Korean privatization has not established the capitalist system, for it relies not only on commerce such as the resale of goods for profit (toegŏri) but also on subsistence-oriented production such as simple food processing. Furthermore, North Korea is yet to develop large-scale industrial production, mass production and consumption, and capital accumulation. Thus, the North Korean economy is characterized not as a market society but as a "marketlike" (*sijangjŏk*) society, a term used by Nee (1989) to describe the Chinese rural economy of the 1980s. This perspective invokes a stage-based theory of capitalist development from merchant capitalism, to industrial capitalism, and then to finance and monopoly capital. It does not anticipate a return to merchant capitalism and subsistence production, as seen in responses by individuals to market reforms in Russia and Poland (Burawoy 2001b; Zbierski-Salameh 2013).

Thirdly, scholars highlight the coexistence of the planned economy and the market economy, whether in their duality, multiple and segmented sectors, or a combination of military rule and economic reform. This approach recognizes the possibility that state surveillance, inequality, market freedom, anomie, and alienation may stabilize the regime. Whereas Yang Munsu (2010) regards the duality of the planned and market economies as a product of the economic crisis of the 1990s, Kim Pyŏngro (2012) dates it to the socialist construction since the 1960s. According to Kim, marketization expanded in the local industry sector, where he locates the rise of individuals as wholesale merchants and middlemen since the mid-1990s. According to Pak Hyŏngjung (2009), the duality exists in almost all economic sectors, including those controlled by the Kim Il Sung family, firms owned by official organizations, firms run by the military and party organizations, the agricultural and cooperative sector, and local markets. Pak argues that this multiple segmentation makes it difficult to separate the formal and informal economies (see also Im Kangt'aek 2014).

Despite their differences, these three divergent perspectives in North Korean studies characterize marketization as extraneous to socialism. In contrast, I argue that the regime theorized capitalist principles as being integral to socialist construction. Under specific historical conditions, the regime formulated its version of permanent revolution and developed its distinctive economic structure. The historicization of socialism and marketization authorizes a serious investigation of North Korea's permanent revolution or its transition to socialism.

JUCHE AS CONTINUOUS REVOLUTION

The anticolonial struggle transforms the theory of permanent or continuous revolution into the pursuit of self-reliance or Juche ideology in North Korea. Studies of North Korea consider this ideology the foundational creed of a theocracy that legitimates totalitarian sovereignty. Scholars have attempted to understand its source in terms of ethnic, familial, religious, and mythic traditions (Hassig and Oh 2009; Myers 2011; Kwon and Chung 2012). Instead, I approach Juche ideology as a program of permanent revolution, which formed political sovereignty through the concrete process of socialist construction. The regime promotes Juche theory as a product of its historical conditions— the legacy of Japanese colonial domination, national division, and American imperialism. Like their Soviet and Chinese counterparts, the North Korean state singled out the development of productive forces as the essential factor for completing the socialist transition. In 1969 Kim Il Sung (1971g) stated that the socialist system frees productive forces from crisis, as state planning allows for the rational use of resources, establishes equilibrium among sectors of the national economy, and fosters rapid technological development and increased labor productivity. As during the Great Leap Forward in China, the people's revolutionary zeal was mobilized to make "the productive forces multiply." In a nutshell, self-reliant development (charyŏk kaengsaeng) since the 1960s pursued heavy industrialization and regulated labor processes to extract surplus from labor. The North Korean regime extended Lenin's vision of the alliance of the proletariat and peasants during the socialist transition while condemning Trotsky's insistence on the dictatorship of the proletariat for politically isolating workers (Kyesok hyŏngmyŏng e kwanhan chuch'e chŏk rihae 1992). Nonetheless, the regime constantly emphasized the hegemony of the working class and the construction of workers and peasants into the masses under the leadership of the supreme leader (suryŏng). Mao espoused continuous revolution in stages from collectivization and industrialization to ideological-cultural and technological struggle. Similarly, the Juche vision underwrites "ideological, technological, and cultural struggle" as the crux of its continuous revolution.[3]

With an idiosyncratic and utopian flair, heavy industrialization and the law of value have become the two pillars of North Korean development through theoretical debates and political struggles over the stages of socialist transition. Sŏ Tongman ascribes the power struggle in the mid-1950s, which was crucial to Kim Il Sung's rise to power, to the debate over stages of socialist revolution (Sŏ Tongman 2005, 2010). The momentous controversy developed over the interpretation of the historical conjuncture marked by completion of land reform and collectivization. In 1956 Song Yejŏng in the Yenan group defined North Korean society as still completing the bourgeois democratic stage, in which anti-imperialist and antifeudal democratic revolution still required an alliance with the democratic bourgeoisie, whose private capital was necessary for restructuring the economy.[4] Song advocated the creation of "state capitalism" in North Korea. Like Lenin's 1921 New Economic Policy, this would permit market exchange of agricultural goods, foster the coexistence of state planning and the market, and pursue balanced economic growth rather than rapid heavy industrialization. In contrast, Kim Il Sung's Kapsan group asserted, in tune with Mao Tse-tung's standpoint of the Chinese development, that the completion of agricultural collectivization completed the transition to socialism and authorized the consolidation of socialism through continuous ideological, technical, and cultural struggles. In 1955, asserting socialism as "an inevitable demand of social and economic development," Kim Il Sung (1971d) saw small peasant economy, commodity production, and private trade and industry as impediments to the growth of productive forces. Under the banner of building "state socialism," Kim Il Sung pursued Stalinist heavy industrialization as the "first and foremost priority" in 1958, although, like Mao, he also attended to the development of light industry and agriculture (Li Myŏngsŏ 1991:144). Kim (1971d:21–22) asserted that the priority to develop heavy industry is the crux of socialist industrialization:

Only with the establishment of a powerful heavy industry is it possible to ensure the development of all industries, transport and agriculture, and the victory of the socialist system. The backwardness and deformation of our heavy industry, the legacy of Japanese imperialist colonial rule, hampered the development of the economy as a whole in our country after Liberation . . . If we do not set up a powerful heavy industry in our country in the future, we shall not be able to shore up light industry which was originally very backward, nor provide the countryside with modern farm machinery, nor ensure radical improvement in the people's living conditions. Only with the establishment of a powerful heavy industry can the independence of the economy and the independent progress of the country be assured.

As of the late 1980s heavy industrialization was still called the foundation of economic development. In a speech delivered to the Central People's Committee Meeting in 1989, Kim Il Sung (1997b:266) reiterated the urgency of prioritizing the development of heavy industry, given that a secure supply of electricity, coal, cement, and steel would make possible the production of modern machinery, fuel, and materials needed by other industries. This development of productive forces under conditions of resource shortage and the fight against imperialist power, argued Kim, requires the revolutionary spirit of self-reliance of the masses under the supreme leader's guidance (*Kyesok hyŏngmyŏng e kwanhan chuch'e chŏk rihae* 1992:14–29).

At first socialist construction was tied to colonial and postcolonial national politics under national division, but it soon fixated on the development of North Korea's economy. At the beginning, the establishment of an independent national economy in North Korea was elevated to the foremost task in creating the democratic foundation for ultimate national unification. The land reforms of 1946 were called "the great historic undertaking of converting North Korea into a firm democratic base for the reunification of the country" (Kim Il Sung 1971a:37). The issue of pro-Japanese collaborators was dealt with far more thoroughly in the North than in the South, where the United States helped to maintain the power of those who had served the Japanese empire in the administration, army, and police. In that conjuncture, rice symbolized a form of national sovereignty. When an independent accounting system was introduced, Kim Il Sung (1996g:363) objected to its extension to agriculture:

> Since we were liberated from Japanese rule, we have provided rice to people at a very low price. . . . If the price of rice is set at market price, households with few children will be alright, while households with many children will not have much left after buying rice. This would not make everyone live well. That's why we have continuously provided rice at a low price. I said, rice itself is communism.

According to Kim, "People without a country [*nara*] are worse than a dog at a funeral." Political conditions, however, determined the process of decolonization even in North Korea, as the purge of Japanese collaborators, for instance, not only was delayed by a wide nationalist front of communists and moderate nationalists in 1945 but also imposed land reform and collectivization on political opponents who resisted the Soviet policies (Chŏn Hyŏnsu 2002). Moreover, the development of a socialist national economy after the Korean War further detached its socialist construction from the drive for reunification. The two Koreas' agreement on peace in 1972 was soon followed by the establishment of two dictatorship regimes across the demilitarized zone and their race for economic growth. Kim Il Sung's speeches on the economy were routinely devoted to the role of the party in developing heavy industry and its connection with light industry and agriculture. The quest for decolonization was transposed onto the memory of armed struggle during the 1930s in Manchuria, which was the basis of the Juche ideology until the present. The issue of national unification perennially appeared only in Kim's interviews with foreign journalists and delegates (Kim Il Sung 1991). Paik Nak-chung, a prominent South Korean critic, characterized North Korean economic development as a loss of self-recognition under the national division (see Sŏ Tongman 2010:157). This fading self-recognition surfaces in cosmopolitan moments of meeting the people of other Third World socialist countries.

In reality, economic planning in North Korea has continuously faltered after some initial success, although North Korean studies in South Korea focus on the crisis of the 1990s and see the pre-1990s as the period of socialist consolidation. The period of rapid economic growth (1957–1970) was afflicted by continual shortages of labor, technology, and capital, which were compounded by pursuit of economic self-reliance. Foreign aid fostered rapid postwar reconstruction from 1954 to 1963. Despite a growth rate of 7.5 percent in the 1960s, the first Seven-Year Plan centered on heavy industrialization beginning in 1961 and took ten years to complete. The decline in foreign aid and global oil shocks slowed the pace of economic growth in the 1970s. Accordingly, the Second Seven-Year Plan (1978–1984) was extended for three years because of difficulties in the strategic sectors of electricity, steel, and nonferrous metal production. The North Korean economy experienced negative growth from 1990 to 1998, which includes the food crisis of 1995 to 1997, and then rebounded to a growth rate of 3.8 percent in 1999 and 2000 (O Suyŏl et al. 1995; Kwŏn Oguk and Mun Inch'ŏl 2011). For outside observers, the economic crisis relates to the planned economy and the personality cult. Inside North Korea, however, it is attributed to the shortage of resources and labor, declining labor productivity, and bureaucracy. From the 1960s onward the regime persistently sought to resolve these problems with institutional measures: the dual economic structure, distinctive industrial organization, and adoption of the law of value. North Korean state continued to integrate capitalist principles into its socialist construction through these measures. The wave of privatization and marketization in North Korea since 1990s must be assessed in the context of this internal debate on socialism and capitalism.

THE DUAL ECONOMY AND MARKETIZATION

In the dual economic structure, planning and allocation of resources and labor for heavy industry were controlled by the state, while oversight of light industry was relegated to provincial and district authorities (Pak Hyŏngjung 2009). From the mid-1950s to the mid-1970s, heavy industry accounted for about 80 percent of the state's total industrial investment in North Korea. As a means to rationalize industrial production to manage shortages of resources and labor, localized light industry producing consumer goods was expected to mobilize underutilized sources of labor, among which housewives were frequently mentioned (Kim Il Sung 1971f). The call to develop local production of light manufacturing was repeated throughout the 1970s and 1980s (Kim Il Sung 1986c). Calling it a miracle in 1980, Kim Il Sung (1996c) reported the creation of nearly four thousand modern local factories, which he said were born out of the ashes of colonial rule and war and provided the people with food, clothing, and housing. The localization of light industry progressed as the proportion of support for local government in the state's total budget decreased from 30 to 35 percent from 1960 to 1964 to about 15 percent from 1973 to 1990 (Kwŏn Oguk and Mun Inch'ol 2011:156).

The localization of light industry is framed as a utopian vision of balanced development that fixed two quintessential forms of uneven capitalist development: between the city and countryside and between accumulation and consumption. North Korea's agricultural traditions and large rural population are seen to give the country a particular advantage in establishing even development, as local industries absorb them. In 1962 Kim Il Sung (1971b:343) characterizes the situation:

In capitalist countries the population is excessively concentrated in cites; in no respect is this good. In our country where socialism is being built in conditions under which capitalism did not develop well, there is no need to allow undesirable population concentration in the cities as in capitalist society. Factories should not be concentrated in the cities only, but built in different places according to the specific features of the provinces. What a splendid job it is to build factories and develop industry in all parts of our country with its beautiful mountains and rivers!

He called for building factories that reflect the specific characteristics of each province. This approach to the development of local industry also was projected to reduce transportation costs and serve strategic interests because the geographic dispersal of production facilities would decrease their vulnerability in the event of enemy attack. Kim states (1971b:342) in the same speech:

How difficult it would be if we built foodstuff, textile, paper and other factories only in cities, and had to bring raw materials from all parts of the country, press oil and produce textiles and send them back to the consumer areas! Suppose we made soy sauce and bean paste in Pyong-yang and sent them to the remote mountain areas. We would have to bring in beans, make the soy sauce and bean paste and send them back there. In sum it would be a two-way transportation.

In 1970 Kim (1986c:33) also stated that "the most important thing in socialist economic construction is to maintain a proper balance between accumulation and consumption and between the production of the means of production and consumer goods." According to Li Myŏngsŏ (1991:131), a North Korean economist, accumulation and consumption are not in principle antagonistic in socialism because "socialist accumulation ultimately aims to serve consumption." However, Li reasons that it would take considerable time to reach that point of socialist accumulation; meanwhile, systematic increase of accumulation over consumption is necessary to expand technology and increase economic development. At the same time, the regime found it impor-tant to provide sufficient consumption goods not only for everyday living but also for increasing material incentives for peasants and workers. In 1962 Kim criticized the tendency for peasant households in cooperatives to pile up their share of rice at home, making rice cakes and giving them away to visiting mar-ried daughters and relatives rather than selling them and thus making them available to others. It was expected that the production of consumer goods would motivate peasants to work harder so that they could increase their cash income and buy more consumer goods (Li Myŏngsŏ 1991:357–58). In this context, the regime, in principle, consigned the production of most consump-tion goods to local industries. Though taken as a means to encourage both frugality and market-based purchase of basic goods, a reduction in the volume of goods available through the system of free distribution is consistent with the ongoing shortage of daily life necessities. For instance, in the 1980s Kim Il Sung (1996f:192, 1996i:405) instructed that one new uniform be distributed to each worker every four years as an inducement for workers be careful with uniforms and buy their own replacement as needed; soldiers received a new uniform every five years. At the same time, the processing of food and fishery products for sale, including cooked mushrooms, dried kelp, and salted and dried fish, was repeatedly encouraged as a means for increasing cash income. Improvements to the packaging and display of goods to increase their value and price were also encouraged, such as selling juice by the glass on the street. Products made by such subsidiary work were sold through three channels: state-owned stores, direct stores run by various organizations and coopera-tives, and farmer's markets (Kim Chinhwan 2010).

FIGURE 7.2 North Koreans processing of potatoes at the Apnok River in 2013. Courtesy of Cho Ch'ŏnhyŏn.

Subsidiary production and market exchange of consumer goods have been and continue to be emphasized. The subsidiary production of consumer goods is known as the 8.3 system, referring to Kim Jong Il's Instruction on August 3, 1984, to increase production by using leftover materials, factory waste, and surplus household labor (Kim Pyŏngyŏn 2009; Yi Sŏkki 2009). Declaring 1989 as the year of light industry, the regime facilitated the production of consumer goods, ranging from processed foods, clothing, shoes, umbrellas, brooms, buckets, and furniture to tires, electric fans, and bicycles. Producers were permitted to sell their goods for income. The July 1, 2002, Instruction, which is North Korea's most ostentatious privatization policy, once again encouraged individuals to refurbish used goods or recycle waste to sell in the market and state-approved stores; the identity of sellers or suppliers of the materials was not required. The 2004 New Management System allowed up to 30 percent of production to be sold at the discretion of managers.

Key changes from the 1990s are twofold: an unprecedented expansion of markets and the introduction of a rudimentary form of private property ownership. The shifting policy on market operations includes the daily People's Market (*inmin sijang*) in three or four places in each province until 1950, the

Farmer's Market (nongmin sijang) in two or three designated places every ten days per province after collectivization in 1958, in one to two places daily in each province beginning in 1984, back to every ten days starting in 1991 during the crackdown on antisocialist activities, and a return to daily trading in 1993. In 2003 the Farmer's Market was changed to the Comprehensive Market (chonghap sijang), and by 2007 these markets numbered close to three hundred and traded about 80 percent of all daily goods (Kim Ch'anghee 2010). The prohibition on trading grain and industrial goods was lifted with the exception of military weapons. The expansion of market activities since the 1990s benefited from the legalization of private property rights. Privatized items under the Civil Law and Family Law of 1990 include housing, household goods, cars, and items needed for agricultural and fishery production, such as fishing boats, livestock, and farm implements. The state legalized 30 to 50 p'yŏng of land per household, about 1,000–2,000 p'yŏng to an entity such as an agricultural cooperative, and 100 p'yŏng for a military household. In the beginning, cultivation was restricted to vegetables but later was extended to corn, beans, and other staples as a result of the food crisis.[5]

The latest economic crisis began to diminish by the late 1990s. The production of coal, electricity, cement, and magnesium reportedly increased since 1999. Industrial factories surpassed production targets, and local industrial firms increased their production of consumer goods. New small- and medium-sized hydroelectric plants improved the supply of electricity. Imports from China eased shortages of resources needed for production. Agricultural production increased with South Korean assistance in the cultivation of grain, potatoes, and other vegetables. In such a conjuncture, the state sought not just to retain its control over subsidiary production and market exchange but also to appropriate their profits. On the one hand, the state repeatedly restricted eligibility to market trading and the range of tradable goods. The July 1, 2002, Instruction vainly ordered workers to return to factories and workplaces and permitted only women to conduct market trading. From 2005 to 2008, the state repeatedly limited market trading to women over forty years old or increased the minimum age to forty-nine, although people evaded the restriction with bribery and falsified permission (Ryu Kyŏngwŏn 2009; Yang Munsu 2012). On the other hand, the state ordered all subsidiary production units run by individuals, households, and neighborhoods (kanae-ban or kanae chagŏppan) to register at administrative units (inminban) and pay a fixed proportion of profits as fees. The state also ordered individuals to pay for release from their official workplaces in order to engage in more profitable production and market activities. In addition, the state also rented market stands with varying fees depending on the price and kinds of goods sold on the stands and the location of the stands (Kim Pyŏngro 2009).

Historical analysis of the dual structure suggests that the increased marketization of local production after the food crisis of the mid-1990s did not break with the socialist economy as assumed in the scholarly literature; rather, the increase was continuous with it albeit accompanied by significant changes. As mentioned earlier, North Korean studies in South Korea define subsidiary market activities as the "informal" or "secondary" economy, in contrast to the formal or state-planned economy. They debate whether the expansion of market activities leads to regime failure and democratization. They also debate whether in the 1990s the regime reversed the priority in economic development from heavy industry to light industry and agricultural production. The shortage of consumer goods and grain had continued long before the crisis of the mid-1990s, however, and was addressed by the development of the dual industrial structure. The current marketization tends to have increased in agriculture and light industry, i.e., local firms and factories owned by districts and provinces that mobilize local resources to produce consumer goods. Markets and the production of consumer goods by individuals, neighborhood organizations, and local firms have all along been characteristics of industrialization in North Korea. Recent efforts by the state to bring the market under its control are not new; they are markers of the continuous struggle to accommodate the market within the state's socialist construction and to cope with the consequent contradictions.

INDUSTRIAL STRUCTURE AND ORGANIZATIONAL NETWORK

The industrial structure in North Korea consists of the independent accounting system (tongnip ch'aesanje) and the combined enterprise system (yŏnhap kiŏpso). The former aims to increase the discretionary power of managers in production, exchange, and the use of profits in order to boost incentives to improve labor productivity and make production more efficient. The latter integrates factories that produce related goods into one industrial unit under the control of the primary factory. Mirroring the business accounting system implemented to offset shortage and declining productivity in the USSR, the independent accounting system was introduced in 1962 in state-owned firms and factories, applied in the early 1970s to local firms, and then expanded in 1984 to all sectors of production and distribution. In the independent accounting system, the funds necessary for production are primarily provided by the state; a firm is expected to submit a designated proportion of income and profit as well as other fees to the state on schedule and is allowed to keep the rest. Until 2002 materials used in production were to be procured through exchange with finished products to prevent firms from favoring production of high-priced or easily producible goods (Kim Sanggi 2004). The prohibition on paying cash to procure resources for production, however, interfered with the independent accounting system because producers were not concerned about pricing and profits.

In 1984 Kim Il Sung (1996i) described the independent accounting system as the only means to improve the poor coordination among officials and organizations. Officials in charge of planning were chastised for setting production quotas without adequately considering actual conditions of production, namely, resources, labor power, and demand for the product. Firms and factories were criticized for meeting quotas at the expense of quality. For instance, in order to meet targets for delivery to thermal power stations, coal mines did not use their coal-dressing machines to purify the coal; when burned to generate electricity, impure coal did not produce sufficient heat, which resulted in malfunctioning equipment and accidents. In Kim's (1986c:35) critique in 1970, the State Planning Commission and other state economic agencies saw "only the big, thick branches of the trees while ignoring the small, slender twigs." The big and thick branches of the trees may well refer to the required amount of production necessary for the development of productive forces, as in the Great Leap Forward of China; and the small and slender twigs may denote details in the actual production process. North Korean leadership sought to resolve the chronic shortage of resources and labor through the increase of material incentives and accountability. The July 1, 2002, Instruction furthered the independent accounting system by authorizing a firm to plan, produce, and sell at least a portion of production at the price set by itself.

Introduced in 1973 on an experimental basis and fully implemented in 1985, the combined enterprise system integrates strategic production plants with the main suppliers and auxiliary factories. Like its counterpart in East Germany during the late 1960s and early 1970s (Grabher 1997), the combined enterprise system in North Korea was an attempt to rationalize the coordination and control of production and offer basic infrastructural services such as training technicians and organizing community affairs. This combined enterprise system is different from the combined company (yŏnhap hoesa), which, like the Soviet type under the Khrushchev regime of the late 1950s, integrates firms producing the same products in a local area or nationwide, for example, to form a mining combined company or a chemical combined company, in order to standardize technology and products. Given that the economy was governed by the principles of unified and detailed planning, a combined enterprise receives its production quota from the state planning committee of the government's administration (Chŏngmuwŏn),[6] and then the combined enterprise plans its own production process. The administration's department of industry instructs the combined enterprises under its control on the use of technology. The primary factory in each combined enterprise decides on the production technology and organization used in the combined enterprise's other factories. Pronounced in North Korea is the importance of securing supplies of resources and the rational use of resources and produced goods by creating an intricate web of co-dependency among factories in a combined enterprise. The combined enterprise system implements the double independent accounting system at the levels of combined enterprise and factory. A combined enterprise on average consists of about ten factories, though a large one comprises twenty to forty factories.[7]

In the late 1960s, Kim Il Sung (1986a:22) articulated the idea of the combined enterprise system by sharply contrasting capitalist and socialist economies: In capitalist society, capitalists do not care one bit about other sectors or factories, as they purchase needed resources in the market; in contrast, in a socialist planned economy, because "all production is carried out according to plan, the egoistic attitude of being satisfied with just the prosperity of one's own sector and one's own enterprise, without paying any attention to others, cannot be tolerated." He attributes the waste of the state's resources to the lack of cooperation among different sectors of the national economy and among factories. For instance, the failure to produce a sufficient quantity and quality of coal causes steel production to decline; that in turn decreases the manufacture of machinery used to weave textiles. The shortage of tractors in the countryside is also traced back to a factory's deficient production of crankshafts, then to the Kangsŏn Steel Plant's insufficient production of thin pipes, and finally to the inability of Hwanghae Iron Works to produce enough sheet steel (Kim Il Sung 1986a). Major components of the Sunch'on Vinalon Combined Enterprise include the primary factory that extracts vinalon from coal and limestone and produces vinalon fabric; chemical factories that use derivatives produced in the extraction, such as a carbide factory and a fertilizer factory; and a fabric dyeing factory. Yet the goal of centralizing industrial production was hampered by the primary factory's inability to command the combined enterprise's other factories in their use of production technology and organization. For instance, the 2.8 Vinalon Combined Enterprise dispensed with the coal factory because of the inability of its primary vinalon factory to direct the technology and organization necessary for coal production.

Although limited in number, studies of the North Korean combined enterprise system are divided about its characteristics. Some characterize it as a centralized system that adopts the Taean management system (Pak Hugŏn 2013), while others attribute its expansion from the mid-1980s to its decentralization of management (O Kangsu 2001). Introduced in 1961, the Taean management system integrates the central party's power over the economy with the mass-line policy, emphasizing the principle that "the upper organs help the lower, superiors help their inferiors" (Kim Il Sung 1971f; see Ch'a Munsŏk 1999). At the same time, the Taean system emphasizes the practice of the mass-line policy that instructs party members to "go deeply among the masses" and collect opinions from workers under the regime's signature motto, "One for the whole, the whole for one." The mass-line is presented as the corrective to the bureaucratic tendencies pervading factories and enterprises. Collective discussion among party cadres, management cadres, workers, and technicians is promoted to accurately determine production capacity and the necessary quantity and quality of labor. The supreme leader who instructs the masses directly through his frequent workplace visits is idealized as the force that unifies all these elements into an organized process of production (Juch'e ŭi kyŏngje kwalli iron 1992:69–106). In contrast, the combined enterprise system is considered to harbor the tendency to decentralize production. Its expansion from the mid-1980s is credited with the decentralization that transferred many functions from Chŏngmuwŏn to combined enterprises concerning production planning and contracts between combined enterprises, in addition to management of resources (O Kangsu 2001). The increased power of local authorities over firms and factories in late 1981 created problems for the coordination of planning and production, when a combined enterprise consisted of factories across different provinces, districts, and cities (Nakagawa 2003b). In response, during the 1980s and 1990s the combined enterprise system in North Korea was restructured several times to make changes in its jurisdiction and managing departments (O Kangsu 2001).

Does the combined enterprise system lead to a horizontal network of integrated production firms capable of instigating resistance against the Workers' Party's authority, as happened in the Soviet Union when the Communist Party director, technical deputy director, and trade union representative at the factory level cooperated to resist the state's production targets in the 1920s?

Or is the combined enterprise system capable of creating a top-down patronage network like that in China, which enabled Deng Xiaoping to enlist the support of the Communist Party and provincial secretaries for his reforms? Padgett (2012:267–315) contrasts these horizontal and patronage networks in his analysis of communist organizational networks. North Korea seems to have developed both of these organizational networks, though further study is needed. The possibility of developing a horizontal network at the level of factory or combined enterprise exists, when party members have power over managers but also are dependent on them for meeting production quotas and realizing profits. Shortages of resources particularly induced the two groups to cooperate closely in evading laws and regulations in order to acquire resources, fulfill the quota, and make profits to pay wages to the workers. Despite the continuous call for ideological and cultural struggle, it is doubtful that the central party succeeded in containing the egoism and bureaucratic tendencies of party members and preempting the formation of a horizontal network at the level of factory or combined enterprise. Kim Il Sung (1971c) in 1962 criticized party functionaries for "rushing around carrying briefcases . . . here and there from early morning on like travelling salesman [sic]." Party functionaries may well have pursued the "thin and long lifestyle"—exercising political influence to access material goods and maintaining the status quo by hoarding and lying about production. In the early 1990s Kim Jong Il was critical that "party secretaries in some factories and enterprises carried out administrative roles such as the allocation of resources, while neglecting their original role to educate the people," and that "party members lost their judgment on whether their intervention in economic matters is right or wrong" (Ch'a Munsŏk 2002). Some patterns of corruption since the mid-1990s expose the network of cooperation at the firm or combined enterprise level. Fraudulent bookkeeping and reporting on production and supply of produced goods to officially designated factories enable a firm or a combined enterprise to sell products on the black market and obtain cash to buy resources for production or for individual profit (O Kangsu 2001). Interviews with t'albukcha show that factories submit about 30 percent of their production to designated factories, sell about 30 to 40 percent to other factories to obtain resources, and sell 20 to 30 percent on the black market (Yi Sŏkki 2004). Some bureaucrats even invest their own money to buy resources and sell them in the market for profit. Using their political network, they also lend the name and the right to do business illegally. For example, a firm operating a railway offered its building and electricity to illegal producers of artificial meat made from the leftovers of soybean oil production (Kim Chongok 2008).

The mass-line policy of the Taean system, which was presented as a corrective to the bureaucratic tendencies pervading factories and enterprises, might deter the development of the horizontal network. Even before the crisis of the 1990s, members of the central party were prompted to consult in person with a factory's party committee and managers as the approach to modify a combined enterprise's planning through mediation by the regional planning commissions; and members of the regional commission were instructed to make personal visits and hold discussions with workers, technicians, and party members in the workplace on details of production, from procuring resources and labor and obtaining product specifications to distributing schedules (Kim Il Sung 1986a:28). State planning departments were established in factories and enterprises to function as "cells" of the regional planning commissions (Kim Il Sung 1986b:91). This mass-line politics was intended to create a patronage system not so much between the party and provincial secretaries as between the party and the masses. The combined enterprise system is promoted as the means to unite party leadership with the mass-line policy for the realization of self-reliance. Kim Il Sung noted that according to Juche ideology, the combined enterprise system is especially important in a country like North Korea that lacks the foreign currency needed to import resources and goods; he also mentioned that he had declined the Soviet Union's offer of electricity because accepting aid could lead to Soviet interference. The tension between centralization and mass-line politics in the Taean system is repressed by the supreme leader's sovereign power, which is elevated as his love for the masses and makes his instructions to them supersede all other policies.

The interdependence of firms in the combined enterprise system means that a failure in the system can cause the crisis to spread like a brush fire. The combined enterprise system, however, seems to be neither a complete failure nor a complete success. The regime affirmed its merits by restoring it shortly after its termination. In 1999 the combined enterprise system was dismantled under the New Economic Strategy in order to divert the state's resources to factories with strategic importance, such as steel plants. However, it was reinstated in the following year because its dissolution worsened shortages of resources. As part of the reform, the right to foreign trade, which Kim Il Sung opposed granting to combined enterprises in order to preserve national independence, was permitted to combined companies. Scholars in South Korea debate whether economic planning and factory management moved from the central party to the state's administrative cabinet with the beginning of economic liberalization in the 1990s. For some experts, the shift from the party to the state was a response to the economic crisis for which the party was blamed: managerial authority over economic policies was made official in late 1993 after the failure of the Third Seven-Year Economic Plan; the 1998 constitutional reform transferred economic management from the party to managers of factories and enterprises; from early 2002, hundreds of economic experts were dispatched to factories and enterprises; and enterprises and factories no longer submitted their budgets to the ministry of finance but instead to the provincial government (Ch'a Munsŏk 2002; Yi Sŏkki 2004; Pak Hyŏngjung 2009). According to Yi Taegŭn (2009), the observed shift of economic planning from the party to the cabinet results from a grave misunderstanding of the North Korean system in terms of the division of the party, the state, and the military. Yi argues that the supreme leader is firmly in power through his control over the party, which in turn controls the military and state administration through party committees. Yi's thorough analysis is, however, restricted to the top level and does not address organizational relations between the top leadership and lower-level functionaries in the party system.

The succession of Kim Jong Il in 1994 and the consequent military-first rule (sŏn'gun chŏngch'i) intensified the feud among scholars in North Korean studies about the changing relationships among not only the party, administrative cabinet, and the military but also the state's economic planning, the market, and the military economy. In 1966 Kim Jong Il established the basis for his succession by creating the post of party secretary that came to control the party. Beginning in the mid-1970s he acquired control over key party offices and by 1980 consolidated his power over the party and the military. Whereas some experts stress the military's wresting of power from the party and the state, others observe a continued unity of the party, the state, and the military.[8] Some others speculate that the military industry (and its foreign trade of lucrative materials), which is largely autonomous from the cabinet's budget and has been separate from the general economy since the early 1970s, maintains the reproduction of the socialist economy (Cho Taesŏk and Yun Sŏngsik 2005). Yet others see it as newly reinforcing the diverse sectors of North Korea's multidimensional economy (Pak Hyŏngjung 2009; Kwŏn Oguk and Mun Inch'ŏl 2011). A major effect on the economy of the military-first rule is the use of the military industry's budget to develop missiles and nuclear facilities. One should not, however, overemphasize the military's political and economic power. Except for the period of 1998 to 2002, when the military budget increased to 29 to 37 percent of GDP, the military budget remained at 22 to 27 percent of GDP from the early 1970s until 2008.

FIGURE 7.3 North Korean soldiers trimming radish in 2013. Courtesy of Cho Ch'ŏnhyŏn.

SOCIALIST LABOR AND THE LAW OF VALUE

The industrial structure in North Korea depends on its labor policy. The labor system simultaneously normalizes and disrupts the institutionalized labor process in North Korea by regulating labor and by mobilizing the shock work movement. The Taean system has institutionalized labor regulations and material incentives while merging them with the mass-line policy and political and ideological incentives. It has standardized the labor process by detailing daily schedules, labor shifts and their procedures, use of tools, and material rewards. At the same time, shock work has been adopted to break the labor routine to set a new standard for the labor process. The New Economic Strategy of 1998 has further enforced this double approach, strengthening the regulations and renewing the so-called Ch'ŏllima movement. New labor heroes have been named as model workers for exemplifying the spirit of self-reliant development and demonstrating determination and creativity by circumventing material shortages, repairing machinery, and exceeding production quotas (Ch'a Munsŏk 2002).

It is commonly assumed that North Korea concentrates on political and ideological incentives and implements free and equal distribution known as "the average principle" and that these North Korean socialist characteristics disintegrated with the economic crisis in the 1990s and the July 1, 2012, Instruction that ended the free distribution of housing and daily essentials

(Koryŏ taehakkyo kich'o hangmun yŏn'gu t'im 2005; Kim Chinhwan 2010). On the contrary, I argue that, despite the importance of political and ideological incentives, the regime has also embedded material incentives in the very conception of labor during the socialist construction. In a report on the work of the Central Committee to the Fourth Congress of the Workers' Party of Korea on September 11, 1961, Kim Il Sung (1971e) emphasized "material stimulus to the working people's enthusiasm for production." Already during postwar reconstruction in the 1950s, workers were subject to specific regulation of their labor, for instance, the number of bricks to be moved each day, receiving a larger stipend for exceeding the labor quota and less for falling short of it (Kim Il Sung 1996e). According to Kim Il Sung (1971e), the principle of socialist distribution is "to eat according to work," so distribution differing according to the quality and quantity of work is defined as "an objective law in socialist society." That is, the principle of "eating according to work" was named as the socialist principle of labor (Kim Il Sung 1996g). The Socialist Law of Labor implemented in 1978 reflects the regime's orientation that "a communist society is not a society where one will have an easy life and not have to work," but a society "based on collectivism, in which all the working people work and live in unity" (Kim Il Sung 1996g). It grants the state the power and responsibility to set piece rates as "the basic form of pay," which are formulated on the basis of data from a model factory in each sector of the national economy (Kim Il Sung 1996a). Setting the labor quota is rationalized as the means to accurately align the amount of machinery and labor in the workplace. The Taean system aims to bring the regulation of labor under the party's central control.

At the same time, the mobilization of shock work has continued in the name of creating a seamless unity of individuals and the collective. Launched in 1957 to fulfill the Five-Year Plan of industrialization ahead of schedule, the shock work was called the storming movement (tolgyŏk undong) modeled after Ch'ŏllima, the legendary winged horse that flies hundreds of miles a day to the land of happiness. It was reported that workers dash forward at the speed of Ch'ŏllima to shorten production time on all fronts of socialist construction across industry, agriculture, transportation, construction, science, education, and culture. By the end of August 1961, 2 million working people joined the storming movement; 4,958 work teams and workshops, involving 125,028 persons, received the title of Ch'ŏllima, and 55 work teams with 1,459 persons were honored with it twice (Kim Il Sung 1971e). The shock work movement has continued in recent years under various names, among them "The Seventy-Day Battle," "The Three Revolutionary Work Team Movement," and "The Three Revolutionary Red Flag Acquisition Movement."

Buck-Morss (2002:111) explores the meaning of "shock" in the shock work that was popular during the First Five-Year Plan in the USSR: "Shock" (*udar*) is "the Russian word meaning a blow or strike with impacting force in the military sense (of an air attack), in the natural sense (of a thunder clap or musical percussion), and also in the medical sense (of stroke or seizure)." As the name given to shock work in North Korea, storming (*tolkyŏk*) shares the image of superhuman rather than the machinelike images of the Taylor system. But the word tolkyŏk describes a concerted attack and platoon-collectivity in military ground forces that count on the coordinated efforts of individual soldiers. The memory of the anti-Japanese armed struggle in Manchuria of the 1930s and 1940s has routinely been evoked to foster political and ideological motivation among workers. The memory of the Manchuria armed struggle came to be equated with Kim Il Sung's heroic struggle, erasing the history of the tumultuous relationship of Korean communists and peasants with both Chinese communists and Japanese colonizers. In his call in 1962 to overcome shortages of resources in local industrial production, Kim Il Sung (1971b) recounted the episode when his guerrilla army in Manchuria extracted nitric acid from cow urine to produce gunpowder for use against the Japanese imperialists. In his appeal in 1982 for the construction of medium- and small-sized hydroelectric plants, Kim Il Sung (1996d) told the tale of the people's determination to use a water mill to hull rice and grain for guerrilla armies. In order to inspire the production of consumer goods and diversification of subsidiary work, in 1984 Kim Il Sung (1996i) presented the underground guerrilla fighter Wang as a role model: he disguised himself as a merchant during the Manchuria armed struggle to accomplish his clandestine work and in doing so earned money to finance the party's publications. To emphasize the importance of inventing and repairing machines and tools, Kim (1997a) spoke in a meeting of the Central Committee of the Workers' Party in 1988 about making "Yŏnkil bombs" during the Manchuria armed struggle by using common items such as hammers and cooking pots, which came to symbolize the development of self-reliance. Kim (1996h) also emphasized the habit of study as key to cultivating the art of socialist leadership, referring to the experience of the Manchuria armed struggle during which study was said to be the foremost duty of revolutionaries. His pardon of guerrillas suspected of being pro-Japanese Minsaengdan spies is taken as displaying his belief in the masses and their dedication to the revolution by becoming self-sufficient (Kim Il Sung 1986d). In 1990 Kim (1997c) also invoked the Manchuria revolutionary spirit when urging the people to make small tractors by themselves and mechanize agriculture instead of waiting for the state to supply them with large Ch'ŏllima tractors.

FIGURE 7.4 Slogans posted on a building in Musan, North Korea, in 2013. Courtesy of Cho Ch'ŏnhyŏn.

The widely reported feud between Hwang Jang Yŏp and Kim Jong Il in 1996 needs to be assessed within this history of socialist labor policy and practice. As an architect of Juche ideology, Hwang held the highest post in the Office of the Secretariat, where documents and speeches about policies are written for the supreme leaders. In a statement about his exile submitted to South Korean intelligence and published in the conservative magazine *Wŏlgan Chosŏn*, Hwang attributes his defection to a fundamental clash with Kim Jong Il over "the importance of material conditions for developing the independence and creativity of the people" (see Kim Chinhwan 2010:307–12). In his own recollection, Hwang advocated marketization of the North Korean economy and the adoption of material incentives, whereas Kim dismissed emphasis on material factors as reactionary bourgeois thought and revisionism that corrode the party. However, these oppositions between socialism and marketization and between material and ideological incentives are problematic. They are nothing new but rather are built into the socialist construction that integrated them. Since the 1950s the development of productive forces has perhaps been the most important imperative in the construction of the North Korean economy. The merger of material incentives and workers' submission to the state also has been the cornerstone of the labor process. The regime long ago rejected the principle of distribution by need as the "averaging principle" or "the unity principle" (chŏnch'ejuŭi) that ignores the individual's contribution. In the mid-1980s Kim Jong Il avowed that "collectivism opposes not the application of material incentives but the practice of placing individuals' interests before those of the group" (Kim Chinhwan 2010:216–17). Kim Jong Il reiterated in 2001 that "those who labor more and better must receive a larger share of both material rewards and political recognition" (Kim Chinhwan 2010:478). The repeated emphasis on the principle of distribution according to work may well be the sign of the contrary tendency of political favoritism. At least it illustrates a basic contradiction in its socialist construction.

When labor discipline is central to rationalizing resources and improving productivity, the looming question concerns the appropriation of surplus value from labor, i.e., the law of value. Theorization of the law of value is central to interpreting the transitional character of the socialist economy in North Korea, as it was in the USSR. Kim Jong Il (2003:1–2) stated in 1961 that proper "utilization" of the law of value is crucial in the transition period when traditional and past modes of production coexist:

> The law of value [kach'i pŏpch'ik] should not be ignored if we are to rationalize the economic management system in a socialist society, where remnants of the old society still exist. Only when the law of value is utilized properly can we strengthen the system of savings, mobilize workers to raise the quality of products, and immediately implement the independent accounting system. . . . In a socialist society, consumer goods are commodities, and workers receive their distribution according to labor [nodong e ŭihan punbae] in the form of money so that they can pay money to buy consumption goods. The law of value is, therefore, bound to operate here.

When answering scholars' questions about the law of value in the Science and Education Department of the Party Central Committee in 1969, Kim Il Sung cautioned about the grave effect of any "Right" or "Left" error on this question. He (1971g:168) explained that in the socialist economy during the transition period,

> the law of value operates not blindly as in capitalist society but within a limited scope, and the state uses it in a planned way as an economic lever for effective management of the economy. Later, when the transition period is over and cooperative property is turned into property

of the entire people so that a unitary form of ownership is established, the produce of society . . . will not be called a commodity but simply the means of production and consumer goods, or by some other name. Then the law of value also will cease to operate.

Kim Il Sung (1996b:179) went on to say in 1978 that the law of value operates with the independent accounting system, which leads to "reduce the per-unit consumption of materials and increase both the output value per employee and the quality of the goods produced."

The adoption of the capitalist principle is theorized only in "form," not in substance. The state's pricing of goods and financial control are theorized as measures to ensure socialist use of the law of value. In his aforementioned 1969 answer to scholars, Kim Il Sung (1971g:170–71) elaborated that production under the independent accounting system and the law of value takes the "form" of commodity production. This occurs because state enterprises operate as if they were under different ownership and use and manage the means of production independently of one another. Independent management gives the impression that the means of production exchanged between them are commodities like those handed over to different ownership; however, with the state's planning, the exchange of commodities is determined by prices set by the state.[9] Taking the state's pricing of stationery goods for school children as an example, Kim Jong Il (2003) emphasized that the law of value serves the need of the people in a socialist society in contrast to its service to capitalists' profit-making. When firms in a socialist economy are forced to buy with their profits and sell for more profits, they do not waste resources and sell or purchase even small means of production. In that way, useless things are not taken and useful things are not left unused, argued Kim Jong Il. This forces firms to produce goods of sufficient quality for market trading.

In this theory of the law of value only in form, banks must gather unused or idle money and supply it to sectors in need by speeding up the circulation of currency (Kim Il Sung 1971g). The rapid circulation of commodities (resources) merged with an equally rapid circulation of money is expected to prevent hoarding and wasted resources. In this way, the socialist monetary system aims to link commodities with the financial and circulation sectors (Li Wŏn'gyŏng 1986:56–119). Currency reforms in 1947, 1959, and 2009 facilitated the circulation of money back to banks by invalidating currency that was held by individuals and firms too long and thus kept out of the circulation. Repeated currency reforms set the maximum amount that can be converted from the old to the new currency. The 1947 reform set the convertible amount according to class and political position—worker, peasant, clerk, adminis-trator, firm, organization, and so on (Li Wŏn'gyŏng 1986:58–67). The 2009 reform limited currency conversion to 100,000 won per household at 100:1, while allowing individuals to convert an additional 50,000 won at 1,000:1. Experts debate the latest currency reform as either an expedient to seize cash in preparation for a succession of power or as a means to bring market activi-ties under the state's planned economy (Kim Ch'anghee 2010). Beyond this debate, currency reform is to be understood in the context of its socialist his-tory of financial control, commodity exchange, and the law of value.

North Korea's theorization of the law of value ironically inverts Marx's the-sis. Marx's (1976) law of value explains profit as originating from surplus value in the form of unpaid labor. While Marx criticized political economists who saw market investment and pricing as sources of profit, North Korean leader-ship similarly turns to the state's pricing to justify labor regulation and the accumulation of surplus value. As debated in the USSR during the 1930s, the political meaning of the socialist use of the law of value would then depend on the nature of the state—whether it benefits the nomenklatura or the people. Discussing the Soviet adoption of the Taylorist labor system, Buck-Morss (2002: 104) noted that Lenin also thought "he could import capitalist forms of labor without their exploitative content" and justified it in the name of the transitional economy. In Lenin's words:

The Russian is a bad worker compared with the people in advanced countries . . . [as a result of] the persistence of the hangover from serfdom. . . . The Taylor system, the last word of capitalism . . . is a combination of the refined brutality of bourgeois exploitation and a number of the greatest scientific achievements in the field of analyzing mechanical motions during work, the elimination of superfluous and awkward motions. . . . The possibility of building socialism depends exactly upon our success in combining the Soviet power and the Soviet organization of administration with the up-to-date achievements of capitalism.

(Buck-Morss 2002:309–10)

But "the capitalist form is its content," according to Buck-Morss (2002:104–5), as factory workers' sensory experience of assembly line production is indis-tinguishable from that in the West. The cult of the machine seems more futuristic in North Korea, given the shortage of machines. However, the similarity between the two socialist regimes is undeniable: both appropriate capitalist dynamics and rationalize the appropriation in the name of eliminating remnants of the old society in the move toward historical progress.

CONCLUSION

This chapter has demonstrated the importance of historicizing the processes of marketization and privatization that have expanded in North Korea since the 1990s. It has shown that the putative current transition to capitalism is embedded in the history known as the transition to socialism. Throughout its socialist construction, like other socialist countries North Korea confronted a clash between the task of capital accumulation for productive forces and the axiom of creating an alternative to capitalist social relations. Contradictions and attempts to resolve them are surprisingly consistent in North Korea. Its socialist economy has been built up through a strategy that has prioritized heavy industrialization while relegating the production of consumer goods to local governments. In the name of rationalizing production and distribution, the regime has implemented an independent accounting system and a distinctive industrial structure. It has also appropriated the law of value by aligning labor regulation with financial control over factories and enterprises. Prevailing scholarly opinion opposes socialism and capitalism, treating them as extraneous to each other. The analysis in this chapter, however, discloses the historical efforts to reconcile socialism with production and appropriation of surplus value and to theorize the uneasy adoption of capitalist principles as the socialist transition. Institutional measures analyzed here are emblematic of North Korea's rendition of permanent revolution.

This analysis of crisis and crisis resolution does not assume a clear demarcation between normalcy and crisis in the North Korean socialist economy. The common periodization that distinguishes the period of crisis since the 1990s from the period of consolidation that preceded it contributes to interpreting the current crisis as a sign of the total failure of North Korean socialism. Instead, it is more viable to consider socialism a critique of capitalist social relations and to comprehend the internal logics and contradictions involved in the arduous process of actualizing such critique in the so-called transition to socialism and communism. Contradictions and crises are inherent in North Korean socialism. This historical perspective allows us to avoid futile predictions about North Korea's inevitable or stalled transition to capitalism. The blend of socialist and capitalist elements is not a recent phenomenon resulting from ad hoc attempts to resolve the current economic crisis but part and parcel of the systematic theorization and realization of socialist transition. Despite significant changes, the current marketization and privatization from the 1990s reconstituted rather than abandoned these contradictions. An adequate explication of this historical context serves as the basis for cogent interpretation of the crisis and its constitutive effect on the state's sovereignty and everyday politics.

8

SPECTACLE OF *T'ALBUK*:
FREEDOM AND FREE LABOR

Border-crossing migration constitutes the everyday politics of economic crisis and a subsequent reconfiguration of socialism, capitalism, and democracy in North Korea. The everyday meaning of freedom, labor, and border crossing is invested with memories of the past and desires for the future. The present is nonsynchronous: it is not continuous with socialism nor is it a linear transition to market democracy. Reconstituted notions of freedom and equality in relation to the new interpretation of socialism become the drivers of border-crossing migration. Central to my analysis of North Korean migration is the narrative of "I didn't have to come [to China and South Korea] but still [I did] . . ." that suggests nondecision and contingency. Interrupting idioms that rationalize border crossing, the narrative defies its experience as a totality with clear causes and effects. The narrative does not allow an easy resolution of the experience of border crossing nor determine its meaning. I characterize the narrative of "I didn't have to come but still . . ." as a discourse of commodification in which one transcends and reinforces one's own commodification in the process of production and market circulation. Rather than turning North Koreans away from market activities, the experience of unequal exchange, uncertainty, and monopoly in the North Korean market drives people to migrate to China and South Korea in further pursuit of market opportunities. In other words, repeated migration from North Korea to China and to South Korea is the Hegelian "negation of negation" without the dialectical resolution of their displacement.

This narrative authorizes a shift of analytic focus from commonplace disputes over the human rights of North Korean refugees to the commodification of their labor. This shift enables us to connect inquiry into state sovereignty with inquiry into commodification and in doing so explore the thorny relationship between freedom and free labor. The popular narrative of t'albuk describes North Korean border crossing as an escape from totalitarian rule and constructs North Korean migrants as refugees whose condition as stateless subjects dispossess them of their inalienable rights as humans. Instead, however, they are refugees in the sense that in the modern history of capitalism, people are repeatedly expropriated from their means of livelihood, are displaced, and become free labor. Fearing social unrest, the state categorizes these displaced people as beggars, robbers, and vagabonds and makes work compulsory despite its scarcity. For Marx (1976:875), this process of primitive accumulation is a history written "in letters of blood and fire." For Polanyi (1944), intellectuals and policy makers make a variety of responses to the commodification of land, money, and labor, including formulation of social welfare programs and the liberal creed in order to recover "the society." Primitive accumulation continues until the present as accumulation by dispossession, according to Harvey (2005), or as the logic of expulsion, according to Sassen (2014). The narrative of "I didn't have to come but still . . ." reveals the historical unconscious of the people expropriated from North Korea and China. At a time when representative political democracy and legalism are foreclosing on the space for critiquing capitalism, I discern a few aleatory subjects, who imagine a new collective politics by reworking socialism's utopian dreams of prosperity, equality, freedom, and work for use value.

The border-crossing migration of North Koreans since the late 1990s marks a new postcolonial moment. Their migration to China, especially for the Korean Chinese community in northeast China, evokes the colonial displacement of more than a half-century ago. The history of colonial migration shared by Korean Chinese and North Koreans translates into ethnic and national affect that mediates the current border-crossing of North Koreans and their commodification. Korean Chinese are the figure of "interposition," who comes between North Korean migrants and their experience of capital accumulation and freedom (see Žižek 2007:4). This interposition inverts the capitalist integration of Korean Chinese, North Koreans, and South Koreans in the post–Cold War era into perverse emotions for one another. The missionary work of Korean Chinese with North Koreans doubles this interposition, establishing spirituality as the foundation for prosperity, thus reversing the Calvinist principle of hard work. Whereas the Cold War era was marked by the sublime goal of unifying the two Koreas, the post–Cold War era is a postunification moment that develops a transnational ethnic community.

This chapter begins with a reading of the unreleased documentary *Kando Arirang* to extrapolate the past and present in the union of North Koreans and Korean Chinese. This leads to my analysis that embeds North Korean migration in the socioeconomic and political changes taking place in North Korea and explores the everyday narrative of repeated migration to China and South Korea. Following this, I construe ethnic nationalism as mediating border-crossing migration and enabling migrants to transcend and repeat their own commodification. Finally, I delineate three aleatory subjects whose politics suspend commodification.

KANDO ARIRANG

The unreleased documentary *Kando Arirang* set in Yanji, China, is an allegory of the relationship between Korean Chinese and North Koreans in the capitalist present. Made by Cho Ch'ŏnhyŏn between 2000 and 2003, the film's poignant love story portrays the impossible union across the border that signifies the surplus of a capitalist present. The title cannily overlays the folk anthem "Arirang" of displaced lovers' heartache and sorrow in the face of drought, war, rebellion, and foreign invasion with the history of Korean displacement to Kando (currently Yanbian Korean Autonomous Prefecture), including the current North Korean migration. The union of Yi Hwasu, a seventy-five-year-old Korean Chinese widower working as a street cleaner in the market, and O Yongshil, a sixty-five-year-old North Korean widow working illegally as a caretaker in a Yanji hospital, symbolizes the unfulfilled communion of the displaced in both societies. While O at first begs him to live together as a last resort because she needs to find safe housing in China, mutual affection seems to have taken root. She suggests that they live together in North Korea when Korea is reunified, saying that her children would treat him well. Yet until then, she feels haunted while shuttling back and forth between North Korea and Yanji in search of her youngest daughter, who was kidnapped by Korean Chinese traffickers during their first trip to China in 1997, five years earlier. She returns regularly to North Korea once or twice per year to take money she earned to her children, and she looks after other North Korean women in China while searching for her abducted daughter. When she goes to North Korea, Yi anxiously awaits her without knowing whether they will meet again, saying whoever "dies first would be happiest for not having to go through the pain of heartache." She wishes to die in North Korea and rest her spirit there, for her children are there and her late husband is buried there.

Her experience of displacement is encapsulated in her sense of "bitterness about the lapsed time" (*sewŏl ŭl wŏnmang hamnida*). In her words:

> The time passed really fast. I came [to China] to earn a living by trading. After food ran out during the food crisis [in North Korea], my husband went to stay with my eldest daughter. One month later, I received a telegram about his death. Then I searched for any means to survive, but couldn't find any. So I took a train to go to stay with her, but got off at Sambong and crossed the Tuman River [to come to China]. Then I lost my youngest daughter. I searched in frenzy for her here and there. . . . If I am in North Korea, I am restless with the thought that I could find my youngest daughter if I go to China. Once I am in China, I am frantically looking for her in vain, while my heart is also racing for my other children in North Korea. I resent the lapsed time. Why do I have to live with this pain and hardship?

As a metonym for the historical present, lapsed time—an unspecified length of time—eludes a clear enunciation. She sings "Harvest Song" [*p'ungnyŏn'ga*] as a substitute for an explanation; its joyful lyrics could not be farther from her emotional state. She also sings a more somber folk song with the lyrics: "There is no place to go [and settle] in this world. Where are you going? Where are you going crossing this field?" She mournfully says, "It is so sad. Where can I go?" She reveals her respectable socioeconomic status in North Korea when she remarks that if her daughter were sold to a rural man as most of the trafficked North Korean women are, she could not endure country life. She confides to the filmmaker that she and her daughter came to China to buy goods for her daughter's marriage (*honsu*). She maintains the appearance of t'albukcha and hides the fact that she is living with Yi Hwasu when she visits churches and NGO-run shelters for assistance. Yet she is critical of the discourse of t'albuk, saying that whenever she was caught on the train in North Korea without a travel permit, she was immediately released without a word of admonishment by North Korean border guards and police (if she told them she was traveling to find food).

O dies suddenly of a heart attack in October 2002 while hiding in a friend's house in China to avoid a government crackdown on illegal North Koreans. Yi bids her farewell at the funeral:

> Goodbye. Let's meet in *kuch'ŏn* [the other world] again. You are happier than I am since you died first. . . . What a pity that your spirit is in a foreign country for having died here. When you go to the other world, beg

your deceased husband to forgive you. How does this happen? *Zaijian* in Chinese. *Sayonara* in Japanese. *Chalga* in Korean.

His trilingual farewell encapsulates the repeated displacement of Koreans under Japanese colonial rule, the Chinese revolution, the Korean War, and the current crisis.

The experience of historical excess momentarily becomes palpable and derives meaning through reference to historical memory. When Yi restlessly awaits O's safe return from North Korea, he is awakened by what his grandfather asked him about "the sorrow of the Tuman River" more than sixty years earlier:

> During Japanese colonization, Koreans flocked here. It [Manchuria] was known as a good place to live. My grandfather moved from Hwanghae Province [to Kando] carrying my then two-year-old father on his back, and then sacrificed himself for the family's survival by working for Han Chinese landlords. When my grandfather asked me whether I understood "the sorrow of the Tuman River," I had no clue, thinking what nonsense it was. However, as I now live with her, it resonates with my heart.

In his innocent boyhood remembrance, his current experience coheres into his perceptual and sensorial world. It captures a broken dream of his grandfather and his generation. His burst of recognition is a form of writing on the memory system, creating a space of contemplation and turning the everyday passage into a substance that releases history from the frozen container of the Chinese socialist history and its history of the Korean Chinese minority. His metacommentary about the Tuman River's sorrow is a self-reflexive moment, which breaks the dams of official and local histories and releases the flow of history across the generations. The sensory memory of displacement stored in his grandfather's body and words is now transferred to his own. A mnemonic return to the colonial era does not guarantee belated recognition of the authentic meaning of colonial or current migration. Instead, mnemonic practices capture the problem of recognition, then and now, and the possibility of a dialectics that leads to a new political subjectivity. In light of Benjamin's insights, remembering the Tuman River's sorrow can awaken one to the colonial experience that was repressed and thus is not yet constituted as "experience"; this awakening can in turn give rise to another political awakening from normative everyday experience in the present moment (see Benjamin 1969).

MARKET DEMOCRACY

The politics of North Korean human rights represent North Korean migrants as refugees from totalitarian rule, or t'albukcha. This representation has garnered significant political and moral weight for advancing South Korean conservative politics of human rights and global politics of anti-terrorism. It also has been challenged by various NGO reports and scholarly studies. During the heyday of North Korean migration in the 2000s, t'albukcha tended not to come from the most impoverished sector of the population, contradicting t'albuk narrative (Kang Ch'ayŏn 2004:63). According to my North Korean interviewees, the actual reasons for their migration are diverse, ranging from the search for food and freedom to boredom, flight from criminal prosecution, search for family members who previously went to China or were separated during the Korean War, search for work, and small-bag trading.[1] Moreover, only a fraction of North Korean migrants plan to go to South Korea when they leave North Korea. Many migrants go back and forth between North Korea and China, return to North Korea after earning money in China, or become long-term migrants who secure residence with real or forged Chinese residency documents. Migrants usually visit home two or three times during stays in China of five to seven years, maintaining contact with their family in North Korea.

Retribution against t'albukcha in North Korea is reduced except for those who sought to go to South Korea and made contact with missionaries. Since it is hard to prove the frequency of border-crossing, t'albukcha can claim starvation as the cause of crossing if they are caught. The image of North Korea's borders as formidable barriers is Cold War posturing rather than reality. Most of the length of the Tuman and Apnok Rivers dividing China and North Korea is not only unguarded but also shallow enough for children to cross by walking or swimming; the waters usually go up to an adult's chest or neck at their deepest. According to my interviewees, people across the rivers communicate by gestures or shouting such that if North Koreans ask for something in the morning, those on the Chinese side can provide it by the afternoon. Border crossing can also be treacherous, for it can involve waiting for hours at night in winter's blustery cold for a signal from the guard on the other side of the border. Crossing is synchronized with the border guards' schedule and regularized through bribes, which were 100 to 200 yuan per each person per crossing in the early 2000s and increased in 2006 after both states attempted to crackdown on migrants without permits. Moreover, South Korea is not the only destination for t'albukcha who also settle in Canada and Europe (Im Kŭnho 2009; Choi Sŭngch'ŏl 2012).

FIGURE 8.1 North Korean children fishing in the Apnok (Yalu) River in 2013. Courtesy of Cho Ch'ŏnhyŏn.

The aporia in characterizing North Korean migrants as escapees from totalitarian rule denotes the impossibility of understanding freedom solely within the framework of state sovereignty and the universal system of freedom and equality. Instead, the narrative of "I didn't have to come but still . . ." suggests that North Koreans' own notions of freedom are grounded in historically specific conditions of their migration, that is, global capitalist integration of North Koreans, Korean Chinese, and South Koreans. The narrative relates to the deregulated nature of their migration, which contrasts with government-sponsored migratory work in Russia. At least until the mid-2000s, North Korean laborers in Russia moved in small groups of two or three, freely searching for work, especially in the logging and mining industries under official contracts between the two states; and they paid half of their wages to the North Korean state (Interview with Cho Ch'ŏnhyŏn on October 22, 2006, in Seoul). In the 1990s, lucrative work in the logging and mining industries in Russia under official contracts between the two states was popular among North Koreans. By the mid-1990s, about 20,000 North Koreans worked as loggers in Russia, though its popularity declined in 2000s, when those leaving their workplace to become undocumented laborers in Russia became less rare (Kim Ch'angbŏm 2009; Ostrovsky 2009). In contrast, migrants to China are commonly depicted as refugees rather than as migrant workers. Beyond different responses to illegal North Koreans in China and Russia, the regional variation of their migration reveals a global production chain that since the 1990s has come to encompass North Korea, China, and South Korea. In China, North Korean migrants fill the labor shortage not only in farming resulting from the exodus of Korean Chinese to South Korea but also in the flourishing service industry in Yanbian fueled by their remittances and savings from South Korea. Even during the food crisis from 1995 to 1998, North Korean men worked as seasonal agricultural laborers from May to October and in the forests cutting lumber. It was common for a North Korean man to return and work for the same household every year (Interview on July 2, 2002, in Seoul). North Korean women worked in restaurants and other service sectors. Comparing with Korean Chinese migrant workers in South Korea, a North Korean woman said in 2001 that she worked in Tumen in China "without paying the broker's fee, while Korean Chinese must pay at least $10,000 to work in South Korea." She earned about 1,000 yuan annually, paying only 100 yuan to North Korean guards when leaving and returning to North Korea (Interview on July 3, 2003, in Seoul). North Korean migrants also find work in labor-intensive factories operated by South Koreans in Shandong and other coastal areas in China. In this chapter I interpret North Korean migrants' representation of freedom and free labor within this global capitalist circuit, and I probe the social character of the migration narrative of "I didn't have to come but still . . ." through the relationship between capitalism and democracy.

"Bold and Short Style"

North Korean migrants represent their border crossing as being prefigured by the prolonged yearning for freedom under socialism. The notion of market democracy fills in the political space opened up by the latest economic crisis. Women, ordinary workers, and the politically marginalized are said to be among the first to become entrepreneurs because they had so little to lose; the powerful and loyalists to the socialist system, known as the "core strata" (*haeksim kyech'ŭng*), were either too ashamed to engage in market trading or feared the state's sanctions even at the risk of starvation (Choi Pongdae 2008; Son Hyemin 2010). A son of a Korean War prisoner recollects that his family's low political status actually made it easier for them to venture into market activities and earn a lot of money well before the catastrophic food crisis. By paying bribes, he and his older brother were assigned to jobs favored in North

Korea, himself as a railway official and his brother as a chauffer. His family thought of escaping to South Korea as early as 1995 and even withdrew their savings from the bank, but the death of Kim Il Sung raised hopes of unification, and they temporarily halted their plan. He spoke of having loved South Korea since childhood:

> I longed to live in South Korea since I was ten years old to the extent that I thought of myself as South Korean. I longed to go to South Korea even more after hearing from Korean Chinese merchants visiting North Korea in 1987 that South Korea is not a colony of imperialist America but an affluent country.
>
> (Interview on August 9, 2002, in Seoul)

His brother, who engaged in illegal trading in antiques with Korean Chinese brokers, found a Korean Chinese security officer who arranged his family's escape to South Korea. His father went to China first, and shortly after his mother, two other brothers, a sister-in-law, a nephew, and he all escaped to China, without speaking of their escape to family members living in other towns, including sisters, another sister-in-law, and other nephews and nieces. They lived in China for a month under the protection of the Korean Chinese security official. In his impression, Korean Chinese did not appear affluent, though he and his family had heard that they were free and prosperous and lived in a real utopia. Given that his father had been a Korean War prisoner and expected to receive more than a half million dollars in South Korea, many Korean Chinese brokers approached them to assist their journey to South Korea. After they arrived in South Korea, their family gave $30,000 to the Korean Chinese security agent out of gratitude for helping them escape. Yet his life in South Korea was far from the future he dreamed about. When I met him in 2002 in Seoul, he worked in a recycling factory, where he sorted disposed items. He consoled himself by saying that his life is better than that of his older brother, who does nothing but rely on a meager government stipend without much prospect of independence. The middle-aged women he worked with affectionately nudged him to find a wife soon.

The notion of market democracy reflects easy access to market trading, as small-scale market trading requires almost no formal skill and only a small amount of capital. In 1999 about $250, or 50,000 to 60,000 North Korean won, was needed to trade agricultural products, and about $500 to trade industrial goods across borders (Chŏng Ŭni 2009; Im Kŭnho 2009:26). Expressing her pride and satisfaction in her accomplishments, a woman in her early twenties recounts her backbreaking work to procure and sell wine, using a narrative framework of freedom and self-control:

> I used to carry ten pounds of rice to the market, sell them, buy rice wine, and carry it back to home. For instance, if I bought rice liquor for 0.8 won, I sold it for 1.2 won, I used the profits for buying daily essentials, while spending the principal to buy another batch of rice wine to continue trading. Though it did not sell well, wine was better than other items since people tended to buy it anyway. I worked on a cooperative farm during the day and sold wine at night in my house. No one controlled or placed me under surveillance. I went to the market to trade rice for wine at 7:00 A.M. and returned around 7:30 or 8:00 P.M. on the same day. I used to walk about four hours each way (70 ri or 28 km) to the market that is open every ten days. I carried rice on my back or, if I was lucky, by cart pulled by oxen. I sold it, bought rice wine, put it in a rubber bag, and carried it home on my back. Once I arrived at home, I diluted it with water before selling it to people.
>
> (Interview on July 3, 2007, in Yanji)

After her parents' divorce when she was thirteen years old, she lived with her mother and sister for few years until they went to China and lost contact with them. When we met in Yanji in 2007, she had remained in China six years, was married to a blind Korean Chinese man, and was raising their five-year-old daughter. She recalled that she liked selling wine, since "no one controlled or placed me under surveillance." Though meager, the profits from selling wine enabled her to make ends meet and even save some money to buy oxen, blankets, kitchen plates, furniture, and wallpaper and to repair her one-room house.

A former technician in an architecture firm in North Korea, who was majoring in nursing in a university in Seoul when I met her in 2002, told me that her yearning to live in a capitalist society grew from her youth in North Korea reading banned novels. She used to wonder about the world beyond the sea's horizon:

> One of the books that impressed me most was a novel called *The Temptation of X* that featured a protagonist in America wronged by a friend. In order to earn money needed for revenge, the protagonist took up three jobs every day, working in a machine factory, in a printing factory, and in another place, leaving only few hours for sleep. This novel made me

see freedom and reward in doing various kinds of work in a capitalist society, which contrasted to our socialist system with the state assigning work to individuals regardless of one's wish. Frankly speaking, I felt that a capitalist society is really a free society.

If this novel concerns the economic aspect of bourgeois society, another novel entitled A *Needle's Eye* made me think about the political and moral aspect. It depicted a woman who tried to protect her family and chastity against the harassment of a policeman in England during World War II. . . . Reading this and other novels, I came to think that capitalism must have characteristics other than the evil features we knew and that a capitalist society could be really free. I came to understand why our society places those who saw this side of capitalism under surveillance after they return from abroad.

(Interview on August 5, 2002, in Seoul)

The desire for freedom is the filter through which one becomes fixated with China as an embodiment of free capitalism. After a month-long visit to a relative in China, a former student at the Fishery University in North Korea, who was in his late twenties and majoring in economics at a leading university in Seoul when I met him in 2002, came to see his regimented life in North Korea as both unbearable and backward:

The university system in North Korea is organized like the military, treating a college as a platoon and a university as a battalion placed under a regiment. The morning is assigned to the lecture, while the afternoon is devoted to the fixed social education program that is followed by administrative work in the evening. We get up at 5:30 A.M. upon the sound of a horn blowing, do the morning exercise, dress in uniform, and walk in group from a dormitory to classrooms. Eighty percent of classes were offered on politics despite the technical nature of my university. I left for China when I was in the third year of a five-year program.

(Interview on August 12, 2002, in Seoul)

During a month-long visit to China, he was not only shocked by the way that people freely referred to Kim Jong Il by name but also felt deceived when he saw the economic prosperity in China. He came to view people in North Korea not as leaders of their own fate, as Juche ideology evokes, but as robots living in acquiescence to the status quo. He was thrilled to see advertisements on Chinese television and impressed by the liveliness of the people in the market, a vitality absent from North Korea since the 1970s. Although he was expected to follow an elite course after graduation, he left North Korea after telling his father that he would come back in six months after earning money and learning skills in China.

Market exchange disaggregates the people into individual consumers. The market is depicted as a democratic force that equalizes the distribution of wealth by elevating the living standards of ordinary people. According to an article in *Imjin'gang*, a journal that reports putatively inside views and information from North Korea, the market brought about an economic miracle; for instance, in Sunch'ŏn, "after the Arduous March [of the food crisis in the mid-1990s], people's lives have become better than before the crisis. . . . They changed their rundown floors into expensive ones; if before the food crisis only 40 percent of households, including those of elites and officials, owned black-and-white television, almost every household owns color television . . . and uses electronic rice cookers, and more than half own VCD players" (Son Hyemin 2009:59–61).

Capital accumulation, monopolization, and increasing inequality, however, accompany grassroots marketization in North Korea. According to Pak Yŏngja (2009), the current North Korean society comprises three strata. The upper stratum in the society comprises foreign traders, military officers, security agents, and engineers such as technicians who repair electric transformers. The middle stratum consists of merchants, self-employed restaurant owners, small-bag traders, and traveling merchants who sell goods in the countryside for grain that they then sell in city. The bottom stratum in Pak's study includes a growing number of people who work in child care or fetch water because there are chronic interruptions of water service; at this level there are also helpers at restaurants, laborers who renovate housing, and those who meet others' labor mobilization requirements, such as in planting and harvesting rice or participating in regular neighborhood meetings. A former foreign trader discloses key methods of wealth accumulation in North Korea:

The most profitable business in North Korea is to get the right to distribute and divert for personal profit aid goods donated by the Red Cross or other world relief organizations, which North Koreans call "beef hit by lightening." The second most profitable way of accumulating wealth is to embezzle state money and property. One must take it like licking ice cream rather than biting it so as not to leave a trace. That's what I did as a foreign trader. For instance, if I was authorized to buy something at $1.00 per unit, I would buy it at $0.60 by using competition among

Chinese wholesalers, fabricate a receipt, and keep the difference. . . .
The third best method is to profit by diverting domestically produced
goods such as tobacco to the black market.

(Interview on October 24, 2006, in Seoul)

T'albuk from North Korea is a customary way out when embezzlement is
exposed. In this former foreign trader's observation, wealth is difficult to accu-
mulate through market trading by ordinary people, "who carry a few kilograms
of beans to exploit price differences by selling them in a different region, and
survive another day with this profit." Those with large amounts of capital and
political connections engage in wholesale border trading. Low-level entrepreneurs use cars and trucks to transport products in bulk and generate larger
profits by selling in small quantities in local North Korean markets (Interview
on October 24, 2006, in Seoul). Since public transportation either breaks down
or is unavailable, ordinary people beg drivers for a ride and pay a fee to sit
on top of the truck's load, whether it is coal or cement. They wait for hours,
holding signs with their names, destinations, and sometimes the fee they are
willing to pay. This former foreign trader used to see them while driving an air-
conditioned car, and he would say, "Why do they bother to live?" This disdain
for the poor as subhuman is echoed in a report from North Korea showing that
in the recent wave of marketization, creditors can treat debtors as slaves and
that everyone accepts that "money yields more money" (Son Hyemin 2009).

Lucrative foreign trade involves competition and monopoly among
powerful operatives, such as the Workers' Party, the People's Force (Inmin
muryŏkpu), the army, the National Security Agency (Powibu), and the
Central People's Committee. The security department mobilizes prisoners
to cut trees and cultivate medicinal herbs, while army units collect lucrative mushrooms with an avarice that threatens their extinction. A central
department of the Workers' Party dominates export of pricey natural
resources such as gold, silver, and zinc as well as other highly profitable
products such as animal skins, herbal medicines, and mountain fruits and
mushrooms, as well as fishery goods. In the border city of Chŏngjin, foreign
trade is conducted by 130 to 140 organizations, including fifty army units,
ten police units, three to four National Security Agency units, and one unit
each of the protection department, municipal party federation, and youth
federation. The People's Force founded the Maebong Corporation in China
to engage exclusively in supplying weapons to rebel groups in Southeast
Asia and gangs in Asia, at the same time supplying foreign tobacco to China
for profit (Chŏng Sejin 2000:133–55).

In an everyday saying in North Korea, the temporality of capital accumulation is characterized as the "bold and short style" (*kukko tchalke*) of entrepreneurship. According to an *Imjin'gang* report on the Group Struggle Against Anti-Socialist Phenomena, those with this business style attract popular admiration for being pioneers who find profitable items before others and decisively pursue production and trade. The bold and short style draws on individuals' desire, instincts, and audacity rather than on reason, rationality, and expertise. It is contrasted to the "thin and long style" (*kanŭlgo kilge*) that studiously obeys party orders and works to realize production goals set by the state (Son Hyemin 2009:51). The bold and short style is embraced as the key to succeeding in business; it is the ability to overcome competition and uncertainty on the one hand, and capricious legal and political conditions on the other, whether through bribery, connections, or favors. *Imjin'gang*'s report ascribes the bold and short style of business to the state's crackdown on entrepreneurial ventures that require such business strategy. However, this coveted style also denotes an overall character of high-risk and short-term profit maximization apart from the state's oppression. Profits in North Korea are not necessarily pursued by applying modern principles of rationalization, long-term investment, and delayed gratification. Rather, they are driven by the rule of instantaneous maximization of profits and short-term capital turnover. North Koreans now learn to sell clothes made at home or smuggled from China quickly even when it means making less profit, because fashion changes so rapidly. Burgeoning numbers of neighborhood and household production units are surprisingly effective at producing goods to meet consumers' desires for fleeting fashions. North Korea's increasing integration into the global capitalist system is also evident in the way its service industry caters to foreign capital, such as subcontracting the production of animation for French producers.

Bold and short accumulation accentuates competition and uncertainty in social relations, which individuals suppress through the opposition of democracy and socialism and the opposition of individuals' market activities and the state's crackdown. The inversion of socioeconomic inequality and dehumanization into the failure of the state's sovereignty works as an imperative in the migration to China and South Korea. The army and the police in the era of the military-first rule are condemned as a group of thugs and profiteers who loot crops and money from people. A former college student in her twenties recollects with revulsion:

When people had nothing to eat, what wouldn't they not dare to do? They steal corn from the cornfields in autumn in order to survive. Facing the dwindling supply in the state's storehouses, Kim Jong Il, however, instructed the army to guard the grain supply. There is no such country where the army holds guns against its own starving people struggling to survive. . . . Doesn't the army exist to defend one's country? . . . People call the Tuman River [Tuman'gang] the "runaway river" [tomanggang, which in Korean is phonetically similar to Tuman'gang, the Tuman River], the river one crosses to survive.

(Interview on August 8, 2002, in Seoul)

Upon arrival in South Korea in 1999, she gave many lectures about state oppression in North Korea and shared her experience as a born-again Christian in churches and social organizations in South Korea while preparing to go to university. In the era of human rights advocacy that defined North Korean migrants as refugees, migrants conventionally began their story with an account of their suffering at the hands of the state, as if to satisfy outsiders' curiosity and obtain their sympathy. Even when I asked North Korean migrants primarily about their work experiences, they still brought up the issue of the brutal and corrupt state. Among ordinary people, the 8.3 system, which under Kim Jong Il's 1984 Instruction incorporates commodity production into its socialist economy, signifies "lack" or "fake" because capitalism is believed to be fettered by old socialist social relations and institutions ("Pukhan sisa yongǒ haesǒl" 2009). These narratives act as representations that sustain belief in market utopia; they cast the state as an evil force that deprives ordinary people from enjoying the desired utopia. Through this new historicism the state and the people continue to objectify each other.

In everyday accounts, China and South Korea exemplify morality and social order, which the crisis in North Korea corrupted. According to a housewife in her late forties who came to Yanji for two months of secret Bible study, "There is no conscience in North Korea. Instead it is plagued with corruption, theft, robbery, and deceit due to economic hardship. Suicide spreads. Fortune tellers are popular. The law is weakest in North Korea though it might appear strongest" (Interview on June 27, 2007, in Yanji). For her, South Korea is a country of altruism, where men sacrifice for their ailing wives and girlfriends and firefighters risk their lives for others—behaviors she saw in South Korean TV dramas such as *Steps of Heaven* and *All-In*.

Risk and failure in market trading also bring North Koreans to China searching for work and other economic opportunities. The crisis does not necessarily stem from the socialist state's regulation of markets, as often assumed in North Korean studies, but from the inherent uncertainty of the markets. According to a former leader of a shock labor brigade who came to South Korea in 1999, he made exorbitant profits as a wholesale trader and then lost everything overnight. Failure prompted him to engage in illegal trading and eventually escape to China, according to the memoir he wrote with the twin hopes of gaining attention from evangelists who could bring him to South Korea and of selling his story to a journalist or publisher. After his hope of joining the party was wrecked by the exposure of his father's collaboration with the South Korean army during the Korean War, he began to pursue market trading in 1991, when he was twenty-four years old:

> I used to buy fishery products such as sea cucumber, swellfish, and octopus in Ongjin, where my brother lived, and sell them in border areas, making a profit of 70 percent. This involved changing transportation three times over a forty-hour period to go from my home to Ongjin to Hoeryŏng, a border city, for another five hours. I repeated the trip two or three times per month. Despite the hard work, earning money was fun. I traveled with soldiers and bribed them for protection. . . . I earned a lot, and everyone was envious as I decorated my house well, now equipped with TV, refrigerator, audio set, and sewing machine.
>
> My savings and business experience enabled me to engage in riskier and more profitable businesses, such as trading gold and forbidden goods such as antiques, narcotics, and copper. But I got swindled and robbed by a crook who teamed up with a policeman, and I even was detained by police for three days. . . . Business was going downhill. I lost every time I traveled to trade. Everything, including my family life and business, collapsed as if a curse struck me.[2]

He came to China to rebuild his life after thinking about committing suicide. He worked on farms and stayed in shelters run by missionaries in China before coming to South Korea.

Deception and swindling sums up the experience of market trading in North Korea for the aforementioned technician in an architectural design office in North Korea. She explains that she quit her job at the design office to engage in market trading to support her family. However, the prevalence of cheating and fraud in the market led her to give up market trading and migrate to China in the hope of finding a job and freedom:

> After my father died, I became the head of household, quit my job, and engaged in market trading to support my family. With the fake

travel permit that I got with a bribe, I traveled between Chunggangjin in north P'yŏngan Province where I lived and Pyongyang to sell dried squids to the wealthy, foreign trading firms, and my relatives. . . . I had only a modest dream during my work days in the design office. I really wanted to be a good wife after marrying a nice man. But it didn't work out since my boyfriend attending a police university backed out of our marriage after my dad killed a policeman during a driving accident and thus endangered my boyfriend's becoming a policeman after his graduation in case of our marriage. I really committed to my job in the office without a single absence. . . .

While engaged in market trading, I came to realize that the reality of market trading was more horrendous [than the threat of starvation]. People are vicious and driven only by self-interest. It was a totally different world. People in North Korea are not all nice. When money intervenes in a relationship between people, they swindle others. That's why I didn't do well in the market trading I did for a year. I sold dried squids four times [by traveling to Pyongyang each time]. But I got exhausted because it was too hard. I wasn't sure whether I wanted to deceive others. Then, an opportunity arose to go to China. As I had resentment about [North Korean] society and felt longing about capitalist society, I wanted to go to China. Unlike people living near the border, I didn't know about the trafficking in North Koreans.

(Interview on August 7, 2002, in Seoul)

In China she was almost trafficked twice, arrested by the Chinese police, cared for by a Korean Chinese family under a missionary's financing, and then brought to South Korea by the fund donated by three churches.

"I Didn't Have to Come but Still . . ."

Socialism is renounced as a thing of the past, and market freedom is embraced as if it were prefigured under socialism. This renunciation of the past brings a moment of awakening from the illusion that the state would guarantee everything and defend society from any threats. It is not that all along the people believed this illusion to be the truth. Rather, the motif of awakening from a socialist illusion naturalizes the market as a democratic force. The market's discipline of labor recasts the problematic of freedom. In principle, socialism grounds freedom and democracy in "common property." According to Marx (1976:171), "Common property is the basis for a new association of free individuals who work with the means of production held in common and expend their various forms of labor-powers in full self-awareness as one single social labor force." Since the economic crisis of the mid-1990s the people were driven away from state-owned and cooperative-owned workplaces and became "free labor" in the market. Free labor is a double-edged concept: it implies freedom from the possession of the means of production and also having the freedom to sell one's labor in the market. Capitalism ties the notion of freedom with that of free labor. Marx (1976) conceptualized the exchange value of labor as socially necessary labor in the context of large-scale industrialization, in which the rationalization of labor processes took the form of scientific management and flexible labor management to increase the efficiency of labor and thus lower the cost of production. In North Korean migrants' narratives, this socially necessary labor time is obfuscated by the migrants' delight in their ability to make a living and buy goods. While the North Korean state, as explored in the previous chapter, has made strenuous efforts to incorporate individual interest into socialist collectivism, individuals confound current forms of privatization and marketization with freedom.

The narrative of "I didn't have to come but still . . ." frames everyday narrations of border crossing. The aforementioned former wine seller recalls that it seemed almost obtuse not to migrate to China: her village is only 50 meters away from the Tuman River, where a shout across the river echoes back from China (Interview on July 3, 2007, in Yanji). Her crossing was as quick and effortless as the blink of an eye; she knew a few border-control soldiers and their schedules, so she knew when to cross the river undetected. A man who was in his early twenties when we met in Seoul in 2002 did not attribute his migration to economic reasons. Leaving North Korea for China in 1998 and arriving in South Korea in 2001, he was living in Seoul on a monthly government stipend without a stable job. While living in North Korea he had engaged in smuggling antiques to China, which eventually led him to visit China without telling his mother, and there he stayed until going to South Korea. He recounted his journey to China as an impulsive act to "have some fun with friends and get some fresh air." He said he ended up staying longer in China because there was no freedom in North Korea, although his family was affluent because of his father's lucrative work in construction (Interview on August 10, 2002 in Seoul). The decision to go to China was equally spontaneous for another man, who had lived in North Korea as kkotchebi (displaced child) since 1994, when he was fourteen years old. At first he survived by stealing rice cakes and noodles from the market. Later he made a lot of money by stealing purses on busy streets and in bustling train stations and shared his loot with police. He enjoyed a good life, dining in restaurants, drinking, and seeing movies, often with police. After he returned home, he made his mother proud of him for a while by selling wood in the same market where she sold fried doughnuts. Yet, after an accident in which he ended up beating a child from a high-status family, he returned to a life of vagabondage in North Korea and then left for China at a friend's suggestion, without saying a word to his mother.[3]

The seemingly spontaneous decision of North Koreans in the narrative of "I didn't have to come but still . . ." implies a certain nondecision about the act of migration. The narrative reveals a transcendental subjectivity that breaks down and continues its commodification only in so far as its logic escapes them, in much the same way consumers think of consumption as a spontaneous act of freedom. This portrayal of their migration as a nondecision or as a fait accompli akin to destiny simultaneously reinforces and transcends their commodification in North Korea and China. This subjectivity encapsulates the Hegelian negation of negation that Žižek (1993:120–21) explores in terms of the Lacanian triad of need-demand-desire: "The subject needs 'natural,' 'real' objects to satisfy needs: if we are thirsty, we need water, etc. However as soon as the need is articulated in a symbolic medium . . ., it starts to function as a demand. . . . [T]he Other is originally experienced as he or she who can satisfy our need. . . . Desire is what in demand is irreducible to need." When a North Korean migrant's need is articulated though the symbolic medium of money, it starts to function as a demand. Even if individuals may get what they ask for in China, the demand is not fully satisfied because their true aim is genuine community. The unfulfilled need sets off a new object, South Korea. In the repeated negation, the original need for freedom, equality, and community is mediated and forever delayed. The repeated migration from North Korea to China to South Korea is a paradoxical act of subjugation to and transcendence of unequal exchange, uncertainty, and monopolies in the market. Repeated migration establishes a metabolism for capital accumulation on a global scale. It reproduces capital accumulation through transcendence of economic crisis. Migration is a moment of both identification and disidentification with capitalist commodification.

ETHNIC AND RELIGIOUS PERVERSION

Ethnic nationalism and evangelism help to portray border crossing as a transcendental act of pursuing freedom and community. Ethnic and religious perversion of Korean Chinese and North Koreans signifies the transference of their socioeconomic failure on each other. For Korean Chinese, it involves the simultaneous denouncement of North Koreans and commitment to save them; and for North Koreans, it leads to concurrent enchantment with and distancing from Korean Chinese in their pursuit of migration to South Korea. Korean Chinese and North Koreans become the figure of interposition for each other, which steps between one's gaze and its "proper" object (see Žižek 2007). How Korean Chinese and North Koreans play this role of mediating money and capital for each other is explored here. In the narrative of "I didn't have to come but still . . . ," the primordialization of ethnic nationhood turns border crossing into performance. It is not that Koreans' original notion of ethnic nation is rekindled, but that it is continuously reconstituted by new interactions among North Koreans, South Koreans, and Korean Chinese. The mutual embrace of North Koreans and Korean Chinese eases the uncertainty, competition, and dislocation associated with labor mobility across borders, as if ethnic nationhood could guarantee unobstructed and fluid crossings. The invocation of an ethnic ethos posits the barriers to the market, e.g., labor skill, turnover time of labor, and shortage of capital, as barriers to ethnic and national homogeneity that could be resolved through cultural modifications of identity and historical memory. Ethnic ethos also translates into "credit," a form of capital: the speculation of one's own value through an intangible identification with each other.

After the initial embrace, Korean Chinese increasingly regard helping North Korean relatives and visitors as an impossible task and liken it to trying to fill a bottomless pot with water. For instance, a North Korean woman in her twenties failed to locate her relatives in China only to receive help from a middle-aged Korean Chinese woman, who treated her as her own daughter because of their similar age, brought her home, found her a job at a barbecue restaurant, and after a year prepared her to return to North Korea by giving her a truckload of goods, including three new color televisions, a refrigerator, new and used clothes, shoes, candy, and umbrellas, among other items, and even paying the cost of transportation to the border. Upon her return home the young woman bought a new fishing boat with the money earned by selling the gifts and asked the Korean Chinese woman for more money a few years later (Interview on July 2, 2007, in Yanji). The latter refused to reply to her out of a sense of betrayal; the North Korean woman stole money from the Korean Chinese woman's purse before she left—money meant to be given to her as yet another gift. According to a view current in the Korean Chinese community, North Koreans never stop begging for more, commit violence if denied, and jeopardize the safety of Korean Chinese because the Chinese state arrests those who aid North Koreans. A Korean Chinese missionary Mr. Shin (pseudonym) in Yanji spoke of the deceptiveness of North Koreans:

> When t'albukchadŭl come to my church to receive help at night, each of them usually brings two backpacks. They get their backpacks filled with rice and leave for North Korea and yet come back before dawn to ask for another backpack load of rice, lying that they lost the whole load to border guards [in North Korea]. . . . They lie because they are like that at the root.
>
> (Interview on June 28, 2007, in Yanji)

North Koreans' attitude toward Korean Chinese people is equally paradoxical. At first North Koreans show deep gratitude for the assistance they receive from Korean Chinese, while at the same time expressing amazement about the prosperity evidenced by their eating rice and meat every day and their bustling markets and streets. The North Koreans' initial envy and appreciation quickly turn into emphatic rejection of Korean Chinese people. According to a former technician in an architecture firm in North Korea who was studying in a nursing college in Seoul when we met in 2002, Korean Chinese see t'albukcha only as a commodity: Korean Chinese "kill two birds with one stone" by appropriating money offered by South Korean churches to care for North Koreans and benefiting from their unpaid work. She elaborates:

> I taught English and mathematics to her [Korean Chinese patron's] daughter, while doing housekeeping work. Since she ran a clothing business, I managed her clothing business and organized all the clothing transactions as well. While at first she must have felt burdened by having me at her place, she didn't want to let me go in the end, even risking to forgo the money from the pastor. It was because I provided such valuable labor power [nodongnyŏk], frankly speaking.
>
> (Interview on August 7, 2002, in Seoul)

Her Christian patron cried a lot after letting her go because they had grown very close. Whenever her patron came to South Korea, she brought all kinds of things as if she were a mother visiting her married daughter. The interviewee's ambivalence toward her patron reflects the process of commodification mediated by ethnicity. Her ambivalence extends to South Koreans too, as South Koreans pick on others' faults, even paying attention to small points of etiquette. She regards Han Chinese as more trustworthy than South Koreans. She attributes her mixed feelings about Korean Chinese and South Koreans to their ethnic national character. However, they also denote ethnic national mediation of global capitalist integration that sets clear parameters on their relations.

The marriage of North Korean women and Korean Chinese men in China is often portrayed by human rights advocates as human trafficking or as a necessary union for the women to survive as refugees. Yet understanding their daily life relationship demands a historical and political sensibility. After a Korean Chinese man marries a woman who came from North Korea illegally, the couple tends to frequently move to avoid attention from neighbors and authorities, leaving their farms and risking the loss of secure income, until the need to send their children to school makes them less mobile. The dread of arrest and deportation of the North Korean wife causes them to suffer from anxiety and distress. Yet it is also widely accepted in Korean Chinese villages near the border that a deported wife tends to return within a year if she wishes. A man I met in 2006 during a visit to Hunchun in China married another North Korean woman, after his first North Korean wife was deported. After his second wife was also deported, he was waiting for her return instead of bringing her back. Although he knew his deported second wife's address in North Korea, he thought she could have already returned if she wanted. When I met him, he was working as a day laborer in construction and logging after having lost his land to brokers who promised him the opportunity to work in South Korea. He was still trying to go to South Korea. In another family I visited, the husband also knew his deported wife's address in North Korea—less than 10 kilometers from his home in Banshi in China. He had not visited her in part because he did not have enough money to buy gifts for her family members there. Although the border and deportation create a barrier to their marriage, it is surmountable with caution and money. Neither state sovereignty nor ethnic consciousness is absolute for either Korean Chinese or North Koreans.

Inverted Calvinism

The transhistorical temporality of Christianity permits both Korean Chinese and North Koreans to transcend the trauma of material failure and sustain their ruptured capitalist desires while undergoing their own privatization. Folk customs and superstitious practices are used to allay anxieties over the risk of market trading. For example, it is believed that carrying red beans or eating tofu before departure averts bad luck while traveling for market trading and that eating noodles is inauspicious and lengthens the journey (Choi Chini 2007:174–77). North Koreans and Korean Chinese also draw on Christianity for similar protection against market uncertainty and workplace competition. However, they invert Calvinism: Calvinism sees one's economic wealth as God's reward for hard work and produces a strong work ethic as the basis of its affinity with capitalism; in reverse, Korean Chinese and North Koreans establish spirituality as the source of economic prosperity. Korean Chinese missionaries omit the virtue of labor when they equate South Korean economic growth to God's blessing, presupposing its prosperity as the essence of its national legitimacy.

According to a Korean Chinese missionary Mrs. Kim (pseudonym) in her sixties, her proselytizing during trips to North Korea started by telling listeners that "God's blessing made corn grow tall in China just across the river, while God's curse ruined the corn in North Korea" (Interview on July 2, 2007, in Yanji). For her, economic opulence in North Korea seems to compensate for her own broken dream in China. After the textile factory where she worked as an inspector went bankrupt, she ventured into small-bag trading between Yanji and Russia, as did many Chinese in the late 1980s and early 1990s. Though she at first earned a lot of money, she lost everything after investing in a textile factory and went into deeper debt after failing in the retail sale of octopus. After these travails were compounded by a bitter divorce and her mother's death, she became a born-again Christian. She has devoted her life to caring for North Korean refugees and uses intermittent funds from South Korean pastors and visitors to visit North Korea and proselytize. In her view prayer enabled her to endure repeated threats of arrest by Chinese authorities, overcome fear, and take the risk of becoming involved with evangelist missions in North Korea. She stayed up the whole night to pray for the Korean nation when North Korea launched its first nuclear test in October 2006.

Whereas her own trauma lurked beneath her resolute sacrifice for North Koreans and was still palpable during my interview, missionary Shin struck me as a shrewd intermediary. Like her, he at first amassed a fortune in the wholesale candy trade and then lost everything on a mining investment. He also regards South Korea's economic development as evidence of God's blessing, and he told North Korean Bible study trainees that they could replicate that success with their belief in God.

When I ask them [North Koreans] how they think South Koreans turned their country from ashes after the Korean War to an advanced country, they usually say at first it was because of the United States' assistance that made South Korea into an American pawn. Yet they couldn't reply when I ask whether a single country can make such a change in another, and whether the North Korean government could do the same for Korean Chinese like me. They still couldn't refute me when I told them that God's blessings have made the Republic of Korea as it is today. They were amazed when I told them it is not human power but heaven's work for a country to be transformed from ashes into an advanced country. . . . They also began to change their views on South Korea after watching [South Korean] DVDs and TV dramas in China. . . . We find signs of God's work in the Bible, for instance, in the passage, "If you seek me and follow me, I will set you above all other nations and make you the greatest nation."

I teach them prayer as a spiritual conversation with God. The essence of prayer is in the passage of Matthew 7:7, "Ask and it will be given to you; seek and you will find; knock and the door will be opened to you." . . . They express very well what they feel [in their appreciation for Kim Il Sung]. It would become an excellent prayer if they were to replace Kim Il Sung with God.

(Interview on June 28, 2007, in Yanji)

Between 2004 and 2007 he brought 126 people from North Korea for a month-long visit for Bible study. He stabilized this operation with assistance from his childhood friend, who operated a billiard store and other businesses in North Korea. The expenses of his apparently comfortable lifestyle and his mission activities were funded regularly by a hospice group of a megachurch in an affluent community south of the Han River (kangnam) in Seoul. When he introduced me to three North Koreans illegally visiting for Bible study, he chose People's Park in downtown Yanji as our meeting place. Reminding me of the danger of arrest, he took us inside the bushes on a steep hill on the park's fringe. Given that all three North Koreans appeared well-fed and healthy and could be mistaken for Korean Chinese, this precaution seemed excessive—in fact, meeting inside the bushes seemed more likely to attract attention. I could not help thinking that the precaution was staged to drama-tize the riskiness of his operation.

Money is figuratively a synonym for Christianity and South Korea. "Money is necessary to proselytize each and everyone in North Korea," said missionary Kim. Whenever she visited North Korea, she took money and hundreds of kilograms of rice and clothing with her to distribute to potential converts. The converts pledged their beliefs to her when they felt their prayer was answered, for instance, when a customer would buy zucchini from her rather than from a neighboring vendor or when a husband was promoted at work (Interview on July 2, 2007, in Yanji). Mr. Shin set his missionary expenses per person at 1,500 yuan, including 500 yuan for bribing border guards, 200 yuan for living expense during training in China, and 800 yuan to be used in North Korea for six months to one year until their revisit. A forty-three-year-old housewife made her second trip for Bible study out of gratitude and curiosity after receiving 10 kg of rice (Interview on June 27, 2007, in Yanji). According to a fifty-two-year-old manager of the Musan Mining factory visiting from North Korea, his determination to save people suffering from North Korea's economic distress was like that of Esther in the Old Testament, who delivered her people from destruction (Interview on June 27, 2007, in Yanji). He spoke of his interest in earning a lot of money and going to South Korea to do the same, and he asked if I could help him. His spiritual confession usually followed talk of his ambition to earn money as if an afterthought. Many North Korean migrants who join Bible studies in China are keenly interested in going to South Korea. According to Mr. Shin, pastors and churches select which North Koreans to send on the basis of their ability to cite the Bible, their confession of faith, and their friendliness.

Through its daily rhythms, evangelism also constructs the socially necessary time of labor in China. Korean Chinese and South Korean employers draw on Christianity as a means to discipline North Korean workers and pay them less than their Chinese counterparts. When a Korean Chinese missionary ran a farm in Yanji as a shelter for t'albukcha with funding from a church in Seoul, a North Korean migrant complained that it had become a business to finance the missionary's house and the university education for his two sons.[4] The previously mentioned student in the Fishery University recollects his work as being enmeshed with Bible study when he was employed at a small furniture factory in Wihae in China:

> The South Korean owner of the furniture factory was a Christian who preached to us after work, although we were exhausted from working since the morning. I felt like I was as tightly controlled as I was in North Korea. . . . In the factory, we were required to get up at 5:00 A.M. and study the Bible. Then we washed our face, ate breakfast, and then went to work. . . . I think of Christianity not as a reality but as a product of the imagination, though I might be wrong. . . . I practiced it, hoping it might give me some consolation. It is because people help us, feeding

us, giving us a place to sleep, and buying us essential things for living. Yet I didn't want to fall deeply into it since it would prevent me from doing other things.

(Interview on August 12, 2002, in Seoul)

Instead of paying him fair wages, the factory owner promised to take him to South Korea. After waiting for years, he took money from the owner after locking him in a room and came to South Korea through a dangerous fourteen-day journey from China to Thailand. When he saw the South Korean factory owner again in South Korea, he felt both anger and gratitude, anger because the owner gave him only 1,500 yuan after five years of work and gratitude because he had given him shelter.

Capitalism penetrates the unconscious of Korean Chinese and North Koreans. The paradoxical emotion Korean Chinese and North Koreans feel toward each other signifies that each group is an ideological figure for the other, who, in Žižek's (1989:48) terms, "stitch up the inconsistency of [their] own ideological system." The mutually equivocal attitude of Korean Chinese and North Koreans may result neither from Korean Chinese' cultural inauthenticity as diaspora nor from North Koreans' lack of moral and human quality. Their passionate fascination with and denunciation of each other involves a metonymic inversion of the concrete into the abstract, whether primordial ethnicity or inalienable humanity. In the Lacanian sense, each Korean group as the ideological figure of the other signifies the desire for the capitalist dream of instantaneous wealth and genuine community that they failed to attain in North Korea and China. The transference of the capitalist relationship onto an ethnic one enables North Korean migrants to "enjoy" their own symptom of desiring capitalist dreams and to renew it in the form of imagining South Korea as a true ethnic nation. Korean Chinese missionaries make a symbolic journey to South Korea, preaching about the South Korean economic miracle to North Koreans. For North Koreans, going to South Korea follows the earlier migration to China as a repetition of displacement and commodification, which restores their desire for money, security, and a new collectivity.

The global capitalist circuit in the present is an excess that cannot be contained by ethnic nationalism. This excess is articulated as "the debt in the heart of Korean Chinese toward North Koreans" and "the fate of Korean Chinese standing on the edge of a sword," which Pak Ch'angwuk of Yanbian University describes as the kernel of Korean Chinese current relations with North Koreans (*Hangyoreh* newspaper, July 29, 2002). Pak insists that North Korean migration to China since the mid-1990s is not an "escape" but an "illegal crossing" (togang), which has been repeated by both Koreans and Chinese for more than a century. In other words, Koreans crossed the Tuman and Apnok Rivers from the late nineteenth century, during the Japanese occupation, during difficult times in the 1960s, and again from the 1990s. More than a half million Chinese migrated to North Korea to avoid famine in the early 1960s. Some of these migrants, who remained in North Korea as overseas Chinese nationals, became merchants facilitating trade between the two countries since the 1990s. Notwithstanding Pak's intention to repudiate the discourse of t'albuk, the debt of the heart and the edge of the sword may in fact denote the specters of difference that belie the supposed unity of Koreans across borders in their new global capitalist network. When the shared ethnic past of North Koreans and Korean Chinese is mobilized to overcome deception and exploitation, the edge of the sword and the debt of the heart may signify historical excess or the repressed reality of the global circuit of production. According to missionary Shin, this circuit stratifies Koreans by country within a hierarchy constructed by globalization. History returns in the form of a debt that Korean Chinese can neither discharge nor disentangle from their knotted emotions. A historical perspective exposes the irreducible disquiet within their present relations with home, whether home is North Korea or China, and interrupts their capitalist present within the global production chain.

IMAGINING A NEW COMMONS

In its aleatory form, humanity resides in the momentous critique of the capitalist promise of prosperity and freedom that is fostered by the trinity of the market, evangelism, and ethnicity. I present three North Korean migrants in China, whose avowal of vagabondage, manual labor, and a stateless nation is central to the construction of the displaced as human beings and the repudiation of their names and places in the juridical order of state power such as t'albukcha, illegal labor, and trafficked women. These figures criticize the metanarratives of democracy championed by human rights activists and missionaries. They also reject the temporal succession from socialism to capitalism. Instead, these subjects find properties of democracy at the moment of working out of their memory of socialism and their experience of its transition. Probing these subjects follows Ranciere's (1989:10) method of writing about labor, which aims not to "scratch images to bring truth to the surface" but rather to "shove them aside so that other figures may come together and decompose here." The following three figures of North Korean migrants come to the fore when the figure of t'albukcha and ethnic national subjects are shoved aside.

Vagabondage

Lurking in the politics of North Korean human rights is the disapproving attribution of North Korean refugees as vagabonds. In this figuration they are beggars who use deception to extort money from South Korean visitors or missionaries; they immediately spend it all on expensive tobacco and alcohol as if there is no tomorrow, and they wander aimlessly and drift from place to place. A young t'albukcha sums up the formula of "deception" (ŏllida in Hamgyŏng Province's dialect):

I tell South Korean tourists and visitors that my mother and father died from starvation in North Korea, that I have nothing to eat but water here in China, and that I want to go home but have no money. If they give me money, I thank them and say good-bye with a big smile. . . . We felt angry if they gave us little. They must give us money. In that way [by lying] we neither plead nor beg for money [pinŭn'ge anigo kugŏl hanŭn'ge anida].⁵

The interpretation of the socialist past defines humanness as the act of giving and receiving charity. According to Cho Ch'ŏnhyŏn, a veteran reporter on issues of North Korean migrants, t'albukcha's formula of deception does not just appeal to Koreans' compassion (chŏng) for t'albukcha as ethnic national kin. More important, it reflects the socialist tradition of self-critique (chaa pip'an) in North Korea that leads people to hide their true feelings and needs. Cho advocates a humanistic approach that regards t'albukcha as any other displaced group such as the homeless and youth vagrants who survive by evoking compassion in others through deceit—telling lies or appearing abject with smelly clothing and unwashed faces. Their deception, notes Cho, shows that they are only humans whose experiences of socialism have taught them survival skills (Interview on October 24, 2002, in Seoul). A South Korean pastor in a large church in Seoul also reflects on the socialist past:

The socialist past accounts for t'albukcha's double or even multifaceted personality marked by discrepancy between word and action. . . . The enforcement of control and surveillance in North Korea destroyed altruistic values such as love, respect, and sacrifice, as one has been taught to perform surveillance on others. Dispossessed of positive ideas about life, t'albukcha tend to steal from others rather than help them.

(Interview on July 24, 2002, in Seoul)

Spearheading the North Korean mission of the Christian Council of Korea (Han'gich'ong), he operated shelters in Yanbian and as of 2005 organized clandestine escape of more than eighty t'albukcha to South Korea through a third country; he ran the North Korean mission with about a dozen t'albukcha in his church in Seoul. What t'albukcha needs, according to the pastor, is not just money, clothing, and other resources but freedom from fear and terror and a new life's purpose that religion can provide. Evangelization, he continues, is a means to eliminate the North Korean regime, which is the ultimate way to save North Koreans. He sent some t'albukcha back to North Korea after their Bible studies, giving them money and copies of the Bible, though this practice drew sharp criticism for endangering their lives because the North Korean state treats contact with missionaries as a serious crime. Missionary Shin also regards North Koreans' customary deception as a deeply ingrained disposition formed by their socialist past (Interview on June 28, 2007, in Yanji).

The attribution of lying to socialist tradition or humanist practice connects the relationship between the socialist past and the capitalist present. Lying embodies North Korean migrants' aspiration to regain sovereignty when appeals to socialism and capitalism coexist to commodify their beings. A North Korean migrant in his early thirties traces lying to the socialist habit of extortion or leveling (chojŏlhada):

Living without one's own efforts is the everyday habit of living off others' back or feet as a freeloader. This habit comes from living in North Korea, where if I give you a glass of wine, you must give me a glass. They pilfer from each other. . . . North Korea is socialist *only in name*, and it is actually *not that different from capitalism* [emphasis added] where people gnaw and tear each other to get things. They come to China with a preposterous idea . . . that money falls down from the sky. . . . If South Koreans don't give money, they seek them out with sad stories or simply demand money.[6]

The long-standing socialist practice of collectivism entailed in leveling is turned into a system of "robbing each other." T'albukcha's appropriation of the collective practice of leveling in the form of deception challenges a commonplace dichotomy of the socialist past and the capitalist present. For decades the North Korean state has sought to reconcile collectivism and individual material incentives. In such a conjuncture, t'albukcha's positing of the temporal continuity of the past and the present affords a political subjectivity that rejects the subterranean capitalist force running through both NGO politics and privatization in North Korea.

Scandalous acts of deception and drifting offer a rare glimpse into subjects who envisage a new terrain of humanness. They signify not so much the entrepreneurial and opportunistic spirit as the paradoxical experience of commodification. On the one hand, the act of lying might be a self-objectification that participates in producing exchange value, turning their subjectivity into a link in the commodity chain. Vagabondage may reinforce the fetishism of money when one envisages money not as the product of one's own labor but as coming from the sky. They sell a particular experience in the marketplace of humanism and national unification, engaging in exchange as independent and free individuals. This leaves them with formal freedom, in which choices are limited by the market's discourses of humanity. On the other hand, their acts of deception and vagabondage are a poignant intervention on the commodification of their body and their labor, rejecting the capitalist notion of productive labor. Their idleness and vagabondage invokes workers' practices of leisure and laziness as platforms of resistance against the labor time imposed on them during early industrialization in England and France (Ross 1988; Ranciere 1989). North Koreans' laziness and excessive consumption challenge the basis of bourgeois accounts of value creation through abstinence from immediate spending for pleasure. Their acts are tantamount to repudiating the accumulation of money and its transformation into capital. Such repudiation breaks the link between production and consumption. It critiques the regimes of labor discipline enforced by evangelism and ethnic nationalism in North Korea and China. In vagabondage, the money they earn is "not capital but revenue" (Marx 1993:546), for it does not realize a new value through investment in production and circulation. Money in vagabondage vanishes into unproductive consumption.

The Defense of Work

Opposed to the vagabond is the figure of labor who postulates manual work as a source of humanity. The insistence on manual work separates this figure from the good and productive worker advanced by dominant strands of social engineering. The dissenting figure's defense of work resides not in a capitalist desire to save money for an entrepreneurial future but in the pursuit of one's own sovereignty through bodily expenditure of one's own energy and sweat. The North Korean migrant in his early thirties cited in the previous section prefers hard work over humanitarian handouts because he believes his own work supports independence and human dignity:

> North Koreans in China do not need pity but rather a method of living through work. The problem is that they [NGOs and churches] just hand out money. T'albukcha is given about 400 to 500 yuan for each visit to a church speaking for a couple of hours with visitors from South Korea or the United States. When I hear that, I get annoyed. I usually earn 250 yuan per month cleaning public bathrooms.
>
> People in church do not help those who live by hard work. I resist the temptation of visiting a church for free money, thinking that "I have to earn money for my siblings [with my own hands]. . . . When I got help from church, I worked harder to return the good will [of the church]. . . . Otherwise I will be no different from those who do nothing and get help without working. There was a time when I went to churches seeking help. But I know now that it is right to live by my own efforts.

He insists on respectability and self-sufficiency, emphasizing the link between humanity and manual labor. He is an aberrant migrant not because work is unimportant in the lives of displaced North Koreans but because of the gambit of human rights discourse. Most North Korean migrants in China work for Korean Chinese and South Korean employers, though working for Han Chinese is not rare. Descriptions of their experiences of exploitation are similar to those of undocumented migrant workers elsewhere, that is, physical and verbal abuse in the workplace, low pay, unpaid back wages, sudden discharge without pay, and employers' threats of reporting them to the police. Their work experiences are irreconcilable with the familiar representation of them as refugees and thus rarely surface in conventional narratives of t'albuk other than in accounts of trafficking of North Korean women.

Cleaning public toilets is a hieroglyph of "unproductive" and contingent labor. It must be the work that locals avoid and are most eager to delegate to undocumented foreigners. It is also far removed from modern forms of labor that involve legal contract, mechanization, and technology. If compared with work within the history of primitive accumulation and labor history in Europe, the work of cleaning toilets does not likely lead to future entrepreneurship, such as the struggle of craftsmen in the 1830s to set up their own workshops and employ other workers. Rather, it is similar to tailors' strikes against their masters in pursuit of human dignity, independence, and equality (Ranciere 1989). The North Korean migrant's insistence on manual work for meager pay epitomizes his appropriation of his own labor power during working hours. This logic counters the capitalist rule of maximizing the market value of one's worth. Although he wants to save money and send it to his sisters in North Korea, he refuses to submit himself blindly to the logic of capital accumulation.

He redefines the meaning of his labor as living labor by associating work with dignity rather than larger exchange value. The defense of manual labor expresses his desire for new social relations based on a new kind of freedom that is different from the one offered by the market. Exploitation in the workplace presupposes private property and profit maximization, and the market renders freedom as a relation between property-owning individuals. Instead, his embrace of working by the sweat of his own brow denotes corporeal work that resists abstract work or socially necessary labor time spent in the exchange of labor and the exchange of words with human rights advocates and factory owners. This subject rejects what Marx (1993:461) characterized as forms of labor that are alienated and independent of one's existence. Labor becomes his own property in this moment of favoring physical labor over future sums of money. In this pursuit of absolute freedom, humanness does not rest on a formal form of equality as the equal exchange in the (labor) market and approximating equality through negotiation of wages and working days through laws or state policies. Such negotiation merely displaces the issue to contractual equality in juridical order. In a utopian move, the defense of manual labor signifies a search for an individuality that is not constrained by collectivist ideas imposed by the North Korean state and NGOs, among others—whether socialist, capitalist, nationalist, or religious. This figure does not call for a new collectivity to fight against exploitation but expresses the shadow image of isolation and individuality. This individuality is irreducible to selfishness and materialism, as a run of bad luck could put him on the streets. He trades security for a new relation with his own body as a new mode of existence.

A Stateless Nation

A new national community is imagined as a new commons, yet with emphasis on its irreducibility both to state (South Korean or North Korean) and ethnic identification with Korean Chinese. This subjectivity is articulated by Mr. Han (pseudonym), an undocumented North Korean man in China who declines migration to South Korea or an immediate return to North Korea but nevertheless regards the nation as the sublime community (Interview on October 13, 2006, in Yanji). Since Han came to China with his father in 1996 when he was sixteen years old, he worked in Yanji and Shandong at farms, an aluminum window frame factory, small restaurants, South Korean–owned textile factories, and tour agencies. During several hours of conversation, he struck me as the most articulate among North Korean migrants whom I interviewed in China and South Korea. Despite little formal education, his intelligence was apparent not only in his mastery of Chinese but also in his incisive opinions about North Korea's nuclear testing and international affairs. His recognition of the importance of the nation (minjok) underlines his experience of migration. When he faces hardship, the only person who could help him is, he says, is a Korean who shares the same blood, whether South Korean or Korean Chinese. He recalled becoming choked up with emotion when he watched on television the joint entrance of athletes of the two Koreas in the opening ceremony of the 2006 Winter Olympics in Turin, Italy. He links his emotion to the late Kim Il Sung's expression that people without a country (nara) are worse than a dog at a funeral. Han's refusal to go to South Korea runs counter to North Korean human rights advocates who assume South Korea as the only legitimate nation. At first he tried to go to South Korea not out of national sentiment but for economic security, but he gave up after brokers repeatedly deceived and swindled him. He also came to know too well that he would be discriminated against in South Korea, as are other t'albukcha.

Han's subjectivity expresses his aspiration for the true nation, though without giving up his own desires embedded in the present capitalist order. This contradictory subjectivity that desires "capitalism without capitalism" is found in Han's deep ambivalence toward North Korea. While he abhors the new material culture, rampant corruption, and inequality in North Korea, he himself is part of the larger global capitalist force that integrates the two Koreas and the Korean Chinese community since the 1990s. For instance, during his secret return to North Korea to bring his sister and mother to China in 2004, he observed that "money works very well in North Korea. While money in the past was considered a capitalist element, it is now said to be a tool of patriotism as individuals are asked to submit a portion of their income [from market activities] to the state." In his observation, the wealthy in Pyongyang and other places live in ways that would make Chinese drop their jaws. He learned that some people sell as much as 20 tons of rice, contradicting the earlier socialist ethos that "rice is communism."[7] According to him, there is no way one can earn that much money by legitimate means; money begets money in North Korea and buys immunity from wrongdoing. He planned to return to North Korea someday to help people and contribute to educating children in North Korea. Yet, North Korea did not seem to stand for the true nation, at least in its current condition. During his visit to North Korea, he also found that his lifestyle surpassed that of ordinary people. He preferred dining in restaurants to eating meals in the house where he stayed, arousing suspicion among the neighbors about his expenditures that led to his arrest. For him, the prison food made of feed corn was even worse than interrogation, and he lost 8 kg in eighteen days. He returned to China with his sister, leaving behind his mother, who wished to remain home. Back in China, he seems to have become entrenched in making money, as he not only mourned his father's premature death in China as a consequence of the lack of money but also sought to buy Chinese residency.

While he desires a new Korean nation, he prefers living in China, at least for the foreseeable future, despite his stateless status. His fluency in Chinese enables him to pretend to be a Korean Chinese though he derides Korean Chinese for losing their national character (minjoksŏng). In order to deflect suspicion in China, he uses Korean Chinese vernacular when speaking Korean, uses three or four pseudonyms, frequently changes his phone number, exchanges text messages rather than phone calls with his sister working in Qingdao in fear of suspicion, and prefers e-mail communication with friends and acquaintances in South Korea to avoid potential wiretaps on phones. He has a Han Chinese girlfriend who protects him from police suspicion, especially when traveling. He minimizes contact with Korean Chinese in fear of being reported to the police and ignores other North Koreans. When asked if it would be better to help each other, he replied, "One has to create one's own fate," borrowing the essence of Juche ideology. For him, it would suffice if North Koreans would not harm each other and if the same minjok would not deceive each other. When I said that undocumented Korean Chinese migrant laborers in South Korea help each other, he replied that they could because they would not be prosecuted in China when they return. For North Koreans in China, when they are caught and repatriated to North Korea, they will be tortured and forced to report other North Koreans whom they met in China. He also added that many returned to North Korea because they found it more comfortable to live there despite poverty and hunger.

A new imaginative political order offers momentary relief to his fragmented subjectivity. This new symbolic order is framed by his distinctions among nara (country), kukka (state), choguk (homeland), and minjok (nation), all of which are rendered synonymous in the modern nation-state system. In his terms, the Korean nation is based on blood ties and encompasses the two Koreas only, excluding Korean Chinese for their cultural and political inauthenticity; his concept of state denotes a political regime, like the Kim Jong Il regime in North Korea; his homeland refers to North Korea; and his country is China, as this designates the importance of the people as its constituents. He elaborates that

> my concept of nation transcends state. Whether Han'guk [South Korea] or Chosŏn [North Korea], they are all the same nation. The framework of state doesn't fit well to explain my concept. We have to consider the two Koreas to be the same descendants of Tan'gun [the mythic founder of Korea] and their relations within the goal of unification. . . . The country and the homeland are similar but different. For me, my country is China as I want to gain residency in China, while my homeland is North Korea. The country and homeland are the same for people living in North Korea. . . . I learned in North Korea that homeland means the country where one's ancestors lived, regardless of where one lives now. For instance, Chosŏn is the homeland of Koreans in Japan with or without North Korean citizenship.
>
> (Interview on October 13, 2006, in Yanji)

Splitting nation and state, he discloses the excess of his subjectivity. His yearning for the true nation and disavowal of the two Koreas in the present moment epitomizes the modern paradox of human rights—or more important, demonstrates the aspiration to overcome it. He yearns to be a citizen of a country, yet he also is aware of the limits to citizenry rights under state sovereignty. On the one hand, he expresses that citizenship is "the proof that I am human" (chŏdo saram iran chŭngmyŏng) and qualified to cast a vote. He has never held citizenship in any country, including North Korea because he left North Korea when he was sixteen years old, one year before being given an official certificate of citizenship (kongminjŭng). Thus he only has his birth record there. On the other hand, he bases his critique of the state on his remembrance of his father's past. That is, his father's life was continuously refracted through his uncertain political origins in North Korea because his orphan status made it difficult to certify his family's class and political background.

By distinguishing nation, state, country, and homeland from one another, he rejects all available identities and instead expresses his desire for the utopian community that was promised but never realized. When this utopian community is articulated in the language of the nation, the nation gives rise to another political phantasmagoria that translates the critique of the capitalist present into a critique of the existing nation-state. The utopia called nation is transference of new social relations onto an expedient idea of the whole. This transference means that negating the present nation-state's condition by appealing to a new national community remains within the same symbolic limits of nation. The nation is an afterimage: it offers an illusory possibility of transcending the contradictory state of "free labor." Yet his juxtaposition of the previous socialist utopia and the capitalist present undercuts this modern phantasmagoria, bringing to his consciousness the shadowy side of the state and its laws. His astute relations with capitalist forces suffuse his unarticulated rejection of the two Koreas; they drove him out of North Korea and created his desire to become a free, mobile, and self-sufficient worker.

Han's vision of community gives a special place once again to Korean unification, with its emphasis on the Korean people. According to him, the old formula for Korean national unification as the formation of a single state (through the absorption of one state by the other) is no longer viable. Unification remains "a dream for people suffering from hunger." As argued in chapter 6, when leftist and right-wing politics in South Korea enter an uncanny consensus on the capitalist system as a force for national unification, they erase the utopian dream of anticolonial struggle that formed the basis for the Korean War and the consequent division of Korea. In such a conjuncture, Han's rejection of both Koreas resists this erasure of the past dream. His practice of a new temporality that invokes the ur-history of the Korean nation marks a radical moment of remembering the unrealized dream that once again is commandeered by the capitalist present.

The politics of the three aleatory subjects in the foregoing discussion are obscured by conventional human rights discourse. These subjects reveal strategies of, and contradictions in, envisaging the new commons. Instead of being canonical images of victims and stalwarts in quest of freedom, these figures embody the disquiet about actualizing freedom under conditions of propertylessness. The momentous critique of the present harbors the humanity of these three subjects. It disconnects the temporality of the present from the universal time of capital, as well as from the homogeneous time of socialism and nation. The struggle for the commons takes place within the multiple temporalities of the present.

CONCLUSION

The paradoxical prose of migration, "I didn't have to come but still . . . ," places the meaning of migration in the realm of everyday practices in North Korea that traverse the state's prohibition and the individual's heroic escape. The latest everyday politics construes socialism and capitalism as opposition. However, border-crossing migration from North Korea to China and to South Korea is a repeated moment of negation: North Koreans simultaneously transcend and continue the commodification of their labor. Migration exerts a fascinating power as the commodity-form through the production of North Koreans as a Kantian transcendental subject.

Marx argues that capitalist exploitation does not involve any kind of "unequal" exchange but is founded on equal exchange, in which workers appear to be paid the full value of the labor power that they sell. His fundamental insight reveals the paradox of capitalist inequality: market exchange does not violate the principle of equality but is inherent in the logic of equality (see Žižek 2009:173). Marx's insight brings the analysis of democratic sovereignty into the process of production and circulation and calls our attention to everyday politics that associates capitalist relations with democracy. In her analysis of industrial modernity, Buck-Morss (2002:209) conceptualizes mass utopia as a form of democracy from which both capitalist and socialist worlds have awakened during the post–Cold War era. The food crisis of the mid-1990s marks another crisis for North Korea's beleaguered mass utopia. This chapter has examined the shift to market utopia that imagines capitalism as a force for freedom and equality. Border-crossing migration is a transcendental act that simultaneously reproduces market utopia and transcends the ills of capitalism.

The perverse emotion of Korean Chinese and North Koreans toward each other denotes that capitalism expands through the production of contradictory desires. Korean missionaries work as healers who vainly try to unite individuals with the nation-state in a seamless whole. Their proselytizing translates market fantasy about neoliberal capitalism into yet another abstract language of spirituality and deciphers the formula of wealth making. In that conjuncture, the three aleatory figures dissemble their present experience of border-crossing migration against the invoked destiny, whether a unified ethnic nation or a capitalist community. The acts of bodily displacement, manual work, and espousal of a stateless nation split the performative mass activity into incongruent monadic fragments of community. These fragments work like mosaics of the dreams that emblazon the universal desire for community on one's body that is the material site and ultimate sovereign space.

CONCLUSION

Korean unification was a decolonizing project during the Cold War era that envisaged territorial unification of the Korean peninsula to establish a single sovereign Korean nation. In this book I have transformed the Cold War problematic of Korean unification into a problematic pertaining to a modern aesthetics of politics. The chiasmus in this book is, therefore, not so much between ethnic national sovereignty and territorial integration as between modern sovereignty and global capitalism. This approach uncovers a momentous shift from the task of Korean territorial unification to the formation of a transnational Korean community in the post–Cold War present. The formation of transnational Korea is inscribed in the experiences of economic crises by capitalist and socialist Koreas and the Korean diasporic communities. Figures of the Korean transnational community are separated from one another, as if islands, in today's world of identity politics and civil society movements: South Korean unionized workers are contrasted with an irregular and migrant workers who are denied job security and organizational representation; Korean Chinese migrant workers are inscribed as "colonial returnees" for having migrated to China during the Japanese colonial era and returned as migrant laborers, and they are opposed to non-Korean migrant workers framed as "cosmopolitan subjects"; and North Korean migrants are named "refugees" escaping the totalitarian regime. This book has shown the intricate linkages of these figures, whose border-crossing relations construct a hierarchical Korean community on a global scale and embody the logics of the latest capitalist and democratic systems. Here I have elucidated the excesses and contradictions that render the transnational community a liminal space for border-crossing Korean migrants.

The transnational Korea entails asynchronous constellations of neoliberal reforms, as each Korean community adopts them to resolve its singular crisis and imagines capitalism as a democratic moment. Progressing across the former socialist and capitalist divide, privatization and deregulation of the economy are variously construed as the rule of law, freedom, and reparation of state violence. Installment of the market and the rule of law are regarded as necessary for a peaceful reconciliation of the two Koreas and protection of human rights. I have conceptualized as market utopia the democratic politics of reparation, peace, and human rights advocacy. In the realm of democratic politics, the rise of market utopia signifies the growing separation of global capitalism from modernist ideals of mass liberation that were bound up with the sovereign power of the nation-state. In the political vacuum left by the dissolution of socialist states and rampant fear of economic crisis, the advent of neoliberal capitalism skews the act of cultural imagination just as industrial modernism (in its capitalist and socialist forms) had done in the twentieth century. I have delineated the logics that are shared by the liberal repertories of reparation, peace, and human rights and that arise from the abstraction of capitalism into market and democracy. These shared logics are the sublimation of private property rights, the rule of law, and freedom from (the state's) violence.

Transnational Korea is a collective unconscious that eludes the discourses and politics of Korean unification. This collective unconscious is the capitalist unconscious, as the appeal for Korean unification has been reconfigured into a transnational form by the new global system of neoliberal capitalism and its utopian politics. The material constituents of transnational Korea comprise neoliberal reforms, a changing nexus of industrial capital, financial capital, and the state, and the cascading migration of capital and labor across Korean communities. These material changes are symbolized in narrative, affective, and corporeal forms to yield a collective unconscious. Recognition of the capitalist unconscious could help South Koreans depart their illusory position as victors in the Cold War struggle and jettison their gazes toward North Koreans and Korean Chinese as objects of their humanitarianism and decolonization. This awakening may ultimately allow South Koreans to confront their own crises of capitalism and democracy, which manifest in stalemated debates about the stages of democratization and neoliberalization. Recognition in South Korea of the capitalist underpinnings of these democratic engagements would in turn promote recognition of the historical changes in ideas about Korean ethnic and national sovereignty wrought by the new system of capitalism since the 1990s. Furthermore, comprehending the dynamics of this emergent capitalist system would lead South Korea to move out of its politico-ethical limbo between continued lamentation over the human tragedy caused by the national division and economic misgivings over the unification of the two Koreas. A solution to the still-divided families and the persistent instrumentalization of North Koreans and the Korean diaspora would be found in the act of understanding the new capitalist network and its performative politics of freedom and the rights that binds them together. This act would lead to drawing a new horizon for the commons beyond normative social categories of people that separate identities and rights in terms of deserving citizens, refugees, unionized workers, migrant workers, ethnic returnees, and so on.

The capitalist unconscious becomes the historical unconscious, as crisis poses a genuine problem for the interpretation of history. The modern usage of the term crisis is tied to a construction of self and community in the historical processes of the Enlightenment, the French Revolution, science, and capitalism (Latour 1993; Jameson 2013; Roitman 2014). According to Koselleck (2004:22), the accelerating temporality of historical change in the midst of the collapse of absolute power, social unrest, and technological innovation compels an escape "into a future within which the currently unapprehendable present has to be captured by historical philosophy." That is, "politics and prophecy" stand in for recognition of the present. Extending the discussion of crisis and modernity, I have explored crisis not only in terms of the socioeconomics of capital accumulation but also as the very problematic of history and everyday experience arising from capital accumulation and its politico-cultural mediation. Confronting the entwined progression of neoliberal reforms and political democratization, South Korea engages in intense debates on historical periodization that pit the 1987 democratization against the 1997 neoliberalization as the marker of the present. In China and North Korea, the state and individuals stage neoliberal reforms as reparation of unfulfilled socialist dreams, rendering the interpretation of the present as a heated political issue.

Debates in Korean communities about the present reflect current theoretical discussions of global capitalism and democracy that postulate the transition theses: the transition from industrial to financial capitalism, the transition from capitalism to socialism to capitalism, and the transition from mass utopia to market utopia. Various terms for the contemporary form of capitalism—predatory, speculative, neoliberal, transnational, financial, or biopolitical—are contrasted with previous ones, including developmental, long-term, job-creating, life-giving, and nation-based modes of industrial capitalism. These influential theses on the latest capitalism do not espouse the notion of progress but instead offer grim testimony to worsening inequality and seek to foster a better democratic alternative. As they seek to discern a new logic from the changing global political economy and posit a temporal rupture, however, they effect a similar shadowing of the present as in the notion of historical progress.

The desire to grasp the present resides in the repudiation of mass utopian politics with the ending of the Cold War. The shift from the minjung (people) movement to the civil society movement and its identity politics in South Korea since the 1990s signifies an attempt to approach the present without a predetermined future. My analysis of these new democratic politics as market utopia has revealed that the capitalist regime has quickly appropriated the desire for unmediated experience of everyday life. The most striking feature of market utopia is its pledge to realize difference, an emblem of identity politics. Today's market utopia fosters presentism, departing from an earlier transcendental logic of utopian thinking. The abstraction of capitalism into the market imagines utopia forever present rather than futuristic. For instance, the debate on the Overseas Korean Act produced one arbitrary criterion for ethnic Korean membership after another—generation, cultural traits, past citizenship, and date of migration. This debate is no mere dispute over difference and identity in the clash between nation and diaspora or between cosmopolitanism and ethnic nationalism, as represented in South Korean politics. It is, rather, the capitalist unconscious that refuses to recognize Korean Chinese as migrant workers with rights to work and mobility. At once animated and stalemated, the debate about national membership of ethnic Koreans amounts to an unconscious refusal by South Koreans to confront their own capitalist and democratic present.

I have pursued the fidelity of logic and history in order to access the historical present, where the putatively dying industrial production, its institutions, and its utopian ideas are articulated with the new in materiality and memory politics. Walter Benjamin (1969) and Ernst Bloch (2009) among others emphasize the significance of recognizing the existence of the old in the present, i.e., the noncontemporaneous contemporaneity. In a similar spirit, I have problematized the transition theses of history that arise out of the crisis of industrial capitalism and conjecture a historical rupture in socioeconomics, politics, and culture. The projected shift from industrial to financial capitalism works as an ideology in South Korea that legitimates the construction of migrant workers as disposable workers. The reconfigured network of industrial capital and finance capital plays a central role in disempowering labor unions in South Korea. One's experience of privatization in socialist China and North Korea is also contingent on the characterization of history, such as the past as failure and the present as the moment of transcendence. Crisis beckons repressed experiences of past events into the present. The return of the past in the present performs the cultural work of interpreting today's crisis and one's place in it. The past does not disappear despite public announcement of the failure of socialist and other utopian politics of emancipation. The past is instead inscribed in one's knowledge, desire, and the unconscious through which one experiences the present. Through narrative, sensory, and corporeal forms, repressed experience of the past constitutes one's subjectivity in the present. The narrative construction of history discussed in this book includes the historical periodization of democratic transition, socialist transition, and neoliberal capitalism, as well as the problematics of the relationship of cosmopolitanism, nationalism, and ethnicity. Sensorial and corporeal expressions, such as hauntings, flashbacks, memories, and bodily displacement, extend the representation of history beyond rationality and bring it into the realms of emotion and the unconscious.

The notion of repetition as the temporality of crisis and its resolution authorizes a new thinking about the coeval temporality of diverse political regimes in relation to capitalism. Different political regimes such as the socialist state, military state, and representative democratic state are routinely posited as antinomies or as being in developmental stages. They are, however, connected to repeated attempts at crisis resolution. In the footsteps of Schmitt and Löwith, Agamben (1998) finds the philosophical ground of fascism and liberal democracy contiguous in their shared belief in the state's production of social life. Adding socialism, I instead approach cotemporality of various political regimes in terms of historical repetition. Namely, crisis time and again generates the impossibility of overcoming itself, and this impossibility fuels repeated attempts to find adequate political forms to contain its effects. Like other political regimes, socialist regime entails the logic of transcendence as it seeks to overcome private property–based capitalism through the creation of a society based on collective or state ownership. Socialism is a utopian vision that emerged and operated within the crisis of capitalism. The inscription of political regimes on social crises leads to an account of their specific content and shared form. Conceptualization of political and economic systems as historical repetition brings to the fore an understanding of the spatiotemporality of capital accumulation and its mediated crisis. The linkage between capitalist crises and political forms inserts politics and history into current discussions of crisis, community, and utopia.

Recognition of historical repetition becomes a political moment capable of critiquing the hegemonic and normalizing politics of crisis. Recognition of the repeated violence of the police and paramilitary in South Korea during the military dictatorship and democratic era breaks down the aporia of democracy that pervades the present. It makes it possible to envisage a new democratic politics beyond the walls of the fragmented politics of identity. Impromptu remembrance by Korean Chinese of the violence of the Chinese Cultural Revolution during their migratory work in South Korea signifies a rejection of both the (Chinese) socialist and (South Korean) democratic states beyond their specific content. The recognition of repetition is a subversive moment, as the memory of past experiences makes the present experience new. In other words, the crisis in capitalism is the real in Derrida's (1994) notion, which is not immediately and completely graspable in everyday experience, but approachable only in haunting proximity through repeated attempts. Like Deleuze's (1994) notion of repetition, my analysis does not privilege any form as an authentic and truthful rendition of the real or settle for a pluralist understanding as if only difference matters; realization of the real is delayed and repeated in difference. Paradoxes in the politics and representation of crises and crises resolution are discernible in the realm of history, where earlier incomplete utopian practices not only refuse to disappear but also haunt ideals and practices in the present. A possibility about the future is located on the interface between old ideals and new challenges that in turn are predicated on the conditions of daily life in a specific place.

Working like an angel in "Angelus Novus" in Benjamin's (1969) reading, the historical figures explored in this book confront storms of historical change. Jarred by enchanted promises and bewildering realities, they spread their vision into history in search of meanings and possibilities. They see the wreckage of socialism, industrialism, and mass utopia amid the allures of private ownership, individual rights, and universal ethics. In this book I have traced constellations of these moments, in which the "tiger's leap into the past" constitutes a moment of the "now" that interrupts the purportedly linear transition of history. In China, the remembrance by the elderly Korean Chinese man of his grandfather's utterance, "the sorrow of the Tuman River," is a dialectical moment of awakening to the present: a momentary exposure of the excesses of colonial experience leads to the recognition of a new historicity of the present marked by the anguish of his love. The remembrance separates the present from the continuous time of history, disordering the official historiography of national suffering, liberation, and socialist revolution. In South Korea, the flashbacks to the 1980 Kwangju massacre, which fueled the democratization movement of the 1980s, suspend the middle-class life of unionized workers and the pride of intellectuals over the 1987 democratization, leading them to envisage an alliance with irregular workers and migrant workers. The struggle of the Ssangyong workers extends beyond its earlier class struggle to the struggle for life itself. They struggle to cope with ill health, depression, and suicide among workers and their spouses. They suffer from physical and psychological trauma from violent attacks from police and private security forces. They are branded as "terrorists" and subject to social expulsion. And they are fearful of losing their homes through court orders to pay for damages to the company's property during the workers' lock-in demonstration. The repercussions of these events on Ssangyong workers as living and dying labor are so encompassing that they cannot be merely called "affect" and opposed to material conditions. Under the new network of the state, industrial capital, and financial capital, their struggles fuse materiality and the human spirit. Their momentary awakenings entail a historical consciousness that Benjamin calls the real state of emergency in the struggle against fascism. The "now" time as the temporality of the present turns on its head the "once-upon a time" narrative that is integral to the transition theses that conjecture the past as discrete from and discontinuous with the present. Dialectical recognition of the moment means neither a reconstruction of past events in the present, as is common in memory studies, nor past experiences as lessons for the present.

Human rights advocacy for North Korea opposes socialism and capitalism, characterizing the former as dictatorship and the latter as the rule of law. This discursive formulation that opposes socialism and capitalism has been challenged by the theoretical analysis that characterizes socialism and capitalism as twins of state capitalism. Whether socialism is conceived as the other or the twin of capitalism, its actual history cannot be, however, dismissed as the state's failed utopian project. Dilemmas, contradictions, and ironies that emerged during socialist history continue to play havoc with the processes of economic privatization and deregulation. They generate the aporia of democracy and the debate on historical periodization in South Korea while fostering the desire for a stateless national community among Korean Chinese and North Korea migrants. The putative transition to capitalism in North Korea and China is embedded in the actual history of the transition to socialism that reinvented socialism through the integration of capitalist features under their historically specific conditions. In this conjuncture, three subversive subjects imagine alternative forms of community based on displacement without fixed belonging, manual labor without accumulation, and stateless nation.

The Capitalist Unconscious is a study of labor in the putative post-labor era. In the past two centuries, industrial workers in a collective entity have reveled in the inaugural theses and practices of socialism and communism. They are now replaced by new emblematic figures of current history that, according to political activism and theories of contemporary capitalism and democracy, include border-crossing migrants, refugees, migrant women, and immaterial intellectual laborers. In transnational Korean politics, these old and new subjects of history are placed in a social order that separates their socioeconomic status and identities from one another, especially in the era of identity politics based on difference. This book has demonstrated that the critique of the transition theses of capitalism and democracy authorizes consideration of these new and old subjects of history in terms of a continuum in order to comprehend their material connections and envisage a new politics of the commons. The inscription of Korean Chinese and North Korean migrant laborers respectively as ethnic returnees and refugees produces their historically specific terms of commodification by obscuring their intrinsic ties with one another, as well as with South Korean domestic workers and non-Korean foreign workers in South Korea. South Korean politics shows that one's recognition of the shared fate of unionized domestic workers, precarious domestic workers, migrant workers, and diasporic returnees disrupts the social ordering of people in the service of the state and capital.

This book's exposition of this shared capitalist and democratic network rests on my theoretical and methodological frameworks of capitalism, democracy, and socialism and their immanent relationship. In theoretical terms, I have merged two canonical paradigms of modern sovereignty: a framework of biopolitics that accounts for the state's exceptional sovereignty; and a materialist framework of living and dead labor that locates the inalienable sovereignty of the people in their labor power. I have reworked the notion of living and dead labor in order to account for the historically constitutive role of the nation-state state and its sovereignty in the production and regulation of labor. This means that one's relationship with the nation-state as citizen or refugee involves one's social status in the private property system. In turn, I have extended biopolitics beyond its original terrain of the state's production of knowledge in order to explain its limit in determining the sociopolitical. This limit relates to an individual's sovereignty, though indeterminate, over his or her own labor power, as capital buys only labor without the sure control over a hired worker's labor power. No matter how the state elevates private property rights as the sublime, capitalists cannot make workers into their private property. Whether the labor regime is despotic, Fordist, or post-Fordist, capitalists confront a limit when attempting to seize complete control over the labor power of workers. Furthermore, the thesis that contemporary capitalism realizes the real subsumption of labor is problematic, whether capitalist discipline is enacted by new production networks and ideologies of nationalism, cosmopolitanism, or an opposition of the two. The people's realization of sovereignty over their bodies is, rather, a historical question, because it is subject to politico-cultural mediation, which has been elucidated here through the analysis of the new democratic politics called market utopia.

As methodological concerns, I have underscored the problematic of recognition and interpretation in the analysis of politics, which reaches beyond the problematic of making an alternative politics capable of challenging contemporary power structures. In this regard, the politics and historical consciousness are in fact unconscious: they take not only the narrative form in rationalizing experiences but also corporeal and sensory forms that manifest in unexpected, often illegible, and transhistorical memory. With these theoretical and methodological frameworks, I have approached history as political, experiential, and philosophical categories by attending to indeterminate process of power and resistance, memory forms, and temporal structures such as modernity, the postindustrial experience, and crisis. In this book history loses the form of totality, for commodified individuals are only humans whose desires for security and freedom wreak havoc on their equally deep longing for community. The tension between the fear of loss and the desire for union leads one's emotions, words, and bodily memories to become disconnected and disembodied. Any transcendental vision for the future is to be realized in the local, where individuals with diverse histories and sensory experiences work together toward their vision of community. Each political practice is marked by a unique historical temporality in simultaneity and repetition.

NOTES

1. THE CAPITALIST UNCONSCIOUS: THE KOREA QUESTION

1. Tariq Ali (1984) points out that the desire for stability among the people after a long period of war and revolution gave an upper hand to Stalin's developmental project over Lenin's or Trotsky's continuous revolution on a world scale. The industrialization in the 1930s endowed the regime with a social support, as it created jobs and offered upward mobility for workers and peasants thanks to economic advances and political purges that created a mass of vacancies in the bureaucracy.

2. For the discussion of history and memory from the liberal assumption about the community, see Paul Ricoeur (2004).

3. See also James O'Connor (1987:113) for his discussion of fascism as an example of crises that became cauldrons not only for capital restructuring but also for utopian politics.

2. THE AESTHETICS OF DEMOCRATIC POLITICS: LABOR, VIOLENCE, AND REPETITION

1. These migrant workers typically are in their twenties and thirties, whereas Korean Chinese workers tend to be much older especially until the mid-2000s, as discussed in chapter 3.

2. Upon the military's concession to the popular protest in July 1987, workers spearheaded the Great Strikes in July and August and achieved their demands for wage increase and unionization. Although unions were formed in mainly large factories owned by conglomerates, Chŏnnohyŏp (Korean Trade Union Congress, KTUC), formed in 1990, is credited with expanding the unionization of smaller

factories and increasing the national integration of unions. Its successor, Minju noch'ong (Korean Confederation of Trade Union, KCTU) was formed in 1995 and has established industry-level unions, among which the Metal Workers' Union (kŭmsok nojo) is known to be most militant and influential. It pursued the political empowerment of workers, namely, the creation of the Democratic Labor Party. Changes in the structure and politics of the labor movement were adopted as measures to go beyond company-level struggles around wages, promotion, and layoffs and to avoid companies' interference with labor unions.

3. Factories that employ fewer than fifty workers are categorized as small; those employing between fifty and three hundred workers are medium sized.

4. For instance, migrant workers are reported to "hunt" for South Korean women for marriage and legal residence, especially preying on mentally and physically handicapped and middle-aged single women. See Chŏn Hyŏnjong (2007).

5. For a succinct reading of Marx's critique of law, see Bob Fine (1984). According to Fine, "the root of this mystique was that private property appeared as a relation between individual and things constructed in private rather than as the expression of a definite social relation between people" (103).

6. This so-called container suppression was first used in the suppression of the 2009 occupy protests by evictees in Yongsan, a former American military base in Seoul. For a documentary film on the suppression, see Tugaeŭi mun (Two Doors), directed by Kim Ilhan and Hong Chiyu and released in 2012.

7. According to Ko Tongmin, director of the Ssangyong Automobile labor union, "money more than 10,000,000 won [$8,500 to $9,000] is just a number for a laid-off worker. One tries to pay the penalty up to that amount, even borrowing money. Who wouldn't hang, drug, or throw off the roof oneself to die, when one is about to lose their house that he barely owned after 15 to 20 years of backbreaking work" (Im Sŏngji 2011:27).

8. My accounts of the social formation debate draw on four volumes of Han'guk sahoe kusŏngch'e ron (The social formation debate in South Korea), edited by Cho Hiyŏn and Pak Hyŏncha'e (Seoul: Chuksan, 1989–1992), in which Cho Hiyŏn and Pak Hyŏnch'ae compiled a vast scope of writings and debates, running to more than five hundred pages in each volume. They provide a chronological framework with a concise summary while mapping key historical events, terrains of dispute, and structural forces.

9. For the study of the Democratic Labor Party and its division into PD and NL lines, see Chŏng Yŏngt'ae (2010).

3. REPARATION: ON COLONIAL RETURNEE

1.   Koreans who acquired neither Japanese citizenship nor South Korean citizenship are called North Koreans by default.

2.   In the late 1990s, overseas Koreans numbered about 5.5 million or 7.4 percent of the total population of the two Koreas (50 million in South Korea and 24 million in North Korea). As of 2013, the population of overseas Koreans increased to 7 million, including Koreans in China (2.5 million, 36.7 percent), in the United States (2 million, 29.82 percent), in Japan (0.89 million, 12.72 percent), and in Russia and Central Asia (0.49 million, 6.95 percent). For details, see the Ministry of Foreign Affairs and Trade (2013).

3.   All of these fees are based on information gleaned from my interviews with Korean Chinese who came to South Korea from the mid-1990s until the mid-2000s.

4.   The appeal by Group 10, among those who participated in the protest from November 2003 to February 2004 at the One-Hundredth Anniversary Hall of the Korean Church. Unpublished document.

5.   For the analysis of Korean nationality and property rights that were at the center of disputes between Chinese and Japanese in Manchuria, see Hyun Ok Park (2005).

6.   Korean Chinese participating in the sit-in-protest at eight churches, "Chungguk chŏngbu e tŭrinŭn kul" (A letter to the Chinese government), November 24, 2003.

4. SOCIALIST REPARATION: ON LIVING LABOR

1.   Korean Chinese living in the Yanbian Autonomous Prefecture are about half of the total 2 million Koreans in China, and those in Heilongjiang Province include four hundred thousand, or about 20 percent. The majority of Koreans in Yanbian came from northern Korea (currently North Korea), beginning in the late nineteenth century, because of the country's geographic contiguity, while those in Heilongjiang Province tend to come from southern Korea, especially since the 1930s as a result of the Japanese colonial policy of the Korean collective settlement. For details, see Hyun Ok Park (2005).

2.   "Pangmun ch'wiŏpche 5-nyŏn, kwigukcha tŭrŭn mwŏrhana?" (The visiting employment system for five years: What do the returnees do?), *Killim sinmun* (Jilin newspaper), December 6, 2012.

3.   For an insightful interpretation of Korean Chinese women's subjectivities from their bodily symptoms, such as disease, death, and physical disabilities, see Yi Mirim (2011).

5. CHINESE REVOLUTION IN REPETITION:
THE MINORITY QUESTION

1. *Chapkwisin* literally means "mixed demons" or "miscellaneous demons." According to Pettid (2014:144), "Spirits, known as . . . *chapkwi* [minor demons], represent untransformed beings who are of neither this world nor the next and accordingly are a constant danger to the living." In light of this definition and in the context of the making of socialist revolution in China, chapkwisin might suggest social practices and consciousness that are neither old nor new (socialist) and pose a threat to socialist revolution.

2. For the history of Chinese nationalism in the Chinese Communist Party and the purge of Korean communists prior to 1949, see Hyun Ok Park (2005).

3. While Deleuze speaks of "systems" of simulacra, I find "moments" of simulacra in the historical actualization of socialism in order to highlight the fragmented socialist history.

4. For Marxist critiques of history as totality, see Martin Jay's (1984) discussion of Adorno and Bloch; also see Walter Benjamin on history as constellation in "Theses on the Philosophy of History" (1969).

5. 1 kŭn equals 0.6 kg.

6. Chu Tŏkhae's biography, *Chu Tŏkhae ŭi ilsaeng*, omits discussion of the politics of Korean independence and the power struggle between the CCP and Korean communists.

    Cho Namgi's biography points out what seems to be the CCP's strategy of domesticating the history of the anti-Japanese struggle of Koreans. Beginning in 1951 the central Chinese state commemorated Korean revolutionaries who fought in northeast China. It also began in 1957 to archive traces of Koreans' anti-Japanese revolutionary struggles in Yanbian, such as propaganda fliers, rice containers, everyday tools, and resources. During the drive to study Mao's thought in the early 1960s, many Chinese officials from Beijing visited Yanbian to pay tribute to the revolutionary struggle of Koreans. See Kok and Chung (2004).

7. While Chosŏn was doubtlessly associated with North Korea in the big-character posters of Yanbian University, many Koreans, especially those from southern Korea living in the northern and southwestern parts of northeast China (Liaoning and Heilongjiang Provinces), must have imagined a not-yet-unified Korea. For details of the multiple-nationality thesis, see *Minjok munje "ttajŭbo" hoejip* (1958). For details of the national rectification movement, see O T'aeho (1993).

8. About five thousand Korean youth in China joined the army and went to North Korea during the war. Another 5,740 Koreans went to North Korea to serve in the areas of intelligence, translation, and transportation. A total of 6,981 Koreans in Yanbian, in addition to Mao's own son, lost their lives in North Korea during the

Korean War. For details, see Yŏnbyŏn tangsa hakhoe (1989:51). At North Korea's request, the Chinese state sent 10,297 Korean Chinese households (52,014 individuals) in 1958 and 1959, a third of whom went to work in the countryside and the rest in factories. See Yi Sangsuk and Wenzhi Song (2012).

9. I call Koreans in Manchuria "Korean Chinese" especially beginning in 1952 when the Yanbian Korean autonomous region was established, although their identities and rights remain contested.

10. Following Stalinist economic orthodoxy while adopting a gradual process, China collectivized agriculture in two phases by the end of 1956: the first phase, from 1952 to 1955, was the creation of low-stage cooperatives, which were replaced in the second phase, in 1956, by advanced cooperatives. For elaboration of China's moderation of the Stalinist policy, see Teiwes (1987).

11. Yanbian Autonomous Prefecture is one of thirty autonomous prefectures in China. There are also sixty-nine autonomous counties like Changpai Korean Autonomous County in Liaoning Province.

12. An estimated sixty-three thousand (5.9 percent) of Koreans in northeast China, with fifty-two thousand in Yanbian alone, joined the Chinese communist army during the three-year period of the civil war (1946–1949); an additional one hundred thousand Koreans in Yanbian offered assistance on the front lines. About five thousand to six thousand Koreans are honored as "revolutionary heroes" (yŏlsa) for dying in the liberation war. A Korean even wrote the anthem of the Chinese People's Liberation Army. Korean Chinese made up 93.96 percent of 15,970 revolutionary heroes in Yanbian during the anti-Japanese struggle and the liberation period combined. For details, see Yi Chinryŏng (2002); Kok and Chung (2004:502); and Chŏnmun munje chŏjak sojo (2005).

13. "Choego chisi: Sam pan punja Chu Tŏkhae ka Mo Taektong sasang ŭl pandae han hanŭl e samuch'inŭn choehaeng ŭl chaba ttenŭn kŏsŭl yongnap hal su ŏpda" (Supreme instruction: We can't allow the antireactionary Chu Tŏkhae to deny that he opposed Mao Tse-tung's thoughts). This is the document in which the New 8.27 Group denounced the Protectionist Group in 1967. On these charges against Chu Tŏkhae and other intellectuals, see also Yanbian daxue geming weiyuan hui jiaoyu geming zu (1969:43).

14. Internal investigations that cleared all charges against Chu Tŏkhae include "Chu Tŏkhae munje e taehan Chunggong killimsŏng wiwŏnhoe ŭi chae simsa kyŏllon pogo" (Report by the CCP's Jilin Provincial Committee on the reinvestigation of the Chu Tŏkhae inquiry), in Chungguk Chosŏn minjok palchach'wi ch'ongsŏ wiwŏnhoe (1993:6–19); and "Chu Tŏkhae tongji ŭi ŏgul han rumyŏng ŭl pŏtkigo myŏngye rŭl hoebok halde taehan Chunggong Yŏnbyŏn chuwi ŭi kyŏrŭi, June 10, 1978" (The decision by the CCP's Yanbian Committee on nullifying the indictment

against comrade Chu Tŏkhae and exonerating him, June 10, 1978), in Chungguk Chosŏn minjok palchach'wi ch'ongsŏ wiwŏnhoe (1993:19–23).

15. "Ch'oego chisi: Chŏn'guk inmin egye allinŭn kŭl" (Supreme instruction: The news to the people in the whole country), August 9, 1967. This document was produced by various organizations that joined the New 8.27 Group.

16. Chuwi chosa yŏn'gusil, "'Chonguk inmin ege allinŭn kŭl' pandong sŏnjŏn ppira nŭn ŏttŏkke nat'anan kŏsinga? (How did the reactionary propaganda flier "The news to the people in the whole country" come to appear?). This internal investigation report of the Korean rebellion report was conducted by the Yanbian Prefecture government in 1978. Another internal investigation report by the Yanbian Prefecture government is Chungguk kongsandang Yŏnbyŏn Chosŏnjok chach'iju wiwŏnhoe, "'panguk p'ongnan,' 'xx t'ŭkmu,' 'chiha Kumindang' tŭng ŏgurhan an'gŏn ŭl chŏngchŏng hagi wihan de kwanhan kyŏlchŏng" (The decision on correcting absurd accusations such as "'rebellion,' 'xx spies,' 'underground Kuomintang'"), June 29, 1978.

6. KOREAN UNIFICATION AS CAPITALIST HEGEMONY

1. On Adam Smith's ambivalence to commerce, which he thought destroyed the courage of humankind and the martial spirit, see Albert Hirschman (1997:106) and Tony Aspromourgos (2007). For an analysis of Adam Smith's theory from the perspective of necropolitics, see Montag (2013).

2. I use "family union" instead of "family reunion" in order to highlight the impossibility of resolving the past.

3. On this waiting list, 41,195 are already deceased; about 40 percent of the survived are between 70 and 80 years of age. For details of family union, see Chae Kyŏngsŏk (2001:546) and Yŏm Kyuhyŏn (2009).

4. Cho Ch'ŏnhyŏn, *Kukkun p'oro samin ŭi sŏnt'aek* (The choice of three South Korean prisoners of war). Broadcast on the Korean Broadcasting System (KBS), November 20, 2004, it is based on Cho's filming of three prisoners of war for three years beginning in late 2000.

5. South Korean memories of the Korean War emphasize individual identity, family unity, amity among soldiers, and senseless violence, all of which distance them from the official history and its emphasis on nationalism and patriotism. For survivors' accounts, see Kim Kwiok (2006) and Yi Yonggi (2003). For a cinematic representation of the Korean War in recent years, see Chŏng Pyŏnggi (2013).

6. For the civil war character of the Korean War, see Bruce Cumings (1981). For a new interpretation in the post–Cold War era that pits individuals against the state and erases the decolonizing struggle of the people as an origin of national division,

see *Pak Myŏngrim* (2002). On new trends in the study of the Korean War, see Son Kyŏngho (2011).

7. The term *kkojebi* (*kkotchebi* in South Korea) refers to children and youth refugees in North Korea. Although it is said to be a Korean pronunciation of the Russian word for "vagabond," kkojebi is often translated in South Korea as "sparrow" because of a similar pronunciation.

8. For a remark by the president of the National Endowment for Democracy, see Carl Gershman, "The Human Rghts of North Koreans: An Issue of Universal Concern," delivered at the Sixth International Conference on North Korean Human Rights and Refugees, 2005. http://www.ned.org/about/board/meet-our-president/archived-remarks-and-presentations/021405.

9. Founded in 2005, the New Right Network distinguishes itself from another New Right group, the National Federation of the New Right (New Right ch'ŏn'guk yŏnhap), which it denounces for serving the interests of individual politicians or political parties.

10. The progressive groups that rejected this US legislation on North Korea included Minbyŏn (Lawyers for a Democratic Society), Sarangbang Group for Human Rights, the PSPD (People's Solidarity for Participatory Democracy, the largest NGO), T'ongil yŏndae, and other leftist Christian organizations such as the Korean National Council of Churches.

11. The entry into the Canadian embassy in China on September 29, 2004, included fourty-four *t'albukcha*, all of whom successfully entered; all twenty of those who entered the South Korean embassy in Beijing on October 15, 2004, succeeded; all twenty-nine who entered a South Korean international school in Beijing on October 22, 2004, succeeded; and only three out of the eighteen people who tried to enter the South Korean embassy in Beijing succeeded on October 25, 2004. All of those who successfully entered were deported to South Korea by China.

12. Interviews on July 5 and July 23, 2002, with To Hiyŏn, a principal organizer of this first forced entry and the director of the Association for Families of South Korean Abductees.

13. Interview with Yi Sŭngyong, director of Good Friends, on July 20, 2012, in Seoul, Korea.

14. For an example of detailed self-critique and ideological conversion in the 1990s, see Kim Taeho (2004).

15. My accounts and citations in this section are based on my interview with Chang Chŏngsun on June 14, 2004, and the recorded narration of O Sunbok by Cho Ch'ŏnhyŏn.

7. NORTH KOREAN REVOLUTION IN REPETITION: CRISIS AND VALUE

1. For a case of the Group Struggle Against Anti-Socialist Phenomena that confiscated cell phones in border areas in 2010, see Choŭn pŏttŭl (Good Friends) (2010).

2. For instance, Elizabeth Perry (2007) takes the state's invocation of revolutionary language and ideology in enforcing privatization since the early 1980s as an indication of the continuity of revolution rather than a rupture in Chinese history.

3. On the stage-theory of permanent revolution and conceptualization of industrial, cultural, and ideological development, see Kim Il Sung (1971h).

4. The Yenan group encompassed Korean communists who had joined the CCP's struggle in China during Japanese colonization; the Soviet group referred to communists who stayed or engaged in the communist movement in the Soviet Union before they returned to Korea upon liberation. The Kapsan group included Korean communists who, together with Chinese counterparts, engaged in the anti-Japanese struggle in northeast China (Manchuria). While Kim Il Sung was part of the Kapsan group, he purged it in 1967 under the charge of feudalism and nepotism when the Kapsan group advocated a slow and even development capable of benefiting the people's lives. For details, see Cho Taesŏk and Yun Sŏngsik (2005).

5. 1 p'yŏng = 35.6 sq. ft. Private property rights are still restricted despite their historic validation. For instance, the market sale of housing requires multilayered approval from administrative units that are almost impossible to obtain without paying bribes, which in turn produces informal exchanges and the sale of rights to use. For details, see Ryu Kyŏngwŏn (2008:4–46) and Choi Chini (2008:18–22).

   On legal changes and privatization of land, see Chŏng Sejin (2000:100–103, 207–10) and Kim Pyŏngro (2009:285–330).

6. The status of Chŏngmuwŏn in relation to the party changed over time. It was downgraded in 1972 from the cabinet in 1972, separated from the security agencies in 1982, reintegrated them in 1986, and then upgraded its status by being renamed as the cabinet in 1998.

7. Nakagawa (2003a, 2003b) regards combined enterprise (yŏnhap kiŏpso) and combined company (yŏnhap hoesa) as different types of the general combined enterprise system, and notes that by 1986 the combined enterprise and companies numbered 120, with 61 under the central authority and 59 under local authority. In this chapter, I separate combined enterprise and combined company.

8. For a study of the military-first rule as a tool for Kim Jong Il to secure his power and his son's succession to power amidst deepening social discontent, see Yun Hwang (2010) and Yi Taegŭn (2009).

9. A book on the socialist currency system, written by Li Wŏn'gyŏng (1986) in North Korea, largely recapitulates the law of value only in "form." It adds the importance of the rapid circulation of money.

8. SPECTACLE OF *T'ALBUK*: FREEDOM AND FREE LABOR

1. "Small-bag trading" (*pottari changsa*) refers to a small-scale and independent trading practice, in which individuals carry bags of goods long distances to sell them and earn small profits from the price differences between one place and another. North Korean small-bag merchants usually bring (dried) vegetables and fishery products to sell in China and buy clothing and other daily essentials in China to sell in North Korea. There are also merchants willing to risk being caught smuggling goods such as antiques, drugs, and frog oil out of North Korea.

2. This is cited from an unpublished memoir by t'albukcha, "Naega saraon iyu" (The reason for which I have lived).

3. Unpublished memoir of a man who came from Chŏngjin to Yanbian in 2000 when he was twenty years old and stayed in a shelter run by a church.

4. Unpublished notes that were made available to me by Reverend Kim in August 2002.

5. Videotaped conversation that Cho Ch'ŏnhyŏn showed me on October 24, 2006, in Seoul.

6. Videotaped conversation that Cho Ch'ŏnhyŏn showed me on October 24, 2006, in Seoul.

7. See chapter 7 for the discussion of the postcolonial character of the socialist construction in North Korea.

BIBLIOGRAPHY

KOREAN AND CHINESE TEXTS

Ch'a Munsŏk. 1999. "Pukhan ŭi kongjang kwalli ch'eje wa chŏlchŏng ki Stalin chuŭi" (The North Korean factory management system and high Stalinism). *Pukhan yŏn'gu hakhoebo* 3, no. 2: 227–50.

———. 2002. "Kim Jong Il chŏnggwŏn ŭi kongjang kwalli ch'eje" (The factory management system under the Kim Jong Il regime). *Pukhan yŏn'gu hakhoebo* 6, no. 1: 91–126.

———. 2007. "Pukhan ŭi sijang kwa sijang kyŏngje" (Market and the market economy in North Korea). *Tamnon 201* 10, no. 2: 77–121.

Ch'ae Chaebong and Kim Ch'ŏllyong. 1993. "'Manyak kŭ mangdong man aniyŏttoramŏn . . .'" ("If that absurd behavior wasn't . . ."). In *Chungguk Chosŏn minjok palchach'wi ch'ongsŏ*. Vol. 7, *P'ungnang* (The compiled history of Korean Chinese in China. Vol. 7, Sea waves), edited by Chungguk Chosŏn minjok palchach'wi ch'ongsŏ wiwŏnhoe, 192–95. Beijing: Minjok ch'ulp'ansa.

Ch'ae Hant'ae. 2005. "Chungguk tongp'o nodongja ŭi pŏpchŏk chiwi e kwanhan koch'al" (An analysis of the legal status of Korean Chinese workers). *Chungang pŏphak* 7, no. 1: 77–99.

Ch'ae Kyŏngsŏk. 2001. "6.15 nambuk kongdong sŏnŏn ihaeng ŭi silch'ŏn kwaje" (Problems in realizing the 6.15 declaration of the two Koreas). *Chŏnnam taehakkyo segye hansang munhwa yŏn'gudan kŭngnae haksul hoeŭi* 40: 539–66.

Chaeoe kungmin yŏngsaguk. 2001. *Chaeoe tongp'o ŭi ch'uripkuk kwa pŏpchŏk chiwi e kwanhan pŏmnyul chunggaejŏng pŏmnyulan e taehan oegyo t'ongsangbu ŭigyŏn* (The opinion of the Ministry of Foreign Affairs and Commerce concerning on the bills to amend the Overseas Korean Act). December 1, Seoul, Korea.

Ch'angjo Consulting. 2011. *Hoesa kyŏngjaengryŏk kanghwa rŭl wihan nosa kwan'gyŏ anjŏnghwa k'ŏnsŏlt'ing cheansŏ* (Consulting proposal to stabilize the management and labor relationship in order to strengthen the company's competitiveness). April 28, 2011, Seoul, Korea.

Chin Chŏngsun. 2010. "Chŏngbu ŭi chiyŏn ŭl t'onghan kaldŭng haegyŏl chŏllyak: Samsŏng chadongch'aŭi sijang chinipŭl chungsimŭiro" (The state's strategy of conflict resolution by procrastination: Focusing on Samsung Automobile's entry into the market). *Han'guk chŏngch'aek yŏn'gu* 10, no. 2: 387–400.

Cho Ch'ŏnhyŏn. 2004a. "T'albuk bŭrok'ŏ kŭ kwanggi ŭi in'gan sanyang" (Brokers for escape, their madness in hunting humans). *Mal*, April 29.

———. 2004b. "Ton pŏri mokchŏk ŭi in'gan sanyang" (Hunting humans for money). *Mal*, November 20.

———. 2006. "Han'gich'ong sanha kanbu t'albukcha sangdae ton changsa" (Officials of the Han'gich'ong who used North Korean escapees as business). *Hanminjok arirang*, March 5.

Cho Chŏnghun. 2014. "83-nyŏn KBS isan kajok ch'atki pangsong ŭn taebuk simni chŏnyong" (The 1983 KBS broadcast of Searching for Separated Families aimed to create anti-North Korea sentiment). *Tongilnews.com*, March 26. http://www.tongil-news.com/news/articleView.html?idxno=106582.

Cho Hiyŏn and Pak Hyŏnch'ae, eds. 1989a. *Han'guk sahoe kusŏngch'e ron I* (The social formation debate in South Korea I). Seoul: Chuksan.

———, eds. 1989b. *Han'guk sahoe kusŏngch'e ron II* (The social formation debate in South Korea II). Seoul: Chuksan.

———, eds. 1991. *Han'guk sahoe kusŏngch'e ron III* (The social formation debate in South Korea III). Seoul: Chuksan.

———, eds. 1992. *Han'guk sahoe kusŏngch'e ron IV* (The social formation debate in South Korea IV). Seoul: Chuksan.

Cho Hojin. 2003. "'Ŏllon i kkaengp'an ŭl noa irŭl mangch'otda'—Sŏ Kyŏngsŏk moksa, kukchŏk hoebok undong p'amun ŏllon e ch'aegim hoep'i" ("The media ruined the work"—Rev. Sŏ evades his responsibility in the controversy over the movement to restore the Korean citizenship of Korean Chinese). *Ohmynews*, December 17.

Cho Kwang-tong. 1996. "Kyop'o eso tongp'o ro" (From overseas Koreans to compatriots). Chicago edition of *Han'guk Ilbo*, May 7.

Cho Min. 2003. "Roh Moo Hyun chŏngbu ŭi p'yŏnghwa pŏnyŏng chŏngch'aek: Chŏnmang kwa kwaje" (The peace and prosperity policy of the Roh Moo Hyun government). *T'ongil chŏngch'aek yŏn'gu* 12, no. 1: 1–32.

———. 2006. "Nambuk kyŏngje kongdongch'e hyŏngsŏng ŭi iron chŏk t'ŭl: P'yŏnghwa kyŏngjeron" (A theoretical framework of the South–North economic community: The thesis of the peace economy). In *Nambuk kyŏngje kongdongch'e hyŏngsŏng chŏllyak*

(Strategy of the formation of the South–North economic community), 55–102. Seoul: T'ongil yŏn'guwŏn.

Cho Taesŏk and Yun Sŏngsik. 2005. "Pukhan ŭi sŏn'gun chŏngch'i wa yebang chŏk sahoejuŭi Bonap'at'isŭm" (The military-first rule and the preventive socialist Bonarpartism). *Pukhan yŏn'gu hakhoebo* 9, no. 1: 51–78.

Cho Tonmun. 2004. "Nodong kyegŭp chŏngch'i seryŏk ŭi Minju Nodongdang ŭi kwaje" (The political empowerment of the labor class and the task of the Democratic Labor Party). *Sanŏp nodong yŏn'gu* 10, no. 2: 1–33.

Cho Yŏngch'ŏl. 2007. *Kŭmyŭng segyehwa wa Han'guk kyŏngje ŭi chillo* (Financial globalization and the direction of the Korean economy). Seoul: Humanitas.

Choe Wugil. 2001. "Chaejung tongp'o chŏngch'aek kwa haeoe tongp'o chŏngch'aek ŭi munjejŏm—chaejung tongp'o chŏngch'aek kwa kwallyŏn hayŏ" (The problems in the policy on overseas Koreans—concerning the policy toward Korean Chinese). In *2001 chaeoe tongp'obŏp kaejŏng ŭl wihan semina* (The 2001 seminar on amending the Overseas Korean Act), edited by Uri minjok sŏro topki undong. Seoul, September 25.

Choi Ch'angdong. 2000. *T'albukcha, ŏttŏk'e halgŏsin'ga?: T'albukcha ŭi pŏpchŏk chiwi wa haegyŏl pangan* (What do we do about North Korean escapees?: Legal status of North Korean escapees and its resolution). Seoul: Turi.

Choi Chini. 2007. "<Misin> p'at" (<Superstition> red beans). *Rimjin'gang* 1 (November): 174–77.

———. 2008. "Chagi ka saldŏn kukka chut'aek ŭl p'anŭn hyŏnjang" (At the scene of selling the state housing where one lived). *Rimjin'gang* 3 (August): 18–22.

Choi Jang Jip. 2002. *Minjuhwa ihuŭi minjujuŭi* (Democracy after democratization). Seoul: Humanitas.

Choi Pongdae. 2008. "Pukhan tosi sajŏk pumun ŭi sijanghwa wa tosi kagu ŭi kyŏngjejŏk kyech'ŭng punhwa" (Marketization of the private sphere of North Korean cities and economic stratification of urban households). In *Pukhan tosi chumin ŭi sajŏk yŏngyŏk yŏn'gu* (Private sphere and people of cities in North Korea), edited by Yi Wuyŏng, 41–76. Seoul: Hanul.

Choi Sangch'ŏl. 1997. "Kŏn'guk hu 29-nyŏn." In *21 segi ro maejin hanŭn Chungguk Chosŏnjok palchŏn pangnyak yŏn'gu* (A study of the development strategy of Korean Chinese in the twenty-first century), edited by Cho Ryongho and Pak Munil, 253–61. Shenyang: Ryonyŏng minjok ch'ulp'ansa.

Choi Sŭngch'ŏl. 2012. "Han'guk ttŏnanŭn 'paeŭn mangdŏk' t'albukchadŭl?" ("Ungrateful" North Korean escapees leaving South Korea?). *Ohmynews*, August 23.

Choi Ŭich'ŏl. 2005. *Yurŏp yŏnhap ŭi taebuk in'gwŏn chŏngch'aek kwa pukhan ŭi taeŭng* (EU's human rights policy toward North Korea and North Korea's response). Seoul: T'ongil yŏn'guwŏn.

Choi Wangyu, ed. 2006. *Pukhan tosi ŭi wigi wa pyŏnhwa* (Crisis and change in Nort Korean cities). Seoul: Hanul.

Chŏn Hyŏnjong. 2007. "Nugu ŭi 'mubŏp chidae' in'ga" (Whose "lawless zone" i this?). *Ohmynews*, October 25.

Chŏn Hyŏnsu. 2002. "Haebang chik'u Pukhan ŭi kwagŏ ch'ŏngsan" (Overcoming th past after liberation in North Korea). *Taegu sahak* 69: 33–60.

Chŏn T'aeil kinyŏm'gwan kŏllip wiwŏnhoe, ed. 1983. *Ŏnŭ ch'ŏngnyŏn nodongja ŭi sam kw chugŭm* (The life and death of a youth worker). Seoul: Tolbegae.

Chŏn Yŏngp'yŏng and Han Sŭngju. 2006. "Sosuja rosŏ oegugin nodongja: Chŏngch'ae kaldŭng punsŏk" (Foreign workers as minority: An analysis of the policy conflict) *Han'guk haengjŏng yŏn'gu* 15, no. 2: 157–84.

Chŏng Chaeŭn. 2014. "Kŏmch'al, yŏniŏ nojo p'agoe hoesa son tŭrŏjwŏ" (The Office o Prosecutors, it repeatedly holds the upper hand of the company that shattered th labor union). *Media Ch'ungch'ŏng*, June 2.

Chŏng Chongnam. 2006. "Ssangyong chadongch'a sarye ka poyŏ chunŭn chabonjuŭ nolli" (The logic of capitalism that the Ssangyong Automobile case demonstrates) *Wŏlgan Mal* 244 (October): 78–81.

Chŏng Insŏp. 2003. "Yurŏp ŭi haeoe tongp'o chiwŏn ippŏp: Han'guk ŭi chaeoe tongp'obŏp kaejŏng nonŭi wa kwallyŏn hayŏ" (The preferential treatment o national minorities by their kin-states in Europe: In relations to the debate on the amendment of the Overseas Korean Act in South Korea). *Kukchebŏp hakhoe nonch'onɡ* 48, no. 2: 189–217.

———. 2004. "Chaeoe tongp'obŏp ŭi hŏnbŏp purhapch'i kyŏlchŏng kwa chŏngbu ŭ taeŭng kŏmt'o" (The decision on the inconsistency of the Overseas Korean Act with the Constitution and the review of the government's responses). *Kongik kwa in'gwŏn* 1, no. 1: 13–29.

Chŏng Kŭnjae. 2005. *Kŭ mant'ŏn Chosŏnjok ŭn ŏdiro kassŭlkka?* (Where did so many Korean Chinese go?). Seoul: Bookin.

Chŏng P'anryong. 1993. "Yŏnbyŏn ŭi <Munhwa taehyŏngmyŏng>" (The Cultural Revo-lution in Yanbian). In *Chungguk Chosŏn minjok palchach'wi ch'ongsŏ.* Vol. 7, *P'ungnang* (The compiled history of Korean Chinese. Vol. 7, Sea waves), edited by Chungguk Chosŏn minjok palchach'wi ch'ongsŏ wiwŏnhoe, 292–307. Beijing: Minjok ch'ulp'ansa.

Chŏng Pyŏnggi. 2013. "Han'guk chŏnjaeng yŏnghwa e nat'anan kukkakwan kwa chŏnjaengkwan" (Perspectives on state and war represented in films on the Korean War). *Kukche chŏngch'i nonch'ong* 53, no. 4: 433–61.

Chŏng Sejin. 2000. *"Kyehoek" esŏ sijang ŭiro* (From "planning" to the market). Seoul: Hanul.

Chŏng Sinch'ŏl. 1999. *Chungguk Chosŏnjok sahoe ŭi pyŏnch'ŏn kwa chŏnmang* (Changes and prospects of Korean Chinese society in China). Shenyang: Ryonyŏng minjok ch'ulp'ansa.

Chŏng Sŏngjin. 2006. "Han'guk chabonjuǔi ch'ukchŏk ǔi changgi ch'use wa wigi: 1987–2003" (The long-term trend and crisis of accumulation in Korea). In *Han'guk chabonjuǔi ǔi ch'ukchŏk ch'eje pyŏnhwa: 1987–2003* (Change in the accumulation regime in Korea, 1987–2003), edited by Kyŏngsang taehakkyo sahoe kwahak yŏn'guso, 17–57. Seoul: Hanul.

Chŏng Ŭni. 2009. "Pukhan ǔi chasaengjŏk sijang palchŏn yŏn'gu (A study of the grass-roots development of market in North Korea). *T'ongil munje yŏn'gu* 52: 157–200.

Chŏng Yŏngt'ae. 2010. *P'abŏl: Minju nodongdang chŏngp'a kaldŭng ǔi kiwŏn kwa chongmal* (Faction: Origins and end of the factional conflicts in the Democratic Labor Party). Seoul: Imaegin.

Chŏnmun munje chŏjak sojo. 2005. *Chungguk Chosŏnjok hyŏngsŏng mit yakkan ǔi yŏksa munje e kwanhan yŏn'gu* (A study of the formation of Korean Chinese in China and some historical issues). Yanji: Chŏnmun munje chŏjak sojo.

Chosŏnjok yŏnhaphoe (Korean Chinese Coalition). 2000. "Chaeoe tongp'obŏp kaejŏng ǔl wihan cheanmun" (The proposal to amend the Overseas Korean Act). Seoul, Korea, May.

Choǔn pŏttǔl (Good Friends). 1999. *Tuman'gang ǔl kŏnnŏ on saramdǔl* (People who came by crossing the Tuman River). Seoul: Choǔn pŏttǔl.

———. 2010. "Kukkyŏng yŏnsŏn chiyŏk. Chungangdang kŏmyŏl kǔruppa p'agyŏn hae sonjŏnhwa hoesu" (In border areas, the central party dispatched the censorship group to confiscate cell phones). *Onǔl ǔi Pukhan* (North Korea today) 339 (April 6).

"Ch'oego chisi: Chŏn'guk inmin egye allinǔn kǔl" (Supreme instruction: The news to the people in the whole country). 1967. This document was produced by various organizations that joined the New 8.27 Group on August 9. Yanbian, China.

"Chu Tŏkhae munje e taehan Chunggong killimsŏng wiwŏnhoe ǔi chae simsa kyŏllon pogo" (Report by the CCP's Jilin Provincial Committee on the reinvestigation of the Chu Tŏkhae inquiry). 1993. In *Chungguk Chosŏn minjok palchach'wi ch'ongsŏ*. Vol. 7, *P'ungnang* (The compiled history of Korean Chinese. Vol. 7, Sea waves), edited by Chungguk Chosŏn minjok palchach'wi ch'ongsŏ wiwŏnhoe, 16–19. Beijing: Minjok ch'ulp'ansa.

"Chu Tŏkhae tongji ǔi ŏgul han rumyŏng ǔl pŏtkigo myŏngye rǔl hoebok halde taehan Chunggong Yŏnbyŏn chuwi ǔi kyŏrǔi, June 10, 1978" (The decision by the CCP's Yanbian Committee on nullifying the indictment against comrade Chu Tŏkhae and exonerating him, June 10, 1978). 1993. In *Chungguk Chosŏn minjok palchach'wi ch'ongsŏ*. Vol. 7, *P'ungnang* (The compiled history of Korean Chinese. Vol. 7, Sea waves), edited by Chungguk Chosŏn minjok palchach'wi ch'ongsŏ wiwŏnhoe, 19–23. Beijing: Minjok ch'ulp'ansa.

Chu Tŏkhae ǔi ilsaeng (Life of Chu Tŏkhae). 1987. Yanji: Yanbian inmin ch'ulp'ansa.

Chungguk Chosŏn minjok palchach'wi ch'ongsŏ wiwŏnhoe, ed. 1993. *Chungguk Chosŏn minjok palchach'wi ch'ongsŏ*. Vol. 7, *P'ungnang* (The compiled history of Korean Chinese. Vol. 7, Sea waves). Beijing: Minjok ch'ulp'ansa.

———. 1994. *Chungguk Chosŏn minjok palchach'wi ch'ongsŏ*, vol. 8 (The compiled history of Korean Chinese, vol. 8). Beijing: Minjok ch'ulp'ansa.

Chungguk kongsandang Yŏnbyŏn Chosŏnjok chach'iju wiwŏnhoe (The Yanbian Autonomous Prefecture Committee of the Chinese Communist Party). 1978. "'Pan'guk p'okran,' 'xx t'ŭkmu,' 'chiha Kukmindang' tŭng ŏgurhan an'gŏn ŭl chŏngjŏng hagi wihan te kwanhan kyŏlchŏng" (The decision on correcting absurd accusations such as "'rebellion,' 'xx spies,' and 'underground Kuomintang'"), Yanji, China, June 29.

Chuwi chosa yŏn'gusil (The investigation committee of the Yanbian Korean Autonomous Prefecture government). 1978. "'Chŏn'guk inmin ege allinŭn kŭl' pandong sŏnjŏn ppira nŭn ŏttŏkke nat'anan kŏsin'ga? (How did the reactionary propaganda flier "The news to the people in the whole country" come to appear?). This is the official investigation report of the Korean rebellion during the Chinese Revolution. Yanji, China.

Federation of Small- and Medium-Sized Factories (FSMF). 2000a. "Oegugin sanŏp yŏnsu chedo ŭi hyŏnhwang mit unyŏng panghyang" (Current conditions and directions of the operation of the Industrial Training Program). Paper presented at Iju nodongja in'gwŏn kwa oeguk illyŏk toip chŏngch'aek ŭi kŭnbonjŏk kaesŏn ŭl wihan t'oronhoe (Forum on the human rights of migrant workers and the fundamental reform of the policy on the employment of migrant workers). National Assembly Forum, Seoul, Korea, July 7.

———. 2000b. *Oegugin sanŏp yŏnsu chedo chŏgyong panghyang* (Direction of the application of the Industrial Training Program). Seoul: FSMF.

Goh Byeong-gwon. 2011. *Minjujuŭi ran muŏsin'ga* (What is democracy?). Seoul: Kŭrinbi.

Han Hyŏngsŏng. 2012. "Pip'an hoegyehak ŭi Marŭk'ŭsŭjuŭi sigak esŏ pon Ssangyong chadongch'a sarye yŏn'gu" (A study of the Ssangyong Automobile case from the Marxist approach to critical accounting). *Marŭk'ŭsŭjuŭi yŏn'gu* 9, no. 2: 82–105.

Han Suyŏng. 2011. "Kwanchŏnsa ŭi kwanjŏm ŭiro pon Han'guk chŏnjaeng kiŏk ŭi tu kaji hyŏngsik" (Two memory forms of the Korean War seen from the transhistory perspective). *Ŏmunhak* 113: 431–59.

Hŏ Sangsu. 2009. "Chŏnsŏn: Kwagŏ ch'ŏngsan ŭi wigi wa kwagŏsa chŏngri kwallyŏn wiwŏnhoe ŭi mirae chihyangjŏk kach'i" (The crisis of reparation and the future-oriented value of the Committee on Reparation). *Minju pŏphak* 38: 125–60.

Hŏnbŏp chaep'anso (Constituional Court). 2001. *Kyŏlchŏng, 99 hŏnma 494* (Ruling, 99 hŏnma 494). November 29.

Hong Ilp'yo. 2004. "Nambuk kyŏnghyŏp ŭi hyŏn chuso wa hyanghu kwaje" (The current conditions of the two Koreas' economic engagement and future agenda). Paper presented at 2004 T'ongil simp'ojium t'oron palche 2 (The second discussion of the 2004 symposium on unification), organized by 6.15 Nambuk kongdong sŏnŏn silhyŏn kwa hanbando p'yŏnghwa rŭl wihan t'ongil yŏndae. Seoul, Korea, July 22.

Hong Sunjik. 2004. "Nambuk kyŏnghyŏp hyŏnhwang kwa kwaje" (The current condition and future agenda of the economic engagement of South and North Korea). Paper presented at *Kukhoe t'ongil oegyo t'ongsang wiwŏnhoe kandamhoe* (A seminar in the Committee of Unification, Diplomacy, and Commerce of the National Assembly). Seoul, Korea, March 24.

Hyŏn Tongil et al., eds. 2000. *Chungguk ŭi kaehyŏk kaebang kwa Tongbuga kyŏngje yŏn'gu* (A study of reform and open policies in China and the Northeast Asian economy). Yanji: Yanbian University Press.

Im Chŏnghwan. 2013. "Pŏbwŏn, kungnae ch'a ŏpkye olsŭt'op wigi 'Yusŏng kiŏp sat'ae' nojoch'ŭk e chiphaeng yuye sŏn'go" (The court-sentenced probation of the labor union in the Yusŏng case that threatened to bring the automobile industry to a halt). *news1*, March 28. http://news1.kr/articles/?1066701.

Im Kangt'aek. 2014. "Pukhan sijang hwalsŏnghwa ŭi sumŭn kŭrim, kukyŏng kiŏp ŭi yŏk'al" (The role of state-owned firms, a hidden picture in the facilitation of North Korean marketization). *KDI Pukhan kyŏngje ribyu* 16, no. 6: 25–40.

Im Kŭnho. 2009. "Salgi wihan t'albuk to choe in'ga?" (Is it a crime to escape to live?). *Imjin'gang* 4: 24–31.

Im Sŏngji. 2011. "Yŏnswae sarin. Ssangyong chadongch'a chibu chojik pujang Ko Tongmin tongji wa int'ŏbyu" (A serial murder. An interview with Ko Tongmin, director of the Ssangyong Automobile labor union). *Chongsewa nodong* 66 (March): 24–30.

Joh Won-kwang. 2007. "Iju nodongja wa idong" (Migrant workers and mobility). In *R: Sosusŏng ŭi chŏngch'ihak* (R: The politics of minority), edited by Goh Byeong-gwon, 123–28. Seoul: Greenbi.

Joint Committee for Migrant Workers (JCMK). 2000. *Tasi matchabŭn son: Che 2-ch'a oegugin nodongja taech'aek hyŏbŭihoe chawŏn hwaldongga yŏrŭm suryŏnhoe* (Hands-in-together: JCMK's second summer camp for volunteers). Seoul: JCMK.

———. 2001a. *Oegugin iju nodongja in'gwŏn paeksŏ* (White paper on foreign migrant workers' human rights). Seoul: Tasan'gŭlbang.

———. 2001b. *Nodong kwa p'yŏngdŭng* (Labor and equality), Vol. 2. Seoul: JCMK.

Juche ŭi kyŏngje kwalli iron (Theory of Juche economic management). 1992. Pyongyang: Sahoegwahak ch'ulp'ansa.

Kang Ch'ayŏn. 2004. "Chaejung t'albuk yŏsŏng tŭrŭi saenghwal silt'ae" (A study of the living conditions of North Korean female refugees in China). *Yŏsŏng yŏn'gu* 19: 59–77.

Kang Kŏn. 2009. "Rodongnyŏk ŭi idong" (Labor mobility). *Imjin'gang* 6: 135–41.

Kang Kukchin. 2003a. "'Hŏnbŏp sowŏn ch'ŏnggu hwaginjŭng' muyongjimul tangsajadŭl kŏsen panbal" (Fierce reactions to the useless "certificate of the appeal to the Constitutional Court"). *ngotimes*, December 12.

——. 2003b. "Chungguk e sŏdo irŏn p'udaejŏp anbadatta" (We were not treated this way even in China). *ngotimes*, December 12.

——. 2003c. "Chajin ch'ulguk hamyŏn naenyŏn ilsunwi pojang?" (Is it going to guarantee their reentries next year, with the most preferred status if they voluntarily leave?). *ngotimes*, December 20.

Kim Chaeguk. 1998. *Han'guk ŭn ŏpta* (There is no South Korea). Mokdan'gang: Mokdan'gang minjok ch'ulp'ansa.

Kim Ch'angbŏm. 2009. "Russia chiyŏk 5-chŏnyŏ t'albuk pŏlmokkong tŭri ttŏdolgo itta" (About 5,000 North Korean t'albuk loggers are drifting in Russia). *Future Korea Weekly*, July 29. http://www.futurekorea.co.kr/news/articleView.html?idxno=19045.

Kim Ch'anggyu. 2011. "P'aŏp ŭi yŏksŏl. Yusŏng kiŏp chuga kŭptŭng 'ŏllŏn podo hu kiŏp kach'i allyŏjyŏ'" (The paradox of the labor strike. The upsurge of Yusŏng stock price "because the firm's value came to be known through the media report"). *Chungangdaily*, May 24.

Kim Ch'anghee. 2010. "Pukhan sijanghwa wa hwap'ye ŭi chŏngch'i kyŏngje chŏk punsŏk" (The political economic analysis of marketization and currency in North Korea). *Pukhan yŏn'gu hakhoebo* 14, no. 2: 49–75.

Kim Chinhwan. 2010. *Pukhan wigiron* (The thesis of North Korean crisis). Seoul: Sŏnin.

Kim Chongguk. 1999. *Segigyoch'e ŭi sigak esŏ pon Chungguk Chosŏnjok* (The Korean Chinese minority seen from the perspective of generational change). Yanji: Yŏnbyŏn inmin ch'ulp'ansa.

——. 2000. "Yŏnbyŏn Chosŏnjok chach'iju kanbu taeo ŭi ryŏksa wa hyŏnhwang mit palchŏn yech'ŭk" (History and the current state of officials in Yanbian Autonomous Prefecture and the prospect of its development). In *Chungguk Chosŏnjok hyŏn sangt'ae punsŏk mit chŏnmang yŏn'gu* (Analysis of the current condition and its prospect for the Korean Chinese), edited by Pak Minja, 134–61. Yanji: Yanbian University Press.

Kim Chongok. 2008. "Pukhan ŭi kwallyo pup'ae wa chibae kujo ŭi pyŏndong" (Political corruption and change in the power structure in North Korea). *T'ongil chŏngch'aek yŏn'gu* 17, no. 1: 371–400.

Kim Chongyŏp, ed. 2009. *87-nyŏn ch'eje ron* (The 1987 thesis). Seoul: Ch'angbi.

Kim Hogi 2009. "87-nyŏn ch'eje in'ga, 97-nyŏn ch'eje in'ga" (Is it the 1987 thesis or the 1997 thesis). In *87-nyŏn ch'eje ron* (The 1987 thesis), edited by Kim Chongyŏp, 121–38. Seoul: Ch'angbi.

Kim Hyŏnggi. 1994. "Han'guk chabonjuui chaesaengsan kujo ui t'ukchil kwa chŏnmang" (Characteristics and future of the reproduction structure of Korean capitalism). In *Han'guk sahoeŭi pyŏndong, minjujuŭi, chabonjuŭi, ideologi* (Social change in Korean society, democracy, capitalism, ideology), edited by Han'guk sanŏp sahoe yon'guhoe, 124–69. Seoul: Hanul.

Kim Il Sung. 1996d. "Chungsohyŏng suryŏk palchŏnso rŭl mani kŏnsŏl halte taehayŏ: Yanggangdo ch'aegim ilgun hyŏbŭihoe esŏ han yŏnsŏl, 1982-nyŏn 8-wŏl 13-il" (On the construction of many medium- and small-sized water power plants: An address given at the meeting of workers in Yanggangdo, August 13, 1982). In *Sahoejuŭi kyŏngje kwalli munje e taehayŏ* (On the problem of the management of the socialist economy), 6: 86–95. Pyongyang: Chosŏn nodongdang ch'ulp'ansa.

——. 1996e. "Inmin kyŏngje kyehoek kwa saŏp ŭl kaesŏn kanghwa halte taehayŏ: Chŏngmuwŏn mit kukka kyoehoek wiwŏnhoe ch'aegim ilgun tŭl kwa han tamhwa, 1982-nyon 12-wol 12-il" (On improving and strengthening of the planning of the people's economy: A conversation with officials and the National Planning Committee members, December 2, 1982). In *Sahoejuŭi kyŏngje kwalli munje e taehayŏ* (On the problem of the management of the socialist economy), 6: 139–54. Pyongyang: Chosŏn nodongdang ch'ulp'ansa.

——. 1996f. "Kyŏnggongŏp ul tagŭch'ŏ inmindŭl ŭi mulchil munhwa saenghwal ŭl tŏwuk nop'ija: Kyŏnggongŏp pumun chido ilgun hyŏbŭihoe eso han yŏnsŏl 1983-nyŏn 3-wŏl 10-il" (Let's advance the material and cultural life of the people by driving the revolution in light industry). In *Sahoechuui kyŏngje kwalli munje e taehayŏ* (On the problem of the management of the socialist economy), 6: 189–99. Pyongyang: Chosŏn nodongdang ch'ulp'ansa.

——. 1996g. "Tongnip ch'aesanje rŭl paro silsi hanŭn tesŏ nasŏnŭn myŏt kaji munje e taehayŏ: Chosŏn minjujuŭi inmin konghwaguk chŏngmuwŏn sangmu hoeŭi esŏ han yŏnsŏl 1984-nyŏn 11-wŏl 18-il" (On a few issues concerning the correct implementation of the independent accounting system: A speech given to the officials of the DPRK). In *Sahoejuŭi kyŏngje kwalli munje e taehayŏ* (On the problem of the management of the socialist economy), 6: 352–68. Pyongyang: Chosŏn nodongdang ch'ulp'ansa.

——. 1996h. "Juche ui kyŏngje kwalli ch'egye wa pangbŏp ŭl ch'ŏlchŏhi kwanch'ŏl haja: Chŏngmuwŏn mit tang chungang wiwŏnhoe kyŏngje pusŏ ch'aegim ilgun tŭl kwa han tamhwa. 1984-nyŏn 12-wŏl 5-il" (Let's accomplish thoroughly the Juche economic management system and method: A conversation with officials of the Central Committee of the Workers' Party in charge of economic policy, December 5, 1984). In *Sahoejuŭi kyŏngje kwalli munje e taehayŏ* (On the problem of the management of the socialist economy), 6: 369–94. Pyongyang: Chosŏn nodongdang ch'ulp'ansa.

——. 1996i. "Chosŏn nodongdang chungang wiwŏnhoe che 6-ki che 10-ch'a chŏnwŏn hoeŭi esŏ han kyŏllon, 1984, 12.16" (A conclusion given at the tenth meeting of the Sixth Congress of the Central Committee of the Korean Workers' Party, December 16, 1984). In *Sahoejuui kyŏngje kwalli munje e taehayo* (On the problem of the management of the socialist economy), 6: 395–423. Pyongyang: Chosŏn nodongdang ch'ulp'ansa.

———. 1997a. "Kongjak kigye kongŏp kwa chŏnja, chadonghwa kongŏp palchŏn esŏ chŏnhwan ŭl irŭk'il te taehayŏ: Chosŏn nodongdang chungang wiwŏnhoe che 6-ki che 14-ch'a chŏnwŏn hoeŭi esŏ han kyŏllon, 1988-nyŏn 1-wŏl 30-il" (On the change in the development of machine industry, electronics industry, automobile industry: Conclusion of the sixth session of the Fourteenth Meeting of the Central Committee of the Workers' Party, November 30, 1988). In *Sahoejuŭi kyŏngje kwalli munje e taehayŏ* (On the problem of the management of the socialist economy), 7: 135–57. Pyongyang: Chosŏn nodongdang ch'ulp'ansa.

———. 1997b. "Minjok chŏk kŭngji wa hyŏngmyŏng chŏk chabusim ŭl kajigo sahoejuŭi kŏnsŏl ŭl tagŭch'ija: Chosŏn minjujuŭi inmin konghwaguk chungang inmin wiwŏnhoe che 8-ki che 27-ch'a hoeŭi eso han yŏnsŏl, 1989-nyon 7-wŏl 9-il" (Let's push for the construction of socialism with the national dignity and revolutionary pride: A speech given at the twenty-seventh session of the eighth Meeting of the Central People's Committee of the DPRK, July 9, 1989). In *Sahoejuŭi kyŏngje kwalli munje e taehayŏ* (On the problem of the management of the socialist economy), 7: 259–93. Pyongyang: Chosŏn nodongdang ch'ulp'ansa.

———. 1997c. "Sahoejuŭi nongch'on munje e kwanhan t'eje rŭl ch'ŏlchŏhi kwanch'ŏl haja: Chosŏn minjujuŭi inmin konghwaguk chungang inmin wiwŏnhoe che 9-ki che 2-ch'a hoeŭi esŏ han yŏnsŏl, 1990-nyŏn 6-wŏl 22–23-il" (Let's carry out thoroughly the principles in building the socialist agriculture: An address made at the second session of the ninth meeting of the Central People's Committee of the Democratic People's Republic of Korea, June 22–23, 1990). In *Sahoejuŭi kyŏngje kwalli ŭi munjee taehayŏ* (On the problem of the management of the socialist economy), 7: 335–69. Pyongyang: Chosŏn nodongdang ch'ulp'ansa.

Kim Insŏn. 2004. *Rossia changsa kil* (On the road to Russia for trading). Yanji: Yŏnbyŏn inmin ch'ulp'ansa.

Kim Jong Il. 2003. *Kach'i pŏpch'ik ŭi riyong esŏ chegi tŏenŭn myŏt kaji munje e taehayŏ: Kim Il Sung chonghap taehak haksaeng tŭl kwa han tamhwa 1961-nyŏn 11-wŏl 9-il* (On a few issues raised in the use of the law of value: A conversation with students of Kim Il Sung University on November 9, 1961). Pyongyang: Chosŏn nodongdang ch'ulp'ansa.

Kim Kangil and Hŏ Myŏngch'ŏl, eds. 2001. *Chungguk Chosŏnjok saehoe ŭi munhwa use wa palchŏn chŏllyak* (The cultural superiority and development strategy of Korean Chinese in China). Yanji: Yŏnbyŏn inmin ch'ulp'ansa.

Kim Kwiok. 2006. "Chiyŏk ŭi Han'guk chŏnjaeng kyŏnghŏm kwa chiyŏk sahoe ŭi pyŏnhwa" (Local experience of the Korean War and change in the local society). *Kyŏngje wa sahoe* 71 (Autumn): 40–71.

Kim Kyuryun. 1999. *Nambuk kyŏngje kyoryu hyŏmnyŏk palchŏn pangan* (Proposal for the development of the South–North exchange and cooperation). Seoul: T'ongil yŏn'guwŏn.

——. 2004. "Nambuk kyŏnghyŏp kwa Tongbuga kyŏngje hyŏmnyŏk kudo" (South–North economic cooperation and the map of economic cooperation in Northeast Asia). *Han-Tok sahoe kwahak nonch'ong* 14. no. 1: 103–25.

Kim Hakno. 2005. "P'yŏnghwa t'onghap chŏllyak ŭrosŏŭi haetpyŏt chŏngch'aek" (The Sunshine Policy as a strategy for peaceful integration). *Han'guk chŏngch'i hakhoebo* 39, no. 5: 237–61.

Kim Namgŭn. 2012. "Ssangyong chadongch'a haego sagŏn ŭl kyegi ro pon chŏngri haego chedo ŭi kaesŏn panghyang" (The direction of reforming the restructuring layoff, taking the case of Ssangyong Automobile's layoffs). *Nodongbŏp yŏn'gu* 33: 247–29.

Kim Panghee. 1993. "Sŭngyongch'a sijang chinch'ul Samsŏng ŭi yamang kwa chŏllyak" (Entry into the automobile market: The ambition and strategy of Samsung). *Sisa Journal* 192, July 1.

Kim Pyŏngho and Kang Kiju. 2001. "Chungguk ŭi sosuminjok chŏngch'aek kwa Chungguk Chosŏnjok sahoe ŭi chŏngch'i'i ŭisik mit minjok ŭisik" (Chinese minority policy and the political and national consciousness of Korean Chinese). In *Chungguk sahoe ŭi munhwa wuse wa palchŏn chŏllyak* (The cultural superiority and the developmental strategy of Korean Chinese society in China), edited by Kim Kangil and Hŏ Myŏngch'ol, 105–11. Yanji: Yŏnbyŏn inmin ch'ulp'ansa.

Kim Pyŏngro. 2009. "Kyŏngje choch'i ihu Pukhan ŭi sahoe chŏk pyŏnhwa" (Social change in North Korea after economic reform). In *7.1 kyŏngje kwalli kaesŏn choch'i ihu Pukhan kyŏngje wa sahoe* (Economy and society in North Korea after the 7.1 Instruction on economic management improvement), edited by Yun Yŏnggwan and Yang Unch'ol, 285–330. Seoul: Hanul.

——. 2012. "Pukhan ŭi punchŏlhwa toen sijanghwa wa chŏngch'i sahoe chŏk hamŭi" (Segmented marketization and its sociopolitical implications). *Pukhan yŏn'gu hakhoebo* 16, no. 1: 93–121.

Kim Pyŏngyŏn. 2009. "Pukhan kyŏngje ŭi sijanghwa" (Marketization of the North Korean economy). In *7.1 kyŏngje kwalli kaesŏn choch'i ihu Pukhan kyŏngje wa sahoe* (Economy and society in North Korea after the 7.1 Instruction on economic management improvement), edited by Yun Yŏnggwan and Yang Unch'ol. Seoul: Hanul.

Kim Pyŏngyŏn and Yang Munsu. 2012. *Pukhan kyŏngje esŏ ŭi sijang kwa chŏngbu* (Market and state in the North Korean economy). Seoul: Seoul National University Press.

Kim Sanggi. 2004. "'Kugyŏng kiŏpso tongnip ch'aesanje e kwanhan kyujŏng' haesŏl" (Interpretation of the "rules on the independent accounting system in state enterprises"). *KDI Pukhan kyŏngje ribyu* 6, no. 8: 12–19.

Kim Soyŏn. 2012. "Ch'angjo k'ŏnsŏlt'ing ŭn ŏttŏn hoesa?" (Which company is Ch'angjo consulting?). *Hangyoreh* newspaper, September 24.

Kim Sunam. 2004. *Miguk ŭi taebuk in'gwŏn chŏngch'aek yŏn'gu* (A study of the US policy on North Korean human rights). Seoul: T'ongil yŏn'guwŏn.

Kim Taeho. 2004. *Han 386-ŭi sasang hyŏngmyŏng* (A 386 generation's revolution in thought). Seoul: Sidae chŏngsin.

Kim Tongch'un. 1995. *Han'guk sahoe nodongja yŏn'gu: 1987-nyŏn ihurŭl chungsim ŭiro* (A study of South Korean workers: Focusing on the post-1987 period). Seoul: Yŏksa pip'yŏngsa.

——. 2000. *Kŭndae ŭi kŭnŭl* (Shadow of modernity). Seoul: Tangdae.

Kim Tonghwa. 1993. "Kŏlch'ul han chŏngch'i hwaldongga Chu Tŏkhae" (The renowned political activist Chu Tŏkhae). In *Chungguk Chosŏn minjok palchach'wi ch'ongsŏ*. Vol. 7, *P'ungnang* (The compiled history of Korean Chinese. Vol. 7, Sea waves), edited by Chungguk Chosŏn minjok palchach'wi ch'ongsŏ wiwŏnhoe, 4–10. Beijing: Minjok chp'ul'ansa.

Kim Unghi. 2004. "Nambuk kyŏngje hyŏmnyŏk ch'ujin hyŏnhwang: Munjejŏm kwa haegyŏl pangan" (The current status of economic engagement between the two Koreas: Problems and solutions). Paper presented at 2004 *T'ongil simp'osium t'oron palche 2* (The second discussion of the 2004 symposium on unification), organized by 6.15 Nambuk kongdong sŏnŏn silhyŏn kwa hanbando p'yŏnghwa rŭl wihan t'ongil yŏndae. Seoul, Korea, July 22.

Kim Wusŏng. 2011. "Yusŏng kiŏp, nosa ch'ungdol lo yuhyŏl sat'ae chiman chuga nŭn sanghanga. Todaech'e 'wae' (Yusŏng firm, its stock price increased despite the bloody clash between the management and the labor union. "Why"). *Ezynews*, June 23. http://www.ezyeconomy.com/news/articleView.html?idxno=15898.

Kim Yŏngmi and Han Chun. 2008. "Naebu sijang ŭi haech'e in'ga ch'ukso in'ga?" (Is this disintegration or reduction of the domestic market?). *Han'guk saehoehak* 42, no. 7: 111–14.

Kok Aeguk and Chung Pumsang. 2004. *Cho Namgi chŏn* (Biography of Cho Namgi). Yanji: Yŏnbyŏn inmin ch'ulp'ansa.

Kong Jiyŏng. 2012. *Ŭijanori* (Musical chairs). Seoul: Humanist.

Koryŏ taehakkyo kich'o hangmun yŏn'gu t'im, ed. 2005. *7.1 choch'i wa Pukhan* (The July 1 Instruction and North Korea). Seoul: Nop'i kip'i.

Ku Chiyŏng. 2013. "Chiguhwa sidae Chosŏnjok ŭi idong kwa chŏngju e kwanhan sogo: Chungguk Ch'ŏngdo rŭl chungsim ŭiro (A study of migration and settlement of Korean Chinese in the globalization era: A focus on Qingdao). *Inmun yŏn'gu* 68: 297–330.

"Kukchŏk hoebok undong ŏttŏkk'e saenggak hasimnikka?" (What do you think about the movement to restore citizenship?). 2003. *Chaeoe tongp'o sinmun*, October issue.

Kukka anjŏn kihoekpu (National Security Agency). 1998. *21-segi kukka palchŏn kwa haeoe hanminjok ŭi yŏk'al* (Development of the state in the twenty-first century and the role of overseas Koreans). Seoul: Kukka anjŏn kihoekpu.

Kŭmsok nojo Ssangyong chadongch'a chibu nodongja yŏksa hannae, ed. 2010. *Haego nŭn sarin ida* (Layoff is murder). Seoul: Hannae.

Kwak Aram. 2013. "Chŏngbu nŭn 200-man tongp'o rŭl pŏrinŭn'ga?: Kukchŏk hoebok chudo Sŏ Kyŏngsŏk moksa 'kohyang sŏ sal kwŏlli chwŏya'" (Does the government abandon 2 million overseas Koreans?: Rev. Sŏ Kyŏngsŏk leads the restoration of citizenship, "the right to live in one's hometown must be given"). *Chosun Daily*, November 15.

Kwŏn Oguk and Mun Inch'ŏl. 2011. "Pukhan kyŏnje chae saengsan kucho ŭi chŏn'gae wa chŏngch'i pyŏnhwa" (Development of the reproductive system in the North Korean economy and political change). *Pukhanhak yŏn'gu* 7, no. 2: 135–71.

Kyesok hyŏngmyŏng e kwanhan chuch'e chŏk rihae (Independent understanding of continuous revolution). 1992. Pyongyang: Sahoe kwahak ch'ulp'ansa.

Li Myŏngsŏ. 1991. *Sahoejuŭi chae saengsan ŭi hamrijŏk chojik* (The rational organization of socialist reproduction). Pyongyang: Sahoekwahak ch'ulp'ansa.

Li Wŏn'gyŏng. 1986. *Sahoejuŭi hwap'ye chedo* (The socialist money system). Pyongyang: Sahoe kwahak ch'ulp'ansa.

Lim Jie-hyun, ed. 2000. *Uri an ŭi p'asisŭm* (Fascism in us). Seoul: Samin.

Lim Kŭnho. 2010. "Sŏn'gun ŭi t'ongch'i pangsik ŭl chip'ŏboda: 2000-nyŏn Hyesan pisa kŏmyŏl kwa kŭ chalmot" (Reflecting on the ruling method of the military-first rule: The Hyesan antisocialism inspection and its errors in 2000). *Imjin'gang* 7 (March): 8–47.

Lim Kwangbin. 2002. "Chaeoe tongp'obŏp kaejŏng ŭl wihan taech'aek hyŏbŭihoe ŭi ipchang" (The position of the Committee for Amending the Overseas Korean Act). Seoul, Korea.

Lim Tŏksil. 2000. *Nyŏ pulbŏp ch'eryuja ŭi ilgi* (The diary of an undocumented woman). Yanji: Yŏnbyŏn inmin ch'ulp'ansa.

Ministry of Foreign Affairs. 1999. "Chaeoe tongp'o ŭi ch'uripkuk kwa pŏpchŏk chiwi e kwanhan pŏmnyul sŏlmyŏng." (Explanation on the law on entry and exit and the legal status of overseas Koreans). Seoul, Korea, August 31.

Minisry of Foreign Affairs and Trade. 2013. *Chaeoe tongp'o hyŏnhwang* (The current conditions of overseas Koreans). Seoul, Korea.

Ministry of Justice. 2001. "Chaeoe tongp'o ŭi churipkuk kwa pŏpchŏk chiwi e kwanhan pŏmnyul kaejŏng pŏmnyuran e taehan ŭigyŏn" (The opinion on the bill on revising the Overseas Korean Act). Seoul, Korea, December 17.

——. 2002. "2002 pulbŏp ch'eryu pangji chonghap taech'aek" (The comprehensive plan to prevent illegal stay in 2002). Seoul, Korea, March 12.

——. 2003. "Chaeoe tongp'obŏp sihaengnyŏng tŭng kaejŏngan ippŏp yego" (On the prospective bill to revise the regulation of the Overseas Korean Act). Press release on September 23.

Ministry of Labor. 2003a. "Chaeoe tongp'obŏp kwa oeguk illyŏk chedo" (The Overseas Korean Act and the policy for employment of foreign workers), February 14.

———. 2003b. "Chisok sŏngjang kwa kiŏp ŭl wihan oegugin koyong hŏgaje" (Employment Permit Program designed for continuous growth and business). Seoul, Korea.

Minjok munje "ttajŭbo" hoejip (Collection of "big-character posters" on the nationality question). 1958. Yanji: Yanbian University Press.

Mun Hyŏngjin. 2008. "Han'guk nae Chosŏnjok nodongja tŭrŭi kaldŭng sarye e kwanhan yŏn'gu" (A study of conflicts among Korean Chinese workers in South Korea). Kukche chiyŏk yŏn'gu 12, no. 1: 131–56.

Mun Pusik. 2002. Irŏbŏrin kiŏk ŭl ch'ajasŏ: Kwanggi ŭi sidae rŭl saenggak ham (In search of lost memory: Rethinking of the era of fanaticism). Seoul: Samin.

Nakagawa Masahiko. 2003a. "Pukhan yŏnhap kiŏpso ŭi hyŏngsŏng" (The formation of the North Korean combined enterprise). KDI Pukhan kyŏngje ribyu 5, no. 3: 48–75.

———. 2003b. "Pukhan yŏnhap kiŏpso ŭi hyŏngsŏng kwa pyŏnch'ŏn" (Formation and change of the North Korean combined enterprise in North Korea). KDI Pukhan kyŏngje ribyu 5, no. 4: 31–42.

Nam Sŏngch'il. 2004. "Che-2 che-3 ŭi 3.8 sŏn ŭl chiwura" (Erase the second and third 3.8 division). Seoul, January 23. Unpublished statement.

National Human Rights Commission. 2001. Chaeoe tongp'obŏp kaejŏng pŏmnyuran e taehan kukka in'gwŏn wiwŏnhoe ŭi ŭigyŏn (The National Human Rights Commission's opinion on the bills to amend the Overseas Korean Act). December 21. Seoul: National Human Rights Commission.

O Kangsu. 2001. "Ch'oegŭn Pukhan ŭi kiŏp kwalli ch'egye kaep'yŏn ŭi t'ŭkching kwa panghyang" (Characteristics and trends in the recent restructuring of the management of firms). KDI Pukhan kyŏngje ribyu 3, no. 2: 1–10.

O Kyŏngsŏp, Yun Yŏsang, and Hŏ Sŏnhaeng. 2008. Kukkun p'oro munje ŭi chonghap chŏk ihae (Understanding the problem of South Korean prisoners of the Korean War). Seoul: Pukhan in'gwŏn chŏngbo sent'ŏ, 2008.

O Suyŏl et al. 1995. "Pukhan kyŏngje ch'egye ŭi naeyong kwa kyehoek ŭi kwajŏng" (Contents of the North Korean economic system and the process of its planning). Honam chŏngch'ihak hoebo 7: 85–102.

O T'aeho. 1993. "Minjok chŏngp'ung undong kaundesŏ saenggin ryŏksa ŭi ohae" (Misunderstanding of the history during the national rectification movement). In Chungguk Chosŏn minjok palchach'wi ch'ongsŏ. Vol. 7, P'ungnang (The compiled history of Korean Chinese. Vol. 7, Sea waves), edited by Chungguk Chosŏn minjok palchach'wi ch'ongsŏ wiwŏnhoe, 129–46. Beijing: Minjok ch'ulp'ansa.

Oka Katzhiko. 2002. "Chaeoe tongp'o e kwanhan pŏpchŏk koch'al: Han'guk e itsŏsŏŭi 'chaeoe tongp'o' kaenyŏm kwa kŭ chŏngch'aek" (The legal analysis of overseas

Koreans: Concept and policy of "overseas Koreans" in South Korea). *Pŏphak yŏn'gu* 12, no. 1: 47–85.

Paik Nak-chung. 1998. *Hŭndŭllinŭn pundan ch'eje* (The national division system is shaking). Seoul: Ch'angjak kwa pip'yŏng.

Paik Nakki et al. 1998. *Chungso kiŏp kŭmyŭng wŏnyulhwa pangan* (Proposals for the fluid flow of capital for small- and medium-sized firms). Seoul: Korea Institute for Industrial Economics and Trade.

"Pak Ch'angwuk kyosu waŭi taedam" (Conversation with Professor Pak Ch'angwuk). 2002. *Hangyoreh* newspaper, July 29.

Pak Hugŏn. 2013. "Pukhan kyŏngje ŭi chae kusŏng – part 1" (Rethinking the North Korean economy, Part 1). *Hyŏndae Pukhan yŏn'gu* 16, no. 2: 214–71.

Pak Hyŏngjung. 2009. "Kwagŏ wa mirae ŭi honhapmul losŏ ŭi Pukhan kyŏngje" (North Korean economy as the combination of the past and the future). *Pukhan yŏn'gu hakhoebo* 13, no. 1: 35–60.

Pak Kyŏngt'ae. 2008. *Sosuja wa Han'guk sahoe: Iju nodongja, hwagyo, honhyŏrin* (Minority and South Korean society: Migrant workers, Chinese Koreans, and mixed-blood Koreans). Seoul: Humanitas.

Pak Myŏngrim. 2002. *Han'guk 1950 chŏnjaeng kwa p'yŏnghwa* (South Korea, 1950: War and peace). Seoul: Nanam.

Pak Minja. ed. 2000, *Chungguk Chosŏnjok hyŏn sangt'ae punsŏk mit chŏnmang yŏn'gu* (Analysis of the current condition and its prospect for the Korean Chinese). Yanji: Yanbian University Press.

Pak Sŏksam. 2002. "Pukhan ŭi sakyŏngje pumun yŏn'gu" (A study of the private economic sector in North Korea). *Hanŭn chosa yŏn'gu* (March).

Pak Sŏkun. 1995. "Han'guk ŭi oegugin nodongja in'gwŏn munje wa taech'aek" (Human rights issues of foreign workers in South Korea and alternatives). *Pŏpkwa sahoe* 11: 273–99.

———. 2000. "Nodong hŏgaje toip ŭi panghyang" (Direction of the institutionalization of the Labor Permit Program). Paper presented at *Iju nodongja in'gwŏn kwa oeguk illyŏk toip chŏngch'aek ŭi kŭnbon chŏk kaesŏn ŭl wihan t'oronhoe* (Forum on the human rights of migrant workers and the fundamental reform of the policy on the employment of migrant workers). National Assembly Forum, Seoul, Korea, July 7.

———. 2002. "Oegugin kŭlloja ŭi nodong hŏga mit in'gwŏn pojang e kwanhan pomnyul ane taehan kŏmt'o ŭigyŏn." In *2-ch'a Chŏnggi unyŏng wiwŏnhoe hoeŭi charyo* (Documents for the Second Annual Executive Committee Meeting), JCMK internal document. Seoul, Korea, November 7.

Pak Sŭngok. 2010. "Nodong undong sŭmultul ŭi Chŏn T'aeil lo tora kara" (Labor movement, return to twenty-two-year-old Chŏn T'aeil). *Nodong sahoe* 155: 40–53.

Pak Yŏngja. 2009. "2003-nyŏn <chonghap sijangje> ihu Pukhan ŭi 'chubyŏn nodong' kwa 'nodong sijang'" ("Marginal labor" and "the labor market" after the 2003 comprehensive market system). *Han'guk chŏngch'ihak hoebo* 43, no. 3: 149–71.

"P'aŏp hamyŏn chuga olla. Yusŏng kiŏp chuga nŏlttwigi" (The stock price increases with the labor strike. The swing of Yusŏg stock price). 2011. *Ch'amnews*, June 30.

"Pangmun ch'wiŏpche 5-nyŏn, kwigukcha tŭrŭn mwŏrhana?" (The visiting employment system for five years. What do the returnees do?). 2012. *Killim sinmun* (Jilin newspaper), December 6.

"Pŏbwŏn, 'kyŏngch'al kwa ch'ungdol Yusŏng kiŏp nojo 4,500 manwŏn paesang ch'aegim'" (The Court, "the responsibility of the Yusŏng union to disburse 45,000,000 won for damage caused by its clash with the police"). 2013. www.newsis.com. May 30. http://www.newsis.com/ar_detail/view.html?ar_id=NISX201 40530_0012952555&cID=10201&pID=10200.

Pŏmryun. 2001. "Illyu p'yŏnghwa ŭi sasang kwa silch'ŏn" (Ideas and practices of peace for humanity). Talk presented at the sixth education conference of Good Friends, *P'yŏnghwa undong ŏttŏk'e hal kŏsin'ga?* (How do we advance the peace movement?). June 1, Seoul Korea. Unpublished document.

"Pukhan sisa yongŏ haesŏl" (Commentary on North Korean vocabularies). 2009. *Imjin'gang* 5: 133.

"Pukhan sisa yongŏ haesŏl 2" (Commentary on North Korean vocabularies). 2009. *Imjin'gang* 6: 171.

Ryu Eun Kyu. 2007. *Yŏnbyŏn munhwa tae hyŏngmyŏng: 10-nyŏn ŭi yaksok* (The Great Cultural Revolution in Yanbian: The ten-year-old promise). Kunp'o: T'ohyang.

Ryu Kyŏngwŏn. 2008. "Chut'aek kŏraewa kŭ pujŏng pup'ae ŭi naemak" (Misconduct and corruption in the housing market). *Rimjin'gang* 3 (August): 4–46.

———. 2009. "Ttodasi kinjang kam hŭrŭnŭn sijang" (New tension again in the markets). *Rimjin'gang* 4: 62.

"Sarye" (case). 2003. A one-page unpublished statement by the people (Group 1) who joined the sit-in demonstration from November 2003 to February 2004 that was organized by the Committee for Amending the Overseas Korean Act. December.

Shin Sŭnggun et al. 2003. "Chaejung tongp'o haebŏp, yŏjŏnhan p'yŏnghaengsŏn" (The solution to Korean Chinese, still parallel). *Hangyoreh* newspaper, November 30.

Sŏ Chaejin. 1995. *Tto hana ŭi Pukhan sahoe* (Another North Korean society). Seoul: Nanam.

Sŏ Kyŏngsŏk. 2002. "Chaeoe tongp'obŏp kaejŏng panghyang" (The direction of the amendment of the Overseas Korean Act). February 1. http://www.koreanchinese.or.kr/board/117.

Sŏ Tongman. 2005. *Pukchosŏn sahoejuŭi ch'eje sŏngnip sa 1945–1961* (The formation of North Korean socialism, 1945–1961). Seoul: Sŏnin.

———. 2010. *Pukchosŏn yŏn'gu* (A study of North Korea). Seoul: Ch'angbi.

Sŏk Wŏnjŏng. 2003. "Iju nodongja munje wa Han'guk sahoe ŭi kwaje" (Issues of migrant workers and tasks of Korean society). In *Saehoe p'orŏm*, 399–405. Seoul, Korea.

Sŏl Tonghun. 1999. *Oegugin nodongja wa Han'guk sahoe* (Foreign workers and South Korean society). Seoul: Seoul National University Press.

———. 2007. "Oeguk kukchŏk tongp'o 'pangmun ch'wiŏpche' sihaeng ŭl aptugo" (Thinking ahead of the implementation of "the visiting employment system" for overseas Koreans with foreign citizenship). *Kukchŏng Briefing*, January 23. http://dhseol.com.ne.kr/publish/mz2007_03.html.

Son Hyemin. 2009. "Pak Kiwŏn, kŭ Sunch'ŏn saram" (Pak Kiwŏn in Sunch'ŏn). *Imjin'gang* 5 (September): 45–73.

———. 2010. "'Scarlet Ohara' wa Chosŏn nyŏsŏng" ("Scarlet O'Hara" and North Korean women). *Imjin'gang* 7 (March): 112–21.

Son Kyŏngho. 2011. "Ch'oegŭn Han'guk chŏnjaeng yŏn'gu tonghyang: 2005-nyŏn ihu yŏn'gu rŭl chungsim ŭiro" (The trend in the study of the Korean War: Focusing on studies after 2005). *Han'guk kŭndaesa yŏn'gu* 56 (Spring): 202–26.

Son Mia. 2009. "Ssangyong chadongch'a nodongja taet'ujaeng ihu muŏsŭl hal kŏsin'ga?" (What must we do after the great struggle of Ssangyong workers?). *Chŏngse wa nodong* 49 (September): 33–60.

Song Chongho. 2006. "Oegugin nodongja chiwŏn tanch'e ŭi hyŏnhwang kwa hwaldong" (Status and activities of the advocacy organizations for foreign migrant workers). *Minjok yŏn'gu* 28: 29–54.

Taehanmin'guk kwanbo (The gazette of the Republic of Korea). 1999. September 2.

Yanbian daxue geming weiyuan hui jiaoyu geming zu, 1969. *Zichan jieji zhishi fenzi tongzhi jiu Yanda: Zuie yi bai lie* (The rule of the former Yanbian University by bourgeois intellectuals: One hundred cases of crime). Yanji, China, December.

Yang Kŏnmo. 2013. "1983-nyŏn isan kajok ch'atki" (The search for the separated families in 1983). *Kyŏnghyang Daily*, June 20.

Yang Munsu. 2010. *Pukhan kyŏngje ŭi sijanghwa* (Marketization of the North Korean economy). Seoul: Hanul.

———. 2012. "2000-nyŏndae Pukhan ŭi pan-sijanghwa chŏngch'aek" (Antimarket policy in North Korea in the 2000s). *Hyŏndae Pukhan yŏn'gu* 15, no. 1: 85–123.

Yang Munsu et al. 2007. *Pukhan ŭi nodong* (Labor in North Korea). Seoul: Hanul.

Ye Tonggŭn. 2010. "Küllobŏl sidae Chungguk ŭi ch'eje chŏnhwan kwa tosi chongjok kongdongch'e chae hyŏngsŏng: Pukkyŏng Wangjing Korea t'aun ŭi Chosŏnjok kongdongch'e sarye yŏn'gu" (A system transition in China and reconfiguration of the urban ethnic community in globalization: A case study of the Korean Chinese community in the Wangjing South Korean town in Beijing). *Minjok yŏn'gu* 43: 159–85.

Yi Changsŏp et al. 2007. "Yŏnbyŏn Chosŏnjok ŭi chayŏngŏp siltae e kwanhan yŏn'gu" (A study of the self-employed business of Korean Chinese in Yanbian). *Han'guk Tongbuga nonch'ong* 44: 31–53.

Yi Chinryŏng. 2002. "Chosŏnin esŏ Chosŏnjok ŭiro: Chungguk kongsandang ŭi Yŏnbyŏn chiyŏk changak kwa chŏngch'esŏng pyŏnhwa, 1945–1949" (From Koreans to Korean Chinese: Domination of the Chinese Communist Party and changes in identity in Yanbian). *Chungso yŏn'gu* 95: 89–116.

Yi Chinsŏk. 2003. "Chosŏnjok kukchŏk hoebok . . . 'happŏp ch'eryu' chagyŏk ŏdŭmyŏn kwihwa sinchŏng kanung" (The restoration of the citizenship of Korean Chinese. It is possible to apply for naturalization if acquiring "legal status"). *Chosun Daily*, November 20.

Yi Hogŭn. 2012. "Chŏngri haego tŭng kiŏp ŭi koyong chojŏng kwa Togil ŭi 'choŏp tanch'uk chiwŏn'gŭm' chedo ŭi koyong anjŏngmang yŏk'al e kwanhan koch'al" (Adjustments of employment, including restructuring layoffs, and the study of stabilization of employment in the case of the program on "the fund for shortening working hours" in Germany). *Nodong chŏngch'aek yŏn'gu* 12, no. 30: 199–214.

Yi Jin-kyung, ed. 2008. *Chŏnjigu chŏk chabonjuŭi wa Han'guk sahoe: Tasi sahoe kusŏngch'eron ŭiro?* (Global capitalism and the South Korean society: A return to the social formation debate?). AlteRevolution 2. Seoul: Kŭrinbi.

Yi Jin-kyung and Goh Byeong-gwon. 2006. "Cheguk ŭi sidae in'ga, Cheguk ŭi hwanghon in'ga: Hanmi FTA rŭl tullŏssan chŏngse e kwanhayŏ" (Is this an imperial era or an imperial sunset?: The politics surrounding the FTA between South Korea and the United States). *Ch'amsesang*, April 24. http://www.newscham.net/news/view.php?board=news&nid=33235&category1=3.

Yi Kŭmsun. 2005. *Pukhan chumin ŭi kukkyŏng idong silt'ae: Pyŏnhwa wa chŏnmang* (Reality of the border-crossing migration of North Koreans: Changes and prospects). Seoul: Korea Institute for National Unification.

Yi Kŭmyŏn. 1999. "The Third National Forum in Solidarity with Migrant Workers, Tokyo '99 ch'amga hago nasŏ" (After Participation in the Third National Forum in Solidarity with Migrant Workers in Tokyo in 1999). In *1999 saŏp charyo moŭm* (Compiled documents of the activities in 1999), edited by JCMK. Seoul, Korea: JCMK.

Yi Kwangkyu. 2001. "Chaeoe tongp'obŏp ŭi munjejŏm" (Problems of the Overseas Korean Act). Paper presented at 2-ch'a chaeoe tongp'o chiwi hyangsang mit chaeoe tongp'obŏp kaejŏng ŭl wihan kongdong semina (The second seminar on the improvement of the status of overseas Koreans and the amendment of the Overseas Korean Act). Seoul, Korea, March 12.

Yi Mirim. 2011. "2000-nyŏndae sosŏl e nat'anan chosŏnjok iju yŏsŏng ŭi t'ajajŏk chŏngch'esŏng" (Representation of Korean Chinese migrant women's subjectivities as others in novels of the 2000s). *Hyŏndae sosŏl yon'gu* 48: 645–72.

Yi Nanju. 2002. "Oegugin nodongja munje, nodong undong i nasŏya handa" (The issues of foreign workers, the labor movement must lead). *Nodong sahoe* 65: 34–40.

Yi Pyŏnghye. 2003. "Sŏ Kyŏngsŏk moksa int'ŏbyu—'Chosŏnjok ŭi hanjokhwa kyŏlk'o pangkwan halsu opta'" (Interview with Reverend Sŏ: "We can no longer ignore sinicization of Korean Chinese"). *Tongbuga sinmun*, November 18.

Yi Pyŏnghwa. 2013. "Han'guk kwa Ilbon ŭi oegugin nodongja chŏngch'aek kwa oegugin nodongja undong: Ijungjŏk simin sahoe wa chŏngch'i kujo" (Policy on foreign workers and the foreign workers' movement in South Korea and Japan: The double-sided civil society and political structure). *Kiŏkkwa chŏnmang* 29: 264–306.

Yi Sangho. 2007. "Wansŏngch'a ŏpch'e ŭi hyŏmnyŏk ŏpch'e taehan saehoe chŏk ch'aegim: Hyŏndae chadongch'a ŭi sarye rŭl chungsim ŭiro" (On the social responsibility of the parent company to subcontracted company: With the focus on Hyundai Automobile). *Tonghyang kwa chŏnmang* 70: 173–208.

Yi Sangsuk and Song Wenzhi. 2012. "1950–1960-nyŏndae Chosŏnjok ŭi Pukhan iju wa puk-chung hyŏmnyŏk" (The migration of Koreans to North Korea and the North Korea–China cooperation in the 1950s–1960s." *Pukhan yŏn'gu hakhoebo* 16, no. 1: 359–77.

Yi Sŏk et al. 2009. *Pukhan kyehoek kyŏngje ŭi pyŏnhwa wa sijanghwa* (Change in the North Korean planned economy and marketization). Seoul: T'ongil yŏn'guwŏn.

Yi Sŏkki. 2004. "1990-nyŏndae ihu Pukhan kyŏngje ŭi t'ŭkching kwa wigi" (Characteristics and crisis of the North Korean economy in the post-1990s). *Tonghyang kwa chŏnmang* 62: 156–207.

———. 2009. "Pukhan kiŏp kwalli ch'egye ŭi pyŏnhwa" (Change in the management system in North Korea). In *7.1 kyŏngje kwalli kaesŏn choch'i ihu Pukhan kyŏngje wa sahoe* (Economy and society in North Korea after the 7.1 Instruction on economic management improvement), edited by Yun Yŏnggwan and Yang Unch'ol, 88–150. Seoul: Hanul.

Yi Sŏngro 2013. "Konggong chŏngch'aek ŭirosŏ hatpyŏt chŏngch'aek e taehan p'yŏngga" (An evaluation of the Sunshine Policy as a public policy). *Tonghyang kwa chŏnmang* 87: 264–303.

Yi Sŏnhi, ed. 2001. *Isan ŭi sŭlp'ŭm: Ton i muŏsigillae* (The sorrow of family separation: What is called money). Seoul: Kyonghan.

Yi Taegŭn. 2009. "Pukhan ŭi kwŏllyŏk kujo pyŏnhwa wa hugye kudo chŏnmang" (The change in North Korean power structure and the prospect of succession). *Pukhan yŏn'gu hakhoe ch'un'gye haksul palp'yo nonmunjip* 2009: 47–73.

Yi Tuwŏn. 2006. "Han'guk kyŏngje kyoryu ka Chosŏnjok kyŏngje e mich'in yŏk'al" (The impact of the South Korea–China economic exchange on the Korean Chinese economy). *Tongbuga kyŏngje yŏn'gu* 18, no. 1: 1–25.

Yi Wŏnsŏk. 2003. "Taehanmin'guk ŭi hanŭl e nallinŭn p'yŏnji" (The letter that flies in the South Korean sky). Seoul, Korea. Unpublished document.

Yi Wuyŏng, ed. 2008. *Pukhan tosi chumin ŭi sajŏk yŏngyŏk yŏn'gu* (The private sphere and people of cities in North Korea). Seoul: Hanul.

Yi Yŏngjae. 2010. "Kwagŏsa p'ihae posang e taehan pip'anjŏk kŏmt'o: Kwangju minjung hangjaeng mit minjuhwa undong e taehan p'ihae posang kwa kukka paesang ŭi pigyo rŭl chungsim ŭiro" (A critical review of reparation of past history: Focusing on reparation and the state's compensation in the Kwangju minjung struggle and the democracy movement). *Kiŏk kwa chŏnmang* 12: 199–234.

Yi Yonggi. 2003. "Maŭl esŏ ŭi Han'guk chŏnjaeng kyŏnghŏm kwa kŭ kiŏk" (Experience and memory of the Korean War in a village). *Yŏksa munje yŏn'gu* 6: 11–55.

Yŏksa munje yŏn'guso, ed. 1995. *Pundan 50-nyŏn kwa t'ongil sidae ŭi kwaje* (Fifty years of national division and the agenda for the unification era). Seoul: Yŏksa munje yŏn'guso.

Yŏllin wuridang t'ongil oegyo t'ongsang wiwŏnhoe. 2004. "Chaeoe tongp'o chŏngch'aek, idaero choŭn'ga?: T'al naengjŏn sidae hanminjok network, ije urasiaro munŭl nŏlp'ija" (The policy on overseas Koreans. Is it alright?: Let's open our gate to Eurasia, making the Korean national network in the post–Cold War). Seoul, Korea, October 22.

Yŏm Kyuhyŏn. 2009. "Isan kajok sangbong hwaktae, chŏngnyehwa haebŏp ŏpna? Ibent' ro chŏllak han isan kajok sangbong, Kŭmgangsan myŏnhoeso tŭng tolp'agu ch'a'jaya" (Is there any solution to expand the family reunion of the separated? The family reunion reduced to an event must find a breakthrough such as the utilization of a meeting place at Kŭmgang Mountain). *Minjok 21* 104: 102–5.

Yŏnbyŏn tangsa hakhoe, ed. 1989. *Yŏnbyŏn 40 nyŏn kisa* (Forty years of news reports in Yanbian). Yanji: Yŏnbyŏn inmin ch'ulp'ansa.

Yoo Yŏnggyu and Yoo Chihe. 2003. "Ittang e harabŏji myoji, nae hojŏk to innŭnde: Kukchŏk hoebok e nasŏn chungguk tongp'o" (There are my grandfather's tomb and my family registration in this land: Korean Chinese and their efforts to restore citizenship). *Taehanmaeil* newspaper, November 15.

Yun Hwang. 2010. "Kim Jong Il ŭi sŏn'gun yŏngdo ch'egye kuch'uk e ttarŭn sŏn'gun chŏngch'i ŭi kinŭng punsŏk." (The analysis of the functions of the military-first rule following the formation of Kim Jong Il's military-first leadership system). *Han'guk Tongbuga nonch'ong* 57: 214–39,

Yun Sujŏng. 2005. "Sosuja undong kwa chwap'a undong" (The Minority movement and the leftist movement). Paper presented at the Second Conference of the Marxist Communale in South Korea. February 17.

Yun Yŏnggwan and Yang Unch'ŏl, eds. 2009. *7.1 kyŏngje kwalli kaesŏn choch'i ihu Pukhan kyŏngje wa sahoe* (Economy and society in North Korea after the 7.1 Instruction on economic management improvement). Seoul: Hanul.

ENGLISH TEXTS

Abelmann, Nancy. 1996. *Echoes of the Past, Epics of Dissent: A South Korean Social Movement.* Berkeley: University of California Press.

Abensour, Miguel. 2011. *Democracy Against the State: Marx and the Machiavellian Movement.* London: Polity Press.

Agamben, Giorgio. 1998. *Homo Sacer: Sovereign Power and Bare Life.* Stanford, CA: Stanford University Press.

Aglietta, Michel. 2001. *A Theory of Capitalist Regulation: The US Experience.* London: Verso.

Ahn, Kyong Whan. 1998. "The Influence of American Constitutionalism on South Korea." *Southern Illinois University Law Journal* 22: 71–115.

Ali, Tariq, ed. 1984. *The Stalinist Legacy: Its Impact on Twentieth-Century World Politics.* Chicago: Haymarket Books.

Anderson, Benedict. 1992. *Imagined Communities: Reflections on the Origin and Spread of Nationalism.* London: Verso.

Appadurai, Arjun. 1996. *Modernity at Large.* Minneapolis: University of Minnesota Press.

——. 1998. "Dead Certainty: Ethnic Violence in the Era of Globlization." *Public Culture* 10, no. 2: 225–47.

Arendt, Hannah. 1951. *The Origins of Totalitarianism.* London: Schocken Books.

Armstrong, Charles. 2003. *The North Korean Revolution, 1945–1950.* Ithaca, NY: Cornell University Press.

Aspromourgos, Tony. 2007. "Adam Smith: Peace and Economics." *AQ* (September-October): 12–40.

Badiou, Alain. 2005. "The Cultural Revolution: The Last Revolution?" *Positions: East Asia Cultures Critique* 13, no. 3: 481–514.

——. 2010. "The Idea of Communism." In *The Idea of Communism*, edited by Costas Douzinas and Slavoj Žižek, 1–14. London: Verso.

Basok, Tanya, and Emily Carasco. 2010. "Advancing the Rights of Non-Citizens in Canada: A Human Rights Approach to Migrant Rights." *Human Rights Quarterly* 32, no. 2: 342–66.

Benjamin, Walter. 1969. "Theses on the Philosophy of History." In *Illumination: Essays and Reflections by Walter Benjamin*, edited by Hannah Arendt, 253–64. New York: Schocken.

——. 2002. *The Arcade Project.* Cambridge: Belknap Press.

Binns, Peter, Tony Cliff, and Chris Harman. 1987. *Russia: From Workers' State to State Capitalism.* New York: Bookmarks.

Bleiker, Roland. 2005. *Divided Korea: Toward a Culture of Reconciliation.* Minneapolis: University of Minnesota Press.

Bloch, Ernst. 1987. *Natural Law and Human Dignity.* Cambridge: MIT Press.

——. 2009. *The Heritage of Our Times.* London: Polity Press.

Braziel, Jana Evans. 2003. *Theorizing Diaspora: A Reader.* London: Wiley-Blackwell.

Brown, Kerry. 2006. *The Purge of the Inner Mongolian People's Party in the Chinese Cultural Revolution, 1967–69: A Function of Language, Power and Violence.* Kent: Global Oriental.

Brown, Wendy. 1995. *States of Injury: Power and Freedom in Late Modernity.* Princeton: Princeton University Press.

Brubaker, Rogers. 1998. *Citizenship and Nationhood in France and Germany.* Cambridge: Harvard University Press.

Buck-Morss, Susan. 1989. *The Dialectics of Seeing: Walter Benjamin and the Arcades Project.* Cambridge: MIT Press.

——. 2002. *Dreamworld and Catastrophe: The Passing of Mass Utopia in East and West.* Cambridge: MIT Press.

——. 2013. "A Commonist Ethics." In *The Idea of Communism 2,* edited by Slavoj Žižek, 57–76. London: Verso.

Burawoy, Michael. 1985. *The Politics of Production: Factory Regimes under Capitalism and Socialism.* London: Verso.

——. 1992. *The Radiant Past: Ideology and Reality in Hungary's Road to Capitalism.* Chicago: University of Chicago Press.

——. 1997. "The Soviet Descent into Capitalism." *American Journal of Sociology* 102, no. 5: 1430–44.

——. 2001a. "Neoclassical Sociology: From the End of Communism to the End of Classism." *American Journal of Sociology* 106, no. 4: 1099–120.

——. 2001b. "Transition Without Transformation: Russia's Involutionary Road to Capitalism." *East European Politics and Societies* 15: 269–90.

Burawoy, Michael, and Pavel Krotov. 1992. "The Soviet Transition from Socialism to Capitalism: Worker Control and Economic Bargaining in the Wood Industry." *American Sociological Review* 57: 16–36.

Butler, Judith, and Athena Athanasiou. 2013. *Dispossession: The Performative in the Political.* Cambridge: Polity Press.

Campbell, Timothy, and Adam Sitze, eds. 2013. *Biopolitics: A Reader.* Durham: Duke University Press.

Cho, Grace. 2008. *Haunting the Korean Diaspora: Shame, Secrecy, and the Forgotten War.* Minneapolis: University of Minnesota Press.

Choi, Seung-Whan. 2011. "Re-Evaluating Capitalist and Democratic Peace Models." *International Studies Quarterly* 55: 759–69.

Chun, Jennifer Jihye. 2009. *Organizing at the Margins: The Symbolic Politics of Labor in South Korea and the United States.* Ithaca: ILR Press.

Clarke, Simon. 1988. "The Marxist Theory of Overaccumulation and Crisis." *Capital and Class* 36: 59–92.

———. 1993. *Marx's Theory of Crisis*. London: Palgrave Macmillan.

Cliff, Tony. 1974. *State Capitalism in Russia*. London: Pluto Press.

Clifford, James. 1992. "Traveling Cultures." In *Cultural Studies*, edited by C. Nelson and P. Treicheler, 96–112. New York: Routledge.

Comaroff, John, and Jean Comaroff. 2009. *Ethnicity, Inc.* Chicago: University of Chicago Press.

Coutin, Susan Bibler. 2005. "Contesting Criminality: Illegal Immigration and the Spatialization of Legality." *Theoretical Criminology* 9, no. 1: 5–33.

Crotty, James, and Kang-Kook Lee. 2002. "A Political-Economic Analysis of the Failure of Neoliberal Restructuring in Post-Crisis Korea." *Cambridge Journal of Economics* 26, no. 5: 667–78.

Cumings, Bruce. 1981. *The Origins of the Korean War, Vol. 1: Liberation and the Emergence of Separate Regimes, 1945–1947*. Princeton: Princeton University Press.

de Soysa, Indra, and Hanne Fjelde. 2010. "Is the Hidden Hand an Iron Fist? Capitalism and Civil Peace, 1970–2005." *Journal of Peace Research* 47, no. 3: 287–98.

Dean, Jodi. 2009. *Democracy and Other Neoliberal Fantasies: Communicative Capitalism and Left Politics*. Durham: Duke University Press.

Deleuze, Gilles. 1994. *Difference and Repetiton*. New York: Columbia University Press.

Derrida, Jacques. 1994. *Specters of Marx: The State of the Debt, the Work of Mourning and the New International*. New York: Routledge.

Dirlik, Arif. 2003. "Globalization and National Development: The Perspective of the Chinese Revolution." *CR: The New Centennial Review* 3, no. 2: 241–70.

Douzinas, Costas. 2010. "Adikia: On Communism and Rights." In *The Idea of Communism*, edited by Costas Douzinas and Slavoj Žižek, 81–100. London: Verso.

Dunayevskaya, Raya. 1944. "A New Revision of Marxian Economics." *American Economic Review* 34, no. 3: 531–37.

Dutton, Michael. 2005. "From Culture Industry to Mao Industry: A Greek Tragedy." *Boundary 2: An International Journal of Literature and Culture* 32, no. 2: 151–67.

Evans, Peter. 2014. "The Developmental State: Divergent Responses to Modern Economic Theory and the 21st Century Economy." In *The End of the Developmental State?*, edited by Michelle Williams, 220–40. New York: Routledge.

Fanon, Frantz. 1967. *Black Skin, White Masks*. New York: Grove Press.

Fine, Bob. 1984. *Democracy and the Rule of Law: Liberal Ideals and Marxist Critique*. London: Pluto Press.

Foucault, Michel. 1978. *History of Sexuality*. Vol. 1. New York: Random House.

Friedman, Gil. 2005. "Commercial Pacifism and Protracted Conflict: Models from the Palestinian-Israeli Case." *Journal of Conflict Resolution* 49, no. 3: 360–82.

Fuller, Lon. 1969. *The Morality of Law*. New Haven: Yale University Press.

Gao, Mobo. 2008. *The Battle for China's Past: Mao and the Cultural Revolution*. London: Pluto Press.

Gartzke, Erik. 2007. "The Capitalist Peace." *American Journal of Political Science* 51, no. 1: 166–91.

Gartzke, Erik, Quan Li, and Charles Boehmer. 2001. "Investing in the Peace: Economic Interdependence and International Conflict." *International Organization* 55, no. 2: 391–438.

Gerber, Theodore, and Michael Hout. 1998. "More Shock Than Therapy: Market Transition, Employment, and Income in Russia, 1991–1995." *American Journal of Sociology* 104 (July 1998): 1–50.

Gershman, Carl. 2005. "The Human Rights of North Koreans: An Issue of Universal Concern." Delivered at the Sixth International Conference on North Korean Human Rights and Refugees, http://www.ned.org/about/board/meet-our-president/archived-remarks-and-presentations/021405.

Goldner, Loren. 2009. "Ssangyong Motor's Strike in Korea Ends in Defeat and Heavy Repression." *Marxism 21* 6, no. 4: 323–37.

Goldstein, Melvyn C., Ben Jiao, and Tanzen Lhundrup. 2009. *On the Cultural Revolution in Tibet: The Nyemo Incident of 1969*. Berkeley: University of California Press.

Gong, Sung-Jin. 2004. "Human Rights Issues in North Korea." In *International Symposium on North Korean Human Rights Issues*, edited by the National Human Rights Commission, 233–40. Seoul: National Human Rights Commission.

Gowan, Peter. 1999. *The Global Gamble: Washington's Faustian Bid for World Dominance*. London: Verso.

Grabher, Gernot. 1997. "Adaptation at the Cost of Adaptability? Restructuring the Eastern German Regional Economy." In *Restructuring Networks in Post-Socialism*, edited by Gernot Grabher and David Stark, 107–34. Oxford: Oxford University Press.

Gupta, Akhil, and James Ferguson, eds. 1997. *Culture, Power, Place: Explorations in Critical Anthropology*. Durham: Duke University Press.

Habermas, Jürgen. 1991. *The Structural Transformation of the Public Sphere: An Inquiry into a Category of Bourgeois Society*. Cambridge: MIT Press.

Hagan, Jacqueline Maria. 2006. "Negotiating Social Membership in the Contemporary World." *Social Forces* 85, no. 2: 631–42.

Halbwachs, Maurice. 1992. *On Collective Memory*. Chicago: University of Chicago Press.

Hardt, Michael. 2010. "The Common in Communism." In *The Idea of Communism*, edtied by Costas Douzinas and Slavoj Žižek, 131–44. London: Verso.

Hardt, Michael, and Antonio Negri. 2001. *Empire*. Cambridge: Harvard University Press.

——. 2011. *Commonwealth*. Cambridge: Harvard University Press.

Harman, Chris. 2010. *Zombie Capitalism: Global Crisis and the Relevance of Marx*. New York: Haymarket Press.

Harootunian, Harry. 2000. *History's Disquiet*. New York: Columbia University Press.

——. 2012. "Deprovincializing Marx." Paper presented at the conference on Marxisms in East Asia. Taiwan, June 6–9.

——. 2015. *Marx after Marx: History and Time in the Expansion of Capitalism*. New York: Columbia University Press.

Harvey, David. 1991. *The Condition of Postmodernity: An Enquiry into the Origins of Cultural Change*. London: Wiley-Blackwell.

——. 2005. *New Imperialism*. Oxford: Oxford University Press.

——. 2011. *Enigma of Capital: And the Crises of Capitalism*. Oxford: Oxford University Press.

Hassig, Ralph, and Kongdan Oh. 2009. *The Hidden People of North Korea*. Lanham: Rowman and Littlefield.

Hayek, Friedrich. 1944. *The Road to Serfdom*. Chicago: University of Chicago Press.

Hegel, G.W.F. 1977. *The Phenomenology of Spirit*. Oxford: Oxford University Press.

Heo, Uk, and Sunwoong Kim. 2000. "Financial Crisis in South Korea: Failure of the Government-Led Development Paradigm." *Asian Survey* 40, no. 3 (May/June): 492–507.

Hilferding, Rudolf. 1910 (reprinted in 1981). *Finance Capital: A Study of the Latest Phase of Capitalist Development*. London: Routledge and Kegan Paul.

Hirschman, Albert O. 1997. *The Passions and the Interests: The Political Arguments for Capitalism Before Its Triumph*. Princeton: Princeton University Press.

Jameson, Fredric. 1981. *The Political Unconscious: Narrative as a Socially Symbolic Act*. Ithaca: Cornell University Press.

——. 2013. *A Singular Modernity: Essay on the Ontology of the Present*. London: Verso.

Jay, Martin. 1984. *Marxism and Totality: The Adventures of a Concept from Lukács to Habermas*. Berkeley: University of California Press.

Kahler, Miles, and Scott Kastner. 2006. "Strategic Uses of Economic Interdependence: Engagement Policies on the Korean Peninsula and Across the Taiwan Strait." *Journal of Peace Research* 43, no. 5: 523–41.

Karatani, Kojin. 2012. *History and Repetition*. New York: Columbia University Press.

Keynes, John Maynard. 1936 (reprinted in 2013). *The General Theory of Employment, Interest, and Money*. New York: Edison Martin Print.

Kim Dae Jung. 1997. *Three-Stages Approach to Korean Reunification: Focusing on the South-North Confederal Stage*. Los Angeles: University of Southern California Press.

Kim Il Sung. 1971a. "The results of the agrarian reform and future tasks: Report to the Sixth Enlarged Executive Committee Meeting of the North Korean Organizing Committee of the Communist Party of Korea, April 10, 1946." In *Selected Works of Kim Il Sung*, 1: 35–55. Pyongyang: Foreign Languages Publishing House.

——. 1971b. "Let us radically improve the people's living standards by strengthening the role of the county and further developing local industry and agriculture: Concluding speech at the Changsong joint conference of local Party and economic functionaries, August 8, 1962." In *Selected Works of Kim Il Sung*, 3: 331–71. Pyongyang: Foreign Languages Publishing House.

——. 1971c. "On further developing the Taean work system: Speech at the Enlarged Meeting of the Party Committee of the Taean Electrical Machinery Plant, November 9, 1962." In *Selected Works of Kim Il Sung*, 3: 423–40. Pyongyang: Foreign Languages Publishing House.

——. 1971d. "Character of tasks of our revolution: From every effort for the country's unification and independence and for socialist construction in the northern half of the republic. April 1955." In *Selected Works of Kim Il Sung: Revolution and Socialist Construction in Korea*, 13–29. New York: International Publishers.

——. 1971e. "Completion of socialist transformation: From report on the work of the Central Committee to the Fourth Congress of the Workers Party of Korea, September 11, 1961." In *Selected Works of Kim Il Sung: Revolution and Socialist Construction in Korea*, 30–52. New York: International Publishers.

——. 1971f. "Socialist construction in the Democratic People's Republic of Korea and the South Korean Revolution: Lecture at the Ali Archam Academy of Social Sciences of Indonesia, April 14, 1965." In *Selected Works of Kim Il Sung: Revolution and Socialist Construction in Korea*, 77–98. New York: International Publishers.

——. 1971g. "On some theoretical problems of the socialist economy: Answers to the questions raised by scientific and educational workers, March 1, 1969." In *Selected Works of Kim Il Sung: Revolution and Socialist Construction in Korea*, 159–82. New York: International Publishers.

——. 1971h. "Great results and new perspectives: From report on the work of the Central Committee to the Fifth Congress of the Workers Party of Korea. November 2, 1970." In *Selected Works of Kim Il Sung: Revolution and Socialist Construction in Korea*, 183–214. New York: International Publishers.

——. 1986a. "On taking good care of state property and using it sparingly and further developing the fishing industry: The concluding speech at the 19th Plenary Meeting of the Fourth Central Committee of the Workers' Party of Korea, June 30, 1969." In *Kim Il Sung Works*, 24: 1–72. Pyongyang: Foreign Languages Publishing House.

——. 1986b. "For further development of the unified planning system: Speech delivered at a consultative meeting of the officials in charge of the planning sector, July 2, 1969." In *Kim Il Sung Works*, 24: 73–91. Pyongyang: Foreign Languages Publishing House.

———. 1986c. "Let us develop local industry and bring about a fresh upswing in the production of mass consumer goods: Speech at the National Conference of Workers in Local Industry." In *Kim Il Sung Works*, 25: 30–58. Pyongyang: Foreign Languages Publishing House.

———. 1986d. "On strengthening the work of establishing the monolithic ideological system of the Party amongst cadres and the work of revolutionizing them: Concluding speech at the 21st Enlarged Plenary Meeting of the Fourth Central Committee of the Workers' Party of Korea, July 6, 1970." In *Kim Il Sung Works*, 25: 119–54. Pyongyang: Foreign Languages Publishing House.

———. 1991. *Answers to the Questions Raised by Foreign Journalists*. Pyongyang: Foreign Languages Publishing House.

———. 1996a. "The Socialist Labor Law of the Democratic People's Republic of Korea." In *Selected Works of Kim Il Sung*, 8: 20–35. Pyongyang: Foreign Languages Publishing House.

———. 1996b. "Let us further accelerate socialist construction through efficient financial management: Speech made at a national conference of financial and banking workers on December 23, 1978." In *Selected Works of Kim Il Sung*, 8: 174–202. Pyongyang: Foreign Languages Publishing House.

———. 1996c. "Let us further develop local industry: Speech at the National Conference of Workers in local industry, June 30, 1980." In *Selected Works of Kim Il Sung*, 8: 292–302. Pyongyang: Foreign Languages Publishing House.

Kim, Jaeeun. 2011. "Establishing Identity: Documents, Performance, and Biometric Information in Immigration Proceedings." *Law and Social Inquiry* 36, no. 3: 760–86.

Kim Soo Young. 2004. "The North Korean Human Rights Act in Comparison with Other U.S. Legislation Concerning Foreign Countries." *KEYS* 18 (Autumn). http://www.dailynk.com/english/keys/2004/18/03.php.

Kim Young Hwan. 2005. "Coming Collapse of the North Korean Regime." *KEYS* 20 (Summer). http://www.dailynk.com/english/keys/2005/20/01.php.

Klug, Heinz. 2000. *Constituting Democracy: Law, Globalism and South Africa's Political Reconstruction*. Cambridge: Cambridge University Press.

Koo, Hagen, ed. 1994. *State and Society in Contemporary Korea*. Ithaca: Cornell University Press.

———. 2001. *Korean Workers: The Culture and Politics of Class Formation*. Ithaca: Cornell University Press.

Kornai, Janos. 1986. "The Hungarian Reform Process: Visions, Hopes, and Reality." *Journal of Economic Literature* 24: 1687–1737.

Koselleck, Reinhart. 2004. *Futures Past: On the Semantics of Historical Time*. New York: Columbia University Press.

———. 2006. "Crisis." *Journal of the History of Ideas* 67, no. 2: 357–400.

Ku Jun Hoe. 2014. "Citizens' Alliance Demonstrates for Passage of Act." *DailyNK*, February 12. http://www.dailynk.com/english/read.php?catId=nk00100&num=11502.

Kwon, Heonik, and Byung-Ho Chung. 2012. *North Korea: Beyond Charismatic Politics*. Lanham: Rowman and Littlefield.

Kwon, Jong Bum. 2005. "In the Crucible of Restructuration: Violence and Forging 'Workers of Iron' in the Transition to a Neoliberal Democracy in South Korea." PhD diss., New York University.

Lankov, Andrei. 2013a. *The Real North Korea*. Oxford: Oxford University Press.

——. 2013b. "Low-Profile Capitalism: The Emergence of the New Merchant/Entrepreneurial Class in Post-Famine North Korea." In *North Korea in Transition*, edited by Kyung-Ae Park and Scott Synder, 179–94. Lanham: Rowman and Littlefield.

Latour, Bruno. 1993. *We Have Never Been Modern*. Cambridge, MA: Harvard University Press.

Lee, Ching Kwan. 2007. *Against the Law: Labor Protests in China's Rustbelt and Sunbelt*. Berkeley: University of California Press.

Lee, Namhee. 2009. *The Making of Minjung: Democracy and the Politics of Representation in South Korea*. Ithaca: Cornell University Press.

Lefebvre, Henri. 2008. *Critique of Everyday Life*. Vol. 2, *Foundations for a Sociology of the Everyday*. London: Verso.

Lenin, Vladimir. 1917 (reprinted in 1969). *Imperialism, the Highest Stage of Capitalism: A Popular Outline*. New York: International Publishers.

Lesser, Jeffrey. 2003. *Searching for Home Abroad: Japanese Brazilians and Transnationalism*. Durham: Duke University Press.

Linger, Danieal Touro. 2001. *No One Home: Brazilian Selves Remade in Japan*. Stanford: Stanford University Press.

Loyalka, Michelle. 2013. *Eating Bitterness: Stories from the Front Lines of China's Great Urban Migration*. Berkeley: University of California Press.

Lu Xiuyan. 1994–1995. "A Step Toward Understanding Popular Violence in China's Cultural Revolution." *Pacific Affairs* 67, no. 4: 533–63.

Lukács, Georg. 1972. *History and Class Consciousness: Studies in Marxist Dialectics*. Cambridge: MIT Press.

Luxemburg, Rosa. 1900 (reprinted in 1973). *Reform or Revolution*. New York: Pathfinder Press.

——. 1913 (reprinted in 2003). *The Accumulation of Capital*. New York: Routledge.

MacFarquhar, Roderick, and Michael Schoenhals. 2006. *Mao's Last Revolution*. Cambridge: Harvard University Press.

Marx, Karl. 1968. *The Eighteenth Brumaire of Louis Bonaparte*. New York: International Publishers.

——. 1976. *Capital I: A Critique of Political Economy.* New York: Penguin Classics.

——. 1977. *Critique of Hegel's Philosophy of Right.* Cambridge: Cambridge University Press.

——. 1992. *Capital III: A Critique of Political Economy.* New York: Penguin Classics.

——. 1993. *Grundrisse: Foundations of the Critique of Political Economy.* New York: Penguin Classics.

McNally, David. 2010. *Global Slump: The Economics and Politics of Crisis and Resistance.* Oakland: PM Press.

Montag, Warren. 2013. "Necro-Economics: Adam Smith and Death in the Life of the Universal." In *Biopolitics: A Reader,* edited by Timothy Campbell and Adam Sitze, 193–214. Durham: Duke University Press.

Moon, Katherine. 2000. "Strangers in the Midst of Globalization: Migrant Workers and Korean Nationalism." In *Korea's Globalization,* edited by Samuel Kim, 147–69. Cambridge: Cambridge University Press.

Myers, B. R. 2011. *The Cleanest Race: How North Koreans See Themselves and Why It Matters.* New York: Melville.

Nee, Victor. 1989. "A Theory of Market Transition." *American Sociology Review* 54: 663–81.

O'Connor, James. 1987. *The Meaning of Crisis.* Oxford: Basil Blackwell.

Oneal, John, and Bruce Russett. 1997. "The Classical Liberals Were Right: Democracy, Interdependence, and Conflict, 1950–1985." *International Studies Quarterly* 41: 267–94.

Ong, Aihwa. 1999. *Flexible Citizenship: The Cultural Logics of Transnationality.* Durham: Duke University Press.

Ostrovsky, Simon. 2009. "N Koreans toiling in Russia's timber camps." *BBC News,* August 26. http://news.bbc.co.uk/2/hi/programmes/newsnight/8221164.stm.

Padgett, John. 2012. "The Politics of Communist Economic Reform: Soviet Union and China." In *Emergence of Organizations and Markets,* edited by John Padgett and Walter Powell, 267–315. Princeton: Princeton University Press.

Park, Hyun Ok. 2005. *Two Dreams in One Bed: Empire, Social Life, and the Origins of the North Korean Revolution.* Durham: Duke University Press.

Pashukanis, Evgeny. 1924 (reprinted in 2001). *The General Theory of Law and Marxism.* New York: Transaction Publishers.

Paterniti, Michael. 2003. "The Flight of the Fluttering Swallow." *New York Times Magazine* 27 (April): 46–51, 62, 112–13.

Perkins, Dwight. 1991. "China's Economic Policy and Performance." In *The Cambridge History of China.* Vol. 15, *The People's Republic.* Part 2, *Revolutions Within the Chinese Revolution, 1966–1982,* edited by Denis Twitchett and John Fairbank, 475–539. Cambridge: Cambridge University Press.

Perry, Elizabeth. 2007. "Studying Chinese Politics: Farewell to Revolution?" *China Journal* 57 (January): 1–22.

Pettid, Michael. 2014, "Shamanic Rites for the Dead in Chosŏn Korea." In *Death, Mourning, and the Afterlife in Korea: From Ancient to Contemporary Times*, edited by Charlotte Horlyck and Michael Pettid, 137–54. Honolulu: University of Hawaii Press.

Polanyi, Karl. 1944 (reprinted in 1971). *The Great Transformation: The Political and Economic Origins of Our Time*. New York: Beacon.

Ranciere, Jacques. 1989. *The Nights of Labor: The Workers' Dream in Nineteenth-Century France*. Philadelphia: Temple University.

——. 1999. *Disagreement: Politics and Philosophy*. Minneapolis: University of Minnesota Press.

——. 2009. *Hatred of Democracy*. London: Verso.

Ricoeur, Paul. 2004. *Memory, History, Forgetting*. Chicago: University of Chicago Press.

Rodrik, Dani, Arvind Subramanian, and Francesco Trebbi. 2004. "Institutions Rule: The Primacy of Institutions over Geography and Integration in Economic Development." *Journal of Economic Growth* 9: 131–65.

Roitman, Janet. 2014. *Anti-Crisis*. Durham: Duke University Press.

Ross, Kristin. 1988. *The Emergence of Social Space: Rimbaud and the Paris Commune*. Minneapolis: University of Minnesota Press.

Rozman, Gilbert. 1987. *The Chinese Debate about Soviet Socialism, 1978–1985*. Princeton: Princeton University Press.

Rusko, Christopher, and Karthika Sasikumar. 2007. "India and China: From Trade to Peace." *Asian Perspective* 31, no. 3: 99–123.

Russo, Alessandro. 2005. "The Conclusive Scene: Mao and the Red Guards in July 1968." *Positions: East Asia Cultures Critique* 13, no. 3: 535–74.

Ryang, Sonia. 1997. *North Koreans in Japan*. Boulder: Westview Press.

——. 2008. *Writing Selves in Diaspora: Ethnography of Autobiographics of Korean Women in Japan and the United States*. London: Lexington Books.

Sachs, Jeffrey. 1992. "The Economic Transformation of Eastern Europe: The Case of Poland." *Economics of Planning* 25: 5–19.

Salvadori, Massimo. 1990. *Karl Kausky and the Socialist Revolution, 1880–1938*. London: Verso.

Sassen, Saskia. 2014. *Expulsions: Brutality and Complexity in the Global Economy*. Cambridge: Belknap Press.

Schiller, Nina Glick, Linda Basch, and Cristina Szanton Blanc. 1995. "From Immigrant to Transmigrant: Theorizing Transnational Migration." *Anthropological Quarterly* 68, no. 1: 48–63.

Schmid, Andre. 2002. *Korea Between Empires*. New York: Columbia University Press.

Schmitt, Carl. 1976. *The Concept of the Political*. New Brunswick: Rutgers University Press.

——. 1985. *Political Theology: Four Concepts on the Concept of Sovereignty*. Chicago: University of Chicago.

Schram, Stuart. 1971. "Mao Tse-tung and the Theory of the Permanent Revolution, 1958–69." *China Quarterly* 46 (April-June): 221–44.

——. 1989. *The Thought of Mao Tse-Tung.* Cambridge: Cambridge University Press.

——. 1991. "Mao Tse-tung's Thought from 1949 to 1976." In *The Cambridge History of China.* Vol. 15, *The People's Republic.* Part 2, *Revolutions Within the Chinese Revolution, 1966–1982,* edited by Denis Twitchett and John Fairbank, 1–106. Cambridge: Cambridge University Press.

Seidman, Gay. 1994. *Manufacturing Militance: Workers' Movements in Brazil and South Africa, 1970–1985.* Berkeley: University of California Press.

Sen, Amartya. 1999. *Development as Freedom.* New York: Knopf.

Seremetakis, C. Nadia, ed. 1994. *The Senses Still: Perception and Memory as Material Culture in Modernity.* Chicago: University of Chicago Press.

Shakya, Tsering. 1999. *The Dragon in the Land of Snows: A History of Modern Tibet Since 1947.* London: Pimlico.

Shank, J. B. 2008. "Crisis: A Useful Category of Post-Social Scientific Historical Analysis?" *American Historical Review* 113, no. 4: 1090–99.

Shin, Gi-Wook, and Kyung Moon Hwang. 2003. *Contentious Kwangju.* Lanham: Rowman and Littlefield.

Shin, Gi-Wook, and Michael Robinson, eds. 2001. *Colonial Modernity in Korea.* Cambridge: Harvard University Asia Center.

Smith, Adam. 1976. *The Wealth of Nations.* Oxford: Oxford University Press.

Soh, Sarah. 2009. *The Comfort Women: Sexual Violence and Postcolonial Memory in Korea and Japan.* Chicago: University of Chicago Press.

Soysal, Yasemin. 1995. *Limits of Citizenship: Migrants and Postnational Membership in Europe.* Chicago: University of Chicago Press.

Stalin, Joseph. 1951. *Economic Problems of the USSR.* Peking (Beijing): Foreign Language Press.

Stark, David, and Laszlo Bruzst. 1998. *Postsocialist Pathways.* Cambridge: Cambridge University Press.

Stasiulis, Daiva, and Abigail Bakan. 1997. "Negotiating Citizenship: The Case of Foreign Domestic Workers in Canada." *Feminist Review* 57: 112–39.

Steger, Manfred. 1997. *The Quest for Evolutionary Socialism: Eduard Bernstein and Social Democracy.* Cambridge: Cambridge University Press.

Sun, Yan. 1995. *The Chinese Reassessment of Socialism, 1976–1992.* Princeton: Princeton University Press.

Szelenyi, Ivan. 2008. "A Theory of Transitions." *Modern China* 34, no. 1: 165–75.

Szelenyi, Ivan, and Eric Kostello. 1996. "The Market Transition Debate: Toward a Synthesis." *American Journal of Sociology* 101, no. 4: 1082–96.

Tait, Richard. 2003. "Playing by the Rules in Korea: Lessons Learned in the North–South Economic Engagement." *Asian Survey* 43, no. 2: 305–28.

Teiwes, Frederick. 1987. "Establishment and Consolidation of the New Regime." In *The Cambridge History of China*. Vol. 14, *The People's Republic*. Part 1, *The Emergence of Revolutionary China, 1949–1965*, edited by Roderick MacFarquhar and John Fairbank, 96–111. Cambridge: Cambridge University Press.

Torpey, John. 2006. *Making Whole What Has Been Smashed: On Reparation Politics*. Cambridge: Harvard University Press.

Trotsky, Leon. 1984. "Socialist Relations in the Soviet Union." In *The Stalinist Legacy: Its Impact on Twentieth-Century World Politics*, edited by Tariq Ali. Chicago: Haymarket Books.

——. 2007. *Terrorism and Communism: A Reply to Karl Kausky*, edited by Slavoj Žižek. London: Verso.

——. 2010. *The Permanent Revolution*. Seattle: Red Letter Press.

Verdery, Katherine. 1999. "Fuzzy Property." In *Uncertain Transition*, edited by Michael Burawoy and Katherine Verdery, 53–82. Lanham: Rowman and Littlefield.

Virno, Paolo. 2004. *A Grammar of the Multitude*. Cambridge: Semiotext(e).

Walder, Andrew. 1996. "Markets and Inequality in Transitional Economies: Toward Testable Theories." *American Journal of Sociology* 101, no. 4: 1060–73.

White, Gordon. 1976. *The Politics of Class and Class Origin: The Case of the Cultural Revolution*. Sydney: Australia University Press.

Yang, Guobin. 2003. "China's Zhiqing Generation: Nostalgia, Identity, and Cultural Resistance in the 1990s." *Modern China* 29, no. 3: 267–96.

Yi, Kŭmsun. 2004. "The Perception of and Reaction to the North Korean Human Rights Act in South Korean Society." In *International Symposium on North Korean Human Rights Issues*, edited by the National Human Rights Commission, 49–68. Seoul: National Human Rights Commission.

Young, Louise. 2012. "Empire in East Asia." Paper presented at the workshop series on *After the Postcolonial Turn: Global Perspectives*. Columbia University, New York, September 19.

Zbierski-Salameh, Slawomira. 2013. *Bitter Harvest: Antecedents and Consequences of Property Reforms in Postsocialist Poland*. Lanham: Lexington Books.

Žižek, Slavoj. 1989. *The Sublime Object of Ideology*. London: Verso.

——. 1993. *Tarrying with the Negative: Kant, Hegel, and the Critique of Ideology*. Durham: Duke University Press.

——. 2002. *Revolution at the Gates: Selected Writings of Lenin from 1917*. London: Verso.

——. 2005. *Interrogating the Real*. New York: Continuum.

——. 2007. *Enjoy Your Symptom!: Jacques Lacan in Hollywood and Out*. New York: Routledge.

——. 2009. *In Defense of Lost Causes*. London: Verso.

INDEX